ISRAELI FILM

Reference Guides to the World's Cinema

Guide to the Cinema of Spain
Marvin D'Lugo

Guide to American Cinema, 1965–1995
Daniel Curran

Guide to African Cinema
Sharon A. Russell

Guide to American Cinema, 1930–1965
Thomas Whissen

Guide to the Silent Years of American Cinema
Donald W. McCaffrey and Christopher P. Jacobs

Guide to the Cinema of Sweden and Finland
Per Olov Qvist and Peter von Bagh

Guide to the Cinema(s) of Canada
Peter Harry Rist, editor

ISRAELI FILM

A Reference Guide

Amy Kronish and
Costel Safirman

Reference Guides to the World's Cinema
Pierre L. Horn, Series Adviser

PRAEGER

Westport, Connecticut
London

Library of Congress Cataloging-in-Publication Data

Kronish, Amy.
Israeli film : a reference guide / Amy Kronish and Costel Safirman.
p. cm.—(Reference guides to the world's cinema, ISSN 1090–8234)
Includes bibliographical references and index.
ISBN 0–313–32144–2 (alk. paper)
1. Motion pictures—Israel—History. I. Safirman, Costel, 1937– II. Title. III. Series.
PN1993.5.I86K76 2003
791.43'095694—dc21 2002028310

British Library Cataloguing in Publication Data is available.

Library of Congress Catalog Card Number: 2002028310
ISBN: 0–313–32144–2
ISSN: 1090–8234

First published in 2003

Praeger Publishers, 88 Post Road West, Westport, CT 06881
An imprint of Greenwood Publishing Group, Inc.
www.praeger.com

Printed in the United States of America

The paper used in this book complies with the Permanent Paper Standard issued by the National Information Standards Organization (Z39.48–1984).

10 9 8 7 6 5 4 3 2 1

CONTENTS

ILLUSTRATIONS

SERIES FOREWORD

For the first time, on December 28, 1895, at the Grand Café in Paris, France, the inventors of the *Cinématographe*, Auguste and Louis Lumière, showed a series of 11 two-minute silent shorts to a public of 35 people, each paying the high entry fee of one gold franc. From that moment, a new era had begun, for the Lumière brothers not only were successful in their commercial venture but also unknowingly created a new visual medium quickly to become, throughout the world, the half-popular entertainment, half-sophisticated art of the cinema. Eventually, the contribution of each member of the profession, especially that of the director and performers, took on enormous importance. A century later, the situation remains very much the same.

The purpose of Greenwood's *Reference Guides to the World's Cinema* is to give a representative idea of what each country or region has to offer to the evolution, development, and richness of film. At the same time, because each volume seeks to present a balance between the interests of the general public and those of students and scholars of the medium, the choices are by necessity selective (although as comprehensive as possible) and often reflect the author's own idiosyncracies.

André Malraux, the French novelist and essayist, wrote about the cinema and filmmakers: "The desire to build up a world apart and self-contained, existing in its own right . . . represents humanization in the deepest, certainly the most enigmatic, sense of the word." On the other hand, then, every *Guide* explores this observation by offering discussions, written in a jargon-free style, of the motion-picture art and its practitioners and, on the other, provides much-needed information, seldom available in English, including filmographies, awards and honors, and ad hoc bibliographies.

Pierre L. Horn
Wright State University

PREFACE

The country of Israel is young, and Israeli film is still a developing industry. As can be seen from an analysis of the quality films produced during the last 10–15 years, the industry has undergone considerable growth and is maturing rapidly. In fact, Israeli films have received critical attention and have been seen in film festivals all over the world, have been broadcast on television internationally, and have gained status and prestige as the cultural and social voice of a nation. In writing this book, we have tried to provide insight into that voice. What are the themes that have been seen on the Israeli screens? How have these themes changed over the years? Who are the people behind the films—and what are they trying to convey?

In "A National Cinema in the Making: An Overview," we have tried to provide a historical and social view of the films. There is no doubt that Israeli cinema reflects the existential dilemmas and the social achievements of both Arabs and Jews within Israeli society. It also reflects political crises and critical voices. Only a careful analysis of trends can provide a greater understanding of the country and the people of Israel. In order for readers to be able to assess these trends for themselves, we have tried to provide detailed information on a large number of Israeli films and filmmakers. The emphasis is on "information"—our intention was to provide as much raw material as possible, including synopsis, credits, biographical material, and so on—in order to supplement the material that already exists in English and in order to provide readers with a valuable resource in assessing the cinematic culture of Israel. It should be noted that a "guide" is not an "encyclopedia"—it does not claim to be all-inclusive. Rather, we have chosen to discuss a diverse selection of Israeli films (information on more than half of the features produced since the establishment of the state in 1948 is included herein) and to offer background on a large number of key film directors, producers, actors and actresses, cinematographers, and composers.

One of the most difficult tasks was to choose which films should be included. Films were chosen based on a number of criteria: cinematic quality, thematic content, success at the box office, reviews of the Israeli critics, and awards, both national and international. The films chosen here reflect historical trends and social issues. They also offer a look at the development of filmmaking in Israel—both as an industry and as an art form. Since documentary filmmaking is also an important part of the film expression of a nation, we have included a representative choice of documentary films made for the cinema (since the 1930s) based on similar criteria. The documentary films appear together with the feature films, listed alphabetically, in the major part of this guide, which is devoted to individual film entries. Each entry includes English title, original Hebrew title (in transliteration), year of production, credits, awards, analysis of the importance of the film, the major issues that it portrays, and a synopsis of the film's narrative. In order to assist readers in searching for additional information, an asterisk (*) signifies a cross-reference to a film entry or to biographical information.

A fair amount of this guide has been dedicated to the people who have produced Israeli films—those who have devoted their lifework to the art of cinema. Some of them were pioneers in the field. Others have taken up the reins where the pioneers left off. All of them, however, have made an important mark on the film industry in Israel. Their brief biographies are presented, together with a filmography of their Israeli films.

Awards presented to films and filmmakers can be an important measure of achievement. They also measure the growth and development of the industry. This guide provides an appendix of international prizes that have been awarded to Israeli feature films—a reflection of the recognition received over the decades. Also mentioned herein are the prestigious national prizes that have been awarded—the prizes of the Israel Film Center of the Ministry of Industry and Trade that were awarded during the 1970s and 1980s; the Israeli Academy Awards, which have become the major prizes of the industry since 1990; and the prizes of the important international film festivals of Jerusalem and Haifa.

In researching the biographical section and in analyzing literally hundreds of films, we took advantage of the insight and experience of many people in the field. We wish to thank the following persons for their input, advice, and patience while being interviewed as part of our research: Gila Almagor, Muhammed Bakri, Uri Barbash, Michal Bat-Adam, Rafi Bukaee, Eli Cohen, Ilan Eldad, Larry Frisch, Amit Goren, Moshe Ivgi, Tsipi Reibenbach, Dan Wolman, and the following, who are no longer with us: Baruch Dienar and Maryana Gross.

The resources amassed at the Jerusalem Cinematheque were invaluable to our ongoing work, and we thank Lia van Leer for making them available to us. We viewed films—both on 35mm editing tables and on video equipment—and we partook of many public screenings of Israeli films. We made use of the library's new database of Israeli cinema and wish to express our appreciation to the staff—Nirit Eidelman, Ilil Barak, Keren Ben-Or, Michal Mendelboym, and Avi Green—for their efforts in organizing and adding to the enormous collection of newspaper clippings and the creation of this database. In researching the production credits that appear for each film entry, we tried to take the information from the films themselves—a method that truly provides the most reliable material. When this was not possible, however, the information was taken from materials at the library of the Jerusalem Cinematheque.

We are indebted to a previous book on Israeli film entitled *World Cinema: Israel*, by Amy Kronish (published in 1996), from which we adapted some of the research and material and built around it a new structure. We also made use of the reference work by Meir Schnitzer, *Israeli Cinema: Facts/Plots/Directors/ Opinions* (published in Hebrew in 1994), which provided us with details that were otherwise difficult to find.

Our thanks to our editors, Eric Levy of Greenwood Publishing Group and John Donohue of Westchester Book Services, for their dedication to this important series. This is one of the paths for different cultural voices to become known internationally and for readers to become acquainted with a variety of cinematic expressions that are so important in helping to spread greater international dialogue and understanding.

We are especially thankful to our families for their advice, assistance, and support during every phase of this project. We would never have been able to complete this guide without their invaluable insight and understanding.

Amy Kronish
Costel Safirman

A NATIONAL CINEMA IN THE MAKING: AN OVERVIEW

Since its inception, Israeli cinema has been preoccupied with issues of a society under siege—the hardships of a situation of ongoing war, problems of Jewish–Arab relations, and the major survival issues of the state. Despite this focus, Israeli filmmaking is in fact much more complex and varied. Indeed, Israeli cinema covers a wide spectrum of issues that have developed during the more than 70 years since the first local production of a feature film in 1932.

Filmmaking in Israel, as in other countries, is a contemporary cultural form of expression and also a political and social expression, reflecting more than the personal point of view of each filmmaker and producer and providing a commentary on social trends, historical challenges, and societal issues. Although films can be considered as individual pieces of work, the thrust of this overview is to show how an understanding of Israeli society can be garnered through a careful analysis of the subject matter, issues, and styles of expression of this unique medium. This analysis provides the reader with a better understanding of Israeli cinema as a national cinema in the making—one that has been developing since its infancy during the early British Mandatory period and flourishing in recent years.

THE BRITISH MANDATORY PERIOD

Filmmaking began in British Mandatory Palestine following World War I with an emphasis on documentary production. This period was characterized by ideological and informational films that were produced to convince foreign audiences of the success of the Jewish pioneering enterprise in Palestine at that time. The films of the period reflected the great enthusiasm for the idealism and dedication to egalitarianism, socialism, and self-defense, all of which characterized the efforts of the early pioneers during the 1920s and 1930s.

A number of the major documentaries of that period were commissioned by the institutions of the embryonic state, such as *Land of Promise* (Judah Leman, 1934), a look at the development of the Jewish settlement in Palestine. Although very different in style, *Avodah* (Helmar Lerski, 1935) also emphasized images of the archetypal pioneers, drilling for water, working in the fields, and making the desert bloom. Lerski's monumental images of people and machinery, however, were offered in contrast to the Palestine that the Jews were trying to change and improve—the barren hillsides, premodern Arabs plowing with old-fashioned methods, and camels slowly lumbering across the screen.

The embryonic film industry in Palestine was struggling and developing during this period. In addition to documentary filmmaking, a number of filmmakers tried their hand at the production of newsreels. The major contribution in this field was made by Nathan Axelrod, who used homemade equipment and worked out of his own laboratory, tirelessly producing Carmel Newsreels, which were screened in the cinemas without interruption for more than 30 years (except during the war years from 1940 to 1945, when the cinemas were closed). Axelrod's newsreels have documented every significant aspect of the growth of the Jewish state in the making, including the establishment of the kibbutzim, the draining of the swamps, the development of the city of Tel Aviv, and the declaration of the state of Israel by David Ben-Gurion in 1948. Together with Haim Halachmi, who came to cinema from the world of theater, Axelrod produced the first dramatic, feature-length film, *Oded the Wanderer* (directed by Halachmi, 1932).

THE HEROIC PERIOD

Following the establishment of the state of Israel in 1948, dramatic filmmaking began to develop, especially with an emphasis on creating the mythical images typical of a young society. Almost all of the dramas of this period provide heroic images of both men and women—pioneers, fighters, and Holocaust survivors—as can be seen in feature-length dramas such as *They Were Ten* (Baruch Dienar, 1960), which looked back on the early pioneers of the nineteenth century, and *Hill 24 Doesn't Answer* (Thorold Dickinson, 1954), about the War of Independence. *They Were Ten* is a sensitive story of heroism and bravery based on the diaries of early Zionist settlers in the 1880s. Shot on location on a hilltop in the western Galilee, the film is significant due to its artistic quality, in-depth characterizations, and striking images. Filmmaker Baruch Dienar is credited with the first Hebrew-speaking feature film to be given recognition internationally—Twentieth Century Fox distributed the subtitled version in 24 countries. *Hill 24 Doesn't Answer*, a film of three episodes, recounts the tales of a group of young soldiers during the last remaining hours of the War of Independence of 1948. The film combines elements of romance and melodrama with authentically evoked incidents based on historical detail.

Following the uplifting victories of the 1967 Six Day War, a second wave of heroic dramas was seen on the screen. Different from the first wave, these films show both cinematic development and societal change. The loneliness of a war widow is sensitively portrayed in *Siege* (Gilberto Tofano, 1969); the motivations that drive men to commit heroic deeds are seen in *Every Bastard a King* (Uri Zohar, 1968); and a dangerous commando mission is portrayed in *Scouting Patrol* (Micha Shagrir, 1967). Although these films reflect a society in which the perils of war are a basic part of life, there are now a growing maturity, a sense of loss, and an understanding of the dangers involved in wartime. This trend toward a more realistic approach to the inevitability of war continued until the image of the invincible heroic Israeli faded entirely from the screen following the 1973 Yom Kippur War, the war that caught Israel unaware, thereby bringing tremendous losses in battle and resulting in a newfound feeling of vulnerability.

THE CENTRALITY OF JERUSALEM

Following the Six Day War, the reunited city of Jerusalem became the focus of a number of films of the period. In addition, there have been a small number of filmmakers over the years for whom Jerusalem is central to their work. The films of Dan Wolman—*Hide and Seek* (1980), *My Michael* (1975), and his short ode to the city, *To Touch a City* (1978)—reflect a filmmaker's obsession with the city—its light and colors, its stones, its history, and its people. *Hide and Seek* deals with the problems and tensions of living in a society under siege. It is a film about maturity—the demands of a society coming of age, the politics of a state in formation, and the maturity of an adolescent boy who gains understanding and learns about the complexities of the world. Wolman's earlier film, *My Michael*, is an award-winning film about solitude. Set in the divided city of Jerusalem during the 1950s, the film's achievement lies in its beauty and gentleness. A reflection of the divided city in which she lives, the heroine becomes melancholic, isolated, and full of loneliness and tension; she gradually abandons herself to a world of fantasies and dreams.

One of the earliest filmmakers to seriously look at the city, documentary filmmaker David Perlov produced the short film *In Jerusalem* (1963). A few decades later, Ron Havilio combined two styles, documentary and personal diary, for his film *Fragments—Jerusalem* (1994), an epic film that was more than 12 years in the making and that interweaves his personal and family connection to the contemporary city with the historical Jerusalem. Other filmmakers who have portrayed the symbolism of Jerusalem as a major element in their films are Moshe Mizrahi (*I Love You, Rosa*, 1972, and *Women*, 1996), Michal Bat-Adam (*Moments*, 1979, and *A Thousand and One Wives*, 1989), and, more recently, Hagai Levi (*August Snow*, 1993), Ye'ud Levanon (*Black Box*, 1993), and Joseph Cedar (*Time of Favor*, 2000).

Jewish thinkers and religious leaders throughout the centuries have spoken of a vision of heavenly Jerusalem, something difficult to fathom and even harder to concretize. With the advent of photography and cinema, everything became more real and concrete, with less being left to the imagination. Thus, Jerusalem, once a heavenly city, became a city of everyday reality, a city of real-life clashes, a city of people and problems instead of vision and future.

THE DEVELOPMENT OF AN INDIGENOUS CULTURAL VOICE

Even before the Six Day War, during the early 1960s, Israeli cinema began to develop a uniquely Israeli film expression. Menahem Golan contributed to the growth of the industry through the large number of ethnic and action films that he produced, thereby providing jobs, experience, and a film culture for an entire generation of film technicians and filmgoers. Filmmakers such as Uri Zohar and Ephraim Kishon contributed through their new themes and unique styles.

Menahem Golan, the most prolific and successful of Israeli producer/directors, is perhaps the figure most responsible for the growth of Israeli cinema during the 1960s and 1970s. Golan directed his first film, *Eldorado* (1963), which starred the then-unknown Haim Topol and was a huge box office success. Golan's low-budget ethnic films are the forerunners of the popular "bourekas" films, which were generally made for audiences of Jews from Arab lands, known as Sephardi Jews. In 1973 Golan created the first Israeli musical film spectacular, based on a popular Israeli stage musical (by Yigal Mossinson), entitled *Kazablan*. The story is about a petty criminal (played by Yehoram Gaon) who is seen as a victim of social prejudice. The film combines elements of the ambitious American musical with a tale of ethnic tension and romance in Old Jaffa. The lyrics and songs became well known; the album was a best-seller; and the film was acquired by MGM for international distribution.

In addition to comedies and musicals, the prolific and diverse Golan has produced and directed Hollywood-style, fast-paced thrillers of international intrigue, terrorism, and underworld crime. Golan, who has been personally responsible for the production and/or direction of over 50 Israeli features, has been heavily condemned by Israeli critics for his popularized style of filmmaking and crass imitation of Hollywood. Golan did not believe in producing pretentious films for a limited audience of art lovers. Instead, he built his entire career on the belief that films must reach out and meet their public. He produced many of the biggest box office successes in Israel, which were not necessarily also the critics' choice. Even though most of his films poke fun at ethnic types, and his adventure films play on the Israeli macho heroic image, it is important to note that Golan has also produced and directed a small number of elaborate and prizewinning films that received praise from the critics.

Uri Zohar's individualistic filmmaking can be characterized as unique, witty, irreverent, and often decadent. As a member of the Palmach generation, Zohar expresses a rebelliousness and a dissatisfaction with the normative, local lifestyle. His early expressions, such as *Hole in the Moon* (1963) and *Take Off* (1970), although fragmented, are brilliant parodies on many aspects of Israeli society. Moreover, his dramas *Three Days and a Child* (1967) and *Every Bastard a King* (1968) proved him to be a capable, serious director, concerned with societal issues both collective and individual. In a completely different style, he is perhaps best known for his trilogy of beach comedies—*Peeping Toms* (1972), *Big Eyes* (1974), and *Save the Lifeguard* (1977). These self-indulgent comedies portray the adolescent fantasy life of grown men. *Peeping Toms* has become a cult film in Israel due to its slang and its portrayal of the hedonistic and secular lifestyle personified by Zohar and other literary figures of that period. Although Uri Zohar abruptly ended his film career by making a complete about-face and becoming an ultrareligious Jew, his contribution to Israeli cinema is remembered for its spontaneity, creativity, and an authentically Israeli irreverence.

Very different in style and background from Uri Zohar, Hungarian-born Ephraim Kishon was also creating a particularly Israeli style of filmmaking during the 1960s. Although both filmmakers used humor, Kishon's sophisticated satire is very different from Zohar's spontaneity, slang, and vulgarity. Zohar's characters lived on the periphery of Israeli society in contrast to Kishon's satires of the little guy, the victim of society. Kishon's films—*The Big Dig* (1969), about a man who breaks out of a lunatic asylum and creates bedlam in Tel Aviv, and *The Policeman* (1971), which portrays a bumbling cop of Moroccan descent, not very effective but well intentioned—contain inimitable insight and satirical social comment. His most important contribution to Israeli cinema is the musical *Sallah* (1964), a parody of the life of the new immigrant family, Israeli bureaucracy, and the political system. Due to its warmth, understanding, and capacity for poking fun at every aspect of Israeli life, *Sallah* was extremely popular with Israeli audiences and became the most successful Israeli film of that period. The first Israeli film to be nominated for an American Academy Award*, it tells the story of a Moroccan Jew (Haim Topol) who has recently brought his large family to Israel and is living in the humiliating conditions of a transit camp. This exaggerated and stereotypical tragicomic look at the life of the new immigrants is the forerunner of many Israeli ethnic films that addressed the needs and moods of the large immigrant population.

*Seven Israeli films have been nominated for Academy Awards. Six features were nominated for Best Foreign Film: *Sallah* (Ephraim Kishon, 1964), *The Policeman* (Ephraim Kishon, 1971), *I Love You, Rosa* (Moshe Mizrahi, 1972), *The House on Chelouche St.* (Moshe Mizrahi, 1973), *Operation Thunderbolt* (Menahem Golan, 1977), and *Beyond the Walls* (Uri Barbash, 1984). One documentary was nominated for Best Documentary: *The Eight-First Blow* (Jacques Ehrlich, David Bergman, and Haim Gouri, 1974).

THE "BOUREKAS" PERIOD

Immediately after the establishment of the state of Israel in 1948, a large wave of immigration brought Jews from Arab lands, such as Morocco, Iraq, Libya, and Tunisia. These so-called Sephardi Jews are often referred to as the "second Israel" due to the fact that they were looked down upon by the "better-educated" Ashkenazi Jews of European descent. By the late 1960s, the Sephardi Jews had learned Hebrew, moved out of the temporary transit camps, and become a viable audience for Israeli films.

A unique genre of locally produced Israeli films, "bourekas" films—named for the Middle Eastern puff pastry—used clearly identifiable ethnic characters in order to appeal to this segment of the population. The films, produced mostly during the late 1960s and 1970s, included both ethnic comedies and heavily laden melodramas based on ethnic stereotypes. Although not terribly serious or artistic in content, these films show great respect for the family and for Jewish values and were very popular with Israeli audiences.

Some of the most memorable images were seen in Ephraim Kishon's *Sallah* (1964), Menahem Golan's *Lupo* (1970), and Alfred Steinhardt's *Salomonico* (1972). In addition, melodramas by George Ovadiah such as *Arianna* (1971) and *Nurit* (1972) and tragicomedies by Ze'ev Revach such as *Only Today* (1976), *Sweet and Sour* (1979), and *A Bit of Luck* (1992) are some of the classic bourekas films. Revach's Sephardi character Sasson, who appears in many of his films, is a man of warmth, wisdom, and insight. During the same period, filmmakers such as Yoel Zilberg and Ilan Eldad were making ethnic films for Ashkenazi audiences.

Some of the *bourekas* films became pop culture classics in Israel. In addition, although not strictly belonging to the bourekas category, the teen teaser films directed by Boaz Davidson (including *Lemon Popsicle*, 1978, and its sequel, *Going Steady*, 1979) also appealed to the mass Israeli audience. The success of these teenage romances can be attributed to their imitation of international filmmaking techniques, especially the use of fast-paced editing and popular rock music.

POST–SIX DAY WAR BRAVADO

The Six Day War of June 1967 gave the country of Israel a sense of military security that it had never had before. The Israelis transformed their prewar vulnerability into a postwar heroism and optimism, which led them to believe that their new strength would bring them long-lasting peace with their Arab neighbors.

Many films, both documentaries and dramas, were produced that reflected the newfound bravado and euphoria. Films portrayed dangerous commando missions in the Sinai desert, and striking images from the documentary films showed the shoes of fleeing Egyptian soldiers and many Egyptian tanks left behind in the desert.

Produced immediately following the war, full-length feature films offered a new psychological portrayal of the Israeli soldier. These dramas, produced in the wake of the war, include *Every Bastard a King* (Uri Zohar, 1968), portraying a swashbuckling Israeli hero; *Siege* (Gilberto Tofano, 1969), a psychological study of the loneliness of a war widow; *He Walked through the Fields* (Yoseph Millo, 1967), originally a stage play that examines the pioneering generation of the War of Independence; and *Is Tel Aviv Burning?* (Kobi Jaeger, 1967), the first Six Day War drama. Although dissimilar in their narratives, all reflect the postwar obsession with military and security issues and the societal need to come to terms with the new feelings of both euphoria and ambivalence that were a result of the war.

"KAYITZ"—YOUNG ISRAELI CINEMA

During the 1960s and 1970s—at the same time that bourekas films were popular—a new understanding of film as an art form was sweeping through an entire generation of young filmmakers in Israel. These filmmakers, heavily influenced by the French nouvelle vague, established a new style of Israeli cinema, entitled "Kayitz," a Hebrew acronym for "Young Israeli Cinema." Often criticized for not taking the commercial viability of their films into consideration, the Kayitz filmmakers covered a variety of subjects—romance, juvenile delinquency, rootlessness, and alienation—but their films appealed only to an intellectual elite in Israeli life. Different from the escapism of bourekas films, their style could be characterized as personal, psychological, sensitive, artistic, and even avant-garde, and they showed a self-conscious awareness of artistic cinematic techniques.

One of the major filmmakers of the Kayitz movement, Moshe Mizrahi, has directed films both in France and in Israel. His Israeli films include *The Traveler* (French co-production, 1970), about a former Gestapo officer who tries to rebuild his life in Eilat, and three Sephardi cultural films, the best known of which is *I Love You, Rosa* (1962), which was nominated for an Academy Award for Best Foreign-Language Film. Mizrahi's films reflect folkloristic influences, an obsession with both Jewish and Nazi survivors of World War II, a sensitivity to the problems of forbidden love, and an authentic grappling with issues of faith and cultural conflict. His work can be seen as an antithesis to the bourekas films of other Sephardi filmmakers since his portrayal of ethnic characters is idealistic rather than stereotypical.

Another of the auteur filmmakers of the Kayitz movement, Dan Wolman, has become Israel's major filmmaker dealing with humanistic and existential themes, such as aging, alienation, and human relationships. Wolman's humanism is apparent in all of his films—*My Michael* (1975), based on the novel by Amos Oz; *Hide and Seek* (1980), dealing with the problems and tensions of living in a society under siege; *The Distance* (1994), depicting the responsibilities of a son toward his aging parents; and *Foreign Sister* (2000), making a plea for human understanding of the plight of foreign workers within Israel.

In addition to the films of Dan Wolman and Moshe Mizrahi, the leading films of the Kayitz movement include Avram Heffner's *But Where Is Daniel Wax?* (1972) and *Cover Story* (1979), which show a preoccupation with the past; the portrayals of alienation by Nissim Dayan in *Light Out of Nowhere* (1973); and Michal Bat-Adam's *Moments* (1979) and *A Thin Line* (1981), which focus on relationships between women.

The Kayitz period was a period of personal filmmaking that emphasized existential themes of relationships, alienation from society, aging, and the universal search for the meaning of life. It is seen as a reaction against a number of issues: the ongoing state of siege, the rootlessness of a society made up largely of immigrants, the psychological complexities of living in the shadow of the Holocaust, and the disillusionment with the contemporary fulfillment of the Zionist dream. Many of these same filmmakers went on to become the leading politically conscious Israeli filmmakers of the 1980s.

A CONSPIRACY OF SILENCE: FILMS ABOUT HOLOCAUST SURVIVORS

The Kayitz filmmakers were not the only ones to make serious and soul-searching films in Israeli society. Those who attempted to confront the Holocaust also made substantive and sensitive films. Following the establishment of the state of Israel and the incredible victories in battle against the Arab armies during the War of Independence, Israelis found it difficult to understand those Jews who had survived the Holocaust without having tried to defend themselves against the forces of evil. Those survivors, who were not part of the mythology of armed resistance, were made to feel embarrassed by their "sheep to the slaughter" past and learned not to speak of it. As a result, a great conspiracy of silence and denial was created.

The small number of films produced during the early years of the state concerning Holocaust survivors focused on hints of their exploitation at the hands of the Nazis and their emotional instability. When the children of these survivors grew to maturity during the 1980s and into the 1990s, a change developed in the perception of survivors. There was a new appreciation for their spiritual resistance and for the simple fact of their survival. Dramas such as Daniel Wachsmann's *Transit* (1980), Tsipi Trope's *Tel Aviv–Berlin* (1987), Eli Cohen's *Summer of Aviya* (1988), and its sequel, *Under the Domim Tree* (1995), deal with the difficulties of survivors adjusting to their new lives and living in the haunting shadows of their memories.

Similarly, the documentaries *Due to That War* (Orna Ben-Dor, 1988), *Choice and Destiny* (Tsipi Reibenbach, 1993), and *Don't Touch My Holocaust* (Asher Tlalim, 1994) are controversial films that deal with the problems of survivors and second-generation survivors and the psychological hardships that they have endured. In her award-winning film *Due to That War*, Orna Ben-Dor (herself the child of survivors) documents the impact of the Holocaust on the lives of second-generation survivors, two popular Israeli rock figures, singer Yehuda Poliker and lyricist Ya'ackov Gilad, and their parents. The fact that Poliker and Gilad's rock album *Ashes and Dust* was so popular and sold so many copies is a clear indication that the younger generation of Israelis was ready to confront an issue mostly hidden by the parents' generation.

During the mid-1980s, Gila Almagor, the "first lady" of Israeli stage and screen, wrote her own personal story of the shame that she had felt as a child, growing up with a mother who was forever tortured by her memories of the Holocaust. Two films were produced based on her autobiographical material: *Summer of Aviya* (1988) and *Under the Domim Tree* (1995), both directed by Eli Cohen. For many years, Almagor had been satisfied with her press image as a Jew of Moroccan descent, a misperception that emerged from the roles that she played on the Israeli screen (*Eldorado, Fortuna, Highway Queen*). She had been hiding her true family story, that her mother was a Holocaust survivor whose experiences had left her scarred and unbalanced all of her life. As a result of her mother's inadequacies, Almagor grew up in a boarding school with other children, many of whom were survivors themselves. During the 1980s, Almagor, now a mature woman, began to come to terms with her own past. At that time, she wrote and performed her own story—with herself playing the role of her mother—first as a one-woman theatrical performance and later as an award-winning film, *Summer of Aviya*.

In the sequel, *Under the Domim Tree*, it becomes apparent that the mother did not actually experience the Holocaust. Rather, she went to Palestine before the war. Her feelings of guilt at having left her family behind and self-deprecation for not having suffered what they suffered bring her to a mental breakdown. She not only imagines that she has suffered the agonies of the Holocaust but tattoos a number on her arm.

In a form of self-censorship, it is interesting to note that there have been no Israeli cinematic portrayals of the atrocities perpetrated by the Nazis. This is in part due to the years of silence and also due to a hesitation on the part of Israeli filmmakers about trivializing and commercializing a subject of such sensitivity.

THE SOCIALIST DREAM

Serious filmmaking in Israel also brought Israeli filmmakers into confrontation with some of the foremost ideological issues of the society. The kibbutz, where members lived a communal life, was the revolutionary contribution of the pre-state pioneering generation. Based on the Marxist principle "from each according to his ability, to each according to his need," the socialist ideology of the kibbutz called for a lifestyle of equality, commitment to the land, and, by necessity, the communal raising of children. Over the years, this ideology proved problematic, and issues arose that required flexibility and adaptability rather than strict adherence to ideology.

During the 1950s, kibbutz communities split apart over ideological issues as it became clear that the old principles needed reworking. As Israeli cities developed, early films reflected the growing tension beween kibbutz and city life. During later periods, films dealing with the kibbutz way of life reflected serious internal crises of ideology. Yitzhak (Tzepel) Yeshurun's *Noa at 17* (1981) shows concern with the issues of a collective society in flux. Films by Nadav Levitan, including *Intimate Story* (1981) and *Stalin's Disciples* (1986), portray problems of collective living—lack of privacy, an individual's need to bend to the will of the group, tensions of group decision making—and the need to adapt to the dynamic world outside the kibbutz framework.

As can be seen through the films portraying the kibbutz, this uniquely Israeli form of socialism underwent major crises in its ideology and was constantly facing change in an attempt to keep up with contemporary reality.

SELF-CRITICISM

Just as the kibbutz movement felt the need for adaptation to outside pressures, all aspects of society must remain flexible, dynamic, and open to criticism, which leads to social growth, development, and change. Conscious of this need, artists feel compelled to use their art form as a platform for social criticism. In all parts of the world, they tend to be more politically left-wing and often choose to dedicate their art to raising consciousness and criticizing societal and political issues. Israeli filmmakers have also shown this tendency. In fact, following the new vulnerability and changing societal attitudes that came about as a result of the hardships on the battlefield during the 1973 Yom Kippur War, Israeli filmmakers began to delve critically into problematic issues such as the responsibilities of military service, the nature of war, Arab–Jewish relations, and the Middle East conflict.

This period of social consciousness and political criticism was ushered in with the production of two groundbreaking films: Yehuda (Judd) Ne'eman's *The Paratroopers* (1977), the first film to ask difficult questions about the Israeli army and the tough discipline of army training, and Daniel Wachsmann's *Hamsin* (1982), which presents Arab characters in depth and poses questions about the superficial relationship between Jewish employer and Arab worker within the state of Israel. As the 1980s continued, a preoccupation developed with issues of army and defense; there was a new sensitivity toward the tragedies of war; and a plea was made for greater understanding of our Arab neighbors. Moreover, the documentary films of Amos Gitai and the television dramas of Ram Loevy show a sense of social responsibility and a tendency toward political criticism in Israeli filmmaking. Feature films that deal with the traumas of war include *Shellshock* (Yoel Sharon, 1988), set during the Yom Kippur War; *Ricochets* (Eli Cohen, 1986), a film produced by the film unit of the Israeli army concerning the War in Lebanon; and *One of Us* (Uri Barbash, 1989), about an army cover-up during the period of the first *intifada* (uprising).

Reflecting on his own fears and hesitations before joining the army, filmmaker Renen Schorr made the prizewinning *Late Summer Blues* (1986), which dramatizes the ambivalent feelings of a group of young people on the verge of conscription. Schorr chose to set his film in the period of the War of Attrition, during the summer of 1970; nevertheless, the film transcends any specific period and reflects the issues and dilemmas facing young people about to be inducted into the army during wartime.

TWO PEOPLES—ARABS AND JEWS

Previously portrayed as primitive characters in peripheral roles, Arab screen characters slowly began to extend beyond stereotypes. The earliest Israeli film to portray an Israeli Arab with depth of character is *My Name Is Ahmed* (Avshalom Katz, 1966), a short film written by Ram Loevy. The film concerns the feelings of a recent high school graduate as he leaves his Arab village to find work in Tel Aviv.

Two major literary adaptations explore Arab–Jewish relations. Based on David Grossman's book, *The Smile of the Lamb* (Shimon Dotan, 1986) is the story of a wise old man who embodies Arab folk wisdom and lives on the fine line between reality and fantasy. The second, *Khirbet Hiza'a* (Ram Loevy, 1978), from the story by S. Yizhar, is set during the 1948 War of Independence between Israel and the surrounding Arab states. Produced for Israel Television, the film explores the feelings of ambivalence and guilt on the part of those involved in forcibly deporting the citizens of an Arab village. Due to its controversial nature, the completed film was initially shelved by the producer/broadcaster for many months until a protest organized by the workers' committee forced Israel Television to relent and broadcast the film.

Arabs continued to be portrayed as one-dimensional characters and visual symbols and only in supporting roles until the Israeli political and psychological realities began to change in the 1980s. At that time, a major feature film was produced that grapples with the relations between Jews and Arabs within Israeli society and is set against the background of life in the agricultural area of the Galilee in northern Israel. *Hamsin* (Daniel Wachsmann, 1982) is a landmark production because of its brutal honesty and intensity and because it was the first attempt at tackling the difficult subject of contemporary Arab–Jewish relations in the Galilee.

Two major Israeli films explore the basic bonds of common destiny between Arab and Jew. In Uri Barbash's *Beyond the Walls* (1986) and Eran Riklis' *Cup Final* (1991), outside forces cause the two groups to forge an otherwise unlikely alliance. Bought for international distribution by Warner Brothers, *Beyond the Walls* challenges political and social stereotypes, portrays larger-than-life characters, and offers a harsh, realistic portrayal of the best and the worst within

Israeli society. Most importantly, it presents a clear metaphor of Arab and Jew being locked up together, uniting against a common enemy, and condemned to mutual acceptance and coexistence.

Similar to *Beyond the Walls, Cup Final* leads the viewer toward the possibilities of mutual understanding; the conclusion, however, is less optimistic. On the background of the War in Lebanon, the film explores the themes of male bonding during wartime, the relationship between captor and captive, and the possibility of coexistence in the politically tense atmosphere of the Middle East.

Any possibility of achieving understanding and coexistence in Israeli society is complicated by the fact that Israel has been in a continuous state of war with some of her Arab neighbors since its existence. For the first 19 years, the Arabs in the region constituted the major power bloc, both militarily and politically. Following the war in 1967, the tables were turned, and suddenly they found themselves as the losers in battle. At that time the Jews, who had been the underdog for thousands of years, found themselves in a position of strength. Rafi Bukaee's *Avanti Popolo* (1986) explores this reversal of roles and makes a plea for understanding the humanity of the Arab enemy. Two Egyptian soldiers are crossing the Sinai Peninsula when they come across an Israeli patrol. Using the only language that they have in common—the language of the theater—one of the Egyptian soldiers, a professional actor, recites a Shylock monologue from *The Merchant of Venice*. Using all his acting ability and considerable charm, he is begging for water and understanding at the same time: "I am a Jew. Has not a Jew eyes, emotions, senses? Do we not bleed?" With this reference to Shylock, director/scriptwriter Rafi Bukaee is saying to his Israeli filmgoing public, You were an oppressed minority in the diaspora; now it is time for you to understand and empathize with the oppressed minority within your midst.

Avanti Popolo is about perceiving the human being behind the face of the enemy. Although it refers to wartime, it is a metaphor for the greater understanding of Arab neighbors in general. The need for developing a better understanding and relationship between Jews and Arabs in Israel is the theme of three other films produced in the 1980s—*Marriage of Convenience* (Haim Bouzaglo, 1988), a comedy told from the middle-class Israeli point of view; *Nadia* (Amnon Rubinstein, 1986), from the perspective of an Israeli-Palestinian teenage girl; and *Night Movie* (Gur Heller, short, 1985), from the point of view of an Israeli soldier who has a fleeting encounter with a Palestinian teenage boy. All three films are about relationships under difficult circumstances.

One of the fears of improved coexistence is that it can lead to romantic entanglements. Three feature films have been produced on the subject of Arab–Jewish forbidden love—*On a Narrow Bridge* (Nissim Dayan, 1985), *Torn Apart* (Jack Fisher, 1989), and *Crossfire* (Gideon Ganani, 1989). *On a Narrow Bridge* and *Torn Apart* importantly reflect the intolerance of both the Jewish and Arab communities, which cannot condone a serious relationship between an Arab woman and a Jewish man. *Crossfire* is different from these two films in that it is set during the period of the British Mandate and is based on a true incident, a tragic love story between a Jewish girl from Tel Aviv and her Arab lover from Jaffa.

A number of the films that deal with the problems of Arab–Jewish relations focus on friendship and betrayal. Yehuda (Judd) Ne'eman has directed several films that reflect growing dissent in Israeli society. His first feature, *The Paratroopers* (1977), portrays the stresses of army service. His next two films, *Fellow Travelers* (1983) and *Streets of Yesterday* (1989), depict the ambivalent feelings of Israelis whose left-wing politics bring them to actively support underground Palestinian organizations. Both are complex narrative films about Israelis who become unwittingly involved in the armed struggle of their Arab friends and, having stretched out their hands to assist them, become caught in a complex and dangerous web of betrayal.

During the 1990s, as the peace process developed, fewer films dealt with Arab–Jewish issues on the Israeli screen. Following Eran Riklis' *Cup Final* in 1991, only two feature films, both allegories, were produced dealing with relations between Arabs and Jews: *The Flying Camel* (Rami Na'aman, 1994) and *Circus Palestine* (Eyal Halfon, 1998). *The Flying Camel* explores a mutual relationship between two men, an Arab and a Jew. In this film, in contrast to others produced before, the two men have parallel desires and dreams. It is a political statement about Jews and Palestinians rebuilding elements of the past and working together for the future. *Circus Palestine*, a complex film of romance and intrigue, tells the story of a Palestinian entrepreneur who brings a circus to a Palestinian town under Israeli army occupation.

Previously obsessed with security problems and issues of how to support masses of new immigrants, Israeli society developed into a proud and self-confident nation, and attention started to be focused on the Arab minority within its midst. During the 1980s and early 1990s, films of depth about Arabs and Arab–Jewish relations began to fill Israeli cinema screens, films that were extremely varied in nature. Quite different from those produced during earlier periods, these films offered a radically new image of the Arab. Arab characters were no longer faceless stereotypes of the enemy; rather, they began to be seen as individuals with political consciousness, human needs, and a sense of humor. Some of the films of this era are deeply pessimistic and end in violence and tragedy. Others offer a vision of coexistence and mutual support, even amid brutality and war, or make a plea for better understanding between the two groups. Yet all reflect a growing consciousness among filmmakers of the new importance of Arab–Jewish relations. This can be seen in a new recognition of each other's histories and current dilemmas and a basic acceptance by Jew and Arab that the other is here to stay.

THE RISE OF PALESTINIAN FILMMAKING

Only recently have films produced and directed by Arab filmmakers from Israel and from the Palestinian Autonomy begun to appear. Born and raised in

Nazareth, Palestinian writer-producer-director Michel Khleifi has been based in Belgium since 1970. He made the first Palestinian feature drama, *Wedding in Galilee* (Belgian-French-Palestinian co-production, 1987), as a foreign production and has also directed, among others, the following feature-length documentaries: *Fertile Memory* (1980) and *Canticles of Stone* (1989). *Wedding in Galilee*, shot on location in Arab villages in the Galilee and the West Bank, portrays the story of generational differences in political consciousness, family tensions, and sexual inadequacies, all in the face of life under Israeli military law. Another film that deals with life under military occupation is Ali Nassar's *The Milky Way* (1998).

Palestinian filmmaker Rashid Mashrawi grew up in a refugee camp in the Gaza Strip. Having begun his career as an art director on Israeli film productions, Mashrawi was the first major Palestinian filmmaker to have made films within the context of the Israeli film industry. His films depict Palestinians as trapped by the political reality. *Across the Border* (short, 1987) portrays a man caught without a passport; *Shelter* (short, 1989) portrays an Arab construction worker locked in a shelter in Tel Aviv at night; *The Magician* (short, 1993) portrays an Arab trapped by his own invisibility within Israeli society; and the feature film *Curfew* (1993) portrays Palestinian citizens confined to their homes during the tedious period of a curfew imposed by the Israeli army. Since the establishment of the Palestinian Autonomy, Rashid Mashrawi has lived and worked in Ramallah. He also directed *Long Days in Gaza* (1991), a documentary for the BBC, and the feature film *Haifa* (1996), a Palestine–Netherlands co-production.

Palestinian filmmaker Elia Suleiman caught international attention with his *Divine Intervention* (2002), which won the Jury Prize at Cannes (2002). This film and his previous *Chronicle of a Disappearance* (1996) are not narrative films in the regular sense. Both films are made up of a series of vignettes and take place on the background of the Israeli–Palestinian conflict.

The films made by Arab filmmakers—both Israeli and Palestinian—offer serious political comment and insight into the plight of the Arab minority within Israel and the Palestinians within the areas of the Palestinian Autonomy and reflect their growing consciousness and nationalism.

A MATURING FILM TRADITION—THE ISRAELI "NEW WAVE" OF THE 1990s

Having overcome the obsession with the larger issues of military service, problems of Arab–Jewish relations, and the self-sacrificing nature of the communal society, Israeli cinema, like Israeli literature, has begun to turn inward, toward the individual within the context of societal issues. With its roots in the trauma of the 1973 Yom Kippur War, this emphasis on the individual on the screen is continuing to evolve. During the 1990s Israeli filmmakers turned their cameras to human stories of love, loss, and relationship as well as social issues, such as drug abuse and poverty, feminism and homosexuality, ethnic assimilation and alienation.

The films of the 1990s reflect a growing maturity—an awareness of individuals with their own personal roots, a consciousness of societal ills, and, at the same time, refreshing new lightness, subtle humor, and in-depth and authentically evoked characterizations. This new emphasis is manifested in films on varying subject matter. Different from the heroic films dealing with the nature of war and relations with Arabs, recent films portray male figures as vulnerable and less macho, such as *Shuroo* (Savi Gabizon, 1990), *Dreams of Innocence* (Dina Zvi-Riklis, 1993), and comedies such as *The Revenge of Itzik Finkelstein* (Enrique Rottenberg, 1993) and *Lovesick on Nana St.* (Savi Gabizon, 1995), all four starring Moshe Ivgi as the antihero.

In addition to images of the contemporary Israeli male, recent filmmaking looks at issues of a decaying society. Assi Dayan takes a critical look at societal ills such as loneliness, suicide, and political extremism in his apocryphal film *Life According to Agfa* (1992). The career of director Assi Dayan, son of the famous politician and war hero Moshe Dayan, is symbolic of the transformation that we see taking place. For more than 20 years, Dayan was best known for his ethnic films and social satires. Then he wrote and directed *Life According to Agfa*, a controversial statement, set in a Tel Aviv pub, about urban alienation, chauvinism, self-destructiveness, and racism. In coming to terms with his own aging, Dayan wrote and directed *Mr. Baum* (1998), which shows a middle-aged vulnerability and weariness and reflects a true turning inward. Also illustrating the new individuality as seen in recent filmmaking, Joseph Pitchhadze's prize-winning film *Under Western Eyes* (1996) is heavily influenced by international literary and cinematic elements. The filmmaker has created a road movie, a cinematic work of art that is an intriguing portrayal of betrayal, alienation, loneliness, and despair.

Homosexuality

Two major feature filmmakers in Israel have begun to offer homosexual images on the screen. The first was Amos Gutmann, whose film *Amazing Grace* (1992) was the first Israeli feature film to confront the loneliness and pain of AIDS.

The second Israeli filmmaker to grapple with homosexual issues is Eytan Fox, known for his popular feature film *Song of the Siren* (1994), the television dramatic series *Florentene* (1997–1999), and the acclaimed television drama *Yossi and Jagger* (2002). Fox's films offer positive portrayals of homosexual characters who are comfortable in their surroundings.

As Israeli society is developing and maturing and is no longer obsessed solely with cosmic and political issues, the new emphasis on human portrayals of the "now" generation should bring more portrayals of gay and lesbian issues to the screen. In fact, as personal existential dilemmas are taking over from the stereotypical heroic images, issues of homosexuality have slowly begun to enter the consciousness of the people via the screen.

Achieving Normalcy

David Ben-Gurion, the first prime minister of Israel, dreamed of a Jewish state that would be normal like other states. If Israeli cinema is a reflection of trends in Israeli society, then we can safely say that we've achieved Ben-Gurion's dream. With the turn of the millennium, during the year 2000, 10 new feature films were released that portray themes no less normal than crime, violence, chauvinism, vulgarity, and exploitation in Israeli life. Joseph Pitchhadze is one of the young filmmakers who have made a name by creating aesthetically ambitious films dealing with a complex and "normal" society. Pitchhadze's *Besame Mucho* (2000), named for the Spanish love song, is a passionate love story about gangsters falling over each other in pursuit of a valuable stolen religious icon. On another level, the film is loosely based on Tarantino's *Pulp Fiction.*

While most of the films of the millennium year reflect the Israeli filmmaking trend that emphasizes "normal" life and films that befit a "nation like all other nations," there are also films dealing with issues of Israeli life—one antiwar film (*Kippur* by Amos Gitai), one film criticizing the rise of religious fundamentalism and the settler movement on the West Bank (*Time of Favor* by Joseph Cedar), and one film dealing with issues within the Bedouin community (*Yellow Asphalt* by Dan [Nokyo] Verete).

Religious Extremism

During the mid- to late 1990s, with the rise of the influence of religious parties within the coalition political system, there were a significant increase in antagonism between secular and ultrareligious Jews and a conscious awareness of the rise of religious extremism. A number of serious feature films were produced that portray the ultra-Orthodox religious communities. Yossi Somer's *The Dybbuk of the Holy Apple Field* (1997) is a moving, modern-day adaptation of Sholem Ansky's classic Jewish play *The Dybbuk* and takes place in the Jerusalem neighborhood of Meah Shearim. Somer's courageous version of this tale of mystical romance combines contemporary elements with rich kabbalistic spiritual symbols. Amos Gitai's *Kadosh* (1999) is set within a cloistered community of Sephardi ultra-Orthodox Jews, also in Meah Shearim. It is a heavily ideological and emotional film, and most of the drama takes place indoors, within closed spaces, providing a sense of the stifling nature of life within this community.

Additional films grapple with issues of religious life—Daniel Wachsmann's *The Appointed* (1990), about corruption, both religious and financial, within the ultra-Orthodox community, and Joseph Cedar's *Time of Favor* (2000), about the dangers of fanaticism and religious extremism.

The Family through Modern Eyes

As the trend moves away from major political issues in film and moves toward grappling with personal stories about individuals, we begin to see films dealing with issues of the family, with marriage, and with touching love stories.

Shemi Zarhin's *Passover Fever* (1995) portrays a holiday gathering at the old family home. It combines elements of family intrigue with hope, love, and dedication to solving family problems. The matriarchal figure and her devoted husband have invited all their children and grandchildren for the Passover holiday. Only the son who was killed in action is missing from this family tableau, and his memory lingers forever in the background. In fact, his memory haunts the family in the same way that terrorism, political insecurity, and memories of war gnawed at the basic fabric of Israeli society of the 1990s, as peace continued to be elusive.

Other films that deal with issues of the family are *Family Secrets* (1998), about a homosexual uncle who brutally rapes his nephew, two tragic films about domestic abuse—*Tell Me That You Love Me* (1983) and *Chronicle of Love* (1998), both by Tsipi Trope, and *Broken Wings* (Nir Bergman, 2002) about dealing with loss within the family.

Contemporary Images of Women

Although the pioneering socialist ideology of the early Zionist movement was built upon equality, in reality women were less equal than men. For example, on the communal agricultural settlements known as kibbutzim, conditions required that women carry an equal share of the work, but they were mostly assigned to child raising and domestic tasks. As an exception, women sometimes worked alongside the men in the fields and orchards. Kibbutz men generally shouldered more of the physically difficult tasks—working in the fields, laying irrigation pipes, and caring for the animals. With increasing industrialization, men also assumed positions of management in the factories.

During the period before the establishment of the state, a small number of women volunteered for combat roles and served side by side with men in the Palmach and on the battlefronts during the War of Independence. Consequently, in the films produced during the early years of the state, women are portrayed as assertive characters and equal fighting partners. Heroic women are seen in combat roles in *Hill 24 Doesn't Answer* (Thorold Dickinson, 1954) and in *Pillar of Fire* (Larry Frisch, 1959). During the later years however, greater emphasis was more and more placed on traditional female roles in the home. As a result, the army began to exclude women from combat roles, and most were assigned clerical and secretarial jobs. Thus, the Israeli army became primarily a male dominion, and women largely disappeared from the screen in films dealing with the military world.

As a result, decades of Israeli filmmaking presented only a small number of complex narrative films about women's issues, including *Siege* (Gilberto Tofano, 1969), *Moments* (Michal Bat-Adam, 1979), and *The Last Winter* (Riki Shelach, 1982). The 1990s, with its shifting emphasis to women's roles and its portrayal of the fading chauvinism of the Israeli male, brought about a major increase in films dealing with strong female images, including Ayelet Menachemi and Nirit Yaron's *Tel Aviv Stories* (1992), a series of three short subjects dealing with women's issues, and Aner Preminger's *Blind Man's Bluff* (1993) about a young woman reaching maturity and independence.

Michal Bat-Adam, the first Israeli-born woman to direct a feature film, made her debut film, *Moments*, in 1979. This was a prizewinning film that expressed emotions and feelings cinematically rather than through the use of dialogue. One of her later films, *Aya, Imagined Autobiography* (1994), is a profound look at the emotional turmoil of a woman's life as she is haunted by memories of the past. Moving between past and present, the film provides fragments from the woman's life. Michal Bat-Adam's filmmaking is characterized by highly personal elements of relationships, the hardships of growing up, and the conflicts of mature women as they grapple with memories of their past.

During the years following the bombings and traumas of the Gulf War of 1990–1991, two films sentimentally portray the period of the war through the story of a woman. *Song of the Siren* (Eytan Fox, 1994) is a romantic comedy, rich in texture, color, and humor. Based on the acclaimed novel by Irit Linur (published in 1991), the film portrays an image of a professional woman who is self-confident, mature, and successful. Award-winning *Yana's Friends* (Arik Kaplun, 1999) portrays two people—one is an arrogant Israeli film student, and the other, Yana, is a new immigrant from Russia—who share a flat in Tel Aviv. Only under the pressures of the missile attacks and hidden by a gas mask is Yana able to permit herself to be seduced by her flatmate. Uncomfortable with her inadequacies in a foreign language and in a foreign culture, Yana has found a way—via the gas mask, which covers her identity as a new immigrant—to adjust to her new reality.

Two films of the 1990s portray foreign women, both journalists on assignment in Israel. In both *Time of the Cherries* (Haim Bouzaglo, 1991) and *Double Edge* (Amos Kollek, 1991) the female character is an American journalist striving for honesty and truth in political reporting. In *Double Edge*, the journalist (Faye Dunaway) is attracted to two men—one is an Israeli, and the other is a Palestinian terrorist. Her journalistic honesty, coupled with her naïveté, leads her into complex and dangerous situations. Similarly, in *Time of the Cherries*, the journalist becomes emotionally involved with the Jewish subject of her reporting. In both of these films, the foreign woman symbolizes an international media standard—a Western work ethic and a higher level of professionalism. In adjusting to Israel, however, she must conquer newfound complexities in the political and artistic arenas.

One of the most prolific actresses on the Israeli screen, Gila Almagor often portrays the Jewish mother, from the prostitute/mother of an institutionalized child in *The Highway Queen* (Menahem Golan, 1971), to the Holocaust survivor in *Summer of Aviya* (Eli Cohen, 1988) and its sequel, *Under the Domim Tree* (Eli Cohen, 1995). She plays the widowed mother who succeeds in finding love and life again in *Siege* (Gilberto Tofano, 1969), the courageous and self-sacrificing single mother in *The House on Chelouche St.* (Moshe Mizrahi, 1973), the activist in *Hide and Seek* (Dan Wolman, 1980), the elegant, yet world-weary, single mother and owner of a Tel Aviv pub in *Life According to Agfa* (Assi Dayan, 1992), the old-fashioned and superstitious mother in *Sh'chur* (Shmuel Hasfari, 1994), and the sophisticated mother of the contemporary dysfunctional family in *Passover Fever* (Shemi Zarhin, 1995). Gila Almagor's diverse screen personae provide insight into the varied images and types of Israeli mothers. She has played roles as the indulgent and self-sacrificing mother. She has also been the self-centered and manipulative mother. She has played the unbalanced Holocaust survivor, the Sephardi mother, the war widow, the prostitute, the single parent, and the matriarch of the modern family—all images found in Israeli society until this very day.

Documentary Filmmaking

As a cultural voice and a tool for political expression, documentary films reflect the sociopolitical reality of a country. They raise issues, grapple with problems, and reflect pressures of life in an authentic way that dramatic filmmaking is unable to do.

Since its earliest days, Israeli cinema has included strong documentary voices. During the Zionist period, before the establishment of the state of Israel, the documentary filmmakers included Helmar Lerski, Ya'akov Ben-Dov, and Nathan Axelrod, among others. After the state of Israel was born, documentary films played an important role in strengthening the voice of the heroic genre, as can be seen in the large number of feature-length documentaries of the post–Six Day War period: *Six Days to Eternity* (Ya'akov Hame'iri, Yitzhak Mimisch Herbst, 1967), *The War after the War* (Micha Shagrir, 1969), *The Twenty Years War* (Paul Smith, 1968), *Follow Me . . . The Six Day War* (Alfred Steinhardt, 1967), and *Three Hours in June* (Ilan Eldad, 1967).

The period of the Eichmann trial (1960–1962) brought the subject of the Holocaust into the mainstream of the national discourse. During the period following the trial, the Ghetto Fighters' House (at Kibbutz Lochamei HaGhettaot) decided to embark on a massive project of collecting archival footage from the vaults of film archives in Europe and produced a trilogy of documentary films. In an attempt to make the gray mist of living in the shadow of the Holocaust slowly disappear and disintegrate through the use of film images, the Ghetto Fighters' House offered films that are epic in scope. The first in the series is *The Eighty-first Blow* (Jacques Ehrlich, David Bergman, Haim Gouri, 1974), a devastating look at the historical details of the Holocaust, using archival footage and pieces of testimony from the Eichmann trial itself. Other major documentaries followed. They were less far-reaching in scope but more interpretive, including *Due to That War* (Orna Ben-Dor, 1988), *Choice and Destiny* (Tsipi Reibenbach, 1993), *Daddy, Come to the Fair* (Nitza Gonen, 1994), *Don't Touch My Holocaust* (Asher Tlalim, 1994), and *Martin* (Ra'anan Alexandrowicz, 1999). The first Israeli television documentary to win an Emmy Award, *Kapo* (1999), directed by Tor Ben Mayor and Dan Setton, grapples with issues of forced collaboration with the Nazis by Jews while under the threat of death.

The personal portrait has also reached the Israeli screen. David Perlov's *Diary* (1988) is an intimate portrayal of one family, yet, at the same time, it is a monumental look at the collective. Ron Havilio has also used this genre in his epic film *Fragments—Jerusalem* (1996), which tells the story of a city filled with difficult challenges and tensions.

Documentary filmmaking is an aesthetic reflection of political, societal, and cultural elements. Contemporary documentary filmmakers such as Amos Gitai and David Benchetrit have made important contributions in the political arena; Amit Goren, Julie Shles, Michal Aviad, Arnon Goldfinger, Tsipi Reibenbach, Asher Tlalim, and Ron Havilio have made equally important contributions in the historical, social, and cultural sectors of Israeli life. In recent years, due to a proliferation of cable television channels within Israel, documentary filmmaking has begun to be a popular voice and art form.

FOREIGN FILMMAKERS

The Lumière brothers were the first to send cameramen to Palestine as part of their early efforts to record faraway and exotic places for French audiences. At that time in 1896, the camera was immobile, but the images moved. During the more than 100 years that have passed since that time, many more filmmakers have been attracted to the Holy Land. Among the earliest filmmakers who made the long trip to the Holy Land were two British directors, Murray Rosenberg, who came in 1911 to document the Jewish images in the Holy Land in his film *The First Film of Palestine*, and Sidney Olcott, who came in 1913 to make the biblical epic *From the Manger to the Cross*.

One of the things that have added to the style, diversity, and growth of the Israeli film industry is the large number of foreign filmmakers who have directed features and documentaries in Israel. Polish filmmaker Alexander Ford arrived in 1933 to direct a story of the pioneers, *Sabra* (Chalutzim), with members of the Habimah Theater, including Hannah Rovina, Raphael Klatchkin, and Aharon Moskin. A co-production of Poland and British Mandatory Palestine, the laboratory work and editing on the film were carried out in Warsaw. During the same period, before the establishment of the state, foreign filmmakers who made documentary films include A. J. Bloome, who directed *Dream of My People* (1934) with Cantor Yossele Rosenblatt, and Helmar Lerski, who directed *Avodah* (1935). Following the establishment of the state, French documentarist Chris Marker directed *Description of a Struggle* (1960). In addition, many Israeli feature films were directed by foreign filmmakers—Thorold Dickinson directed *Hill 24 Doesn't Answer* (1954), Denys de La Patellière directed *Sabra—Death of a Jew* (1969), Barbara Noble directed *Worlds Apart* (1979), the well-known Irish actor Richard Harris directed *Bloomfield* (1970), and the Hungarian-born Hollywood cinematographer Zsigmond Vilmos directed *The Long Shadow* (1992).

Foreign influences have also been felt through the contribution of new immigrant filmmakers. During the early years of the state, filmmakers such as Larry Frisch, Nuri Habib, George Ovadiah, and Aryeh Lahola brought with them cultural backgrounds and filmmaking styles that helped to mold the unique expression of Israeli cinema as it grew and developed. In more recent decades, successful filmmakers from the former Soviet Union who interrupted their careers to relocate to Israel include Mikhail Kalik (*Three and One*, 1975) and the documentarist Herz Frank (co-director of *The Man of the Wall—A Documentary Mystery*, 1998).

CONCLUSION

Israeli film is an art form in the making over the past 70 years that depicts the self-image of the people of Israel. In its short history, Israeli cinema has moved from crude films, almost primitive in style, some propagandistic and some melodramatic, to a more developed and sophisticated cinematic style that includes depth of character and complexity of plot. Thematically, Israeli cinema has moved from an emphasis on the community to an understanding of the individual, from the sacrifices of the pioneering period to the materialism and personal egotism of the contemporary period, from stereotypic heroic images to more complex and problematic images of the Israeli in a continually changing society, from one-dimensional portrayals of Arab characters to a reaching out for an understanding of one's Arab neighbors.

Although growing and developing, Israeli cinema is riddled with many problems. These problems include issues of government support, limited audience, inadequate budgets, and a lack of professionalism and experience in the field of scriptwriting. In addition, Israeli cinema suffers from identity problems; is it possible to be an indigenous Israeli art form, or does the road to success require that one produce films that are international in nature? Those filmmakers who have tried to appeal exclusively to the international market have lost their Israeli appeal. This identity problem, however, is being resolved as quality films are winning international acclaim and as a uniquely Israeli stylistic and thematic filmmaking expression is developing. Israeli films of recent years have also won the attention of Israeli critics and the Israeli filmgoing public for their artistic expression and their authentic reflection of societal issues.

ISRAELI FILMS

Films are arranged alphabetically by English title. A full biography and film entry can be found for those marked with an asterisk. The following abbreviations have been used: Dir. (Director), Prod. (Producer), Sc. (Scriptwriter), Ph. (Cinematographer), Edit. (Editor), Narr. (Narrator).

AGAIN, FOREVER (Roman Be'Hemshachim), 1985.

Dir.: Oded Kotler*; Prod.: Nurit Shani; Sc.: Yitzhak Ben-Nir, based on his novel; Ph.: Hanania Bar; Edit.: Anat Lubarsky; Music: Shem-Tov Levy*; Cast: Haim Topol*, Galia Topol, Efrat Lavie, Uri Levy, Anat Topol, Natan Datner, Sari Tzuriel, Aliza Rosen, Gabi Amrani, Shmuel Shiloh, Shoshana Duar.

On the background of the political situation of 1977 (when the Labor Mapai party lost the national elections and Menachem Begin's right-wing Likud party gained power for the first time), the film tells a story about politics, responsibilities, relationships, unobtainable dreams, soul-searching, and the fear of time passing you by.

Effi (Topol) is an overworked lawyer, married to a sensitive woman, a poet, and they have a little girl. This is his second marriage. His ex-wife is also remarried with a small child. They both seem to want to get back together, but after 10 years, it is not meant to be. Effi is also involved in politics and begins to notice the dirt and corruption of the ruling party.

AMAZING GRACE (Hesed Mufla), 1992.

Dir. & Sc.: Amos Gutmann*; Prod.: Dagan Price; Ph.: Amnon Zlayet; Edit.: Einat Glaser Zarhin; Music: Arkadi Duchin; Cast: Gal Hoyberger, Sharon Alexander*, Rivka Michaeli, Aki Avni, Hina Rozovska, Devorah Bartonov, Karen Ofir, Igi Wachsman, Hasida Stoleru, Ada Varlerie-Tal.

Awards: Silver Palm, Valencia (1992); Honorable Mention, Houston (1992); Honorable Mention, Torino (1992); Wolgin Award, Jerusalem (1992); Critic's Jury Prize, Haifa (1993).

A story of homosexual love, the film provides a study of the complicated relationships between homosexual men and their mothers, including a sensitive scene of homosexual desire in which the picture from a magazine comes to life in the fantasy of the male reader, a fantasy that is more erotic in what is implicit than in what is explicit on-screen.

Thomas (Sharon Alexander), a 30-year-old New York homosexual, has returned "home" to Tel Aviv for a visit. Although Thomas is dying of AIDS, there are only hints of his disease in the film; in fact, he makes great efforts to hide his condition from everyone. He is befriended by 18-year-old Jonathan (Gal Hoyberger), who is still smarting from his breakup with his previous lover. When Thomas asks him if he wants to sleep with him, Jonathan answers, "I don't want to get used to someone who won't be here tomorrow," but for Thomas this has a completely different meaning.

Jonathan has a surprisingly healthy relationship with his family—his younger sister; high school brother, eager to have his first heterosexual experience; and his mother, for whom he works in a children's shelter. Thomas, on the other hand, has a complicated relationship with his bedridden and bitter grandmother and his aloof mother (Rivka Michaeli), who does not know how to reach out to her ailing son. There is another image of a mother in the film—the mother of Jonathan's ex-lover, Mickey (Aki Avni), who is convinced that she is acting in the best interests of her "deviant" son when she informs the military police of his whereabouts in order to force him to behave like a "man" and shoulder his responsibilities by serving in the army.

AMERICAN CITIZEN (Ezrach Amerikai), 1992.

Dir. & Sc.: Eitan Green; Prod.: Marek Rozenbaum*, Avi Kleinberger; Ph.: Dani Shneur; Edit.: Ira Lapid; Music: Adi Renart; Cast: Guy Garner, Itcho Avital, Eva Haddad, Baruch David, Haim Banai, Danny Roth, Menashe Warshavski, Ayala Neuman, Rafi Adar, Doron Tsabari.

The film is the story of a friendship between two men, one a professional basketball player, the other a journalist, and the help that they give each other in meeting their potential. Film director Eitan Green is also a film critic and edited books about film. His other feature films include *Lena* (1982) and *When Night Falls** (1985).

Michael (Guy Garner) is an American who plays professional basketball. He is hired to play for the Ashdod team in order to help them improve and move up a league. Yoel (Itcho Avital), a local journalist, obsessed with the game of basketball, was once a talented pianist, but he gave it up because of epilepsy. Michael encourages Yoel to play piano again. Yoel pushes Michael, who is suffering from a knee injury, to coach the team and to play some great basketball, thereby saving the team from losing its standing in the league.

Tzvi Shissel (left) and Shuli Rand (center) in *The Appointed* (Daniel Wachsmann, 1990). Photo courtesy of the Jerusalem Cinematheque, reprinted with the permission of Daniel Wachsmann.

THE APPOINTED (Hameyu'ad; Alternative title: *The Intended*), 1990.

Dir.: Daniel Wachsmann*; Prod.: Enrique Rottenberg, Ehud Bleiberg; Sc.: Daniel Wachsmann, Shmuel Hasfari*, Razi Levinas; Ph.: Ilan Rosenberg; Edit.: Zohar Sela; Music: Uri Vadislavski; Cast: Shuli Rand, Tzvi Shissel, Ronit Elkabetz*, Yitzhak (Babi) Ne'eman, Shabtai Conorti, David Danino.

Awards: Wolgin Award, Jerusalem (1990); Best Film, Haifa (1990); Best Cinematography, Best Art Director (Avi & Anat Avivi), Israeli Academy Awards (1990).

About religious extremism, the film deals with ancient religious practices, corrupt leadership, supernatural powers, and forbidden love. Loosely based on the real-life story of the son of the spiritual leader the Baba Sali, the film is the story of a figure chosen to lead a religious sect. It explores the attraction of two opposing forces, both with supernatural powers—one a Messianic figure and the other an agent of Lilith. The setting of the film is in the Galilee, a region in the north of Israel, where writers, poets, artists, and religious thinkers have found the nature and beauty of the surroundings to be compelling.

Shemaya Ben David (Shuli Rand) is a telepathy artist, playing the circuit of Galilee nightspots. One day he meets Oshra (Ronit Elkabetz), a haunting, dark-haired figure capable of creating fire by her psychic powers. She is a messenger of the devil, seen lurking in shadows, darkness, rain, and haze. Shemaya and Oshra take to the road, performing magic acts in nightclubs across the Galilee. When Shemaya's father, the leader of a religious group in Safed, becomes ill, messengers are sent to bring his son back to lead the community, but the son finds it difficult to accept his predestined role as their leader. Eventually, he repents, becomes a miracle healer, and offers cures, prayers, and blessings to the faithful. His business manager (Tzvi Shissel), having decided to join his friend in his new venture, sets out to commercialize his religious leadership. Shemaya finds that the burden of living up to the legend created around him is too great. Although he has become engaged to another woman, he finds it difficult to refuse Oshra's sexual advances. Full of deep religious torment, Shemaya realizes that, like before, he is just a cheap crowd pleaser, and he prays to God not to forsake him. Against the background of the hills of Galilee, Oshra watches from afar as Shemaya struggles with the demons within himself and is then consumed by fire.

ARIANNA, 1971.

Dir.: George Ovadiah*; Prod.: Michael Shvili; Sc.: Michael Shvili, George Ovadiah, Ada Ben-Nahum; Ph.: Ya'ackov Kallach; Edit.: Dov Hoenig; Music: Haim Tzur; Cast: Dassi Hadari, Yitzhak Shiloh, Avi Toledano, Tova Pardo, Arieh Elias, Gabi Amrani, Penina Gray, Rahel Terry, Shlomit Segal, Leah Shlanger, Avraham Ronai.

The film mixes melodrama and sentimentalism with music and song and combines class division and ethnic tension to add tragedy to the romantic element—a successful recipe that Ovadiah repeated in many of his following films, including *Nurit** and *West Side Girl**.

Arianna's mother was a young Sephardi woman who had the misfortune to have an affair with a well-known Ashkenazi lawyer (Yitzhak Shiloh). Finding herself pregnant and not wanting to have the abortion that he so shockingly offers to pay for, she goes to live with friends in a slum area of old Jaffa, where she dies in childbirth. Twenty years pass and her daughter, Arianna (Dassi Hadari), becomes involved with Gadi (singer Avi Toledano), the son of a wealthy family. When Arianna becomes pregnant, Arianna's stepparents sue Gadi's family. The well-known lawyer (who coincidentally had tried to pay for her mother's abortion years ago) is representing Gadi's family in the courtroom. In the most unusual circumstances, he admits that he is the father of Arianna, and he encourages Gadi not to make the same mistake that he made in his own life. Since Gadi and Arianna are in love, they agree to marry, and all ends well.

ATALIA, 1984.

Dir.: Akiva Tevet; Prod.: Shmuel Shiloh, Dani Schik, Omri Maron; Sc.: Tzvika Kretzner, based on a story by Yitzhak Ben-Nir; Ph.: Nurith Aviv*; Edit.: Ruben Korenfeld; Music: Nahum Heiman; Cast: Michal Bat-Adam*, Yiftach

Katzur, Yossi Pollack, Dan Toren, Raphael Klatchkin, Gali Ben-Nir, Ruth Geller, Shifra Millstein, Yair (Koya) Rubin.

Award: Best Actress (Michal Bat-Adam), Israel Film Center (1984).

Made against the background of the 1973 Yom Kippur War, the film revolves around a nonconformist war widow, her bereavement, and her antimilitary and antisocial tendencies. She is seen as an antithesis to societal norms in the stifling communal atmosphere of the kibbutz.

Atalia (Michal Bat-Adam) lost her husband in the 1956 Sinai campaign and assuages her perpetual loneliness by having affairs with many of the men on her kibbutz. When 18-year-old Matti is released from military service due to a heart problem and returns to the kibbutz, he has an affair with Atalia. Atalia's teenage daughter, who lives with the shame of an eccentric mother who has never found her place in the social fabric of the community, experiences bereavement when she loses her young boyfriend at the beginning of the 1973 Yom Kippur War. Similar to the other members of the kibbutz, she is aghast and hurt by her mother's affair with Matti, and this ultimately leads to Atalia's downfall.

ATTRACTION (Ko'ach Meshicha; Alternative title: *Power of Attraction*), 1988.

Dir.: Naftali Alter*; Prod.: Eran Viezer; Sc.: Naftali Alter, Hagit Rachavi; Ph.: Yvonne Miklosh; Edit.: Moshe Ivgi*; Music: Dani Robbes; Cast: Hanan Goldblatt, Irit Alter, Alona Kimchi, Itzik Weingarten, Ofra Weingarten, Liat Farris, Ron Appleberg.

Based on the male fantasy of enjoying the sexual favors of two women, the film takes a comic look at the crisis of midlife to the absurd.

Yali (Hanan Goldblatt) is a married father of two and a successful producer of television commercials. He is bored with his marriage and his work until he meets Noga, a much younger woman (Alona Kimchi). When his wife (Irit Alter) discovers his infidelity, she offers a brilliant yet unorthodox solution. Noga moves into their home and becomes an integral part of their family, but Yali finds it impossible to keep up with two women. When he goes away with his wife for their anniversary, and Noga arrives to join them in bed, Yali flees. He has learned his lesson.

AUGUST SNOW (Sheleg Be'Ogust), 1993.

Dir. & Sc.: Hagai Levi; Prod.: Hagai Levi, Jorge Gurvich, Anat Asulin; Ph.: Jorge Gurvich; Edit.: Hadara Oren, Music: Haim Elfman; Cast: Rami Hoyberger, Avigail Arieli, Gali Ben-Nir, Rita Shukrun, Hillel Ne'eman, Nissim Zohar, Sandra Sadeh, Ya'ackov Banai, Yossi Yablonski, Danny Muggia.

Merging the real and the surreal, the film depicts the tensions between the ultra-Orthodox Ashkenazi community and the more modern and liberal Italian one in Jerusalem. In addition to this feature film, director Hagai Levi has written film criticism and makes television dramas and documentary films.

Ruth Segal, Edna Fleidel, and Hannah Meron (left to right) in *Aunt Clara* (Avram Heffner, 1977). Photo courtesy of the Jerusalem Cinematheque, reprinted with the permission of Avram Heffner.

Gabriel (Rami Hoyberger), a young man from the Italian community, wakes up one morning having experienced a surreal vision in which his religious girlfriend, Na'ama (Avigail Arieli), has been spirited away to some form of bizarre religious ritual. Gabriel questions the meaning of the dream and is consumed with worry about Na'ama. He sets out to find her with the assistance of a young woman from his own community. Meanwhile, Na'ama, who is confused and unable to decide for herself, seeks out the advice of Vera, Gabriel's aunt, who, years ago, married into the ultra-Orthodox community and was forced to separate herself from her Italian roots. Vera's advice to Na'ama is not to choose a boy from outside her own community. While uncovering a stifling world of religious coercion and fanaticism, Gabriel eventually arrives at a guarded yeshivah for girls, surrounded by barbed wire, where he finds Na'ama hiding within.

AUNT CLARA (Doda Clara), 1977.

Dir. & Sc.: Avram Heffner*; Prod.: Rudi Cohen; Ph.: David Gurfinkel*; Edit.: Avi Cohen; Music: Alexander (Sasha) Argov; Cast: Hannah Meron*, Edna Fleidel, Ruth Segal, Yosef Carmon, Shmuel Rodensky*, Shmuel Bunim.

An ethnic comedy about three Ashkenazi sisters, the film provides insight into personal relationships and the burden of family responsibilities, combining humor, Yiddish expressions, and moving performances by well-known theater actors. The film tells the story of the epitome of the Jewish mother, sacrificing and meddling not in one Jewish family, but in three!

Clara (Hannah Meron), Rouga, and Leah are sisters who jointly run a boutique for wedding gowns. The narrative construct has declared Clara, by virtue of her wisdom and age, to be the matriarch of the entire extended family, providing direction and advice to her sisters and their husbands. Only one of the sisters has a child. Although not Clara's daughter in the literal sense, she runs to her Aunt Clara, the head mother, whenever she has problems, even when she needs advice before her wedding. She is the metaphorical heir to Aunt Clara, and she will also become a Jewish mother; even her new husband tells her, "You are always right!" Although manipulative and meddling, Clara is well intentioned and has fully shouldered her family responsibilities with the knowledge that they have forced her to make decisions where others were unable.

AVANTI POPOLO, 1986.

Dir., Prod., & Sc.: Rafi Bukaee*; Ph.: Yoav Kosh*; Edit.: Zohar Sela; Music: Uri Ophir; Cast: Salim Dau*, Suheil Haddad, Danny Roth, Dani Segev, Tuvia Gelber, Barry Langford, Michael Koresh, Shalom Shmueli.

Awards: Golden Eye of the Leopard, Locarno (1986); Critic's Jury Prize, Best Actor (Salim Dau), Haifa (1987); Second Prize, Israel Film Center (1986–1987).

The film explores the reversal of roles that took place during the Six Day War of 1967—the Jews, who had previously been the underdog, suddenly found themselves in a position of strength, and the Arabs were no longer the major power bloc. The film portrays the fine line between the real and the surreal in wartime and, at the same time, offers a metaphor for the need to perceive the human being behind the face of the enemy. Two Egyptian soldiers are trying to find their way back to the Suez Canal shortly after the cease-fire. Searching for water, the two come across a deserted United Nations jeep with a dead Swedish soldier in the back. Under the seat, these two Muslims (who have never tasted alcohol before) discover two bottles of liquor. This narrative element permits the two soldiers to become highly inebriated for some of the following scenes.

When they come across an Israeli patrol, one of the two soldiers, Khalid (Salim Dau), a professional actor on the Cairo stage, uses the language of the theater to beg for water and understanding at the same time. Reciting Shylock's famous monologue from *The Merchant of Venice*, he says: "I am a Jew. Has not a Jew eyes, emotions, senses? Do we not bleed?" In this brilliant and ironic interchange, the Egyptian soldier/actor is begging for his own humanity and honor. When the Israeli soldier laughs and tells the others, "I think he has confused his role," the viewer realizes that the Arab, having found himself in the position of the underdog, suddenly better understands the Jew. Now he requests the same understanding in return.

Arab and Jew march along in the desert twilight singing "Avanti Popolo,"

Salim Dau in *Avanti Popolo* (Rafi Bukaee, 1986). Photo courtesy of the Jerusalem Cinematheque, reprinted with the permission of Rafi Bukaee.

the Italian Communist anthem. When the Israeli soldiers mistakenly enter a minefield, the Arabs run to try to save the lives of their supposed enemies. The tragic ending has the two Arabs symbolically caught between bullets from both sides in the conflict, mistakenly hunted by Israeli troops for having caused the death of their soldiers caught in the minefield and simultaneously shot at by their own troops as they attempt to cross the Suez Canal.

AVODAH (Alternative title: *Work*), 1935.

Dir. & Ph.: Helmar Lerski*; Prod.: Paul Boroschek; Music: Paul Dessau.

A monumental documentary, the film focuses on the agricultural and technological achievements of the pioneers of the 1930s. It opens with an introductory section of feet walking through barren terrain, splashing through water, and trudging over hills until arriving in Palestine. There are glimpses of the local population of Arabs and their primitive agricultural methods—individuals working in the fields; a camel driving a waterwheel; and a shepherd with his goats. Then follows the major part of the film—planting, paving of the roads, harvesting, production of bricks, the communal life of the kibbutz, drilling for water and the triumphant gushing of a natural water source, making the parched land come to life.

The cinematic quality of the discovery of water, as seen through the use of camera angles, dramatic music, and editing, is still remarkable today. The film makes use of shadow, composition, extreme camera angles, close-ups, and stark and contrasting images (such as the juxtaposition of man and machinery). It is a film in the style of socialist realism, dwelling on images that glorify the worker and the monumental achievements; however, no emphasis is placed on the individual. Shot as a silent film, the sound track of music and effects was added in a sound studio in Budapest.

AYA, AN IMAGINED AUTOBIOGRAPHY (Aya, Autobiografia Dimyonit), 1994.

Dir. & Sc.: Michal Bat-Adam*; Prod.: Marek Rozenbaum*; Ph.: Yoav Kosh*; Edit.: Boaz Leon; Music: Amos Hadani; Cast: Michal Bat-Adam, Michal Zoaretz, Shira Lev-Munk, Liat Goren, Gedalia Besser*, Levana Finkelstein*.

A touching, personal document, the film moves between past and present and is about relationships between mother and daughter, the hardships of young girls growing up, and the conflicts of mature women as they grapple with memories of their past. A reflection of the emotional memory of Michal Bat-Adam, the film represents the accumulation of little fantasies and important things that occur in one's mind; these are the elements that make up the "real" or "imagined" autobiography. "God exists in the little things," says the protagonist-filmmaker, as the film concludes and the pages of her film script whirl in the wind around her.

Aya (Michal Bat-Adam), a grown woman, haunted by memories of her past, is making a film about her own life, using vignettes from her childhood and adolescent years to illustrate her memories of tender moments between her parents (Levana Finkelstein and Gedalia Besser), her mother's erratic behavior as she was on the verge of a nervous breakdown, and her own first love affair on the kibbutz where she went to school. The scenes of Aya's past are often played twice, as actors portraying the scene for her film within a film intermingle with her memories of the past.

BAR 51 (Alternative title: *Orphans of the Storm*), 1985.

Dir.: Amos Gutmann*; Prod.: Enrique Rottenberg; Sc.: Edna Maziah, Amos Gutmann; Ph.: Yossi Wein; Edit.: Tova Asher; Music: Arik Rudich; Cast: Juliano Mer, Smadar Dayan-Kalchinsky, Ada Valerie-Tal, Alon Aboutboul*, Irit Sheleg, Moscu Alcalay, David Patrick Wilson, Poli Reshef, Blanka Metzner, Rachel Shor.

Awards: Second Prize for Film, Best Actress (Smadar Dayan-Kalchinsky), Best Cinematography, Israel Film Center (1985).

About the special relationship and spiritual bond between a brother and a sister, this film deals with sexuality and incest, aging and loneliness, and the loss of one's naïveté.

When their mother passes away, Thomas (Juliano Mer) takes his high school sister, Marianna (Smadar Dayan-Kalchinsky), to discover big-city life. Thomas has trouble holding down a job, and in the dark and haunting world of nighttime Tel Aviv, they struggle to support themselves and to find a place to live. They are befriended by an eccentric older woman, Apollonia (Ada Valerie-Tal), an "artistic" type who takes them home to her decaying and claustrophobic apartment, where they exchange the memories and possessions of their youth for the stuffy and cluttered furnishings of Apollonia's decadent lifestyle.

BEFORE TOMORROW (Lifnei Machar), 1969.

Dir.: Ellida Geyra; Prod.: Ram Ron, Alexander Hacohen; Edit.: Jacques Ehrlich; Sc.: Ellida Geyra, Yoram Kaniuk; Ph.: Amnon Salomon*, Adam Greenberg*; Music: Melvin Keller, Alex Weiss; Cast: Yisrael (Poli) Poliakov, Rina Ganor, Arieh Elias, Ruth Harris.

American-born filmmaker Ellida Geyra is the first female to direct a feature film in Israel. The film is made up of two parts, *Spring* and *Autumn*, both about love and courting.

Spring is a vignette of two young lovers (Yisrael Poliakov and Rina Ganor) who, like Adam and Eve, seem to be the only people alive. In a modern setting, their flirting and passion are erotic and almost wordless. *Autumn*, on the other hand, is an old-fashioned romance, filled with dialogue. It is about two older and very different people, a Sephardi man (Arieh Elias) who makes a living selling falafel and an educated Ashkenazi woman (Ruth Harris). He imagines buying a car in order to drive her around. She imagines him as a rugged and strong soccer player. Both are hesitantly looking, in the autumn of their lives, for a way out of their loneliness.

BERLIN–JERUSALEM, 1989.

Dir.: Amos Gitai*; Prod.: Marek Rozenbaum*; Co-prod.: Israel-France-Germany; Sc.: Amos Gitai, Gudie Lawaetz; Ph.: Henri Alekan, Nurith Aviv*; Edit.: Luke Barnea; Music: Markus Stockhausen; Cast: Lisa Kreuzer, Rivka Neuman, Juliano Mor, Keren Mor, Vernon Dubtcheff, Benjamin Levi.

Awards: Special Citation, Italian Film Critics' Association, Venice (1989); Special Jury Prize, Istanbul (1990).

The film presents fragments from the lives of two visionary women—Manya Shochat, a Russian revolutionary, member of the intellectual circles of Berlin, and founding member of the kibbutz and Israeli Labor movement, and Else Lasker-Schuler, a German expressionist poet who fled from Berlin during the years of the Third Reich. In comparing Manya Shochat's socialist lifestyle in Palestine to Else Lasker-Schuler's Berlin of the 1920s and 1930s, the film is looking at cultural history and taking a harsh look at the Zionist period. Both women lose their loved ones to senseless violence.

Manya (Rivka Neuman), called Tanya in Palestine, is ideological, feminist, and hardworking. During the early years of the century, she is instrumental in radicalizing the members of her kibbutz so that women could share equally in the agricultural work and men could work in the kitchen. Else (Lisa Kreuzer), on the other hand, is a poet, self-indulgent and giving more attention to dress and appearance. Whereas Manya comes to Israel searching for a utopian vision, Else comes in the shadow of the Nazi period. The contrasts are also visual—the extreme sunlight of Palestine against the darkness of German nightlife; the healthy outdoor environment of the kibbutz against the cramped and stylized German theater, music, poetry, and cafés. There are also striking similarities, especially the starkness of both places: Palestine's desert landscape and the barren fields, which lead to the controversy with the neighboring Arabs and the killing of Manya's lover, and Berlin's bare trees, empty of their leaves, representing the barren society, the rise of Nazism, the burning of books, and the death of Else's son at the hands of the Nazis.

As Else flees Berlin, she is wandering, searching for a new place. "If I knew of a river as deep as my life, I would throw myself into its water," she says. Arriving in Palestine, she is shocked to discover the Israel of 1989 instead of the Palestine of her dreams. Else, who actually died in 1945, is seen stalking the streets, contemplating the stark reality of the violence and brutality of the period of the Palestinian uprising, *intifada*.

BESAME MUCHO, 2000.

Dir. & Sc.: Joseph Pitchhadze*; Prod.: Mosh Dannon, Shai Goldman, Joseph Pitchhadze, Dov Steuer; Ph.: Shai Goldman; Edit.: Dov Steuer; Music: Barry Sakharof, Rea Moshiach; Cast: Ryan Early, Carmel Betto, Eli Denker, Ayala Verete, Ezra Kafri, Moni Moshonov, Laila Malcos, Menashe Noy, Michael Sarne, Shira Farber, Gili Shoshan, Eyal Shechter.

Award: Wolgin Award, Jerusalem (2000).

Named for the Spanish love song, the film is a story about gangsters in pursuit of a valuable stolen religious icon. It is also a passionate love story, love that cannot withstand the pressures of the world of crime. Utilizing elements of film noir, the film is a humorous takeoff on Tarantino's *Pulp Fiction*, as can be seen in the film's neatly complex and interwoven plot, the lovable criminals and hit men, and the clear visual and script references.

Carmi (Carmel Betto) and Alter (Moni Moshonov) are old friends. Carmi is just being released from prison, having been caught in a job that he did with Alter two years ago. Meanwhile, Alter has purchased a nightclub with the money from that job. The two become involved in stealing a Christian icon from an underworld figure. While Alter is obsessed with a quirky female character, Carmi raises the stakes with the underworld figure by stealing away his girlfriend, the singer at Alter's club.

Muhammed Bakri (center) in *Beyond the Walls* (Uri Barbash, 1984). Photo courtesy of the Jerusalem Cinematheque, reprinted with the permission of Nitzhona Gilad.

BEYOND THE WALLS (Me'Achorei Hasoragim), 1984.

Dir.: Uri Barbash*; Prod.: Rudi Cohen; Sc.: Benny Barbash*, Eran Preis; Ph.: Amnon Salomon*; Edit.: Tova Asher; Music: Ilan Wurtzberg; Cast: Arnon Zadok*, Muhammed Bakri*, Hillel Ne'eman, Assi Dayan*, Rami Danon, Boaz Sharabi, Adib Jahschan, Roberto Pollack, Haim Shinar, Nafi Sallach, Lotuf Nuesser, Ya'ackov Eyali, Dana Katz.

Nomination: Nominated for an American Academy Award for Best Foreign Film (1984).

Awards: Critics' Jury Prize, Venice (1984); First Prize, Salerno (1984); Best Film, Best Director, Best Actor (Arnon Zadok and Muhammed Bakri), Best Screenplay, Best Supporting Actor (Rami Danon), Best Editing, Israel Film Center (1984).

The film portrays Arab political prisoners and Jewish hard-core criminals living side by side in a maximum security prison. Challenging political and social stereotypes and portraying larger-than-life characters, the film presents a metaphor of Arab and Jew being locked up together, both victims of the conflict around them, condemned to mutual acceptance and coexistence.

Uri (Arnon Zadok), imprisoned for armed robbery, is the leader of the Jewish cellblock, which includes a drug addict, a songwriter, common thieves, and a

Jewish political prisoner. Issam (Muhammed Bakri), an ideological, political leader imprisoned for terrorist activity, is the leader of the Arab cellblock.

In the tense prison atmosphere, which includes homosexual rape, arson, and murder, Jews and Arabs are brought together as victims of the exploitative warden, who manipulates them in order to keep total control. He controls the smuggling of drugs into the prison, visitation rights, granting of parole, and even petty requests, such as permission to view a television broadcast of a song contest in which one of the inmates participates. Having written a song of peace and reconciliation for this contest, the inmate (renowned singer Boaz Sharabi) sings, "Give Me Your Hand" (which became a hit song).

As the warden's cruelty continues, the inmates realize that their strength lies in their banding together in common cause with a joint hunger strike. The warden tries to break the strike by offering Uri parole and by dangling before Issam the prospect of a visit from his wife and his young son, whom he has never seen. At the tense climax of the film, the cell door is opened, and Issam peeps out to see his wife and son waiting for him at the end of the corridor. His first reaction is to return to the cell. Encouraged, however, by the demanding clapping of his fellow prisoners and strongly tempted, he tearfully makes his way down the corridor. Issam, however, does not betray the solidarity of the prison inmates, and he tells his wife to go home. Uri and Issam resist the personal bribes offered by the warden, and together they demand concessions for all the prisoners as the hunger strike continues.

Sequel: *Beyond the Walls II* (also directed by Uri Barbash, 1991).

THE BIG DIG (Ta'alat Blaumlich; Alternative title: *Blaumlich Canal*), 1969.

Dir., Prod., & Sc.: Ephraim Kishon*; Ph.: Manny Wein; Edit.: Peter Musgrave; Music: Noam Sheriff; Cast: Shraga Friedman, Nissim Izikari, Yoseph (Bomba) Tzur, Avner Hezkiyahu, Oded Teomi, Rina Ganor, Miriam Gavrielli, Moscu Alcalay, Nathan Walpovitz, Shaike Ophir*.

Awards: Lady of Umbrella, Barcelona XI Semana de Cine en Color (1969); FIPRESCI Special Mention, Monte Carlo TV Festival (1971).

A satire of municipal bureaucracy and ineptitude, the film tells a story that borders on the absurd. A runaway from the local lunatic asylum (Yoseph Bomba Tzur) digs up the streets of Tel Aviv with a stolen pneumatic drill. Each city official suspects the other of having begun what appears to be a massive improvement of the city's infrastructure. Some see it as harassment. Others are jealous that another department is trying to outshine them. No one figures out how to stop the work in the city, and eventually the streets of Tel Aviv link up with the Mediterranean Sea, creating a system of canals similar to those of Venice.

BIG EYES (Eynayim G'dolot), 1974.

Dir.: Uri Zohar*; Prod.: Yitzhak Kol; Sc.: Ya'ackov Shabatai, Uri Zohar*; Ph.: David Gurfinkel*; Edit.: Anna Gurit; Music: Miki Gabrielov; Cast: Uri

Zohar*, Arik Einstein*, Sima Eliyahu, Elia Zohar, Talia Shapira, Menashe Warshavski, Tzvi Shissel.

Popular for the songs sung by well-known singer and actor Arik Einstein, this film is about love, jealousy, and ambivalence in human relationships. The hero, who previously has shown no emotional involvement with women but has used them as a sign of adolescent achievement, shows some development as he begins to realize things about himself. As in *Peeping Toms**, Zohar portrays two very different male friends; the married man is in conflict about remaining faithful to his wife, and the bachelor desires to be a family man. Benny (Uri Zohar), a Tel Aviv basketball coach, is usually successful in juggling his many sexual affairs with his home and family life. He is currently involved with a young woman who takes care of the uniforms and equipment for the team. His previous flame was a gymnastics teacher who has become smart to his antics. His best friend, the team's star player (Arik Einstein), warns him about playing around with the lives of others and throwing away what he's got. When the truth finally reaches his wife, who is very sensitive about his lying to her, his lifestyle begins to crumble, and he begins to realize how he is humiliating and manipulating the people around him. At a wedding of one of the basketball team members, Benny gets drunk, embarrasses his wife, and makes a fool of himself. Returning home in the early hours of the morning and glimpsing his pretty neighbor in a state of undress, he must decide how to continue his life.

Trilogy: *Peeping Toms**, *Big Eyes**, *Save the Lifeguard**, all directed by Uri Zohar.

A BIT OF LUCK (Tipat Mazal), 1992.

Dir.: Ze'ev Revach*; Prod.: Yoram Globus*, Boaz Davidson*; Sc.: Hanan Feld, Ze'ev Revach, based on a story by Ze'ev Revach; Ph.: Yoav Kosh*; Edit.: Zion Avrahamian; Music: Dov Seltzer*; Cast: Ze'ev Revach, Zahava Ben, Arieh Moscuna, Jacques Cohen, Yossi Keinan, Ya'ackov Ben-Sira, Brie Simon, Chen Gueta.

The film is a musical about a father and his daughter who come from Morocco and includes colorful costumes, memorable moments of nostalgia, scenes in Morocco, and authentic Moroccan-Jewish music.

JoJo (Ze'ev Revach) is a talented singer in Morocco who, wearing a red fez and a white robe, entertains at Jewish celebrations together with his wife, who is a belly dancer. When she leaves him the night before they are to leave for Israel, JoJo decides to make the journey with his little daughter. They arrive in Israel, experience the difficulties of life in a transit camp, and eventually settle down in the small town of Atlit (south of Haifa), where JoJo sings in the local café.

As the years pass, JoJo's daughter grows up to be a beautiful young woman (Zahava Ben). When her father goes blind as a result of heavy drinking, she starts singing to earn the money needed to take care of him. In a touching parallel scene between father and daughter, the blind father sings to his daughter,

Ze'ev Revach (center) in *A Bit of Luck* (Ze'ev Revach, 1992). Photo courtesy of the Jerusalem Cinematheque, reprinted with the permission of Yoram Globus.

intercut with images of her over the years, while the daughter sings to her father in front of a large number of guests at a fancy wedding. Later, when JoJo's blindness is cured, father and daughter return to sing together in the small café in Atlit.

THE BLACK BANANA (Habanana Hashechora), 1976.

Dir.: Benjamin Hayeem; Prod.: Benjamin Hayeem, Alice Hayeem; Sc.: Benjamin Hayeem, Alexander Klein; Ph.: Emil (Milek) Knebel; Edit.: Avraham Leibman; Music: Moritz Usherovich; Cast: Danny Kinrot, Genia Maimon, Jesse Nchisi, Orna Orshan, Yossele Yosilevitz, Pnina Mankin, Ivan Nissim, Shalom Zilber, Dafna Ophira, Nazim Jabarin, Benjamin Zemach, Eric Mankin, Muhammed Azam.

An experimental fantasy, the film parodies (in the slapstick style) many aspects of Israeli life and culture from the Hassidic community to the chronically inept police force. The story revolves around three young people all fleeing their parents—a hippie Hassid, who is escaping a prearranged marriage; his American friend, hiding from his overbearing Texas parents; and a young actress who is running from her stifling religious background. In addition to this one feature film, Indian-born filmmaker Benjamin Hayeem made documentaries and public service films.

BLACK BOX (Kufsa Shechora), 1993.

Dir.: Ye'ud Levanon*; Prod.: Gideon Kolirin; Sc.: Nomi Sharron, Ye'ud Levanon, based on a book by Amos Oz; Ph.: Avi Koren; Edit.: Tali Halter-Shenkar; Music: Adi Renart; Cast: Bruria Albeck, Ami Traub, Matti Seri, Amnon Moskin, Roni Ayalon, Sivan Elshayech, Keren Mor, Irit Gidron, Reuven Dayan, Renen Schorr*.

Adapted from a well-known piece of Hebrew literature by Amos Oz, this is a complex narrative film of passion, betrayal, memories, and misunderstandings, all against the background of political issues. Woven together through different periods of time, the story is told via letters between a woman and her ex-husband. Although divorced for seven years, they are strongly connected to each other. Amos Oz's works that have been adapted to film—*My Michael** and *Black Box*—mix national issues with personal themes of desire and loneliness.

Alex is a professor at a London university and the author of a book on the politics of violence. Ilana (Bruria Albeck) is now married to a right-wing, religious activist—the antithesis of Alex in culture, politics, and style—and they have a young daughter. As such, Ilana is the link between two dynamic tendencies within society: the secular, cultured left wing and the insular, superstitious, religious right.

Both Alex and Ilana are survivors not only of their wrecked marriage but also of their memories, desires, and destructiveness. They are obsessed with memories of their past, their love for each other, visions of their moments of passion, and confusion as to how to relate to their teenage son, Boaz. When Alex discovers that he is dying of cancer, he returns to the old homestead to rebuild his relationship with Ilana, to reach out to Boaz, and to die in peace.

BLAZING SANDS (Cholot Lohatim), 1960.

Dir., Prod., & Sc.: Raphael Nussbaum; Co-prod.: Israel-Germany; Ph.: Yitzhak (Mimisch) Herbst, Wolf Geta; Edit.: Erica Shtigman, Aliza Fogut; Music: Siegfried Wegener; Cast: Dalia Lavie, Hillel Ne'eman, Uri Zohar*, Avraham Barzilai, Oded Kotler*, Gila Almagor*, Oded Teomi, Natan Cogan, Avraham Ronai.

The film tells the story of a group of young people who make the dangerous expedition over the desert, across the Jordanian border to Petra. There was considerable public controversy about the film, some claiming that it encouraged young people to undertake reckless forays to Petra. In addition to this feature film, Raphael Nussbaum (1931–1993) directed documentary films and one more feature, *Sinai Commando* (1967).

Dina (Dalia Lavie) has left the kibbutz where she was brought up to live in Tel Aviv, dreaming of one day going to Paris to become a famous dancer. She puts together a group to search for her boyfriend, who is hurt and stranded in the caves at Petra. The group includes a shady character who has put up the money for the expedition; her boyfriend's best friend from the kibbutz (Uri Zohar); a naive youngster (Oded Kotler), around whom all the humor revolves;

and a university student of archaeology. Stopping at the Beersheba Bedouin market to buy camels and clothes, they disguise themselves as a Bedouin caravan and set off on their journey. Although the group succeeds in reaching Petra, finding Dina's boyfriend and a set of ancient forbidden scrolls, which bring danger and tragedy to all those who covet them, the story ends in tragedy and only one member of the group survives to tell the tale of their adventure.

BLIND MAN'S BLUFF (Golem Bema'agal; Alternative title: *Dummy in a Circle*), 1993.

Dir.: Aner Preminger*; Prod.: Haim Sharir; Sc.: Tal Zilberstein, Aner Preminger, based on a book by Lily Perry Amitai; Ph.: Ya'ackov Eisenman; Edit.: Tova Asher; Music: Haim Permont; Cast: Hagit Dasberg, Nicole Casel, Gedalia Besser*, Anat Wachsmann*, Dani Litani, Albert Cohen, Itcho Avital.

Awards: Antigone d'Or, Montpellier (1993); First Prize for first film, Montevideo (1994); Golden Jaguar, Special Jury Prize, Cancun (1994); Wolgin Award, Jerusalem (1993); Israeli Critics Award for Best Actress (Hagit Dasberg), Haifa Film Festival (1994); Best Actress (Hagit Dasberg), Israeli Academy Awards (1993).

The film portrays a professional young woman who must learn to live not only by the expectations of others but also according to her own needs, and depicts her mother as creating stifling and manipulative demands upon her. The Hebrew title refers to the cocoon of family and friends that must be broken in order to reach full maturity.

Mickey (Hagit Dasberg) is studying to be a concert pianist. She is an only child, a single woman, and a second-generation Holocaust survivor. Her overbearing mother (Nicole Casel) is a major obstacle in her path to independence and maturity. Mickey is also frustrated in her relationships with men—a ruthless violinist who uses her to build his own career, a lawyer who leads her on, her aging grandfather, and her weak yet understanding father (Gedalia Besser). Mickey plays piano for her mother's ballet school, but she dreams of more. Befriended by a young prostitute sporting outrageously flamboyant clothes (Anat Wachsmann), Mickey slowly begins to find her own way.

BOYS AND GIRLS (Hasimla), 1970.

Dir. & Prod.: Yehuda (Judd) Ne'eman*; Sc.: Orna Spector, Rachel Ne'eman, Yehuda (Judd) Ne'eman; Ph.: Yachin Hirsch; Edit.: Tova Biran, Nellie Bogor-Gilad; Cast: Yair (Koya) Rubin, Amir Orion, Gabi Eldor, Assi Dayan*, Liora Rivlin, Motti Barkan, Rina Ganor, Judy Katz.

The film is a compilation of three short stories, each reflecting the hopes and frustrations of the disconnected world of young people. The characters in each episode are searching for support, trying to attain love and to achieve inner satisfaction and change. However, each story is punctuated by a feeling of failure.

The Dress is about a girl who tries to attract a young man in the library where she works by buying a new, expensive dress. When they go together to her apartment, he seems to be more interested in her roommate. *The Letter* portrays a government clerk, bored with his work, who advertises in the newspaper for girls to send in their photographs. Quite taken by one beautiful face, he becomes obsessed with finding the girl. However, the girl, finally discovered, is not as enchanting as her photograph. *Thomas Returns* shows a young actor, thrown out of his apartment by his landlady, who goes to the home of his estranged wife. Amused at finding her new boyfriend there, Thomas stays to spend the night with them both.

BRAIDS (Tzamot), 1989.

Dir. & Sc.: Yitzhak Halutzi; Prod.: Azriel Gamliel; Ph.: Arieh Paldi; Edit.: Shimona Kleiner-Tal; Music: Arik Rudich; Cast: Netta Sobol, Adib Jahschan, Techiya Danon, Hannah Azoulai-Hasfari*, Yoseph Shiloah*, Yehudit Millo, Arieh Elias.

The film is a full-length feature film produced for television. Based on a true story about the inner strength of female political inmates in an Iraqi prison, the film is set during the period of Israel's emerging independence.

Suad (Netta Sobol) is a 14-year-old girl who lives in a small Iraqi town during the late 1940s. In the basement of her building, secret Zionist meetings take place. The emissary from Palestine, David, gives Suad a code name. She is arrested when the police find her in possession of a Hebrew newspaper. Incarcerated for several years in a Baghdad prison, Suad develops a special relationship with another Jewish woman, Monira (Hannah Azoulai-Hasfari), a Communist activist. Monira believes strongly that Jews belong in the Arab lands, where they have a responsibility to help overcome poverty and illiteracy. Offering courage and vision to the Muslim women in her cellblock, she leads a revolt among the female inmates. As the years pass and Suad learns to endure the humiliation and deprivation of prison, she develops into a dedicated young woman who never loses sight of her purpose.

BREAD (Lechem), 1986.

Dir.: Ram Loevy*; Prod.: Dana Kogan; Sc.: Meir Doron, Gilad Evron, Ram Loevy; Ph.: Meir Diskin; Edit.: Rachel Yagil; Cast: Rami Danon, Rivka Bachar, Moshe Ivgi*, Etti Ankri.

Award: Prix Italia for TV drama, 1986.

A feature film produced for television, the film is a socioeconomic look at life in the development town of Yerucham in the northern Negev. The complex narrative provides insight into the frustrations, traditional values, economic hardships, and claustrophobic atmosphere of life in the town.

Navah (Etti Ankri) is a young woman who studies in Tel Aviv and comes home only periodically, in order to visit her family. Navah's "old world" father, Shlomo (Rami Danon), a Jew of North African descent, has worked in the local bakery for 20 years. His son, Baruch (Moshe Ivgi), is getting married and dreams of opening a video game shop in the little town, but someone else beats him to it. A video game machine stands in the house as a silent reminder of the family's frustrations.

Shlomo is very proud of his daughter and looks to her for assistance. He tells her the story of a financial crisis at the bakery and asks her to help by being the spokesperson for the workers in their negotiations with the management. When the bakery closes and Shlomo loses his job, he is deeply humiliated. He comes home and discovers that in order to help support the family, his wife has been working at a clothing factory without his knowledge. Devastated by the loss of self-esteem, Shlomo decides to go on a hunger strike.

BROKEN WINGS (Knafayim Shvurot), 2002.

Dir. & Sc.: Nir Bergman; Prod.: Assaf Amir; Ph.: Valentin Belonogov; Edit.: Einat Glaser-Zarhin; Music: Avi Belleli; Cast: Orly Zilbershatz-Banai, Maia Meron, Nitai Gvirtz, Vladimir Friedman, Dani Niv, Dana Ivgi, Daniel and Eliana Magon.

Awards: Grand Prix, Tokyo (2002); Prize for first film, Palm Springs (2003); Wolgin Award, Jerusalem (2002); Best Film, Best Director, Best Actress (Orly Zilbershatz-Banai), Best Supporting Actress (Maia Meron), Best Screenplay, Best Editing, Best Cinematography, Best Art Direction (Ido Dolev), Best Sound (David Lis, Gil Toren), Israeli Academy Awards (2002).

The film is a touching drama about the disintegration of a family living with loss. The story takes place following the death of the father from an allergic reaction to a bee sting, something so tragic, trivial, and apparently senseless that it can be seen as a parallel to the senseless deaths that Israelis are facing all too often in reality. The focus of the film is on the relationship between the mother (Orly Zilbershatz-Banai) and her teenage daughter (Maia Meron).

Dafna is a 43-year-old midwife, working night shifts at a Haifa hospital, widowed, mother of four, trying desperately to make ends meet and to keep her family from unraveling. Her teenage children, a boy and a girl, are as different as night and day. One is having a psychological crisis, hiding from reality dressed up in a mouse costume, and the other bends over backwards to help out at home taking care of the younger brother and sister. The family members are suffering terribly from the death of the father, but they are unable to reach out to each other. When the 10-year-old brother, who is still wetting his bed, is hospitalized in a coma after jumping from a diving board into an empty swimming pool, the family faces a new crisis. Eventually, they begin to pull together.

BURNING LAND (Adama Chamah; French title: *Terre Brulante*), 1984.

Dir. & Sc.: Serge Ankri; Prod.: Ye'ud Levanon*, Doron Eran*; Ph.: Ya'ackov Eisenman; Edit.: Benny Kimron; Music: Gerard Feliciano; Cast: Jacques Ovadiah, Meir Suissa, Dalia Malka, Yitzhak Goren, Miriam Nataf, Gerard Ben-Imo, Laurence Sanderovich (in Arabic, French, and Hebrew).

Awards: Critics' Prize, Torino (1986); Best Musical Score, Israel Film Center (1984).

The film portrays the wealthy, French-speaking Jews of Tunisia, whose culture was caught between the colonial French, the surrounding Arabs, and their own traditional Jewish roots. A strong political statement about being uprooted from one's land and a family story of three generations, the film is about Jewish life and identity, anti-Semitism, intermarriage, and changing Jewish values in the special context of a North African Jewish community. Tunisian-born film director Serge Ankri also directed *Strangers in the Night* (1993) and the documentary *Mama's Couscous* (1993).

Tunisia, 1954. An aging couple lives in the countryside where they brought up their three children and made a living from their olive grove. They are clinging to their Jewishness and to their land. The oldest son, Daniel, is a teacher married to a French Catholic girl; he knows and cares nothing about his Jewish roots and wants to move to France. The daughter and her husband are both still bound to family traditions but are more interested in business than in the ancestral homestead. The youngest son, Andre, is a mechanic who dreams of leaving for Israel.

The patriarch clings to his land, believing that it has brought him equality and respect in the eyes of his non-Jewish neighbors. He is proved wrong, however, when he is pressured by the local Arab religious authorities to sell his property so that they can expand the nearby cemetery. The conflict reaches a peak at a family Rosh Hashanah dinner, when he passes on, and the local Arabs set fire to the olive press. The film concludes with the inevitable uprooting of the olive grove, a scene that recalls the opening sequence of the film, a short prologue presenting a contemporary episode of the uprooting by Israeli soldiers of an olive grove in the occupied West Bank.

BURNING MEMORY (Resisim), 1988.

Dir.: Yossi Somer*; Prod.: Ami Amir; Sc.: Yossi Somer, Ami Amir, based on an idea by David Avivi; Ph.: Yoav Kosh*; Edit.: David Tour, Ya'ackov Dagan, Rifka Yogev; Music: Jan Garbarek, Yossi Elphant; Cast: Danny Roth, Poli Reshef, Shmuel Edelman, Etti Ankri, Alon Olearchik, Yosef El-Dror, Reuven Dayan, Yahli Bergman, Cobi Hagoel, Avi Gilor, Dor Shweitzer.

Award: Best Screenplay, Israel Film Center (1988–1989).

The film deals with the subject of postwar trauma and is based on personal stories of soldiers who suffered during the Yom Kippur War and later during the War in Lebanon and on the experiences of the director, Yossi Somer, who served as a paramedic during the War in Lebanon.

Opening scene: a hellish scene of destruction, a moonscape of fire, smoldering metal, dead bodies, scattered weapons, and mud. A surviving soldier walks among the bodies. The film is the story of this soldier, Gary (Danny Roth), and his fears, his haunting memories of this final battle, his guilt for what he did and did not do to save his friends, his slow rehabilitation in an army clinic, and his struggle to resume his life.

BUT WHERE IS DANIEL WAX? (Le'an Ne'elam Daniel Vax?), 1972.

Dir. & Sc.: Avram Heffner*; Prod.: Bill Gross; Ph.: Amnon Salomon*; Edit.: Jacques Ehrlich; Music: Ariel Zilber; Cast: Lior Yaeni, Yishai Shahar, Esther Zebko, Yael Heffner, Yosef Carmon, Zivit Avrahamson, Miriam Gavrielli, Amnon Moskin, Aliza Rosen.

Awards: Best Film, Best Screenplay, Israel Film Center (1973).

An ironic view of Israeli soul-searching and dissatisfaction, the film also looks at the delusions of middle age. Including the mundane details of everyday life (scenes of people going up stairs and going down stairs, turning lights on and off), the film is a look at a search for youth and the universal theme of searching for the illusory past.

A successful singer (Lior Yaeni) returns home to Israel, where he meets an old school friend who has become a doctor (Yishai Shahar). Both men are dissatisfied with life; they are victims of unstable marriages and, as a consequence, they spend time together reminiscing about their younger days. They gossip about old friends and begin a search—at first informal, later more obsessive—for Daniel Wax, the charming, popular, and brilliant classmate of their youth. Finally, as the singer is slowly losing his own delusions about his youthfulness, he encounters the object of his search. Daniel Wax (Amnon Moskin) has inevitably lost his glamour and become a balding, middle-aged family man.

CEASEFIRE (Hafuga), 1950.

Dir. & Ph.: Amram Amar; Prod.: Yigal Caspi; Sc.: Roger Attali, Amram Amar; Music: Harry Tzelner; Cast: Esther Frieder, Nissim Mizrachi, Ruth Gavrielit, Yitzhak Frej, Eliezer Behar, Yehoshua Mizrachi, Ruth Gottlieb, Rahel Gurion, Ya'akov Greener, David Yerushalmi.

The first Hebrew-speaking feature film produced after the establishment of the state of Israel, the film combines comedy with elements of a love story and period shots of Jerusalem and a nearby kibbutz. The tension between life on the kibbutz and life in the city is portrayed through the romantic story of a young woman from the city and a man from the kibbutz.

The film opens with a documentary montage of scenes of the battle for Jerusalem, which is followed by a comic sequence in which an Israeli soldier, hearing ominous noises from an abandoned ruin, storms the building only to find a little puppy inside. The story focuses on a kibbutznik who decides to try city life.

THE CELLAR (Hamartef), 1963.

Dir.: Nathan Gross*; Prod., Sc., & Music: Shimon Yisraeli, based on his own story; Literary advisor & dialogue: Ya'ackov Malkin; Ph.: Ya'ackov Yunilovitz; Edit.: Dani Schik; Music arranged by Eddie Halperin; Cast: Shimon Yisraeli, with the Voice of Zaharira Harifai, the Hair of Hannah Kahane, and the Shadow of David Semadar.

Award: Jugend Film Prize, Berlin (1963).

One of the earliest Israeli films to deal with the subject of the Holocaust head-on, the film is a stylized, one-actor production, that portrays the hero's memories and conflicts.

Emanuel (Shimon Yisraeli), a survivor of Dachau, lives in Tel Aviv, traumatized by his memories. Fifteen years earlier, he lived in a small town in Germany. His classmate Hans, who killed his father, is now living in his home and married to his sweetheart. The additional characters are all portrayed through the use of voice, silhouette, and shadow.

CHARLIE AND A HALF (Charlie Ve'Chetzi), 1974.

Dir.: Boaz Davidson*; Prod.: Simcha Zvuloni; Sc.: Eli Tavor; Ph.: Amnon Salomon*; Edit.: Alain Jakubowicz; Music: Yair Rosenblum; Cast: Yehuda Barkan*, Ze'ev Revach*, Arieh Elias, Edna Fleidel, Chaya Katzir, Geula Nuni, Elisheva Michaeli, Natan Cogan, Tuvia Tsafir, Moshe Ish-Kassit, Reuven Shefer, Tikvah Aziz, David Shushan.

An ethnic comedy, the film pokes fun at the tendency to debase oneself in the face of wealthier and more successful people and encourages a 12-year-old boy to pull himself out of the slums and create for himself a better future. Filled with superstition, chauvinism, chase sequences, and scenes of eating, the film depicts the gap between rich and poor and between Ashkenazi and Sephardi.

The story revolves around Charlie (Yehuda Barkan) and his neighborhood nemesis, Sasson (Ze'ev Revach). Both are uneducated and unemployed, but Charlie is confident, lovable, and fun-loving, with the intention to make something better of himself, whereas Sasson is a superstitious lout, always the butt of Charlie's jokes. Charlie's mother is depicted as a warm, salt-of-the-earth character, dispensing advice to all the neighbors. A special relationship develops between Charlie and 12-year-old Miko, who lives with his sister in a slum on the outskirts of the city. Miko idolizes Charlie, perhaps as a replacement father figure. The two become an inseparable pair until Charlie gets involved with a wealthy girl from an Ashkenazi family.

CHOICE AND DESTINY (Habechirah Ve'Hagoral), 1993.

Dir. & Sc.: Tsipi Reibenbach*; Ph.: Avi Koren, David Gurfinkel*; Edit.: Ziva Postek.

Awards: Silver Sesterce, Nyon (1993); Prix de la SCAM, Cinéma du Réel Festival, Paris (1994); Journalist's Union Award, Festival for Women's Films, Créteil (1994); Grand Prize, Yamagata (1996).

With painstaking care, the filmmaker portrays the details of her parents' lives—their routines, obsessions, and memories. The lingering camera emphasizes small gestures and habits in its intimate portrayal of the everyday lives of these two Holocaust survivors. During most of this documentary film, the filmmaker's father, Yitzhak Grinberg, relates stories from his past, and her mother, Fruma Grinberg, lurks in the shadows, a silent image, a woman who never spoke about her Holocaust experiences throughout all the years of her daughter's growing up. Suddenly and spontaneously, her mother opens up emotionally. Her father talks about Auschwitz: "You get used to death; you know that death is waiting for you." One of the more memorable scenes portrays the routine-turned-compulsion with which the parents lock the door of their home.

CIRCLES (Ma'agalim Shel Shi-Shabbat; Alternative title: *Weekend Circles*), 1980.

Dir. & Sc.: Idit Shechori*; Prod.: Yehezkel Alani, Ya'ackov Kotzky; Ph.: Nurith Aviv*, Gadi Danzig; Edit.: Ludmila Goliath; Music: Avner Kenner; Cast: Rahel Shein, Hava Ortman, Noa Cohen-Raz, Galit Gil (Roitman), Eldad Yaron, Moti Dichneh, Yoel Lerner, Amos Lavie, Yigal Even-Or, Poli Reshef, Albert Eluz.

About women searching for opportunity and self-definition in life, the film portrays one evening in the life of four Tel Aviv single women.

Dorit (Rahel Shein) is a swinger who knows everyone and seems to sleep with everyone she knows. Her best friend, Tamara (Hava Ortman), is a depressed divorcée. Gilli (Noa Cohen-Raz), a new flatmate, is an innocent girl who grew up in a small town and has just completed her army service. Lior (Galit Gil [Roitman]) is a lesbian. The narrative follows their developing relationships, their worries and pains, set against a bustling Tel Aviv nightlife of parties, concerts, drinking, smoking hashish, sitting at Dizengoff Center, getting one's hair done, searching for someone to spend the night with, and skinny-dipping at dawn in the Mediterranean.

CIRCUS PALESTINE (Kirkas Palesteena), 1998.

Dir. & Sc.: Eyal Halfon*; Prod.: Marek Rozenbaum*, Uri Sabag, Haim Sharir, Einat Bickel; Ph.: Valentin Belonogov; Edit.: Tova Asher; Music: Shlomo Gronich*; Cast: Yoram Hattab, Yevgenia Dodina, Amos Lavie, Bassam Zuamut, Vladimir Friedman.

Awards: Best Film, Best Screenplay, Best Actor (Yoram Hattab), Best Supporting Actor (Amos Lavie), Best Musical Score, Israeli Academy Awards (1998).

A political satire, the film narrative takes place on the background of the *intifada* (Palestinian uprising) of the early 1990s. The Palestinian people are symbolized by a lion, caged up and longing to be set free. The quirky characters are Fellini "types"—the military commander is a manipulative and corrupt egomaniac; the Palestinian entrepreneur is aspiring to greatness; the circus characters are artistes, not conscious of their political surroundings; and the settlers are wild and arrogant.

A Russian circus is brought to a small West Bank town by a local businessman (Bassam Zuamut). When the circus lion escapes, Bleiberg (Yoram Hattab), one of the soldiers stationed in the area, is assigned to lead the operation in finding the dangerous animal. Bleiberg falls in love with Mariana (Yevgenia Dodina), the wild and untamed lion tamer. After they succeed together in getting the lion back, it becomes clear that the colonel (Amos Lavie) wants to keep him as a mascot for his military base. Bleiberg and Mariana whisk the lion away in the night and set him free in the hills.

CLOUDS OVER ISRAEL (Sinaia), 1962.

Dir.: Ilan (Ivan) Eldad (Lengyel)*; Prod.: Matti Raz; Sc.: Moshe Hadar; Ph.: Marco Ya'acobi; Edit.: Dani Schik; Music: Noam Sheriff; Cast: Yiftach Spector, Shimon Yisraeli, Dina Doron, Shaike Levi, Naveh Sha'an, Yitzhak Barzilai, Yitzhak Binyamini, Hadara Azoulai, and the children: Ehud Banai, Sinaia Chamdan.

Based on the true story of a little girl who was saved by an Israeli pilot and who today is living near Beersheba, the film is about tolerance and the need for compassion toward the local Arab population. The only Israeli feature film to be produced against the backdrop of the 1956 Sinai War, it portrays two Israeli soldiers stranded in a Bedouin encampment in the Sinai desert. Although the Bedouin in this film are depicted as background figures in the clash between the two Israeli soldiers, they are also portrayed in-depth, as individuals with feelings.

An Israeli pilot (Yiftach Spector) has engine trouble and parachutes down over the Sinai desert. As he treks along, he comes across the charred wreck of his plane, which has apparently destroyed a Bedouin encampment. Only a young Bedouin mother and her two children have survived. When two Egyptian soldiers who have found the parachute come looking for the pilot, she protects him and doesn't reveal his hiding place. Soon another Israeli soldier, an infantryman (Shimon Yisraeli), comes along, and together they hatch a plan to escape in an Egyptian plane. The young pilot, who feels troubled by the fact that he has brought his war to the local population, destroying their tents and killing their people, wants to take the Bedouin woman and her children with them for medical attention. The infantryman, on the other hand, feels animosity toward the Bedouin and treats them harshly.

The young Bedouin mother (Dina Doron) is the lone adult survivor in this desert encampment. Although she has no language in common with the pilot, she is able to communicate her feelings. The pilot takes off with the Bedouin mother and her two children, and they crash; only the infant survives. The infantryman, who was still on the ground, picks up the infant and continues on.

COFFEE WITH LEMON (Cafe Em Limone), 1994.

Dir.: Leonid Gorovets; Prod.: Zvi Shapira, Gady Castel; Sc.: Leonid Gorovets, Simeon Vinokur; Ph.: Valentin Belonogov; Edit.: Alain Jakubowicz; Music: Haim Elfman; Cast: Alexander Abdulov, Bruria Albeck, Tatyana Vasilyeva.

Dealing with issues of immigration, the film examines the professional hardships and frustrations of adapting to a strange land. This is a tale about starting again and about whether to live with reality or to choose to live in one's own past. Before coming to live in Israel, Russian-born film director Leonid Gorovets directed the prizewinning *Ladies' Tailor* (1990), which portrays the anguish and conflicts of a Jewish family in Kiev as they await deportation the night before Babi Yar. *Coffee with Lemon* is his first Israeli feature film.

Valery (Alexander Abdulov) is a successful stage actor who immigrates to Israel from Moscow. After arriving with his wife and son, they go directly to a stark caravan park. Valery is very involved in his work, but he finds it difficult to learn Hebrew. He realizes that he is unable to adjust, either to his new surroundings or to the difficulties of learning his lines and working as an actor in a foreign language. He returns to Moscow alone, leaving his wife and child in the caravan park. He is searching for the success and appreciation that he left behind, but everything has changed in Moscow. On that day that the Russian White House is burning, Valery is killed by a random shot on the street, a victim of strange historical circumstances.

COVER STORY (Parshat Vinchell; Alternative title: *The Winchell Affair*), 1979.

Dir. & Sc.: Avram Heffner*; Prod.: Ya'ackov Kotzky; Ph.: Dani Shneur; Edit.: David Tour; Music: Naomi Shemer; Cast: Tal Nativ, Oded Kotler*, Esther Zebko, Dov Feigin, Shimon Finkel, Tova Piron, Rafael Tzvi, Devora Kastelnitz, Hazi Carmel, Naveh Sha'an.

Searching into the past, the film portrays a case of political murder and intrigue, reminiscent of a factual murder case that remains unsolved to this day. It raises issues concerning the difficulties of living in the wake of a founding generation of pioneering visionaries.

Ilana is a journalist, and Yehudit is a photographer. The two women, close friends in their personal lives, become interested in an unsolved murder case from the period of the British Mandate (1930s). They decide to investigate and begin by talking with Ilana's father, who himself was involved with the political intrigue and social clique surrounding the victim, Lord Winchell. They meet with Kogan, whose son had to flee the country because of his involvement in the affair, and with Zakkai, an elder statesman who with a little bit of prodding is willing to help them piece together information. While conducting the search, Ilana is also heavily involved with the problems of her own personal life—her desire to become pregnant and her difficult relationship with her husband. These are interconnecting themes—the young woman's study of the past, the way in which the previous generation influences people living today, and the concern with continuity of these forces manifested in the desire to mother a child.

CROSSFIRE (Esh Tzolevet), 1989.

Dir.: Gideon Ganani; Prod.: Marek Rozenbaum*; Sc.: Benny Barbash*; Ph.: Dani Shneur; Edit.: Dani Schik; Music: Eldad Lidor; Cast: Sharon Hacohen,

Dan Turgeman, Sinai Peter, Miriam Gavrielli, Dani Friedman, Arieh Elias, Shlomo Tarshish, Gabi Shoshan.

Awards: Best Editing, Best Art Direction (Ariel Roshko), Israel Film Center (1988–1989).

Set during the period of the British Mandate in 1940s Palestine and based on a true incident, the film tells the tragic story of a love affair between a Jewish woman and an Arab man. Film director Gideon Ganani has directed dozens of documentary films for television in Israel and abroad and played a role in the establishment of the Israeli Second TV Channel.

Miriam (Sharon Hacohen), a young Jewish woman from Tel Aviv, works in her family's restaurant on Sheinkin Street and is learning dance. She is attracted to George (Dan Turgeman), an educated Arab from Jaffa. Miriam's older brother, Shraga, is active in the Haganah, smuggling illegal immigrants into Palestine, and he harasses George one day in an ugly confrontation. George's friends harbor virulent anti-Jewish feelings, but George does not seem to care for politics. Miriam and George become lovers, oblivious to the tumultuous historical events and political sentiments surrounding them and unaware of the dangers that inevitably lie ahead.

CUP FINAL (G'mar Gaviya), 1991.

Dir.: Eran Riklis*; Prod.: Micha Sharfstein; Sc.: Eyal Halfon*, based on an idea by Eran Riklis; Ph.: Amnon Salomon*; Edit.: Anat Lubarsky; Music: Raviv Gazit; Cast: Moshe Ivgi*, Muhammed Bakri*, Salim Dau*, Bassam Zuamut, Yusuf Abu-Warda, Suheil Haddad, Gassan Abbass, Sharon Alexander*, Johnny Arbid, Sami Samir, Meir Suissa.

Awards: Second Prize, Valencia (1991); Honorable Mention (Moshe Ivgi), Jerusalem (1991); Best Actor, Haifa (1991).

The film takes place during the 1982 War in Lebanon and explores the themes of male bonding during wartime, the relationship between captor and captive, and the possibility of coexistence in the politically tense atmosphere of the Middle East.

Cohen (Moshe Ivgi), a boutique owner, is serving in the war as a reserve soldier. When his troop carrier receives a direct hit, he is taken captive by a Palestine Liberation Organization (PLO) unit retreating to Beirut. The unit, under the command of Ziyad (Muhammed Bakri), comprises a diverse group of PLO fighters, including fanatics, idealists, and even an inexperienced and young soccer supporter. Since the two leading PLO fighters are studying in Italy, they are supporting the Italian team in the upcoming World Cup and are surprised to discover that Cohen is holding tickets to the games in his pocket. The group breaks into a luxurious home looking for a television set in order to watch the final game.

The complex narrative includes touching moments—a soccer game played by Ziyad, the PLO leader, against Cohen, the Israeli hostage; a local wedding scene that becomes tense when Israeli soldiers arrive; and a billiards game in which

Moshe Ivgi (center) in *Cup Final* (Eran Riklis, 1991). Photo courtesy of the Jerusalem Cinematheque, reprinted with the permission of Eran Riklis.

Cohen suddenly finds himself playing for all the Arab cities of Palestine. In a humorous, yet touching, scene, two of the PLO fighters go to a nearby Phalangist village in order to obtain insulin for the youngest in their group, and they enter an Israeli military base in order to "requisition" supplies. As the film draws toward its conclusion, the PLO soldiers gaze upon their destination in the distance, the glittering lights of Beirut (filmed overlooking the Israeli city of Haifa), and contemplate what they have experienced together during the last few days and how close they have come in escaping the Israeli army, which virtually surrounds them.

DADDY, COME TO THE FAIR (Abbaleh, Bo Leluna Park), 1994.

Dir.: Nitza Gonen; Prod.: Shmuel Vilozhny, Ido Bahat; Ph.: Leshem Vinitzky; Music: Arik Rudich.

Stand-up comedian Shmuel Vilozhny travels to Poland with his father and sister to search for their roots. Father and son have a special relationship, which grows and develops during the course of the film. At the beginning, Shmuel bitterly accuses his father, a Holocaust survivor, of not sharing his past with his family. As this documentary film draws to a close, however, Shmuel himself better understands his father's silence of many years. Instead of becoming reticent in speaking about the past, however, his theatrical flair helps him to share his experiences.

Comedian Shmuel Vilozhny creates comic moments that intertwine with the serious nature of the film. He reacts through song, soliloquy, and pantomime. The travelers find the little house in which the father grew up, and he tells his son and daughter about his parents, about their life in this little house, and about Shabbat celebrations. Standing together, father, son and daughter celebrate *havdalah* (ceremony concluding the Sabbath). The film concludes with Shmuel prancing along the beach as in a Fellini-like circus parade, singing and gesturing to the viewer to come along with him, to come and understand.

DALIA AND THE SAILORS (Dalia Ve'Hamelachim), 1964.

Dir.: Menahem Golan*; Prod.: Mordechai Navon*; Sc.: Manya and Yosh Halevi, Menahem Golan; Ph.: Harry Waxman; Edit.: Nellie Bogor-Gilad; Music: Yitzhak Graziani; Songs: Naomi Shemer; Cast: Veronique Vendell, Shaike Ophir*, Arik Einstein*, Shraga Friedman, Bomba Tzur.

This comic farce about an attractive girl stowed away aboard an ocean freighter makes for humorous situations. The film is filled with Israeli flavor and Israeli slang, and popular Israeli comedians play the roles of the members of the crew.

Dalia (played by the French actress Veronique Vendell) is an Israeli girl who was taken to Canada as a child by her emigrating parents. Years later, determined to return home to her uncle in Haifa, she hides out on a freighter bound for Israel. As a result of the mysterious disappearance of numerous items from the kitchen, her presence is soon discovered by the crew, who endeavor to conceal her from being discovered by the ship's captain. Always aware of what is happening on his ship, the captain (Shraga Friedman) also aids the girl by pretending not to know that she is aboard. The story develops, as do the relations between the crew and the young stowaway.

DAUGHTERS, DAUGHTERS (Abu El Banat), 1973.

Dir.: Moshe Mizrahi*; Prod.: Menahem Golan*; Sc.: Moshe Mizrahi, Shaike Ophir*, based on a stage monologue by Shaike Ophir; Ph.: Adam Greenberg*; Edit.: Dov Hoenig; Music: Alex Cagan; Cast: Shaike Ophir, Zaharira Harifai, Yoseph Shiloah*, Michal Bat-Adam*, Gideon Zinger, Avner Hezkiyahu, Naomi Greenbaum, Baruch David.

A satire about male chauvinism, the film pokes fun at the traditional preference for male offspring. It is the story of a man plagued by the women in his life—from his loving little girls, to his teenage daughters, his plump wife, and his mistress.

Shabbatai (Shaike Ophir) is a prosperous family man, the father of eight girls. Tormented by the fact that he has no heir to inherit his property and say *kaddish* when he dies, he consults a mystic. Nine months later, his wife (Zaharira Harifai) gives birth to another girl. Shabbatai is determined not to visit his wife or newborn daughter in the hospital. Consequently, his wife deserts him, leaving him to care for the one-week-old baby. At first he turns to his mistress, but together with his friend and foreman (Yoseph Shiloah), he slowly learns to care for and love the little girl. Following a reconciliation with his wife, they find that their eldest daughter (Michal Bat-Adam) is pregnant. After her marriage, she too has a baby girl.

DAY AFTER DAY (Yom Yom), 1998.

Dir. & Sc.: Amos Gitai*; Prod.: Eyal Shiray, Laurent Truchot, David Mandil, Michael Tapuach; Ph.: Renato Berta; Edit.: Nili Richter; Cast: Moshe Ivgi*, Hannah Meron*, Yusuf Abu-Warda, Dalit Kahan, Juliano Mer, Natali Atiah.

Awards: Wolgin Award and Lipper Award for Best Israeli Screenplay, Jerusalem (1998).

On the background of ordinary life in Haifa and by focusing on the mundane, the film is an ironic look at social issues of contemporary Israeli life. Haifa is a complex city where Jewish and Arab life intersects, and thus Jew and Arab are interwoven in the very fabric of the family of the film—a Jewish mother and an Arab father.

Mosh (Moshe Ivgi) is the 40-year-old son of Hannah (Hannah Meron) and Muka (Yusuf Abu-Warda). Mosh is a middle-aged hypochondriac, solely concerned with himself, totally apathetic about the social and national issues of his country. His mother, on the other hand, is very politically involved and is desperately trying to imbibe some of her political consciousness to her son. Divorced, with a young girlfriend, Mosh works in the family bakery. The political irony is palpable when a real estate developer comes around to try to make a deal concerning the sale of Muka's family home, the home that he grew up in.

Trilogy: *Devarim, Day after Day*, and *Kadosh**.

DEAD END STREET (Kvish Le-Lo Motzah), 1982.

Dir.: Yaki Yosha*; Prod.: David Shapira, Yitzhak Kol; Sc.: Eli Tavor, Yaki Yosha; Ph.: Ilan Rosenberg; Edit.: Dani Schik; Music: Yitzhak Klepter; Cast: Yehoram Gaon*, Anat Atzmon*, Gila Almagor*, Tiki Dayan, Moti Shirin, Uri Gavrieli, Hannah Meron*, Gabi Amrani, Eyal Geffen, Moscu Alcalay.

Awards: Best Actress (Anat Atzmon), Israel Film Center (1982).

Dealing with the subject of women who work the streets, the film provides a look at how they are unable to escape the relentless nature of their reality. Excruciatingly realistic, the film provides an added dimension of realism, authenticity, and social commentary through the element of the film within the film.

Alice (Anat Atzmon) is a 17-year-old girl who does not mind her work as a prostitute so much but has been terrorized by her pimp, who milks her for her money, beats her, cuts her hair, and threatens her with a knife. Alice manages to survive on her dreams of someday becoming a model and having her own place. When a television director (Yehoram Gaon) wants to make a documentary film about her, she is resistant at first. The documentary is being produced by a woman (Gila Almagor) who is interested only in exploiting the social issue of prostitution as a good subject for a film. The director, however, becomes involved with Alice and tries to get to know her and to understand her. Alice, a lonely girl whose parents have disowned her, eventually agrees to appear in the film, even though she is sufficiently worldly-wise to understand that once she is seen in a film as a prostitute, she will never be able to escape the world of turning tricks, police roundups, and street violence.

DESCRIPTION OF A STRUGGLE (Hatzad Hashlishi Shel Hamatbaya; French title: *Description d'un Combat*), 1960.

Dir. & Sc.: Chris Marker; Prod.: Wim van Leer; Co-prod.: Israel-France; Ph.: Ghislain Cloquet; Edit.: Eva Zora; Music: Lalan.

Award: Golden Bear, Berlin (1961).

A documentary film of stark juxtapositions, the film portrays Jews and non-Jews, tranquil desert scenery against the noise and beat of multiple languages, holiday celebrations, and outdoor markets. This is a poetic film, filled with humor and pathos, that succeeds in capturing the pulse and the constantly changing and developing reality of life in Israel. A portrait of the land emerges through symbols and images—water, land, and people. The film also combines newsreel footage, stills, and lyrically photographed footage of a vibrant land. The title of the film is taken from a Kafka story in which a man's combat with another man is found to have been a struggle with himself. French filmmaker Chris Marker (b. 1921) is an internationally recognized maker of documentaries. His impressive filmography includes *Le Joli mai* (1963), *La Jetée* (1962), *Cuba Si!* (1961), *Lettre de Sibérie* (1957), and *Dimanche à Pekin* (1956).

DESPERADO SQUARE (Kikar Hahalomot), 2000.

Dir. & Sc.: Benny Torati; Prod.: Amir Harel, Haim Manor; Ph.: Dror Moreh; Edit.: Yosef Grunfeld; Music: Shem-Tov Levy*; Cast: Yona Elian*, Muhammed Bakri*, Yoseph Shiloah*, Uri Gavrieli, Nir Levi, Sharon Rejeano.

Awards: Antigone d'Or, Montpellier (2001); Bronze Tree and Best Script, Valencia (2002); Best Supporting Actor (Yosef Shiloah), Best Art Direction (Elchanan Torati, Dalit Inbar), Best Costume Design (Dalit Inbar, Batya Rosenthal), Best Musical Score, Israeli Academy Awards (2000).

This romantic comedy salutes the days before television, when people went to the old neighborhood movie houses and saw films that were wonderfully emotional and romantic. The film mixes the nostalgia of the Italian film *Cinema Paradiso* (Giuseppe Tornatore, 1988) with a tribute to the Israeli "bourekas" films, which were ethnic melodramas and comedies. Filled with quirky characters and nostalgia and heavily laden with romance, the story takes place in the Hatikvah Quarter on the outskirts of Tel Aviv, where people live in ramshackle structures, and there is a mix of regular people and people who are somewhat unbalanced due to poverty and boredom. Film director Benny Torati characterizes this film, his first feature, as a nostalgic return to the days of naïveté, overpowering love, and big-screen neighborhood movie houses, before television, video, and ratings took over our lives.

Two brothers (Nir Levi, Sharon Rejeano) decide to reopen their father's old cinema on the anniversary of his death. It seems that he closed the cinema 25 years ago, following a feud with his brother, Avram (Muhammed Bakri). The two sons are convinced by the old neighborhood projectionist to mark the occasion by obtaining and screening the cinema's greatest hit, the emotional film classic from India *Sangam* (Raj Kapoor, 1964).

Their mother, Seniora (Yona Elian), is an elegant woman, insistent on furthering her husband's memory. Therefore, she is angry when she learns that his brother has returned to the neighborhood. As the story progresses, it becomes clear that her husband had been jealous of Avram since he was in love with Seniora, and they used to sit together, watching *Sangam*, in the old movie house. The film's climax is the screening of *Sangam*—wonderful clips are woven into the film—and Seniora and Avram sit together watching the film, late into the night, until the sun comes up the next day.

DIARY (Yoman), 1988.

Dir., Sc., & Ph.: David Perlov*; Prod.: Mira Perlov; Music: Shem-Tov Levy*; Edit.: Jacques Ehrlich, Noga Darevsky, Yosef Grunfeld, Levi Zini, Yael Perlov, Shalev Vayness, Bracha Kletchefski, Sharona Levitan, Dan Arav, Boaz Leon; Narrators: David Perlov, Reuven Morgan.

Not a documentary in the standard sense, the film is a personal diary that provides a view of the world through the eyes of one family and shows how changing reality affects them. By exposing the intimate issues and identity of the family of the filmmaker, the film adds insight into the national identity of an entire people. Shot with a small 16mm lingering camera, the film, 10 years in the making (1973–1983), is in the style of stream of consciousness. It was pre-sold to Channel 4, England, in its six-hour format.

Perlov begins by filming his family—his wife, Mira, and his twin daughters, Yael and Naomi—their routine, and the milestones in their lives. Reality creeps in via the television and as his canvas expands to include family friends, views through the window and then trips abroad. The film was shot and edited in chronological order. Part I (1973–1977), for example, includes the Yom Kippur War and how it creeps into their lives, a visit to Brazil, a lesson with Isaac Stern, their move to a new apartment, elections for the Knesset, a visit to Paris, and Sadat's arrival in Jerusalem. In documenting his travels, Perlov expresses nostalgia for other places—São Paulo, Paris, Düsseldorf, Amsterdam, and Brussels. The additional parts: Part II (1978–1980), Part III (1981–1982), Part IV (June 1982–February 1983), Part V (March–July 1983).

Sequel: *Updated Diary* (1990–1999).

THE DISTANCE (Hamerchak), 1994.

Dir., Prod., & Sc.: Dan Wolman*; Ph.: Victor Bilokopitov; Edit.: Shoshi Wolman; Music: Slava Ganelin; Cast: Haim Hadaya, Genya Chernik, Ruth Farchi, Yitzhak Shiloh, Miriam Nevo, Batsheva Noam.

Awards: Wolgin Award, Jerusalem (1994); Critic's Jury Prize, Haifa (1995).

This human story deals with themes of family separation and the responsibility of a son to his aging parents and his homeland. The film interweaves two parallel sets of emigration in the contemporary period—that of Israelis to the United States and that of Jews from the former Soviet Union to Israel.

Oded (Haim Hadaya) is an Israeli-born architect who has moved thousands of miles away to the United States, where he lives with his American-born wife and child. Attracted by the offer of a job in Israel, he returns to visit his parents, who are still entertaining the hope that he will come "home." In the opening scene, Oded's mother, wistfully reminiscing about her son, is teaching the "foreign" Svetlana (Genya Chernik) how to pickle cucumbers just the way Israelis like them. Similar to Oded, Svetlana has left her parents (in the former Soviet Union) to try her luck in a distant land.

Oded arrives and finds that his father is ailing, their old housekeeper has become senile, and his bedroom has been usurped by Svetlana and her son, who are boarding with his parents. Because of his guilt at having left his parents, Oded feels resentment and hostility toward Svetlana—hastily judging her and jumping to conclusions about her lifestyle—and toward her son, who has taken the place of his own child as a grandson to his parents.

DIZENGOFF 99, 1979.

Dir. & Sc.: Avi Nesher*; Prod.: Roni Ya'ackov, Arnon Milchan, David Shapira; Ph.: John Bufti; Edit.: Yitzhak Tzhayek; Music: Cobi Oshrat; Cast: Gidi Gov, Meir Suissa, Anat Atzmon*, Gali Atari, Rahel Goldenberg, Shosh Marciano, Gilat Ankori, Anat Harpaz, Orly Zilbershatz-Banai, Yoni Chen.

A light comedy, filled with popular songs, that became a cult film with young audiences, the film concerns itself with a young generation of Tel Avivians, struggling with ideals and striving for success, coming to terms with a modern, permissive society in which anything goes, and resisting compromising their standards in order to make it in the film world. Dizengoff no. 99 is an address in Tel Aviv, the major metropolis in Israel, which is portrayed as a dynamic city, and the young hero is restless, as seen through the hectic, episodic pace of the film.

Natti (Gidi Gov), a self-confident young fellow who enjoys fooling around, and his two friends—Ossi and Mushon, a guy and a girl (Meir Suissa and Anat Atzmon)—all move in to live together. Against a backdrop of romantic involvements and show-business adventures and motivated by Natti's desire for success, the group decides to produce a film. Although the film is not successful, they try again. The second time, they compromise with their own standards, and their film wins acclaim. Having spent a hectic year together, the group, all of them now more mature, splits up, and Natti, affected by the compromises that he made, leaves to go abroad.

DON'T GIVE A DAMN (Lo Sam Zayin), 1987.

Dir.: Shmuel Imberman*; Prod.: Yisrael Ringel, Yair Pradelsky; Sc.: Hanan Peled, based on a novel by Dan Ben-Amotz; Ph.: Nissim (Nitcho) Leon*; Edit.: Atara Horenshtein; Music: Benny Nagari; Cast: Ika Zohar, Anat Wachsmann*, Liora Grossman, Shmuel Vilozhny, Shlomo Tarshish, Shmuel Shiloh, Idit Tzur, Dudu Ben-Ze'ev.

Award: Best Editing, Israel Film Center (1986–1987).

The film addresses not only the problems of disabled veterans and how they deal with physical and psychological wounds but also the fears of all young men who serve in combat units. It portrays two sides of military service—the problems of returning to life and love after being crippled in battle and an obsession with living life to the fullest before it is too late.

Rafi (Ika Zohar) and Yigal are best friends. Enjoying their last flings before being drafted into an army combat unit, Rafi meets and falls in love with Nira. Even during Rafi's basic training and military service, they continue to see each other on weekends. Hunting down a terrorist, Rafi is wounded in the stomach. After his emergency treatment, he is sent to a rehabilitation unit, where it soon becomes clear that he will always be wheelchair-bound. He refuses to see Nira and turns his anger and jealousy against his friend Yigal, who is healthy and whole. Finding it difficult to deal with Rafi's feelings, Yigal is driven to prove himself by signing on for an officer's training course. Shortly afterward, he is killed in the line of duty. Rafi becomes obsessed with cripples and prostheses, photographing them and decorating his room with the pictures. As his depression and frustration deepen, he turns against his family and drives Nira away. Before it is too late, however, he realizes that in order to keep his dignity, he must fight for what he wants, and he sets out to win Nira back.

DON'T TOUCH MY HOLOCAUST (Al Tigu Li B'Shoah), 1994.

Dir., Sc., & Edit.: Asher Tlalim*; Prod.: Dan Setton, Daniel Paran; Ph.: Yoram Millo, Asher Tlalim.

Awards: Award for Excellence, Jerusalem (1994); Best Documentary, Israeli Academy Awards (1994).

This hard-hitting documentary film, a three-hour production, investigates issues of memory and the influence of the Holocaust on contemporary Israeli society and German society. In some ways each society is a reflection or mirror image of the other—Israeli society chooses to remember; German society chooses to forget. Including footage of the award-winning, controversial, and innovative theatrical performance *Arbeit Macht Frei*, directed by Dudi Ma'ayan and performed by the Acco Theater Company, and documenting its creative process, the film includes interviews with members of the company—Madi and Dudi Ma'ayan, Haled Abu-Ali, and Moni Yosef—and affirms the concept that we are all survivors of the Holocaust. In portraying a theater production, the film reflects the connection between cultural expression and historical memory. It also examines memory from a number of points of view—Sephardi and Ashkenazi, Israeli Arab, and contemporary German.

DOUBLE EDGE (Shlosha Shavuot Be'Yerushalayim / Lahav Hatzui; Alternative title: *Three Weeks in Jerusalem*), 1992.

Dir. & Sc.: Amos Kollek*; Prod.: Amos Kollek, Rafi Reibenbach; Ph.: Amnon Salomon*; Music: Mira J. Spector; Edit.: David Tour, Vicki Hayet; Cast: Faye Dunaway, Amos Kollek, Muhammed Bakri*, Makram Khoury*, Michael Schneider, Shmuel Shiloh, Anat Atzmon*.

Interviews with: Mayor Teddy Kollek, Abba Eban, Ziad Abu Zayyad, Hanan Ashrawi, Meir Kahane, Naomi Alteretz.

An American journalist has her illusions shattered in this film about the dilemmas and difficult position of a foreign reporter who becomes unwittingly involved in the unfolding of political events. The conclusion of the film was considered controversial due to the implied use of violence against children.

An American reporter (Faye Dunaway) goes to Israel to cover the story of the Palestinian uprising (*intifada*). During her three-week stay in the country, she becomes inexplicably attracted to two men—one a Jew (Amos Kollek) and the other a Palestinian activist (Muhammed Bakri). The reporter becomes involved in a murder as the Palestinian uses her to lure a collaborator to his death. When she decides to naively use an action photo without the permission of the censor, she is shocked and saddened to learn that, as a result of her action, revenge is taken against the Israeli soldier who was seen in her photo arresting a Palestinian. The film concludes dramatically as the reporter's life is threatened by a group of Palestinian children. Shaken with fear, she finds herself pulling a gun.

DREAMBOAT (Oolai Tirdu Sham), 1964.

Dir.: Amatsia Hiuni, Yisrael (Putcho) Wessler; Prod.: Amatsia Hiuni; Sc.: Yisrael (Putcho) Wessler, based on his children's book; Ph.: Nissim (Nitcho) Leon*; Music: Dov Seltzer*; Edit.: Dani Schik; Cast: Yehuda Gur-Aryeh, Emanuel Shefer, Mordechai Arnon, Uri Zohar*, Arik Einstein*.

Portraying a friendship that develops between two dreamers—an old man and a child—the film is like a dream itself. There is little dialogue yet much feeling and warmth. The title song, written by Dov Seltzer, became extremely popular at the time.

Walking along the beach one day, Zumba (Yehuda Gur-Aryeh) befriends a 10-year-old boy named Gil (Emanuel Shefer). Zumba is an old man who dreamed all his life of becoming a sailor. Gil and his friends build a ship on the roof of a building in Tel Aviv, they become Zumba's crew, and he is their captain. In a touching scene, Gil names the boat the "Roof Boat," and Zumba adds only a few letters so that it becomes the "Dreamboat."

THE DREAMER (Hatimhoni; Alternative title: *The Morning before Sleep*), 1970.

Dir. & Sc.: Dan Wolman*; Prod.: Ami Artzi; Ph.: Paul Glickman; Edit.: Barry H. Prince; Music: Gershon Kingsley; Cast: Tuvia Taby, Berta Litvina, Liora Rivlin, Shlomo Bar-Shavit, Bronka Salzman, Natan Cogan, Devora Halter-Keidar.

In his first feature film, Dan Wolman portrays his fascination with aging and the elderly. A film about emotion, conflict, and mood, it is set against the backdrop of the mystical city of Safed. The film portrays the interdependence of young and old and the tension between the modern, secular lifestyle (as represented by the young woman) and the older, familial, more rooted life (as seen in the old woman).

A lonely young man (Tuvia Taby) becomes emotionally attached to the elderly residents of an old age home in which he works as an attendant. He develops a special relationship with one elderly woman in particular (Berta Litvina), sketching her portrait and spending time with her. A conflict develops between his devotion to her and his feelings for a young woman (Liora Rivlin) who comes one day to collect the belongings of her grandfather, who recently passed away.

DREAMS OF INNOCENCE (Sipor Sh'Matchil Be'Halvayah Shel Nachash), 1993.

Dir.: Dina Zvi-Riklis; Prod.: Katriel Schory*, Marek Rozenbaum*; Sc.: Avi Mograbi, based on a book by Ronit Matalon; Ph. Dani Shneur; Edit.: Rachel Yagil, Anat Lubarsky; Music: Shem-Tov Levy*; Cast: Moshe Ivgi*, Rita Shukrun, Nissim Sossi, Efrat Aviv, Levana Finkelstein*, Maya De-Vries, Tomer Even, Avner Hezkiyahu, Razia Yizraeli.

A story of broken illusions, the film is told from the point of view of two maturing children who comprehend life and its illusions better than their own father. The father is an immigrant, uprooted from the world of his youth, uncomfortable with his new surroundings, and forever searching for his childhood dreams. The story is told by the daughter, Margalit, as a voice-over narrator, who is reading from letters that she wrote. This is the first feature film of film director Dina Zvi-Riklis, known for her documentary films and her short dramas, including *Cordania* (1984) and *Look-out* (1991).

Benjamin, a 13-year-old boy, and his younger sister, Margalit, live with their mother and grandmother in a moshav, far from the center of the country. Their father, Monsieur Robert (Moshe Ivgi), is a dapper fellow who travels often. Margalit dreams of becoming an acrobat, and Benjamin, wanting to prove himself to the world, kills a snake in the opening sequence. The children go on a journey to Tel Aviv, searching for their lost dog. There they find their father, living poor and alone. Margalit realizes that what her mother has been saying is true—her father lives in a world of dreams. He still imagines making it big—importing parrots from Africa, inventing a bicycle for four, and becoming somebody. These are his dreams.

DRIFTING (Nagua), 1983.

Dir.: Amos Gutmann*; Prod.: Enrique Rottenberg, Malka Assaf; Sc.: Edna Maziah, Amos Gutmann; Ph.: Yossi Wein; Edit.: Anna Finkelstein; Music: Arik Rudich; Cast: Jonathan Sagall*, Ami Traub, Blanka Metzner, Ben Levin, Dita Arel, Boaz Turgeman, Hadas Turgeman, Rashid Mashrawi, Mark Chassman.

Awards: Best Cinematography, Best Actor (Jonathan Sagall), Best Musical Score, Israel Film Center (1983).

First produced as a short drama in 1979, the film is an episodic story of the pain and loneliness of a Tel Aviv homosexual who is obsessed with telling his story. It is an introspective work based on autobiographical elements of Gutmann's life.

Robby (Jonathan Sagall) is a depressed and unsuccessful filmmaker who comes to terms with his own homosexuality while he searches for the backing for his film. Living with his grandmother, Robby blames the problems in his life on his mother, who left for Germany when he was 14 and sends him money to assuage her conscience for having left him, and on his father, a Holocaust survivor who comes around to visit periodically, spouting sentimentality.

DUE TO THAT WAR (B'Glal Hamilchamah Hahi; Alternative title: *Because of That War*), 1988.

Dir. & Sc.: Orna Ben-Dor (Niv)*; Prod.: Shmuel Altman, David Shutz; Ph.: Oren Shmukler; Edit.: Rachel Yagil; Music: Yehuda Poliker.

Awards: FIPRESCI Prize, Berlin (1989); Honorable Mention, Leningrad (1989); Critic's Jury Prize, Haifa (1988).

This award-winning film documents the impact of the Holocaust on the lives of two second-generation survivors—singer Yehuda Poliker and lyricist Ya'ackov Gilad, popular rock figures (of rock band Benzine fame). The film tells the story of Sephardi and Ashkenazi, of working-class and intellectual.

Poliker's father, Jacko, is from Saloniki and was deported by the Nazis to an extermination camp. Gilad's mother, Halina Birnbaum, is a writer and poet from Warsaw whose memories haunt her work. Both Jacko and Halina went to Israel after the war.

This documentary links the two families together, interweaving interviews with the parents and sons and mixing them with performances of their rock songs, which deal with Holocaust memories. Poliker and Gilad produced the rock album *Ashes and Dust*, which includes songs that became popular with the younger generation of Israelis (and which has sold more than 50,000 copies). The title song of the album refers to Gilad's lyrics: "Eternity is only ashes and dust, Years and nothing's forgotten." In the song about Treblinka Station, which appears in the film, one cannot buy a return ticket, and they "cook only with gas." In a particularly emotional sequence in the film, Poliker discusses his own problem of stuttering. He recalls that his father used to gobble his food, a habit from his experiences in the death camp. When Poliker was a little boy, his father choked badly on a piece of bread, and the young boy was sent for help. At that time, he felt the terrible weight of his father's life resting on his shoulders. Although he has become a successful singer, he has stuttered ever since.

THE DYBBUK OF THE HOLY APPLE FIELD (Ahava Asura), 1997.

Dir.: Yossi Somer*; Prod.: Rudiger Findeinsen, Yossi Sommer; Co-prod.: Israel-Switzerland; Sc.: Yossi Somer, Eyal Sher; Ph.: Manu Kadosh; Edit.: Dov Steuer; Music: Rick Wentworth; Cast: Ayelet Zuarer, Yehezkel Lazarov, Mosh Ivgi*, Orna Porat, Yigal Naor.

Awards: Best Foreign Film, Houston WorldFest (1999); Best Cinematography, Best Editing, Best Art Direction (Ya'akov Turgeman), Best Costume Design (Laura Dinulescu), Best Soundtrack (Yoav Sarig, Dov Steuer), Israeli Academy Awards (1997).

An adaptation of the classic Jewish play *The Dybbuk*, by Sholem Ansky, the film is set in the contemporary period in the ultra-Orthodox Jerusalem neighborhood of Meah Shearim. In addition to being about fantasy, mysticism, and kabbala, this is a film about passion, commitment, and betrayal.

Hanan is a secular youth who goes to Meah Shearim searching for his religious roots. He is inexplicably drawn to Leah (Ayelet Zuarer), an ultra-Orthodox young woman living a sheltered life in the care of her father and her grandmother (Orna Porat). Long ago, Hanan and Leah's fathers were friends and swore that their children would be wed. However, Leah's father breaks this promise and wishes to betroth her to another.

Strange visions bring Hanan to search out a rabbi (Moshe Ivgi) who will lead him into the world of mysticism. Invoking powerful spirits, Hanan dies trying to create a spiritual alliance with his beloved. When his dybbuk (spirit) enters the body of Leah, the rabbi attempts an exorcism. However, the two lovers cannot be divided. In fact, they can be together only in death.

EIGHT AGAINST ONE (Shemona B'Ekevot Achat), 1964.

Dir.: Menahem Golan*; Prod.: Micha Cagan, Menahem Golan; Sc.: Uriel Ofek, based on a book by Yamima Tschernovitz; Ph.: Yitzhak (Mimisch) Herbst; Edit.: Dani Schik; Music: Dov Seltzer*; Cast: Shaike Ophir*, Bomba Tzur, Geula Gill, Elisheva Michaeli, Eitan Priver.

Reflecting the Israeli preoccupation with security and intelligence, this film is a combination comedy-musical-spy story. Filmed on location at a kibbutz in northern Israel, the film provides for all children the realization of a dream—success at discovering a real spy (especially one who speaks with a German accent) and winning military honors as a result.

A group of kibbutz children are surprised one day to find that their favorite hideout, an old castle, is occupied by a scientist from Hebrew University. The scientist, Dr. Berger (Shaike Ophir), spends a lot of time with the children, teaching them about insects, telling them stories, and asking them questions. When the children become suspicious of Dr. Berger's questions, they uncover his espionage operation, just in time to save an air force jet from being blown up by a bomb planted to go off during a festive air display.

THE EIGHTY-FIRST BLOW (Hamakah Hashmonim Ve'Echad), 1974.

Dir.: Jacques Ehrlich, David Bergman, Haim Gouri; Prod.: Avraham Shapira, Dani Schik; Sc.: Haim Gouri; Music: Yossi Mar-Chaim; Edit.: Jacques Ehrlich.

Nomination: Nominated for an American Academy Award for Best Documentary.

This documentary film relates the history of the Holocaust. It is meticulous in its scope and devastating in its subject matter. The filmmakers do not flinch from telling the complete story of the horrors or from showing the atrocities.

Arranged chronologically, the film covers the major elements of the history of the period: Kristallnacht, the Nuremberg laws, the ghettoization, the deportations, and the labor and extermination camps. The story of the Warsaw Ghetto is told in detail, including the hunger and fear, the life-and-death struggle for documents, the despair, and, finally, the uprising. There is mention of some interesting historical footnotes, including the sailing of the ill-fated ship the *St. Louis*, which was forced to return from Cuba, and the heroism of Dr. Janus Korczak, who bravely cared for the orphaned children in his charge and accompanied them to their death. This historical document is a compilation of footage and stills shot by the Nazis themselves. The sound track, mixed with mournful ballads, mainly comprises fragments of testimony from the trial of Adolf Eichmann, which took place in Jerusalem in 1961.

The title of the film refers to a young man's story of how he survived 80 lashes in a labor camp. The fact, however, that no one actually believed the stories of the horrors that he endured—their unwillingness to listen to the tale or to believe that it actually happened—was the 81st blow.

Part of a trilogy produced by the Ghetto Fighters' House at Kibbutz Lochamei HaGhettaot.

Sequels: *The Last Sea* (1980), about the postwar illegal immigration to Palestine, and *Flames in the Ashes* (1985), about Jewish armed resistance to Nazi terror.

ELDORADO, 1963.

Dir.: Menahem Golan*; Prod. Mordechai Navon*; Sc.: Leo Filler, Amatsia Hiuni, Menahem Golan, based on a play by Yigal Mossinson; Ph.: Nissim (Nitcho) Leon*; Edit.: Nellie Bogor-Gilad; Music: Yochanan Zarai; Cast: Haim Topol*, Gila Almagor*, Tikvah Mor, Yossi Yadin, Shaike Ophir*.

Already with his first directorial effort, Golan is shifting the focus of the Israeli film industry outward, to an emphasis on films produced for possible distribution abroad. Golan combines a uniquely Israeli atmosphere with elements of ethnic melodrama and suspense and tries to capture international audiences by including a bedroom scene (which created quite a furor in Israel) and by creating an authentic gangster milieu. The title of the film is taken from the name of an underworld hangout in the port area of Jaffa.

Recently released from prison, a man (Haim Topol) tries desperately to start a new life. Much to his chagrin, he finds that the local prostitute (Gila Almagor) is still devoted to him and that he will forever be the object of police suspicion. In addition, his old friends try to convince him to return to his old life of crime. Trying his best to adjust to the requirements of life in normal society, the ex-con is determined to prove his innocence in newly trumped-up charges against him. When one good cop comes along and takes it upon himself to expose the frame-up, the film concludes with a chase scene and a final confrontation between the criminals and the police.

AN ELECTRIC BLANKET (Smicha Cheshmalit U'Shema Moshe), 1994.

Dir. & Sc.: Assi Dayan*; Prod.: Yoram Kislev*; Ph.: Ofer Yanov; Edit.: Zohar Sela; Music: Arkadi Duchin; Cast: Shmil Ben-Ari, Uri Ran Klausner, Rivka Neuman.

Awards: Best Film, Valencia (1998); Best Screenplay, Best Actor (Shmuel Ben-Ari), Israeli Academy Awards (1994).

A black comedy about prostitution and drugs, the film tries to make some sense out of a meaningless existence.

Levi, Moshe, and Malka are three small-time crooks. Malka (Rivka Neuman), a street hooker who performs services for her eccentric boarder, dreams of becoming a famous singer. Her inexperienced pimp, Levi (Shmil Ben-Ari), is the self-proclaimed leader of the bunch, and he is assisted by Moshe (Uri Ran Klausner), who is desperately in love with Malka. Moshe lives on a park bench and dreams of buying an electric blanket, which he would plug into a streetlight to keep him warm at night.

ELECTRIC MAN (Ish Chashmal; Alternative title: *Rutenberg*), 2001.

Dir.: Eli Cohen*; Prod.: Omri Maron, Ruth Lev-Ari; Sc.: Yaron Zelig, based on an idea by Ruth Lev-Ari; Ph.: David Gurfinkel*; Edit.: Yitzhak Tzhayek, Tal Sheffy; Music: Shem-Tov Levy*; Cast: Menashe Noy, Mark Ivanir, Ayelet Zuarer, Lior Ashkenazi, Natasha Vitkovich.

Awards: Best Art Direction (Yoram Shayer), Best Costume Design (Rakefet Levi), Israeli Academy Awards (2001).

Based on the life of a historical figure, the film takes place during the early years of the twentieth century, years of political upheaval and legendary figures, which lead to the later establishment of the state of Israel. The electrical power plant at Naharayim, built by Pinchas Rutenberg, provided electricity until 1948, when it was destroyed during the War of Independence.

Rutenberg (Menashe Noy) was a man of vision and action. After fleeing Russia for the assassination of a double agent, he puts all of his energies into laying the foundations for the first power plant in Palestine. Together with his brother (Mark Ivanir), he chooses a site at Naharayim, where the waters of the

Jordan River can be harnessed to create electricity. Rutenberg goes to London to meet Churchill and to obtain a license for his project. Then, he puts all of his own personal resources into the building of the power plant. During one stormy weekend in 1931, flooding creates havoc at the almost completed power plant. Rushing to Naharayim to survey the damage, Rutenberg recalls his past—his revolutionary days in Russia and his relationships with some of the people who assisted him along the way. Upon reaching Naharayim, he realizes that the damage is extensive, but he is committed to finding the strength to continue and complete the project.

THE END OF MILTON LEVY (Sofo Shel Milton Levy; Alternative title: *The Death of Milton Levy*), 1981.

Dir. & Sc.: Nissim Dayan*; Prod.: Nissim Dayan, Natan Hakeini; Ph.: Yachin Hirsch; Edit.: Dani Schik, Lina Kadish; Music: Avner Kenner; Cast: Oshik Levy, Rahel Dayan, Dov Glickman, Yoseph Shiloah*, Avner Hezkiyahu, Lilith Nagar.

A film about friendship, marriage, the seduction of a freewheeling lifestyle, and the dangers of organized crime, this is the story of a regular guy who becomes involved in something he can't handle—he becomes part of a ruthless world that sweeps him along and leads eventually to his violent death.

Milton Levy (Oshik Levy) is a young man married to a woman who no longer attracts him. He is deeply in debt; his salary as a machinist does not cover their needs or those of his drug addict friend. He borrows more and more and, in order to cover his debts, gets involved in underworld dealings. Milton leaves his wife and child and spends his time with friends who are part of an exciting and carefree lifestyle of drink, drugs, and sex. Milton gets summoned by the head of the Mafia to pull off a job in return for all the favors that he has received. When Milton's drug addict friend robs his old grandmother, Milton goes after him, yelling that he has gone too far. The friend, glassy-eyed, shoots him dead.

ERVINKA, 1967.

Dir. & Sc.: Ephraim Kishon*; Prod.: Ephraim Kishon*, Haim Topol*, Shlomo Mugrabi; Ph.: Alexander Thompson; Edit.: Dani Schik; Music: Dov Seltzer*; Cast: Haim Topol, Gila Almagor*, Avner Hezkiyahu, Ya'ackov Ben-Sira, Yossi Banai, Shraga Friedman, Edna Fleidel, Shaike Ophir*, and the Gashash Trio: Yisrael (Poli) Poliakov, Shaike Levi, Gavri Banai.

Starring Haim Topol as Ervinka, the film is a satire about police stupidity and municipal bureaucratic inefficiency. It reflects an integration of Ephraim Kishon's cynicism and satire with Haim Topol's good, healthy fun.

Ervinka is a charismatic fellow who enjoys fooling around, flattering women, crashing bar mitzvah parties, and pulling gags on his neighbors. When his motorbike gets a parking ticket, he reports the bike stolen to the police and has the ticket canceled. Since his one dream in life is to win the national lottery, he devises a scheme to rob the lottery coffers with the assistance of his friends (the

Gashash Trio). Seeing that they are making a film of a supposed robbery of the lottery, the local police chief (Shaike Ophir) unwittingly cooperates in the scheme. Ervinka, however, finds himself falling hopelessly in love with a pretty young policewoman, and, in the end, much to his own surprise, he returns the stolen money.

ESCAPE TO THE SUN (HaBricha El Hashemesh), 1972.

Dir. & Prod.: Menahem Golan*; Co-prod.: Israel-France-Germany; Sc.: Menahem Golan, Yoseph Gross, based on a story by Uri Dan; Ph.: David Gurfinkel*; Edit.: Fred Zarap; Music: Dov Seltzer*; Cast: Laurence Harvey, Lila Kedrova, Josephine Chaplin, Jack Hawkins, John Ireland, Yehuda Barkan*, Clive Revill, Yehuda Efroni, Gila Almagor*.

The film is based on the famed Leningrad hijacking trials of 1970, when a group of Jews made a desperate attempt to flee the Soviet Union. Shot entirely abroad, the film is a serious human and political statement that criticizes the Soviet restriction on the emigration of Jews.

Eight citizens of a totalitarian state decide that they want to leave their country and live where they please. Each makes the decision for his or her own reasons. Among the group are two young lovers (Josephine Chaplin and Yehuda Barkan) who have pledged to build their lives together elsewhere. The story develops around the suffering and persecution to which these people are subjected, their organization as a group, and their attempt at escape.

EVERY BASTARD A KING (Kol Mamzer Melech), 1968.

Dir.: Uri Zohar*; Prod.: Avraham (Pashanel) Deshe, Haim Topol*; Sc.: Eli Tavor, Uri Zohar; Ph.: David Gurfinkel*; Edit.: Anna Gurit; Music: Michel Colombier; Cast: Pier Angeli, Yehoram Gaon*, Oded Kotler*, William Berger, Tami Tzafroni, Uri Levy, Reuven Morgan, Moshe Yanai.

Awards: Best Direction, Best Color Photography, Chicago (1968).

Combining drama with documentary, the film portrays life in the shadow of war. The war sequences include documentary newsreel footage and a reconstruction of an actual armored tank battle.

An American journalist (Pier Angeli) arrives in Israel to report on the developing crisis prior to the Six Day War. Accompanied by his Israeli-born girlfriend, who later becomes his wife, and shown around the country by his carefree driver-guide Yehoram (Yehoram Gaon), the journalist develops a sympathy toward Israel. He is impressed by the people whom he meets, such as Rafi—based on a historical figure who flew to Egypt in an attempt to single-handedly bring about peace. When the war breaks out, Yehoram reports for duty and becomes a hero when he rescues a wounded soldier. The film climaxes with a scene in which the journalist, particularly influenced by his experiences in Israel during the war and feeling himself part of the people, bravely attempts a rescue in a minefield at Yehoram's kibbutz.

FAITHFUL CITY (Kirya Ne'emana), 1952.

Dir.: Joseph Leytes; Prod.: Joseph Leytes, M. Yona Friedman; Sc: Ben Barzman; Ph.: Gerald Gibbs; Edit.: J. D. Guthridge; Music: Edward Ben-Michael; Cast: Jamie Smith, Avraham Ben-Josef, John Slater, Rahel Marcus, Israel Hanin, Juda Levi, Amnon Lifschitz, Dina (Doron) Peskin, Didi (Ramati) Zonenfeld.

A heroic story on the background of the War of Independence, the film is about children who have survived the Holocaust and are brought as refugees to a youth village in Jerusalem. Originally, the film was produced in English. Later, however, in 1967, a second version was released with Hebrew voice-over and an epilogue of scenes depicting the capture of Jerusalem during the Six Day War. Film director Joseph Leytes was an internationally recognized documentary filmmaker in Poland before going to Israel in 1943. In addition to this film, he directed two feature-length docudramas in prestate Israel.

A group of Holocaust survivor youngsters is brought to a youth village that is staffed by Sam (Jamie Smith), a World War II American war veteran studying at Hebrew University, and the director, himself a survivor with a number on his arm. The youngsters are a difficult group—they play cards, smoke, and tell stories about their past. Anna's (Dina Doron Peskin) stories hint at the exploitation that was endured by women at the hands of the Nazis. Max (Israel Hanin), the ringleader, is a troublemaker; he steals Sam's watch in order to raise the money needed to return to Europe. As time passes and the state of Israel is declared, a feeling of solidarity grows between the youngsters and the staff. When war breaks out, Max finally proves himself by taking on responsibility and mobilizing the other youngsters to sandbag the buildings. There is a terrible water shortage in Jerusalem, and when the water truck cannot get through, Sam heroically drives the truck through a barrage of sniping in order to bring water to the youngsters.

FANTASIA ON A ROMANTIC THEME (Fantasia Al Noseh Romanti), 1978.

Dir.: Vitek Tracz; Prod.: Dani Tracz; Sc.: Hanoch Levin; Ph.: Hanania Bar; Edit.: Dani Schik; Music: Rafi Kadishzon; Cast: Alex Munte, Nissim Izikari, Ruth Segal, Yardena Gurevitz, Yehuda Fuchs, Leon Young, Ilan Toren, Nathan Walpovitz, Yisrael Gurion, Raphael Klatchkin, Avram Heffner*.

Awards: Third Prize, Best Screenplay, Best Actress (Ruth Segal), Best Cinematography, Best Musical Score, Israel Film Center (1978).

Nothing is sacred in this unrestrained satire, which includes crude scenes of parody. Everyone is made fun of—from ugly people to ballet lessons for little girls, from old people to royalty, from the Israeli myth of the beautiful Swede to funerals and suicide. The film also pokes fun at films of beautiful people, such as the Greta Garbo film *Queen Christina* (Rouben Marmoulian, 1933). Scriptwriter Hanoch Levin (1943–1999) was a major figure of contemporary Israeli theater, having written 50 plays, characterized by a combination of satire and tragedy together with crudity and humor. He wrote the scripts for two feature films—*Fantasia on a Romantic Theme* and *Floch** (Dan Wolman, 1972).

Kolf (Alex Munte) is a middle-aged man who has lost the will to live. Neither his best friend nor the love of a kind, albeit ugly, woman Gluska (Ruth Segal), can save him. Kolf tries to hang himself over his mother's grave, which is near the grave of the Unknown Soldier, where Queen Christina of Sweden (who has traveled to Israel searching for a husband) is placing flowers. In an effort to restore Kolf's desire for life, the Queen takes time off from interviewing suitors and devotes an evening to a gala event at a local community center, where she dances with him. Kolf, imagining that the Queen truly loves him, threatens to commit suicide if the beautiful Queen does not marry him. It is Gluska, instead, who takes her own life, having been rejected by Kolf.

FELLOW TRAVELERS (Magash Hakesef), 1983.

Dir.: Yehuda (Judd) Ne'eman*; Prod.: Yehuda Ne'eman, Renen Schorr*; Sc.: Amnon Lord, Yehuda Ne'eman, based on an idea & dialogue by Ruchama Marton; Ph.: Hanania Bar; Edit.: Anat Lubarsky; Music: Rafi Kadishzon; Cast: Gidi Gov, Yossi Pollack, Shmuel Kraus, Yusuf Abu-Warda, Daliah Shimko, Suheiru Hany, Muhammed Bakri*, Nurit Galron; Guest appearances: Peter Freistadt, Michal Bat-Adam*.

Awards: Best Supporting Actor (Yusuf Abu-Warda), Best Editing, Israel Film Center (1983).

A complex political thriller, the film poses a complex moral issue. The story is about an Israeli who has been living in West Germany for many years and is sympathetic to the Palestinian cause.

Yoni (Gidi Gov) grew up on a kibbutz and served in the Israeli army. Currently living in West Germany, he strongly believes in the importance of furthering Palestinian cultural development. He agrees to carry a large sum of money, earmarked for the opening of a university, from his German professor to the group in Israel. He arrives in Israel, where he meets Jamila, head of the Israeli group. Much to his dismay, he learns that Jamila and her group are working toward armed struggle and are planning to use the funds to buy arms. Unwilling to assist in this endeavor, Yoni hides the money and becomes embroiled in a web of intrigue and violence—between the Israeli Secret Service (Shin Bet), members of the Palestinian group, the owner of a Tel Aviv nightclub, the German authorities, and an American arms dealer. Caught up in a dangerous game, Yoni finds that things can end only tragically.

FIELD DIARY (Yoman Sadeh; French title: *Journal de campagne*), 1982.

Dir. & Sc.: Amos Gitai*; Prod.: Richard Copans; Co-prod.: Israel-France; Ph.: Nurith Aviv*; Edit: Scheherazade Saadi.

Award: Golden Sesterce, Nyon (1982).

This documentary film provides a harsh look at the Israeli occupation of the West Bank and the Gaza Strip. Setting out with his crew to film a diary of the occupation, Gitai finds incidents related to the expropriation of land and water resources, such as Palestinian women demonstrating as bulldozers uproot olive trees to make way for a new settlement. Suddenly, the War in Lebanon breaks out, and the film reflects some of those tumultuous events. Rather than using an intrusive voice-over commentary, Gitai allows the searching lens of the camera and the juxtaposition of situations and memories to speak for themselves.

FIFTY-FIFTY (Chetzi Chetzi), 1971.

Dir.: Boaz Davidson*; Prod.: Assi Dayan*, Moshe Golan; Sc.:Assi Dayan, Nissim Izikari, Boaz Davidson; Ph.: David Gurfinkel*; Edit.: Jacques Ehrlich; Music: David Karibushi; Cast: Ze'ev Berlinski, Nahum Buchman, Assi Dayan, Baruch David, Yossi Pollack, Tzvi Shissel, Nissim Izikari, Shmuel Wolf, Dori Ben-Ze'ev, Aliza Yitzhaki.

An entertaining comedy filled with authentic characters, the film portrays the clash between the modern and the old. Two friends share in the purchase of a lottery ticket, cutting it in two, each keeping his half. When one friend dies, and it becomes apparent that the holder of this ticket is the big winner of the lottery grand prize, the chaos and comedy begin. A frantic search ensues for the missing half of the ticket, involving an unfaithful husband, a pair of thieves, and a strange person from a kibbutz who has arrived in the big city.

FIRST LOVE (Ahavah Rishonah), 1982.

Dir. & Sc.: Uzi Peres; Prod.: Ruth Peres; Ph.: Avi Karpick; Edit.: Ilana Ben-Ari; Music: Frances Levin; Cast: Gila Almagor*, Yiftach Katzur, Hanan Goldblatt, Uri Levy, Debby Hess.

The film is about a man's midlife crisis and his return, after 20 years, to his first love. Swiss-born film director Uzi Peres (1951–1992) directed feature films both in France and in Israel. In addition to *First Love*, his Israeli films include *Love without Pity Is Cruel* (1983).

Ziva (Gila Almagor) is a 40-year-old woman, a happily married mother of two. At her birthday celebration, in walks her first boyfriend, Yitzhak (Hanan Goldblatt), who has been living on a kibbutz. It becomes clear that he has not been able to forget her and that he has come to renew their love affair. The appearance of Yitzhak awakens in Ziva memories of their passionate love of many years ago. He stays the night in the family's guest room, and Ziva goes to his room. Matters become terribly complicated when both of Ziva's teenage children, a son and a daughter, become involved.

FLOCH, 1972.

Dir.: Dan Wolman*; Prod.: Alfred Flein, Haim Zeldis; Sc.: Hanoch Levin, Dan Wolman; Ph.: Ya'ackov Kallach; Edit.: David Millstein; Music: Alex Cagan; Cast: Avraham Chalfi, Ofra Doron, Yisrael Segal, Lula Yackobovitz, Arnon Tzafir, Savich Goldreich, Tom Levy, Hanoch Levin.

Award: Third Prize, Israel Film Center (1973).

A tragicomedy, this film reflects both the harsh satire of scriptwriter Hanoch Levin and the compassionate, psychological approach of the filmmaker, Dan

Wolman. Hanoch Levin wrote the script for one other feature film, *Fantasia on a Romantic Theme** (Vitek Tracz, 1978).

Floch (Avraham Chalfi), an elderly man, has lost his only son and the son's family in a car accident. As a result of an overpowering drive to have descendants, he decides to divorce his wife of many years and to search for a young woman with whom he can have a child. Floch's experiences, after leaving his wife, include a series of surrealistic encounters in which he becomes a pitifully sad and, at the same time, amusing caricature of an old man.

THE FLYING CAMEL (Hagamal Hame'ofef), 1994.

Dir. & Sc.: Rami Na'aman; Prod.: Marek Rozenbaum*; Ph.: Yoav Kosh*; Edit.: Tova Asher; Music: Shem-Tov Levy*; Cast: Gideon Zinger, Salim Dau*, Laurence Bouvard.

Combining humor and fantasy, the film portrays the development of a mutual relationship between a Palestinian and an Israeli as they are both searching for remnants of the past. With complex and in-depth characterizations, the film takes a look at a society in which everyone is slightly obsessed and somewhat crazy, "but no more crazy than anyone else."

Bauman (Gideon Zinger) is an eccentric university professor, a collector of strange treasures of the past. Phares (Salim Dau) is a Palestinian garbage collector from Gaza who is searching for the long-gone orange groves that once belonged to his father. Together they search for pieces of the old statue of a flying camel—the symbol of the 1930s Tel Aviv Levant Fair. One day, an Italian nun, Gina (Laurence Bouvard), shows up in a camper and parks in the yard of Bauman's little house. She is a carefree spirit and brings light into the otherwise tense relationship between Bauman and Phares.

In order to restore Tel Aviv to its former glory, Gina, Bauman, and Phares plot to steal the wings of the flying camel from a nearby restaurant. The owner of the restaurant and his hooligan sons come after them and set fire to Bauman's house and his junkyard. The scaffolding that Phares built for the flying camel collapses, and there is a vision of the camel flying off into the night. The next morning, Bauman asks Phares to help him rebuild his house. Phares responds, in a metaphor for the Israeli–Palestinian peace process, "I will help you rebuild your house if you let me have my orange grove."

FORCED TESTIMONY (Edut Me'Ones; Alternative title: *Forced Witness*), 1984.

Dir.: Raphael Rebibo; Prod.: Yoram Globus*, Menahem Golan*; Sc.: Raphael Rebibo, Eli Tavor; Ph.: Maurice Fellous; Edit.: Alain Jakubowicz; Music: Dov Seltzer*; Cast: Anat Atzmon*, Uri Gavrieli, Dalik Volonitz, Shlomo Tarshish, Irit Frank, Moscu Alcalay, Natan Datner, Miri Fabian, Oshik Levy, Avi Kleinberger, Tzadok Tzarom, Itai Keren, Shmuel Vilozhny.

Against a background of ethnic crime, the film is about the rape of an Ashkenazi middle-class woman by a Sephardi tough guy. In addition to making films abroad, the Moroccan-born film director, Raphael Rebibo, has also directed the Israeli feature film *A Place by the Sea* (1988).

Ronit (Anat Atzmon) hears her neighbor's screams and sees the rapist fleeing. Committed to making the rapist pay for what he has done, she decides to testify against him, even in the face of threats and torment from the rapist's brother and his uncouth, underworld friends. When the rape victim, Ronit's neighbor, commits suicide, the case is dismissed. But the rapist's brother remains obsessed with punishing Ronit. As a divorcée with a young son who is also threatened, Ronit reacts like an animal protecting herself and her young.

FOREIGN SISTER (Achot Zara), 2000.

Dir., Prod., & Sc.: Dan Wolman*; Ph.: Itamar Hadar; Edit.: Shoshi Wolman; Music: Slava Ganelin; Cast: Tamar Yerushalmi, Askala Markos, Zvi Salton, Miriam Nevo, Neli Tagar, Yossi Vasa.

Award: Wolgin Award, Jerusalem (2000).

Dealing with the issues and problems of foreign workers in Israel, the film tells of a relationship that develops between two women—one a middle-class Jewish professional and the other an Ethiopian Christian working illegally in Israel. The two women come from different worlds and know very little about each other but eventually form a bond of friendship and understanding. It is a film about stereotypes, patronizing attitudes, lack of understanding, and apathy. It is also a film about how these attitudes can be changed.

Naomi (Tamar Yerushalmi) is a middle-aged woman, married, mother of two. She is overworked from the stresses at home and at work. When her mother becomes unable to continue to care for herself, she hires Genest (Askala Markos), a Christian woman who is trying desperately to earn money for her family back in Ethiopia. However, Genest's pride forces her to quit her new job when it becomes clear that Naomi's mother is an old-fashioned bigot. When Naomi asks Genest to help with her son's bar mitzvah party, they spend more time together, and slowly Naomi begins to understand her new friend's life. She becomes involved with Genest's friends and their difficulties with the immigration authorities, their employers, and their problems in finding medical care. When Naomi finds herself witness to a violent death, she doesn't even bother to tell her family about it—they won't understand anyway.

THE FOX IN THE CHICKEN COOP (Hashu'al B'Lool Hatarnegolot), 1978.

Dir. & Sc.: Ephraim Kishon*; Prod.: Yitzhak Kol, Ephraim Kishon; Ph.: David Gurfinkel*; Music: Nurit Hirsch; Edit.: Hadassah Shani; Cast: Shaike Ophir*, Shoshana Shani, Zaharira Harifai, Ya'ackov Bodo, Sefi Rivlin, Nitza Shaul, Moscu Alcalay, Mordechai Ben-Ze'ev.

The film is a satire on political life and on the supposed advantages of local government. The political fox comes to the chicken coop to offer the advantages of political bureaucracy and corruption.

An aging politician (Shaike Ophir) collapses from exhaustion after a day filled with speeches and political appearances. In the ambulance on the way to the hospital, he imagines himself resting in a small rustic village in the Galilee, reminiscent of the Eastern European shtetl, far removed from petty politics and the pressures of work. The politician begins to change the village for the "better," bringing political consciousness and bureaucracy to the village. People in his imagined town look like people from his own life; in fact, he has a romance with the innkeeper's wife, who is actually his wife! The cobbler's daughter, a deaf-mute, gives herself freely to the politician's assistant, symbolizing the simple naïveté of those who neither hear nor speak the corrupting language of politics. But, as the townspeople become familiar with the ways of politics, greed and corruption spread, and a shotgun wedding is quickly arranged.

FRAGMENTS—JERUSALEM (Shivrei T'munot—Yerushalayim), 1986–1996.
Dir., Prod., Sc. & Ph.: Ron Havilio*; Edit.: Tor Ben Mayor.
Awards: Documentary Prize, Edinburgh (1998); FIPRESCI Prize, Berlin (1998); Grand Prize, Yamagata (1997); New Foundation of Cinema and Television Prize, Jerusalem (1996).

A personal documentary, the film is an ongoing diary of a filmmaker's personal impressions and memory on the background of the history and story of the city of Jerusalem. Layer upon layer, the images of the city are combined with one family's narrative, thus becoming part and parcel of an integrated whole. The film is of epic proportions and includes two "cycles," each approximately three hours. Each cycle is broken into parts:

Cycle One: Mamilla, Days Long Past, Engravers of Metal—Painters of Light
Cycle Two: Sarina Menachem, Within the Walls, Jaffa Road, Abba.

Incorporating unique still photographs and early moving images of the city, the film shows the filmmaker's attraction to the old neighborhood of Mamilla near the Jaffa Gate, built along the divide between old and new, east and west, Arab and Jew. Most of the old buildings of the neighborhood have now disappeared, replaced by upscale housing developments, but the filmmaker's images remain.

GET ZORKIN (Hasamba ve'Na'arei HaHefker), 1971.
Dir.: Yoel Zilberg*; Prod.: Yitzhak Nahar; Sc.: Yigal Mossinson, based on the book by Yigal Mossinson; Ph.: Adam Greenberg*; Edit.: Nellie Bogor-Gilad; Music: Misha Segal; Cast: Shlomo Artzi, Ze'ev Revach*, Dubi Gal, Mani Pe'er, Amos Tal-Shir, Dudu Yardeni, Avi Oriah, Shlomo Tarshish, Galia Gopher, Guest: Yossi Graber.
Award: Gran Premio Platero, Gijon Festival for Youth, Spain (1972).

Adapted from a popular children's book, the film portrays a children's crime adventure. Hasamba is the name of a secret organization of youngsters equipped with sophisticated police gadgets and devoted to the fighting of crime and lawlessness. They are on the track of Zorkin (Ze'ev Revach) and his gang of four young thieves. One member of Hassamba (Dubi Gal) infiltrates the Zorkin gang and gains access to their secret hideaway. When robbing a bank vault, Zorkin exchanges the money and jewels for his own penny jewels and for sand. The Hassamba organization traces the gang, Zorkin is caught by the police, and the reward money from the bank is used to purchase food for the poor.

Sequel: *The Undercover Kids* (Hillel Damron, 1985).

GIRAFFES (Girafot), 2001.

Dir. & Sc.: Tzahi Grad; Prod.: Yitzhak Shani, Tzahi Grad; Ph.: Giora Bejach; Edit.: Shimon Spector, Joelle Alexis; Music: Israel Bright; Cast: Meital Dohan, Liat Glick, Tinkerbell, Micha Selektar, Gal Zeid, Elisheva Michaeli, Avraham Selektar.

Award: Lipper Prize for Best Screenplay, Jerusalem (2001).

This is the story of three young women whose relationships are all intertwined. In this film of suspense and crime, things are not always what they seem, nor are they always visible to the eye. The film opens with a chase scene in which a girl falls from an abandoned building. As the story develops, the viewer tries to understand the meaning of this chase scene and to discern the difference between reality and illusion.

Efrat (Meital Dohan), Dafna (Liat Glick), and Avigail (Tinkerbell) are single women in their 20s, living in the same apartment building. Avigail, a writer, mistakenly gets into a car that has been sent to pick up Dafna, an actress. Dafna mistakenly gets into the car of Avner, a lawyer who has come for his blind date with Efrat. Efrat is left behind and ends up wandering the streets, alone, until she becomes unwittingly involved in a crime. Fleeing the crime scene, Efrat finds refuge living with an elderly woman in a pastoral setting with an abandoned building nearby. The story slowly unfolds as Efrat develops a talent for art and becomes the talk of the town. But what has happened to the money missing from the scene of the crime? Efrat tries to convince Avner to help her prove her innocence. Meanwhile, Avigail and Dafna are producing a film based on partial facts of the story.

THE GIRL FROM THE DEAD SEA (Fortuna), 1966.

Dir. & Sc.: Menahem Golan*; Prod.: Menahem Golan, Yoram Globus*, based on a story by Menahem Talmi; Ph.: Yitzhak (Mimisch) Herbst; Edit.: Dani Schik; Music: Dov Seltzer*; Cast: Pierre Brasseur, Ahuva Goren, Shmuel Kraus, Saro Urzi, Mike Marshall, Gila Almagor*, Yossi Banai, Avraham Mor, Avner Hezkiyahu.

A tragic melodrama, the film portrays the difficulties of a Jewish girl in love with a non-Jewish man and the conflict between the traditional versus the more modern ways of life. Criticized for its distorted and exaggerated portrayal of the lifestyle of Jews of Moroccan descent, the film delves into life in the small desert town of Dimona near the Dead Sea. The patriarchal father figure is contrasted with Fortuna, a stubborn young girl determined to marry the man of her choice even against her father's wishes. Emphasizing this clash, Fortuna appears in the nude (a stand-in was used for the heroine) while embracing her lover under a waterfall at nearby Ein Gedi. The fresh, life-giving waters of Ein Gedi can be seen in direct contrast to the sand of the desert and the salt of the inorganic Dead Sea.

Fortuna (Ahuva Goren) is the only daughter of a family living in Dimona, a remote town in the desert. Engaged to the son of a neighbor, now residing in Paris, she disappoints her iron-willed father (Pierre Brasseur) by falling in love with a newly arrived French engineer (Mike Marshall) at the factory where her brothers work. In a devastating scene, Fortuna's sister-in-law (Gila Almagor) is sent by the stern father to shear off Fortuna's beautiful, long hair, thereby humiliating her for all to see. The arrival on the scene of the aging fiancé causes Fortuna terrible distress, and she decides, with the help of her brother (Yossi Banai), to run away to her engineer. Matters become complicated when another brother (Shmuel Kraus), in a rage, decides to chase after her.

GIVEAWAY (Ke'Shenotnim Kach), 1982.

Dir.: Alfred Steinhardt; Prod.: Yair Pradelsky, Yisrael Ringel; Sc.: Michael Greenstein; Ph.: Nissim (Nitcho) Leon*; Edit.: Atara Horenshtein; Music: Martin Moskovitch; Cast: Ya'ackov Bodo, Rahel Dayan, Carol Feldman, Ya'ackov Halperin, Irit Me'iri.

The film is a musical comedy about two brothers, one a popular Yiddish singer and the other a shy yeshivah student. Polish-born film director Alfred Steinhardt (b. 1930) directed six feature films and numerous documentaries, army training films, instructional films, and commercials during his career.

Mike is a popular singer who enjoys his adventures with women. When a Yiddish-speaking American tourist falls in love with Mike's singing voice, a matchmaker approaches Mike for a meeting. Full of conceit and sure that he will not like the American woman, Mike is not interested. He tells the matchmaker that he will come in disguise, and in his place he sends his ultrareligious brother, thus creating a comedy of errors.

GREEN FIELDS (Sadot Yerukim), 1989.

Dir. & Sc.: Yitzhak (Tzepel) Yeshurun*; Prod.: David Tour; Ph.: Gadi Danzig; Edit.: Tova Asher; Music: Adi Renart; Cast: Amit Lior, Lia Dultzkaia, Shmuel Shiloh, Shmuel Edelman, Ruth Harlap, Sharon Hacohen, Doron Tsabari.

Awards: Grand Prize, Rio de Janeiro (1989); Best Supporting Actor (Shmuel Edelman), Israel Film Center (1988–1989); Wolgin Award, Jerusalem (1989).

Set against the background of the first Palestinian *intifada* (uprising), the film is a modern morality tale of jealousy, murder, guilt, and political apathy toward the situation in the occupied territories. It tells the story of how one family is profoundly changed.

Three generations of the Braverman family are on their way to an army ceremony at Beth-El on the West Bank. Having missed their bus, they get a lift in a bread van, become involved in an incident in an Arab village, and then board a military ambulance. Through this series of errors, they find themselves caught in the midst of the stone-throwing and shooting of the *intifada*. The grandfather (Shmuel Shiloh), who suffers a stroke, represents a generation that is slowly disappearing, and he stands by and does not see or understand what is happening around him. The generation of the middle-aged father, Shmulik (Shmuel Edelman), who has left Israel to live in America, represents the generation that has left the responsibility for dealing with the *intifada* in the hands of the young; however, he proceeds mistakenly to murder a young Arab, for no real reason except that he is angered. The younger generation, burdened with the political reality, is symbolized by the son, Rami (Amit Lior), who feels guilty for not having prevented the murder.

HALFON HILL DOESN'T ANSWER (Givat Halfon Ayna Onah), 1976.

Dir.: Assi Dayan*; Prod.: Naftali Alter*, Yitzhak Shani; Sc.: Assi Dayan, Naftali Alter; Ph.: Ya'ackov Kallach; Edit.: David Tour; Music: Naftali Alter; Cast: Yisrael (Poli) Poliakov, Shaike Levi, Gavri Banai, Tuvia Tsafir, Nitza Shaul.

The film showcases the Gashash comedy trio, a popular comedy group of the 1970s—Poliakov, Levi, and Banai. A parody of some of the absurdities of army life, the film was very successful at the box office. In later years, it became a cult film, especially with young audiences that learned to recite entire comic sequences of the script by heart.

Two men are called up for reserve army duty. One is in love with a young woman who runs away from home and follows him to the army base. Her father chases after her. Becoming lost along the way, the father is taken hostage by the enemy. In order to get him back, the others kidnap an Egyptian soldier, dress up as UN observers, and implement a hostage exchange.

HAMSIN (Alternative title: *Eastern Wind*), 1982.

Dir.: Daniel Wachsmann*; Prod.: Ya'ackov Lifshin; Sc.: Daniel Wachsmann, Dan (Nokyo) Verete, Ya'ackov Lifshin; Ph.: David Gurfinkel*; Edit.: Levi Zini; Music: Raviv Gazit; Cast: Shlomo Tarshish, Yasin Shawap, Hemda Levy, Ruth Geller, Shmuel Shiloh, Tzvi Korenfeld, Meir Suissa, Yossi Keinan.

Awards: Silver Leopard, Locarno (1983); Human Rights Prize, Strasbourg (1984); Best Film, Best Director, Israel Film Center (1982).

The first Israeli film to tackle the difficult subject of contemporary Arab–Jewish relations in the Galilee, this film touches on conflicts of land expropriation, the difficulties of Arabs being accepted in Jewish society, the growth of Arab nationalism, and the sensitive subject of sexual relations between Arab and Jew. For the first time in Israeli cinema, Arab characters are portrayed with complexity and insight, no longer relegated to stereotypes.

Hamsin (Daniel Wachsmann, 1982). Photo courtesy of the Jerusalem Cinematheque, reprinted with the permission of Daniel Wachsmann.

Gedalia (Shlomo Tarshish) is a farmer on a moshav (cooperative farming community) in the Galilee. Gedalia is a loner, living in the shadow of his pioneering father, who had a special relationship with a local Arab family on whose land Gedalia now grazes his cattle. He hears that the government is about to confiscate this land, since it has never been officially registered in the name of the Arab family. In order to obtain the grazing land for himself, he makes an offer to buy it from the Arab family. The patriarch of the family is willing to sell to Gedalia, until pressure is exerted upon him by newly nationalistic young Arabs in the area. It is a hot summer, the eastern desert wind (hamsin) is oppressive, and there is a suffocating tension in the air.

In contrast to the other young Arabs, Khalid (Yasin Shawap), Gedalia's young Arab hired hand, is depicted as sensitive and politically moderate. He is attracted to Gedalia's younger sister, Hava (Hemda Levy), who has returned home from her music studies in Jerusalem; they have an affair in an old house on the farm. Gedalia, ruthless in his business dealings, bitter over losing his grazing land, and patronizing in his attitude toward his Arab neighbors, is outraged at the newly developing audacity of the young Arab. The film ends in tragedy, with the heat wave broken and the rains falling on Gedalia's empty cattle pen—water washing away the tension, as well as the blood.

Assi Dayan in *He Walked through the Fields* (Yoseph Millo, 1967). Photo courtesy of the Jerusalem Cinematheque, reprinted with the permission of Ya'akov Steiner.

HE WALKED THROUGH THE FIELDS (Hu Halach Be'Sadot), 1967.

Dir.: Yoseph Millo; Prod.: Yitzhak Agadati, Ya'ackov Steiner; Sc.: Charles Haldeman, Moshe Shamir, Yoseph Millo, based on a novel and play by Moshe Shamir; Ph.: James Allen; Edit.: Nira Omri, Dani Schik; Music: Alexander (Sasha) Argov; Music Arrangement: Vladimir Cosma; Cast: Assi Dayan*, Iris Yotvat, Shraga Friedman, Yoseph Millo, Gideon Zinger, Yossi Graber, Uri Levy, Shmuel Atzmon, Hannah Aden, Eli Cohen*, Ya'ackov Ben-Sira, Ninette Dinar, Kobi Richt.

Originally presented as a stage play by Moshe Shamir in 1948, which was also directed by Millo, the film tells the story of the heroism of the Palmach generation and the pioneering ethic of self-sacrifice. Moshe Shamir (b. 1921) is a prizewinning Hebrew novelist and prolific playwright whose plays have been performed both in Israel and abroad. Czech-born film director Yoseph Millo (1916–1997) was the founding-director of the Cameri Theater in Tel Aviv (1944) and the Haifa Municipal Theater (1961). He won the prestigious Israel Prize for his outstanding contribution to Israeli theater as an actor and director.

This is his only feature film. Members of the crew were brought from abroad—scriptwriter Charles Haldeman and cinematographer James Allen from Hollywood and the composer, Vladimir Cosma, from Paris.

The screen adaptation is told in flashback as a young soldier reflects on the story of his parents. His father, Uri, was a young kibbutznik, and his mother, Mika (Iris Yotvat), was a new immigrant. The story centers around Uri, who returns to his kibbutz, having graduated from Kadoorie, an agricultural school, that trained many leaders of the pioneering generation, to discover that things have changed on the kibbutz and that there were tensions between the old-timers and the new immigrants. Unlike the nationalistically motivated hero in Moshe Shamir's novel, the film character of Uri (Assi Dayan) is brash, unsentimental, moody, and apparently uninterested in political and nationalistic considerations. Uri seems to be concerned mainly with his romance with Mika, a Holocaust survivor from Warsaw who is different from Uri in every way—she is sensitive and sentimental and a dreamer.

Eventually, Uri faces up to his obligations and leaves Mika to join the Palmach, the elite troops of the newly forming Israel Defense Forces. He is sent on a deadly mission to blow up a bridge and create a diversion for a ship of illegal immigrants that is landing during the night. Uri moves from his personal concerns to a heroic willingness to sacrifice for his homeland—a complex type of new Israeli whose personality reflects the newly developing emphasis on the individual in Israeli society, combined with the heroism and the self-sacrifice demanded during wartime.

THE HERO'S WIFE (Eshet Hagibor), 1963.

Dir: Peter Frye*; Prod.: Peter Frye, Bomba Tzur; Sc.: Batya Lancet, Yosef Netzer, based on a story by Margot Klausner*; Ph.: Marco Ya'acobi; Edit.: Menachem Shuval; Music: Melvin Keller; Cast: Batya Lancet, Gideon Shemer, Shmuel Omani, Baruch Kelem, Lilli Kelem, Eitan Ivri, Ofra Shein.

A psychological drama, the film is about the tension between the socialist, pioneering spirit of the communal kibbutz life and the concerns of the individual. The story is about a woman who lost her husband 15 years earlier during the War of Independence and finds it impossible to love again.

Rachel (Batya Lancet) is a Hebrew teacher on the kibbutz, where she lives with the memories of Eli, her dead husband who, years ago, rescued her from the concentration camps of Europe and brought her to Israel. She has one close friend in the kibbutz, Joseph (Gideon Shemer), who was her husband's friend years ago. He provides her with a discreet kind of friendly protection and encourages her to live in her memories. One of Rachel's Hebrew students is Jerry (Shmuel Omani), who has left his wife and child behind in Mexico to come to the kibbutz as a volunteer. Even though the kibbutz members have criticized Jerry for his individualism, he risks his own life to save the kibbutz from the hazard of exploding barrels of oil during a night of heavy shelling from the Syrian-controlled Golan Heights. The tension of the night's dangers and Jerry's insistence that Rachel stop hiding behind her own self-sacrificing combine to draw her out, push her memories aside, and leave her free to love again.

HIDE AND SEEK (Machbo'im), 1980.

Dir.: Dan Wolman*; Prod.: Dan Wolman, Jeffrey Justin; Sc.: Dan Wolman, Avi Cohen; Ph.: Ilan Rosenberg; Edit.: Shoshi Wolman; Music: Amnon Wolman; Cast: Gila Almagor*, Doron Tavori, Efrat Lavie, Haim Hadaya, B. Armon, Rachel Shor.

Award: Second Prize, Best Cinematography, Israel Film Center (1980).

Set against the background of Jerusalem during the British Mandate period, the film portrays the demands of conformity and loyalty when living in a society under siege. Basing his story at a difficult time in the history of the nation and adding to it a tale of homosexual love, Wolman weaves together the private anguish of an individual with the external pressures and political events of the times. He also uses the theme of a Jew with an Arab lover, a well-known motif from Hebrew literature. The main character, an adolescent boy, represents the society in formation—a closed society that requires maturity in order to understand that things are not so black and white as they seem.

Uri (Doron Tavori) lives with his grandfather, because his parents are working in Europe. He is a difficult youngster, the leader of a small group of boys who pull pranks on the neighbors and play war games with each other. When Uri's mother (Gila Almagor) returns from Europe with a boatload of children who have been rescued from the Holocaust, she focuses her energies on taking care of the children and brings home twin girls in an attempt to get them adopted by her own sister.

Uri eventually develops a warm, trusting relationship with his Jewish tutor, who, not interested in joining the Haganah and later seen with a young Arab man, is suspected of being an informer. Wanting to protect him, Uri follows the tutor and peeks in on him at home, where he witnesses a love scene between the tutor and his Arab friend. No longer the object of suspicion, the tutor is nonetheless beaten by the Haganah and thrown out of his school teaching job.

THE HIGHWAY QUEEN (Malkat HaKvish), 1971.

Dir. & Prod.: Menahem Golan*; Sc.: Menahem Golan, Gila Almagor*, based on an idea by Gila Almagor; Ph.: David Gurfinkel*; Edit.: David Treuherz; Music: Dov Seltzer*; Cast: Gila Almagor*, Yehuda Barkan*, Lia Koenig, Miriam Bernstein-Cohen, Asher Tsarfati, Arieh Moscuna, Dudu Yardeni, Rami Ben-Ari.

A film of social comment, the story is about a prostitute who tries to climb out of the gutter. The gang rape scene is shockingly explicit and violent.

Margalit (Gila Almagor) is a mature woman of the streets, obsessed with her situation and her future. An independent Sephardi woman, toughened by her experiences, she is the mother of a deformed child from an earlier marriage.

Doron Tavori in *Hide and Seek* (Dan Wolman, 1980). Photo courtesy of the Jerusalem Cinematheque, reprinted with the permission of Dan Wolman.

Margalit has a brief love affair with Arik (Yehuda Barkan), a kibbutznik truck driver. She also has a close friendship with her neighbor, the mother of two children. In order to be able to leave her profession and to have a healthy child of her own, Margalit is working hard to earn a lot of money. She goes to Arik's kibbutz, purposefully seeking him out, wanting him to father her child. When she gets pregnant, she stops her work as a prostitute and begins to work as a waitress. One day, four young hooligans come to her restaurant. One of them recognizes her from her previous work. They convince her to go with them on a joy ride, take her to a desolate spot, and violently gang-rape her. Margalit loses her baby and returns to the streets.

HILL 24 DOESN'T ANSWER (Giva 24 Aina Onah), 1954.

Dir.: Thorold Dickinson; Prod.: Thorold Dickinson, Peter Frye*, Zvi Kolitz; Co-prod.: U.S.A.-Israel; Sc.: Peter Frye, Zvi Kolitz, based on stories by Zvi Kolitz; Ph.: Gerald Gibbs, Edit.: Joanna & Thorold Dickinson; Music: Paul Ben-Haim; Cast: Edward Mulhare, Michael Wager, Zalman Levioush, Margalit

Oved, Haim Eynav, Arik Lavie, Azaria (Zuska) Rappaport, Chaya Hararit, Yitzhak Shiloh, Shraga Friedman, Matti Raz; Guest appearances: Shoshana Damari, Yossi Yadin (in English).

Award: Homage of the Jury for simplicity and sincerity (Chaya Hararit), Cannes, 1955.

The film is a series of three episodes of the 1948 War of Independence. During the period of the siege of Jerusalem, a group of four soldiers—three men and one woman—has been chosen to secure one of the hilltops on the road to Jerusalem, before the UN cease-fire comes into effect. On their way to the hilltop, the soldiers swap their stories. The entire film is told in flashback, and therefore the viewer knows at the start that the four soldiers will not survive the mission. Thorold Dickinson (1903–1984) was a well-known British filmmaker who made both documentaries and dramas and went to Israel to make *Hill 24*, which was his last feature film.

The first episode is a romance played against the background of the British Mandatory government's struggle against the Jewish underground. James Finnegan (Edward Mulhare) was a British soldier serving in Palestine when he met and fell in love with a young woman, Miss Mizrachi (Chaya Hararit), involved in underground activities. He recalls how he first met Berger, then an officer in the Jewish underground, during a night in 1946 when illegal immigrants were landing on the beach. He meets him a second time when the Jews blow up a radar installation, and Finnegan, assigned to follow him, traces him to the home of Miss Mizrachi, with whom he ultimately falls in love.

The second episode is the story of Goodman (Michael Wager), an American Jew who went to Israel for a visit and ended up fighting in a Mahal unit (unit for volunteers from abroad). He is wounded in a battle for the Old City of Jerusalem and hospitalized in Misgav Ladach Hospital and then later evacuated with the civilians from the Jewish Quarter.

The third episode is the tale of an Israeli-born soldier (Arik Lavie), fighting in the Negev, near Avdat, who finds himself in hand-to-hand combat against an Egyptian soldier (Azaria Rappaport). He drags the wounded soldier into a cave, and when he is applying first aid, he discovers, much to his surprise, that his enemy has an SS insignia tatooed on his chest. The Israeli soldier has difficulty in killing the mercenary, even though it is on the battlefield.

The fourth soldier, Esther (Margalit Oved), has no tale to tell from her past. Rather, she plays the important role of the flag bearer. The following day, when the UN forces check the status of the hill, even though four dead bodies are found, they award the hill to Israel, since a flag is found clutched firmly in Esther's hands.

HIMMO, KING OF JERUSALEM (Himmo, Melech Yerushalayim; Alternative title: *Bell Room*), 1987.

Dir.: Amos Gutmann*; Prod.: Enrique Rottenberg, Ehud Bleiberg; Sc: Edna Maziah, based on a novel by Yoram Kaniuk; Ph.: Jorge Gurvich, Amnon Zlayet;

Edit.: Ziva Postek; Music: Ilan Wurtzberg; Cast: Alona Kimchi, Dov Navon, Amiram Gavriel, Amos Lavie, Aliza Rosen, Yossi Graber, Ofer Shikartzi, Itcho Avital, Ada Valerie-Tal, Ya'ackov Halperin.

Set in a makeshift hospital in Jerusalem during the 1948 War of Independence, the film presents a psychological study of the victims of war. The visual elements include nightmarish and claustrophobic compositional effects and the special use of lighting and shadow, all combining to offer a comment on the societal outcasts who are victims of a glorified and heroic war.

Hamutal (Alona Kimchi), having lost her boyfriend in the war, volunteers to work at a temporary hospital that has been established in a Jerusalem monastery during the siege on the city. Assigned to work in the monastery's belfry, which houses the ward of the most seriously wounded soldiers, she dedicates most of her attention to Himmo, who has been the most gruesomely maimed. As she gradually falls in love with him, the others in the ward begin to feel neglected, perhaps not wounded badly enough and jealous of her favors. Their battle for life becomes a battle against Himmo. However, Himmo is longing for death and begs Hamutal to put him out of his misery.

As the state of Israel is declared and the siege on Jerusalem is lifted, Hamutal gives Himmo a lethal injection and rings the monastery bells. Based on Yoram Kaniuk's novel, the literary symbolism is quite clear: the suffering and sacrifice of the Jesus figure, Himmo, who is called "King of Jerusalem" ("King of the Jews"), facilitate the rebirth of the Jewish state.

HOLE IN THE MOON (Chor Belavanah), 1965.

Dir.: Uri Zohar*; Prod.: Mordechai Navon*; Sc.: Amos Kenan; Ph.: David Gurfinkel*; Edit.: Anna Gurit; Music: Michel Colombier; Cast: Uri Zohar, Avram Heffner*, Shoshana Shani, Ze'ev Berlinski, Shmuel Kraus, Arik Lavie, Dan Ben-Amotz, Shaike Ophir*, Yisrael Gurion, Daphne Eilat.

A comic and episodic satire, the film uses improvization to illustrate the clash between fantasy and reality in real life. Although conceived in the style of Mekas' *Hallelujah the Hills* (1962), it is an authentically Israeli satire, an openly rebellious and individualistic expression that pokes fun at the sacred myths of earlier Zionist films. The technique of film within the film is used to portray film as a reflection of the imagination, a miracle based on dreams and fantasies that take on concrete characteristics—parallel to the miracle of Israel, the dream that has become reality. Although not a commercial success, the film was considered by many to be an important turning point toward quality and thematic filmmaking.

A new immigrant, Tzelnik (Uri Zohar) arrives at the port of Jaffa. He goes to live in the Negev desert, where he opens a kiosk in the middle of nowhere. Mizrachi (Avram Heffner) comes along and opens a competing business across the way. The two make a living by selling to each other. As there is nothing there, they decide to create a world out of their imagination. They build a cardboard film set, which slowly takes on real dimensions—the buildings turn

Shaike Ophir (left) and Gila Almagor (center) in *The House on Chelouche St.* (Moshe Mizrahi, 1973). Photo courtesy of the Jerusalem Cinematheque, reprinted with the permission of Yoram Globus.

to concrete, people come to audition for parts in the "film," and builders arrive to construct apartment buildings. In one sequence, Arab actors come and ask the filmmakers for better screen roles because they are tired of always being portrayed as the bad guys. After briefly conferring, the filmmakers turn positive to negative, black into white, and the Arabs are given the role of pioneers who plow the land and sing Zionist songs. The imagined world of the filmmakers becomes so real that eventually they lose sight of the thin line between fantasy and reality.

THE HOUSE ON CHELOUCHE ST. (Habayit B'Rechov Chelouche), 1973.

Dir.: Moshe Mizrahi*; Prod.: Menahem Golan*; Sc.: Moshe Mizrahi, Yerach Guber; Ph.: Adam Greenberg*; Edit.: Dov Hoenig; Music: Dov Seltzer*; Cast: Gila Almagor*, Ofer Shalhin, Michal Bat-Adam*, Yoseph Shiloah*, Avner Hezkiyahu, Shaike Ophir*, Yossi Pollack, Etti Grottes, Ariel Forman, Elad Ophir.

Nomination: Nominated for an American Academy Award for Best Foreign Film (1973).

An autobiographical portrayal, the film tells the story of a teenage boy coming of age, set against the background of tension and conflict during the period of the British Mandate, immediately preceding the 1948 War of Independence.

Clara (Gila Almagor) is a widowed mother of four. Having come from a wealthy family in Alexandria, she finds it difficult to work washing floors in order to support her family. However, she learns to subjugate her own desires in order to protect and provide for her four children in the face of wartime dangers. Sami, her oldest, is a proud teenager who is forced to leave school to work as a carpenter's apprentice. He develops a relationship with an educated young woman who works in a bookstore (Michal Bat-Adam), and his political consciousness develops as one of his friends at work tries to unionize the carpentry shop. Sami also becomes friends with Haim (Shaike Ophir), her mother's suitor. A strong mother–son relationship develops, where each depends on the other in the absence of the father, until Sami decides to enlist in the Israeli underground army.

I LIKE MIKE, 1962.

Dir.: Peter Frye*; Prod.: Yitzhak Agadati, Mordechai Navon*, Ya'akov Steiner; Sc: Peter Frye, Edna Shavit, Shlomo Bandakover, Ya'akov Steiner, based on a play by Aharon Meged; Ph.: Nissim (Nitcho) Leon*; Edit.: Nellie Bogor-Gilad; Music: Arie Levanon; Cast: Batya Lancet, Gideon Zinger, Ilana Rovina, Ze'ev Berlinski, Haim Topol*, Sy (Eitan) Gitin, Geula Nuni, Geta Luca, Meira Shor, with Sheikh Suleiman, his sons and members of the El Huzeil Tribe, and the Alumim Dance Group directed by Uri Shauli.

A comedy comparing city life with life on the kibbutz, the film deals with societal values and tells the story of an American tourist whose father is a Texas millionaire.

Having just arrived in Israel, Mike (Sy Gitin) is taken by his taxi driver home to the driver's sister as a boarder. The sister (Batya Lancet) is a caricature of a Jewish mother who shops too much, talks too much, and bosses everyone around. The son of a millionaire is too good to be true, she thinks, and she decides to arrange a match between Mike and her daughter Tamar (Ilana Rovina). Tamar, however, already has a steady boyfriend, Micha, who is a soldier/kibbutznik. When Mike goes on a trip to the Negev and his car breaks down, he gets towed by Micha to the kibbutz. There he falls in love with a beautiful, dark-skinned girl. Meanwhile, Tamar's meddling mother is planning a large party in the city to announce the supposed engagement between her daughter and Mike.

The edited montage at the end of the film portrays and juxtaposes two simultaneous parties—one in the city and one at the kibbutz. In the city, the guests dance cha-cha and do yoga. At the kibbutz, the young people sing Israeli songs and drink coffee around the campfire with the local Bedouin, and Mike sings American cowboy tunes. Both parties culminate in Israeli folk dancing, and the film concludes with a double wedding.

I LOVE YOU, ROSA (Ani Ohev Otach Rosa), 1972.

Dir. & Sc.: Moshe Mizrahi*; Prod.: Menahem Golan*; Ph.: Adam Green-

Michal Bat-Adam and Gabi Oterman in *I Love You, Rosa* (Moshe Mizrahi, 1972). Photo courtesy of the Jerusalem Cinematheque, reprinted with the permission of Yoram Globus.

berg*; Edit.: Dov Hoenig; Music: Dov Seltzer*; Cast: Michal Bat-Adam*, Gabi Oterman, Yoseph Shiloah*, Avner Hezkiyahu, Levana Finkelstein*.

Nomination: Nominated for an American Academy Award for Best Foreign Film (1972).

Awards: First Prize, Best Director, Best Actress (Michal Bat-Adam), Israel Film Center (1973).

Based on stories told by the filmmaker's grandmother about Jewish life in late nineteenth-century Jerusalem, the film is a love story played out against the strict religious laws of that period and against the backdrop of the alleyways of the Old City of Jerusalem. The narrative raises issues concerning traditional Jewish gender roles and the independence of women.

Rosa (Michal Bat-Adam) is a young widow. Following the death of her husband, in accordance with the biblical laws of levirate marriage, she must marry his unmarried brother, who, in this case, is much younger than she. The young brother, Nissim, comes to live with her. As the years pass, they learn to love each other. However, Rosa's independent spirit complicates matters and prevents her from marrying him when he comes of age. Instead, Nissim, out of his love for Rosa, agrees to cast her off in the traditional manner. Thus, he provides her with her own choice of whom to marry. Now an old woman, she tells the story of her love for Nissim to his namesake, their grandson.

I WAS BORN IN JERUSALEM (Ani Yerushalmi), 1971.

Dir.: Yehoram Gaon*; Prod.: Yehoram Gaon, Mike Stolovitzki; Sc.: Yehoram Gaon, Yoram Kaniuk; Ph.: Adam Greenberg*; Edit.: Nellie Bogor-Gilad; Music: Dov Seltzer*; On-screen: Yehoram Gaon, Rahel Zimmerman.

Produced in the post–Six Day period when the city of Jerusalem was reunited, this film is a musical ode to the city. Internationally known actor and singer Yehoram Gaon offers his own tribute to the city that he loves. Through the combination of striking visual backdrops and stirring melodies, Gaon takes the viewer on a tour of the city, old and new, combining nostalgia, mysticism, religious significance, and music.

AN INTIMATE STORY (Sipur Intimi), 1981.

Dir.: Nadav Levitan*; Prod.: Eitan Even, Nissim Levy; Sc.: Nadav Levitan, Dalia Mevorach, based on a story by Nadav Levitan; Ph.: Gadi Danzig; Edit.: Yitzhak Tzhayek; Music: Nahum Heiman; Cast: Hava Alberstein, Alex Peleg, Shmuel Shiloh, Shmuel Wolf, Dan Toren, Gilat Ankori, Peter Freistadt, Orna Sapir.

The film is a study of the pressures of living in the communal environment of the kibbutz. Many scenes are shot through windows, emphasizing the lack of privacy, on the one hand, and the loneliness and isolation of an intense, collective society, on the other.

Leah (Hava Alberstein) is a lonely and unhappy woman whose repeated miscarriages have caused a rift in her 10-year-old marriage. Because they are childless, her schoolteacher husband feels inadequate and embarrassed in front of the other kibbutz members. Their marriage deteriorates as Leah becomes attracted to a young kibbutz member and her husband becomes attracted to one of the volunteers from abroad.

THE INVESTIGATION CONTINUES (Haboleshet Chokeret; Alternative title: *The Investigation*), 2000.

Dir. & Prod.: Marek Rozenbaum*; Sc.: Haim Merin; Ph.: Valentin Belonogov; Edit.: Anat Lubarsky; Music: Efi Shoshani; Cast: Moshe Ivgi*, Aki Avni, Osnat Fishman, David Danino, Asi Levi, Itzik Juli, Sharon Zelikowsky, Eyal Roseles, Reynan Haim.

Awards: Best Foreign Film, Houston (2001); Lipper Prize for Best Screenplay, Jerusalem (2000).

Against the background of crime, brutality, and the terrible abuse of women, the film uses complexity of character and plot in its story of the fine line between being an overzealous cop and a brutal killer. It tells the story of a hardworking police detective who eventually resorts to brutality out of frustration in his dealings with an overconfident, small-time crook.

Opening scene: armed robbery and murder. Micha (Aki Avni), the police detective working the case, pulls in Shalom (Moshe Ivgi), a petty criminal. Right from the start, Shalom has a tremendous ability to unnerve Micha, his interrogator, without letting Micha unnerve him. Micha becomes obsessed with Shalom's wife, trying to convince her of her husband's infidelities and trying to protect her from the terrible dangers involved in knowing too much. The story is complicated by two villains who are trying to get their hands on the loot and who terrorize Shalom's wife. After uncovering the gun that was used in the caper, Micha takes Shalom out to force him to reenact the crime and dig up the buried loot, providing the setting for the inevitably violent ending.

IRIS, 1968.

Dir. & Sc.: David Greenberg; Prod.: David Greenberg, Uri Ohali; Ph.: David Gurfinkel*; Edit.: Dani Schik; Music: David Karibushi; Cast: Gideon Shemer, Shmuel Kraus, Bracha Ne'eman, Ya'ackov Bodo, Mandy Rice-Davis, Nissan Yatir, Liora Ramon, Hannah Rovina, Halit Katmor, Shmuel Wolf.

A film about relationships, obsession, and trust, the story portrays a man torn between what society and his aging mother demand from him and what he wants for himself. Film director David Greenberg (1931–1990) played an important role in developing an Israeli film culture as a film critic, film producer, and the editor and publisher of the film magazine *Omanut HaKolnoa*. In addition to the feature film, *Iris*, he directed documentary films and television programs.

Yoel (Gideon Shemer) is a recently divorced journalist. He takes a roof apartment, where he meets Iris (Liora Ramon), who is many years younger than he. Iris likes to borrow books from Yoel. They flirt together, go rowing on the Yarkon River in the pouring rain, and prance about on the beach in the cold wind of winter. Yoel's mother (Hannah Rovina), living in an old-age home, still thinks that Yoel is married to his first wife. He is unable to tell her about the divorce, since she has her heart set on grandchildren. Meanwhile, he becomes obsessed with Iris, especially with her naïveté and her youthful charm.

IRIT, IRIT (Alternative title: *Mrs. vs. Miss*), 1985.

Dir. & Music: Naftali Alter*; Prod.: Yitzhak Kol; Sc.: Naftali Alter, Jay Frank, Assi Dayan*, Irit Alter; Ph.: Gadi Danzig; Edit.: David Tour; Cast: Irit Alter, Liora Grossman, Hanan Goldblatt, Roni Finkovitz, Michal Ovadiah, Aryeh Cherner, Shmuel Tenneh, Oded Be'eri, Yael Ophir, Gidi Gov, Dov Glickman.

Award: Best Editing, Israel Film Center (1985).

The film is a morality tale, a humorous look at the tensions between career and family, and a portrayal of the ultimate friendship between two women—the sharing of the same man.

Two neighbors are both named Irit, one a housewife (Irit Alter) and the other a career woman (Liora Grossman). The housewife, married to a successful surgeon (Hanan Goldblatt) with two children, dreams of romance. The career woman, a lawyer, self-confident and single, is involved with many men at one time. The housewife envies the freedom of the lawyer, and the lawyer envies the security and traditional role of the housewife. They begin to exchange places, the housewife living out her sexual fantasies and the lawyer beginning to settle down to domesticity and family. A few years later, they have completely switched roles—the lawyer is living with the housewife's husband and family, a newly domesticated woman serving a home-cooked dinner with a little baby crying upstairs, and the housewife is a successful artist, traveling to shows at galleries and entertaining gentleman friends at her home next door.

THE ITALIANS ARE COMING (Ha'Italkim Ba'Im), 1996.

Dir.: Eyal Halfon*; Prod.: Haim Sharir, Massimo Cristaldi; Sc.: Eyal Halfon, Fabrizio Bettely; Ph.: Amnon Salomon*; Music: Tal Yaniv; Cast: Franco Nero, Asher Tsarfati, Yona Elian*, Avraham Mor, Vincenzo Crocitti, Avraham Selektar, Gur Ya'ari, Miri Fabian, Aviatar Lazar.

Using humor and romance, the film deals with two major themes—the crisis of the middle-aged male and the trend away from socialism toward capitalism in the kibbutz of the 1990s.

Daria (Yona Elian), the kibbutz financial manager, is trying desperately to save the kibbutz from bankruptcy. Amos (Asher Tsarfati) is the coach of the kibbutz water polo team. Twenty years ago, Daria and Amos had an affair. During that same period, Amos played in an international water polo championship, and his team lost to the Italians. His friend and nemesis Luigi (Franco Nero), from the winning team, is today the coach of an Italian team that comes to the kibbutz for a play-off game. There are tensions between the two friends. Both are interested in Daria; however, Amos is tired and uncommunicative, and Luigi, on the other hand, is still charming, idealistic, and devoted to the old values of the Italian Communist Party. Amos finds it difficult to raise moral support for his team, which is no longer seen as an important element of communal life in the kibbutz, where the old values are deteriorating and being replaced by an emphasis on the individual and on material goods. Through the encounter with Luigi, however, the members of the kibbutz are encouraged to reassess their communal values and to better understand the importance of team sports as part of their communal existence.

KADOSH, 1999.

Dir.: Amos Gitai*; Prod.: Michel Propper, Amos Gitai; Sc: Amos Gitai, Eliette Abecassis; Ph.: Renato Berta; Edit.: Kobi Netanel, Monica Coleman; Music: Louis Sclavis; Cast: Yael Abecassis, Yoram Hattab, Meital Barda, Sami Hori, Uri Ran Klausner, Yusuf Abu-Warda, Lia Koenig, Rivka Michaeli.

In its portrayal of a pious man who is devoted to his wife at the same time that he is obliged to spurn her due to the fact that she is unable to provide him with a child, the film asks difficult questions about the dogma, insular lifestyle, and attitude toward women of the ultra-Orthodox community.

Meir (Yoram Hattab) and Rivka (Yael Abecassis) have been married for 10 years. He is a devoted husband. The film opens with a long scene, shot in real time, of Meir performing his morning rituals—washing, praying, and dressing, sanctifying himself from the moment that he awakens. Meir's father, the rabbi of their small community, informs Meir that he is obliged to divorce Rivka and marry another so that he can perform the commandment "be fruitful and multiply," thus helping to defeat the threat of the secular society.

Having undergone a series of tests, Rivka learns that she is indeed fertile. The doctor suggests that perhaps the problem lies with her husband, but Rivka refuses to humiliate her husband by telling him about the results of the tests. Meir agrees to divorce his wife and marry another. At the same time, Rivka's younger sister, Malka (Meital Barda), is forced into an arranged marriage with a young man whom she does not love. The awkward and brutal sexual encounter on their wedding night emphasizes the young man's clumsiness, inexperience, and callous attitude toward his bride.

The film ends in tragedy when Malka is unable to live without her lover, a man who left the closed world of their community, and Rivka is unable to live without Meir, her true love, and dies of a broken heart. The film is the third part of a trilogy portraying three Israeli cities; *Devarim* takes place in Tel Aviv, *Day After Day** takes place in Haifa, and *Kadosh* takes place in Meah Shearim in Jerusalem.

KAZABLAN, 1973.

Dir. & Prod.: Menahem Golan*; Sc.: Menahem Golan, Haim Hefer, based on a story by Yigal Mossinson; Ph.: David Gurfinkel*; Edit.: Dov Hoenig; Music: Dov Seltzer*; Choreography: Shimon Braun; Cast: Yehoram Gaon*, Efrat Lavie, Yossi Graber, Yehuda Efroni, Arieh Elias, Etti Grottes, Geta Luca, Avraham Ronai, Ya'ackov Ben-Sira, Misha Oshorov.

The first Israeli film spectacular, the film is a screen adaptation of a popular Israeli stage musical and combines elements of the ambitious American musical with a particularly unique tale of ethnic tension, social prejudice, and romance. A fast-paced, full-fledged musical, the film, which was acquired for international distribution by MGM, is highlighted by scenes of marvelously choreographed, frenetic dancing by a cast of hundreds of dancers and singers. The lyrics and songs (such as "Democratia" and "Rosa") became popular in Israel, and the album was a best-seller.

The film tells of the problems faced by an immigrant from Morocco, nicknamed for his hometown. A hero of an Israeli war, Kazablan (Yehoram Gaon) is now living a frustrated life in the old slum of Jaffa, where he has become the leader of a neighborhood gang involved in petty crime. Kazablan falls in love with Rachel (Efrat Lavie), whose snobbish parents do not approve of the

Yehoram Gaon (pointing to the sky) in *Kazablan* (Menahem Golan, 1973). Photo courtesy of the Jerusalem Cinematheque, reprinted with the permission of Yoram Globus.

match. They are Ashkenazi Jews from Poland and do not permit their daughter to have any contact with the Moroccan. The Hungarian shoe store owner is also in love with Rachel, and in order to remove his opponent, he arranges for Kazablan to be implicated in a crime of theft. As a result of his having saved a police officer's life during the war, Kazablan is given the chance to prove himself; he succeeds in solving the crime and retrieving all of the money stolen from the neighborhood redevelopment fund, thereby winning Rachel and duly impressing her parents.

KIPPUR, 2000.

Dir.: Amos Gitai*; Prod.: Amos Gitai, Michel Propper, Laurent Truchot; Co-prod.: Israel-France-Italy; Sc.: Amos Gitai, Marie-Jose Sanselme; Ph.: Renato Berta; Edit.: Monica Coleman, Kobi Netanel; Music: Jan Garbarek; Cast: Liron Levo, Tomer Ruso, Yoram Hattab, Uri Ran Klausner, Guy Amir, Juliano Mer, Kobi Livne, Ran Kauchinski, Liat Glick-Levo.

Award: Best Sound (Eli Yarkoni, Alex Claude, Gil Toren), Israeli Academy Awards (2000).

Set during the opening days of the Yom Kippur War of October 1973, the film is a very strong portrayal of the horrors and unrelenting nature of war and provides the viewer with a visceral experience. It is based on the director's wartime experiences as a medic on the Golan Heights as the Syrians pushed forward and used the advantage won by the surprise attack against Israel. The film uses documentary reconstruction with fictional elements to portray the story. The characters' names are taken from the names of the actors portraying them, adding to the authenticity of the film, but the realism needs no supporting elements; the battle scenes, shot in real time, are devastating, traumatic, and grimly realistic.

The narrative of the film opens and closes with an erotic love scene in which the main character, Weinraub (Liron Levo), the alter ego of the director, is indulging in art-sex with his girlfriend. They use artist's colors that blend together to cover each other's bodies. When the siren sounds, Weinraub departs, driving through the eerie streets of Tel Aviv (the streets are empty on Yom Kippur) in his old Fiat. He collects his buddy Ruso (Tomer Ruso), and they drive to the Golan Heights to search for their unit. In the chaos of war, they become disoriented.

Along the way, they stop to help Klausner (Uri Ran Klausner), a doctor whose car has broken down. He asks them to help him get to his airborne rescue unit. Thus, commandeered to work in a rescue unit for the duration of the war, Weinraub and Ruso are given the dangerous mission of entering by helicopter into areas under Syrian gunfire to evacuate the wounded and take them to Israeli field hospitals. They become involved in very difficult and bloody missions, trudging through the mud, pushed to the very limits of their emotional and physical capabilities.

No longer the same person, Weinraub eventually returns to his waiting girlfriend. They make love, again in the wash of colors—a violence of colors that blend together to become the brown of mud, the mud that the viewer recognizes as part and parcel of the carnage of war.

KOKO AT 19 (Koko ben 19), 1985.

Dir. & Sc.: Dan (Nokyo) Verete; Prod.: Natan Zehavi; Ph.: Yossi Wein; Edit.: Zohar Sela; Music: Shlomo Mizrachi; Cast: Udi Cohen, Meir Dadon, Shifra Ha'efrati.

The film tells the story of a rock group in Jerusalem. In addition to this film, film director Dan (Nokyo) Verete was a co-scriptwriter for *Hamsin** (Daniel Wachsmann, 1982) and directed *Yellow Asphalt** (2000).

Two good friends, Koko and Pini, play guitar and are the lead singers in a rock group. They make good music together, but another group sings Koko's song on the radio, and it is clear that Koko is not going to get the credit. Together, Koko and Pini break into a store, crossing the line into crime.

THE KOMEDIANT (HaKomediantim), 1999.

Dir.: Arnon Goldfinger; Prod.: Amir Harel; Sc.: Oshra Schwartz; Ph.: Yoram Millo; Edit.: Einat Glaser-Zarhin, Moshe Lutzki.

Award: Best Documentary, Israeli Academy Awards (1999).

A look at the history of Yiddish theater in the United States through the story of one extraordinary family—Pesach'ke Burstein, his wife, Lillian Lux, and their talented children, Susan and Mike. This documentary film is an epic family saga that spans decades. At 15, Pesach'ke ran away from home to become an actor and joined a traveling troupe. In 1923, Boris Thomashefsky, the great American impresario, brought Burstein to America, where he became a star of the Yiddish theater of New York's Second Avenue. There he met a young actress named Lillian Lux, who became his wife. They took off on a theater tour of South America and Eastern Europe and returned to New York just in time, before the outbreak of war in 1939. In 1945, Lillian Lux gave birth to twins, a boy and a girl who from the age of seven appeared regularly onstage with their parents. Their daughter, Susan, became a ventriloquist, and their son, Mike Burstyn, became a popular entertainer in Israel and played leading roles on Broadway.

The filmmaker does not shy away from the bittersweet and human stories, such as the difficulties in acclimating to Israel during the years in which Yiddish culture was stigmatized, the hardships of bringing up children as the family was on tour, and the clash when the children inevitably broke away from their parents.

LACKING A HOMELAND (B'Ein Moledet; Alternative title: *Hatikvah, the Hope*), 1956.

Dir., Sc. & Edit.: Nuri Habib; Prod.: Leo Fuld; Ph.: Nuri Koukou; Music: Moshe Wilensky; Choreographer: Vera Goldman; Cast: Shoshana Damari, Shaike Ophir*, Sa'adia Damari, Ethan Freiber, Kadouri Shaharbani, Amos Arikha, Amnon Mingen, Ezra Levi, Avraham Omer, Ilan Ovadiah, Shlomo Bashami, Yeruham Cohen.

The first Israeli color film, this is the story of a small band of Jews who traveled on foot from Yemen to Israel in 1926. The film makes use of remarkable images of Jews trudging through the sands, silhouetted against the darkening sky with the sun setting in the distance. Iraqi-born film director Nuri Habib made films in Iran before going to Israel in 1954. He directed one additional feature film in Israel, *Rachel* (1958), before going to live in New York.

Naomi (Shoshana Damari) is a Jewish woman who was orphaned as a child and works as an entertainer in a coffeehouse. There is anti-Semitism in the town, and when a little Jewish boy's parents are murdered by marauding Arabs, the local people take the boy to live with Naomi. At this time, a group is forming to make the trek to Israel, and Naomi and the little boy join the group. Zadok (Shaike Ophir) is a Zionist emissary who has been sent to lead the group on the grueling journey. The story includes a range of Jewish types—the quiet shepherd who loves Naomi since their childhood; the money swindler who dies of thirst in the desert, lying among his jewels; the learned Jew offering understanding to Naomi; and the heroic representative from Israel sent into dangerous circumstances to rescue Jews. There is not enough food or water, and there are many trials along the way. When a band of nomads attacks them, they are rescued by an armed group of Jewish men who miraculously take them across a body of water to safety and to their destination.

LAND OF PROMISE (Lechayim Hadashim), 1934.

Dir.: Judah Leman; Prod.: Leo Hermann; Sc.: Maurice Samuel; Ph.: Charles W. Herbert; Music: Boris Morros; Narrated by: David Ross; Songs: Daniel Sambursky; Lyrics: Natan Alterman.

Award: Prize, Venice (1935).

Produced for fund-raising purposes, this documentary film provides a glimpse of the glorious life of the pioneers: working on the land, living communally, bringing life and water to the desert, and singing while they work. There are classic shots of pioneering men and women using the tools of harvesting and toiling to make the desert bloom. In a moving and somewhat humorous sequence, the kibbutz members gather around the piano in the common dining room and sing the stirring "Song of the Emek," about the Jezreel Valley, which was specially written for the film by the celebrated national poet Natan Alterman. This is the only film made in Israel by Polish-born filmmaker Judah Leman (1899–1975), who later made his career in Hollywood.

THE LAST LOVE AFFAIR OF LAURA ADLER (Ahavata Ha'Achronah Shel Laura Adler), 1990.

Dir. & Sc.: Avram Heffner*; Prod.: Marek Rozenbaum*; Ph.: David Gurfinkel*; Edit.: Lina Kadish; Music: Shem-Tov Levy*; Cast: Rita Zohar, Menashe Warshavski, Avraham Mor, Shulamit Adar, Ya'ackov Shapira, Sally-Ann Friedland, Betty Feldman, Menorah Zahav, Bella Luciano

Awards: Best Actress (Rita Zohar), Salerno (1992); Wolgin Award, Jerusalem (1990); Best Film, Best Director, Haifa (1991); Best Actress (Rita Zohar), Best Musical Score, Israeli Academy Awards (1990).

The film is an elegy to the world of Yiddish language and theater that is no more. The story focuses on one middle-aged woman—a great lady of the Yiddish stage, a woman of pride, vanity, inner strength, and joy of life, all of which fade as she succumbs to cancer. On another level, the film portrays both the joys and difficulties of a small theater troupe—working on a shoestring budget, rehearsing endlessly, and suffering through dreary trips at night on the road.

Laura (Rita Zohar) is a talented actress, outshining all the others in their small Yiddish theater company and an elegant woman, reaching out for one last love affair before it is too late. When she is diagnosed as having cancer, she refuses to receive treatment, stating, "I will die with all my hair, on stage, where I belong." Laura lives with Becky (Shulamit Adar), a quiet and self-effacing woman, very different from her friend Laura. Becky has dedicated her entire life to caring for her friend and is now afraid of losing her to the foreign filmmaker who wants Laura to star in her next film or to a member of the troupe who is obviously in love with her or even to her fatal illness.

THE LAST WINTER (Hahoref Ha'Acharon), 1982.

Dir.: Riki Shelach (Nissimoff); Prod.: Ya'ackov Kotzky, Mota Gorfung, Avi Lerner; Sc.: John Herzfeld, based on an idea by Dan Wolman*; Ph.: Amnon Salomon*; Edit.: Kavin Connor; Music: Nahum Heiman; Cast: Kathleen Quinlan, Yona Elian*, Stephen Macht, Zipora Peled, Michael Schneider, Brian Aaron (in English).

Awards: Best Cinematography, Best Musical Score, Israel Film Center (1982).

The film portrays the anxieties and tensions of women left behind in wartime as the men go off to fight. Against the background of the 1973 Yom Kippur War, the film deals with the developing relationship between two women anxiously awaiting news about their husbands, both missing in action on the Egyptian front. During the period of the war, foreign news services provided footage of the prisoner-of-war camps across the border. It was common for families of those missing in action to gather and scrutinize the foreign newsreels for the faces of their loved ones. Bulgarian-born film director Riki Shelach (Nissimoff) worked with Cannon Films in the United States and produced the Israeli film *Trumpet in the Wadi** (Lena and Slava Chaplin, 2001).

At a newsreel screening in Israel, two women, Maya and Joyce, identify the same blurry image as their husband—both husbands are missing in action. Maya (Yona Elian) is an Israeli journalist, and Joyce (Kathleen Quinlan) is an American housewife whose Israeli husband rushed back to join his unit when war broke out. Very different from each other, the two women are initially wary of each other, angry that the other is trying to steal her own certainty that her husband is alive.

Over time, a special bond forms between them, based on the fact that both are undergoing the same fears, anger, and anxiety and that both are suffering the same pity from others around them. When Joyce's husband (Stephen Macht) is released, after an extended period as a prisoner of war in Egypt, he has difficulty readjusting to his life and to his family. He feels ashamed that he did not return as a war hero but as a POW. Worried that he might not be able to perform sexually, Joyce provides an opportunity for her husband to avail himself of the favors of Maya, whose husband has not returned, thus expressing female intimacy and friendship with her friend and at the same time helping her husband to readapt and emerge from the traumas of war.

LATE MARRIAGE (Chatunah Me'ucheret), 2001.

Dir. & Sc.: Dover Kosashvilli*; Prod.: Marek Rozenbaum*, Edgard Tenenbaum; Ph.: Dani Shneur; Edit.: Yael Perlov; Music: Joseph Bardanashvili; Cast: Lior Ashkenazi, Ronit Elkabetz*, Moni Moshonov, Lili Kosashvilli.

Awards: Wolgin Award, Lipper Prize for Best Screenplay, Jerusalem (2001);

Best Screenplay, Best Actress (Ronit Elkabetz), Thessaloniki (2001); Best Film, Kiev (2001); International Critics Award, Best Actress (Ronit Elkabetz), Buenos Aires (2002); Best Film, Best Director, Best Actor (Lior Ashkenazi), Best Actress (Ronit Elkabetz), Best Supporting Actor (Moni Moshonov), Best Supporting Actress (Lili Kosashvilli), Best Screenplay, Best Editing, Best Soundtrack (Oleg Kaiserman, Alex Claude), Israeli Academy Awards (2001).

About the difficulty of rebelling within the family framework, the film is a very human story of one man still tied to his Jewish mother (and if that isn't Freudian enough, the filmmaker has cast his own mother in that role!). Using in-depth characterization and portraying a memorable love scene of considerable passion and nudity, the film provides a glimpse into the traditional values and lifestyle of the Jewish community that went to Israel from the Georgian Republic of the former Soviet Union.

Zaza (Lior Ashkenazi) is a 31-year-old bachelor, studying for his doctorate in philosophy at Tel Aviv University. His traditional Georgian parents (Moni Moshonov and Lili Kosashvilli) want him to marry, and they have been trying, unsuccessfully, to arrange a marriage for him with a suitable young woman of Georgian background. But Zaza has a woman on the side, a divorcée (Ronit Elkabetz) of Moroccan background, with a young daughter. The family is not to be dissuaded. They show up one evening at the divorcée's house and create a humiliating scene for Zaza, in which his mother proves to be a formidable opponent. Having been witness to all this, the divorcée realizes that Zaza is unable to break his family ties, especially with his mother, and she breaks off their relationship.

The film concludes with a wedding scene; Zaza is marrying a beautiful young woman that his family has chosen for him. Drunk and morose, he grabs the microphone, calls up his young bride to the stage, and tells the crowd that he has the most beautiful bride in the world. But, he continues, he has a more beautiful woman on the side. After a few moments of shock, the family saves the day by bringing up Zaza's mother onto the stage—she is his "other" woman on the side.

LATE SUMMER BLUES (Blues Lechofesh Hagadol; Alternative title: *Let It Never End*), 1986.

Dir.: Renen Schorr*; Prod.: Ilan de Vries, Renen Schorr, Doron Nesher; Sc.: Doron Nesher, Renen Schorr; Ph.: Eitan Harris; Edit.: Shlomo Hazan; Music: Rafi Kadishzon; Cast: Yoav Tsafir, Dor Zweigenbom, Shahar Segal, Noa Goldberg, Vered Cohen, Omri Dolev, Sharon Bar-Ziv, Ariella Rabinovich, Edna Fleidel, Miki Kam, Moshe Chavatzelet, Slava Chaplin.

Awards: First Prize, Best Screenplay, Best Musical Score, Israel Film Center (1986–1987).

A sensitive coming-of-age story, the film takes place during the War of Attrition (1969–1970), which is also the period of the student antiwar movement in Europe and the United States. Portraying a group of Israeli youths, the film

Late Summer Blues (Renen Schorr, 1986). Photo courtesy of the Jerusalem Cinematheque, reprinted with the permission of Renen Schorr.

grapples with what it means to be graduating from high school in an atmosphere of ongoing war—their reactions to the death of a close friend, the needs of their parents and schoolteachers to shield them as if they were still children, and their ambivalent feelings toward army service.

It is the end of 12th grade. Fun-loving Yossi (Omri Dolev) is the first of his friends to be drafted. Margo (Shahar Segal), a self-proclaimed Fellini, cannot join the army because of his diabetes. Therefore, he sees himself as an outsider, perpetually looking at his friends through the lens of his super-8 camera. His filming contributes a home-movie dimension to the film. Areleh (Dor Zweigenbom), an antiwar activist, spray-paints the walls of the city with antiwar slogans. Mossy (Yoav Tsafir), a talented musician, is tempted to join the Army Entertainment Troupe instead of a combat unit. Cobi and Shosh are engaged to be married. When the friends get over their shock at the news of Yossi's death in a military accident, they decide to prepare a graduation performance in his honor and put on a very impressive "protest" show, singing "We don't want them to tell us what's right and wrong; we don't want wars, orphans, tombstones," and the film concludes with an ironic rendering of the song "It's Good to Die for Your Country."

LEMON POPSICLE (Eskimo Limon), 1978.

Dir.: Boaz Davidson*; Prod.: Menahem Golan*, Yoram Globus*; Sc.: Boaz

Davidson, Eli Tavor; Ph.: Adam Greenberg*; Edit.: Alain Jakubowicz; Cast: Yiftach Katzur, Tzachi Noy, Jonathan Sagall*, Anat Atzmon*, Ophelia Shtruhl, Devora Halter-Keidar, Menashe Warshavski, Rahel Steiner, Savich Goldreich.

Awards: First Prize, Best Director, Best Actor (Yiftach Katzur), Best Cinematography, Israel Film Center (1978).

Set in 1950s Israel, this is an upbeat, fast-paced film, including music from the late 1950s, teenage pranks, warmth, humor, and attention to period detail, such as hairdos, Elvis posters, motorcycles, jukeboxes, and the selling of blocks of ice on the street. Inspired by *American Graffiti* (George Lucas, 1973), the film focuses on the sexual awakening and teenage mores of three 17-year-old boys at a Tel Aviv high school. The film and its popular sequel, *Going Steady* (1979), turned the young, inexperienced yet talented actors into stars overnight. Both films present a genuine reflection of the anti-Establishment feeling of the time.

The adolescent boys in these films have no use for the pioneering values of the communal endeavor that characterized their parents' generation. Instead, they are exclusively interested in themselves, girls, and sex. Three teenage boys are best friends. Momo (Jonathan Sagall) is outgoing, handsome, and popular with the girls; Benz (Yiftach Katzur) is shy, sensitive, and thoughtful; Yudele (Tzachi Noy) is overweight and hypersensitive and tries very hard to please. Benz is infatuated with Nili (Anat Atzmon), who, however, is in love with his best friend, Momo. There are escapades, such as the boys' first sexual experience with an eccentric older woman, a stolen car that rolls down the beach into the Mediterranean Sea, and the complication of an unwanted pregnancy. When Nili gets pregnant, Benz uses his own money for the abortion and takes cares of Nili until she is well, but Nili eventually returns to Momo.

Sequels: *Going Steady* (Boaz Davidson, 1979), *Hot Bubblegum* (Boaz Davidson, 1981), *Private Popsicle* (Boaz Davidson, 1982), *Private Maneuvers* (Tzvi Shissel, 1983), *Baby Love* (Dan Wolman, 1983), *Up Your Anchor* (Dan Wolman, 1985), *Alex in Love* (Boaz Davidson, 1986), *Lemon Popsicle—The Party Goes On* (Tzvi Shissel, 2001).

LIFE ACCORDING TO AGFA (Hachayim Alpi Agfa), 1992.

Dir. & Sc.: Assi Dayan*; Prod.: Yoram Kislev*, Rafi Bukaee*, Ph.: Yoav Kosh*; Edit.: Zohar Sela; Music: Naftali Alter*; Cast: Gila Almagor*, Shuli Rand, Irit Frank, Avital Decker-Ben Porat, Dani Litani, Smadar Dayan Kalchinsky, Sharon Alexander*, Akram Tabwi.

Awards: Honorable Mention, Berlin (1993); Best Film, Best Director, Best Screenplay, Best Actor (Shuli Rand), Best Supporting Actor (Sharon Alexander), Best Supporting Actress (Avital Decker-Ben Porat), Best Cinematography, Best Musical Score, Best Sound (David Lis, David Uzichov), Israeli Academy Awards (1992); Special Prize in memory of Wim van Leer and Honorable Mention in Wolgin Competition, Jerusalem (1992).

A comment on Israeli life, this film depicts a violent nightmare that takes place as a result of society's ills—loneliness, despair, suicide, chauvinism, discrimination, alienation, and callous relationships. The film takes place during the course of one evening in a Tel Aviv pub, a microcosm of contemporary society, and is loosely based on the Humphrey Bogart film classic *Casablanca* (Michael Curtiz). The major difference between the two films is that the earlier film classic portrays a romanticized version of life in which faithfulness and honor are higher values than personal happiness, while *Life According to Agfa* presents a tough political satire leading to an apocalyptic and chilling ending.

A weary pub owner (Gila Almagor) is suffering from unrequited love. The piano player (Dani Litani) in her pub is a left-wing poet who writes soulful songs and dedicates them to individuals passing through during the course of the evening. The local police officer (Shuli Rand), lurking at the bar all evening, is full of self-importance—a cold and smug individual, he cares nothing for the suicidal young woman who is clinging to him as her last connection to life. In addition to these characters, the pub features a mosaic of Israeli nightlife—a young waitress sniffing cocaine, trying desperately to obtain a visa to enter America; a Palestinian kitchen worker; and a female bartender drawing the viewer's attention to details and characters as she photographs them. When a group of macho Israeli soldiers enters the pub, the parallel to the beer-guzzling German soldiers of Rick's Café is made loud and clear. Reminiscent of the final scene of *Casablanca*, in which Rick sees the woman he loves walk off into the mist with her husband, *Agfa*'s pub owner watches as her lover, sick and dying, strolls into the mist with his wife. As the evening progresses, a group of boorish, boozing, attention-demanding Sephardi Jews arrive on the scene, and violence becomes inevitable.

LIGHT OUT OF NOWHERE (Or Min Hahefker), 1973.

Dir.: Nissim Dayan*; Prod.: Ya'ackov Elkov; Sc.: Nissim Dayan, Ya'ackov Elkov; Ph.: Shmuel Calderon; Edit.: Ed Orshan; Music: Albert Piamante; Cast: Nissim Levy, Shlomo Bassan, Abie Saltzberg, Esther Eshed, Nicole Casel, Victor Atar, Rolf Brinn.

Produced during a period of heightened ethnic consciousness and the growth of the Israeli Black Panther movement (whose aim of fighting discrimination paralleled that of the U.S. organization from which it took its name), the film portrays a social and political look at the hopelessness and the roots of crime among poor and uneducated Sephardi Jews of Israel. The film was shot on location in the streets of the old Shabbazi Quarter of Tel Aviv.

Having just returned from boarding school, 17-year-old Shaul (Nissim Levy) is confronted with a deteriorating world of petty criminals and delinquents. In contrast to the unemployment of the other neighborhood boys with whom he spends his time, he takes a job in a local garage. Shaul finds himself torn between the old values of family and community, which his working-class father is struggling to maintain, and the world of drugs and violence of his older brother.

LITTLE MAN (Shraga Hakatan), 1978.

Dir.: Ze'ev Revach*; Prod.: Baruch Ella, Ze'ev Revach; Sc.: Hillel Mittelpunkt, Ze'ev Revach; Ph.: Gadi Danzig; Edit.: Zion Avrahamian; Music: Shem-Tov Levy*; Cast: Ze'ev Revach, Nitza Shaul, Yosef Carmon, Tzachi Noy, Yitzhak Hezkiya, Hillel Mittelpunkt, Lia Dultzkaia, Liora Tikotsky, Raphael Klatchkin, Tzadok Krauss.

A serious drama, the film deals with the subject of facing one's responsibilities. Shraga (Ze'ev Revach) is a Jew of North African origin who has worked hard to become a factory foreman and to win the boss' daughter. During his army reserve duty on the Golan Heights, a young girl from a nearby, small town comes to "entertain" the troops. Later, when it becomes apparent that she has become pregnant, the men are uncertain how to deal with it. They are too wrapped up in their own lives to concern themselves with the girl. Shraga, however, eventually becomes attracted to the quiet persistence and vulnerability of the pregnant girl.

LOVE AT SECOND SIGHT (Ahava Mi'mabat Sheni), 1998.

Dir., Sc., & Prod.: Michal Bat-Adam*; Ph.: Yoav Kosh*; Edit.: Boaz Leon; Cast: Michal Zoaretz, Yossi Yadin, Natan Cogan, Alon Aboutboul*, Ruth Geller, Devorah Bartonov.

Using autobiographical elements, the film is an intergenerational and cultural look at the subject of love, mixing the contemporary period with memories of the past. The film portrays a woman who, instead of analyzing her feelings cerebrally, has the courage to act upon her gut emotions.

Nina (Michal Zoaretz) is a 25-year-old photojournalist who rents a room from an 80-year-old widower named Froumine (Natan Cogan). One day as she is developing a photograph from her routine work, she discovers the image of a man who stirs her curiosity. As she sets out to find this man, about whom she does not know anything, he slowly takes over her life. Becoming obsessed with her search, Nina cannot stop from imagining him as her destiny. The film is also about other stories of love—Froumine's love for his wife, now passed away, and Nina's infatuation with her grandfather (Yossi Yadin), who was also a photographer, from whom she inherits, in addition to his camera, his love of photography and his obsession with memories of the past.

THE LOVER (Hame'ahev), 1986.

Dir.: Michal Bat-Adam*; Prod: Menahem Golan*, Yoram Globus*; Sc: Michal Bat-Adam, Tzvika Kretzner, based on a novel by A. B. Yehoshua; Ph.: David Gurfinkel*; Edit.: Tova Asher; Music: Dov Seltzer*; Cast: Michal Bat-Adam, Yehoram Gaon*, Roberto Pollack, Fanny Lubitsch, Avigail Arieli, Yves Hativ, Noa Itzik.

A literary adaptation, the film is about unfulfilled love, family tensions, and relations between Jews and Arabs within Israeli society, set against the background of the period of the Yom Kippur War. The middle-aged main character symbolizes a slumbering Israeli society, searching for fulfillment and caught unaware by the perils of the war. Two feature films (*The Lover* and *Three Days and a Child**) are adaptations based on novels by A. B. Yehoshua, whose works reflect antisocial main characters who battle societal elements in order to better adjust to their surroundings. A third film based on a novel by A. B Yehoshua is *The Return from India* (Menahem Golan, 2002).

Asia (Michal Bat-Adam) is a schoolteacher married to Adam (Yehoram Gaon), a garage mechanic. One day, Gavriel, a young, scholarly man, comes into the garage with an old 1947 car but is unable to pay for the necessary repairs. Adam brings him home, and as he assists Asia with the translation of documents for her thesis, she becomes attracted to him.

When Adam brings a young Arab worker from his garage home to help around the house, he trusts him and even gives him keys to the house. However, when the young Arab sleeps with the willing teenage daughter, Adam, who is unable to bring himself to banish Gavriel, his wife's lover, quickly throws out his daughter's young Arab lover. Adam wants desperately to love his wife but lets Gavriel love her in his place. Refusing to fight in the war, Gavriel hides in Jerusalem's ultra-Orthodox community, where Adam eventually tracks him down by cruising the roads at night in his tow truck.

LOVESICK ON NANA ST. (Choleh Ahavah B'Shikun Gimmel), 1995.

Dir. & Sc.: Savi Gabizon*; Prod.: Anat Asulin, Savi Gabizon; Ph.: Yoav Kosh*; Edit.: Tali Halter-Shenkar; Music: Ehud Banai; Cast: Moshe Ivgi*, Hannah Azoulai-Hasfari*, Avigail Arieli, Tuvia Gelber, Shmil Ben-Ari, Menashe Noy, Uri Gavrieli, David Danino, Nissim Zohar; Guest appearance: Dan Wolman*.

Awards: Audience Prize, Special Mention for Acting (Moshe Ivgi), Mannheim (1996); Jury Award, São Paolo (1996); Best Film, Best Director, Best Actor (Moshe Ivgi), Best Actress (Hannah Azoulai-Hasfari), Best Screenplay, Best Editing, Best Musical Score, Best Soundtrack (David Lis, Zion Avrahamian, David Uzichov), Israeli Academy Awards (1995); Wolgin Prize and Lipper Prize for Best Screenplay, Jerusalem (1995); Critics' Prize (Moshe Ivgi), Haifa (1996).

The film is a tragicomic satire on Israeli vulgarity, chauvinism, ethnic humor, and earlier ethnic films. Using humor and quirky characterizations, the film provides insight into areas such as unrequited love, romantic obsession, and stalking and explores the fine line between fantasy and reality.

Victor (Moshe Ivgi) runs the local pirate cable television station in a working-class neighborhood not far from the city. Still living with his mother, Victor spends his time bragging about his sexual exploits and making up erotic fantasies for the locals. He becomes obsessed with a new face in the neighborhood, that of Michaela, an actress who is living with her boyfriend and teaching drama nearby. Victor pursues Michaela in his own unique way, bringing two musicians to serenade her late at night, sending dozens of bouquets of flowers, and broadcasting messages to her via his cable station. Even though Michaela rejects

Victor's overtures, he continues, and it becomes a cause célèbre for the entire neighborhood.

Eventually, Victor's romantic attentions become disturbing and annoying. He loses touch with his own grasp on reality and is hospitalized in the nearby mental hospital. The story continues poking fun at the local rabbi, two neighborhood thugs, and an unloved rabbi's wife (Hannah Azoulai-Hasfari) who is sharing Victor's bed in the hospital. In the background, there is the screaming of a mental patient; he is screaming for Eveline, the love of his life. When Eveline comes to visit, however, the mental patient greets her politely and then continues screaming her name; his dream of Eveline, his obsession with her, his screaming for her are an end in themselves.

LUPO, 1970.

Dir. & Sc.: Menahem Golan*; Prod.: Menahem Golan, Yoram Globus*; Ph.: Yechiel Ne'eman; Edit.: David Treuherz; Music: Nurit Hirsch; Cast: Yehuda Barkan*, Gabi Amrani, Arik Lavie, Shoshana Shani, Aviram Golan, Esther Greenberg, Moti Giladi, Lia Koenig.

A series of hilarious situations, the film is a popular ethnic comedy in the style of a fairy tale in which all ends well. Produced in Hebrew for the Israeli audience, the film was distributed abroad in an English-language version sprinkled with Yiddish expressions. Twenty-five-year-old Yehuda Barkan plays the role of the cantankerous folk hero, even providing the ponderous shuffle of the middle-aged man.

Lupo, a 50-year-old widower, a Jew of Ashkenazi background, refuses to move from his dilapidated shack in a Tel Aviv slum that is destined for demolition. He is a junk dealer, still using a horse and wagon for his trade, unwilling to accept the modern ways around him. His beautiful daughter, Rachel, a young army recruit, is in love with the son of a wealthy banker and is ashamed of her father. When his horse gets hit by a car, Lupo decides to change his lifestyle; he learns to drive, sells his old shack, and marries the widow who has long been secretly in love with him.

Sequel: *Lupo Goes to New York* (Boaz Davidson, 1976).

MARCO POLO—THE MISSING CHAPTER (Marco Polo—Haperek Ha'acharon), 1996.

Dir., Prod., & Sc.: Rafi Bukaee*; Ph.: Avi Karpick; Edit.: Zohar Sela; Music: Uri Ophir; Cast: Shuli Rand, Avital Decker, Peter Firth, Alon Aboutboul*, Owen Teale, Richard Edson, Orly Zilbershatz-Banai, Zhang Wei Wei, Sharon Alexander*.

Awards: Best Cinematography, Best Art Director (Ya'akov Turgeman), Best Costume Design (Rona Doron), Best Sound (Eli Yarkoni, Chen Harpaz), Israeli Academy Awards (1996).

An allegorical film about the Inquisition, the story is told against the background of a tale of Crusader warriors in the Holy Land mixed together with elements of the absurd. This is the story of a man's overwhelming yet destructive love for a Jewish woman.

The year is 1298, and Marco Polo (Shuli Rand) has been accused of heresy by the Inquisition and imprisoned by the rulers of Genoa in their political struggles against Venice. In his cell, he relates his adventures to the scribe Rosticello. The story that he tells is about his love for Tamara the Jewess (Avital Decker) and their travels to the Holy Land. The two meet Aris (Alon Aboutboul), a local desert nomad who falls in love with Tamara and is determined to help her learn to attain sexual pleasure, an episode that climaxes in a baptismal scene in the Jordan River.

MARRIAGE JEWISH STYLE (Chacham Gamliel/Mischakei Nisuim), 1973.

Dir.: Yoel Zilberg*; Prod.: David Avraham, Shimon Herman; Sc.: Moshe Hadar; Ph.: Amnon Salomon*; Edit.: Dani Schik; Music: Nurit Hirsch; Cast: Yossi Banai, Oshik Levy, Yossi Pollack, Dov Friedman, Aviva Gera, Miri Aloni, Nahum Shalit, Ya'ackov Banai, Margalit Ankori.

Combining humor and satire, the film portrays a religious sage whose understanding of life and people sometimes shows great wisdom. His medicinal concoctions sound terrible, and his insight is meant to soothe: "God will take care of you. After all, he loves losers. That's why he created so many of them!"

Uzi (Dov Friedman) is the Ashkenazi foreman of a quarry, engaged to a spoiled Ashkenazi girl. His friend at work, Nissim, takes him home to meet his father, the town's wise man—Gamliel (Yossi Banai), a Sephardi religious sage. In a joke, Uzi puts a ring on the finger of Nissim's sister, Dina (Aviva Gera), and already the wise man says that they are married. Already engaged to one woman, Uzi is now legally married to another. After a divorce is arranged, Uzi cannot forget Dina.

MARRIAGE OF CONVENIENCE (Nisuim Fiktiveem; Alternative title: *Fictitious Marriage*), 1988.

Dir.: Haim Bouzaglo*; Prod.: Micha Sharfstein; Sc.: Haim Bouzaglo, Yossi Savaya; Ph.: Amnon Salomon*; Edit.: Tova Asher; Music: Yitzhak Klepter; Cast: Shlomo Bar-Aba, Irit Sheleg, Ofra Weingarten, Yossi Savaya, Idit Teperson, Adib Jahshan, Eli Yatzpan.

Awards: Best Actor (Shlomo Bar-Aba), Haifa, 1988; Best Film, Best Director, Best Cinematography, Best Editing, Best Supporting Actress (Idit Teperson), Israel Film Center (1988–1989).

The film explores issues of identity and distrust between Arabs and Jews, demonstrating that we are all playing out our roles, whether consciously or not. It is a satire containing humorous caricatures of people who want to be what they are not.

Eldi (Shlomo Bar-Aba), a married schoolteacher with two children, is having a midlife crisis. Supposedly going on a trip abroad, he leaves his family in Jerusalem and takes a taxi to the airport, where he leaves his suitcase behind and continues on to Tel Aviv. Eldi changes his identity and experiments with different roles and relationships. He passes as a visitor from New York at a cheap hotel, where he meets a young Israeli woman (Idit Teperson) dreaming of becoming an American and an Arab bellboy (Eli Yatzpan) trying hard to be an Israeli.

During the daytime, changing his identity entirely, Eldi masquerades as a Palestinian construction worker and joins a team of workers who are presented as voyeurs—outsiders looking in on Israeli society. In his role as an American, he has an affair with one woman, and in his role as a Palestinian, he has an affair with another. Meanwhile, the police, having found his abandoned suitcase at the airport, become involved, and a bumbling investigator gets on his trail.

Eldi builds a seemingly trusting relationship with the other construction workers, and one of them invites him home to Gaza on the weekend. On their return from Gaza, they take an old tire to hang near the construction site for the Jewish children to play on. Eldi's basic distrust of his fellow Arab workers, however, leads him to break out of his role and to shout a warning to the children, for fear that the tire contains a bomb. When it becomes apparent that there had been no intention to hurt anyone, Eldi returns home, having failed in his attempt to build a relationship with his co-workers.

A MARRIED COUPLE (Zug Nasui), 1983.

Dir. & Sc.: Yitzhak (Tzepel) Yeshurun*; Prod.: Yair Pradelsky, Israel Ringel; Ph.: Nissim (Nitcho) Leon*, Ya'ackov Eisenman; Edit.: Tova Asher; Music: Alex Cagan; Cast: Yaron London, Miri Fabian, Ruth Harlap, Zivit Avrahamson, Amnon Dankner.

Awards: Best Film, Best Director, Best Actress (Miri Fabian), Israel Film Center (1983).

The film deals with a man's midlife crisis and the resulting impact on his static marriage. The husband worries that life is passing him by, and he attempts to regain his youth. Micha (Yaron London) is a selfish, 40-year-old journalist, married, father of two. He has become stale in his work and unhappy with his family life. A midlife fling with Maya (Ruth Harlap) brings his relations with his wife, Aviva (Miri Fabian), to crisis proportions. Aviva also is having a crisis, finding it difficult to cope with their two sons and with Micha's adolescent and hostile daughter.

A MATTER OF REPUTATION (Odot Hamonitin), 2000.

Dir. & Sc.: Yoram Kislev*; Prod.: Haim Meckelberg, Haim Avni; Ph.: Nimrod Hiram; Edit.: Zohar Sela; Music: Boaz Avni; Cast: Assi Dayan*, Efrat Ben-Zur, Nir Levi, Alon Dahan, Arik Lavie, Yitzhak Hezkiya, Michael Koresh, Arik Mishali, Liron Levo, Yosef Tzerpinski.

A film about death and dying, the complex narrative moves between two story lines and eventually links them, leaving the viewer with questions about fantasy and reality. There is the story of an aging film director who is writing his last film script. At the same time and running parallel, there is the story of his script, which is being played out on the screen. When the two stories intersect and clash, the viewer is left wondering if the script is a real story or if it has taken over the life of the character and become real for him.

The aging filmmaker (Assi Dayan) is an alcoholic whose mother has just died and who has recently broken up with his latest girlfriend. He is hired by a sleazy producer to write a script and make a film about a young pianist (Nir Levi). As he writes the story, the viewer sees the pianist accompanying a singer at a piano bar. Late one night, the filmmaker is attacked by a bunch of thugs. The pianist, who is obviously also involved in crime, shoots one of the thugs, thereby saving the life of the filmmaker, who is writing the script of his life.

THE MEGILLAH (Hamegillah '83), 1983.

Dir.: Ilan Eldad*; Prod.: Tommy Lang; Co-prod.: Israel-Germany; Sc.: Haim Hefer, Ilan Eldad, Tommy Lang, Guy Walter, based on the *Book of Esther* and on poetry by Itzik Manger; Ph.: Ilan Rosenberg; Edit.: Naomi Peres-Aviram; Music: Dov Seltzer*; Narr: Jonathan Sagall*; Cast: Jonathan Sagall, Nitza Shaul, Michael Schneider, Shlomo Bar-Aba, Aviva Paz, Jerry Hyman.

Award: Best Musical Score, Israel Film Center (1983).

The film is a Purimshpiel—a musical takeoff on the story of Purim—and also an interpretive piece on the meaning of the Holocaust. Based on Yiddish poetry and featuring an on-camera narrator, the film mixes elements of the Yiddish theater with different filmmaking styles—surreal, cabaret, rock musical, and futuristic—and is rich in color, detail, and choreography.

On a visit to an East European shtetl, the narrator meets Esther, who is about to become involved in a Purim play. The Purim story is about a Jewish woman, named Esther, living in Persia, who marries the king and has the opportunity to save her people from destruction when the king's prime minister, Haman, masterminds a plot to kill all the Jews. The stories are mixed, between Persia of the past and Eastern Europe of the twentieth century. In Esther's shtetl, all the Jews are tailors. In her Purim story, Esther, the queen, wears a bejeweled pincushion to show that she identifies with her people. "The tailor's village is gone now, it belongs to yesterday," having been wiped out by Hitler, a modern-day Haman. Using the heaps of clothing portrayed in documentary films about Auschwitz as a visual symbol, the filmmaker has created a sequence of clothes flying through the air, clothes without human bodies, and thousands of buttons falling to the earth. This particularly cinematic sequence conveys the enormity and horror of the tragedy that befell the Jews.

THE MILKY WAY (Shvil Hahalav), 1998.

Dir., Prod., & Sc.: Ali Nassar*; Ph.: Amnon Salomon*; Edit.: Ira Lapid, Tova Asher; Music: Nahum Heiman; Cast: Muhammed Bakri*, Suheil Haddad, Makram Khoury*, Yousuf Abu-Warda, Mahmoud Abu-Gazi, Salim Dau*, Michaela Mitrache, Ahmed Abu-Salaoom.

Award: Best Actor (Suheil Haddad), Valencia (1998).

The film, a metaphor for life under the Israeli Occupation of the West Bank, tells the story of a small Galilee Arab village during the period of military government of the early 1960s. The village is ruled by the Arab Mukhtar, who gets his support from the Israeli military governor of the area.

Mahmoud (Muhammed Bakri) and Muhammed, the son of the Mukhtar (Makram Khoury), harbor animosity toward each other. When Muhammed is killed, it is generally assumed that Mahmoud is the culprit. Fearing for his life, Mahmoud flees the village. His friend, Mabruc (Suheil Haddad), the village fool who lost his parents near the Lebanese border during the 1948 war, persuades Mahmoud to return and to confront the Mukhtar.

MOMENTS (Rega'im; Alternative title: *Each Other*), 1979.

Dir. & Sc.: Michal Bat-Adam*; Prod.: Moshe Mizrahi*; Co-prod.: Israel-France; Ph.: Yves Lafayé; Edit.: Sophie Coussein; Music: Hubert Rostaing; Cast: Brigitte Catillon, Michal Bat-Adam, Assi Dayan*, Avi Pnini.

Award: First Prize, Israel Film Center (1979).

The film, seen mostly in flashback, expresses emotions and feelings cinematically rather than through the use of dialogue. It challenges traditional relationships and portrays a metaphysical lesbian love affair. The chance meeting between two women develops into a complex, intense relationship that includes a powerful love expressed without physical contact and later through the sexual sharing of the same male partner. The film is shot on location at the American Colony Hotel in east Jerusalem, which lends a feeling of charm and beauty to a film in which sensitivities and emotions are of the utmost importance.

Yola (Michal Bat-Adam), a pensive young writer, meets Anne (Brigitte Catillon), a French tourist, on the train from Tel Aviv to Jerusalem. Having decided to book into the same quaint and luxurious hotel, the two women spend a few intense days together. Yola finds herself surprisingly jealous of Anne's one-night fling with the hotel security guard; as a result, she impetuously travels to Tel Aviv to find her boyfriend, Avi (Assi Dayan). After her return, Avi appears at their hotel. The film climaxes in a love scene in which Avi makes love to each woman as the other watches. In this way, Yola expresses her love for Anne, sharing with her a sexual experience. Five years later, Anne returns to visit. Yola is now married to Avi, and they have a child. The two women find that they are still attracted to each other.

MR. BAUM (Mar Baum), 1997.

Dir. & Sc.: Assi Dayan*; Prod.: Yoram Kislev*, Haim Meckelberg; Ph.: Avi Koren; Edit.: Zohar Sela; Music: Boaz Avni; Cast: Assi Dayan, Rivka Neuman, Tomer Sharon, Gil Alon, Yosef Carmon, Natan Zehavi, Adam Baruch, Shira Geffen, Idan Alterman, Shmil Ben-Ari, Uri Klausner.

Awards: Best Screenplay, Best Actor (Assi Dayan), Israeli Academy Awards (1997); First Prize, Haifa (1997).

The film is a pessimistic film d'auteur that represents a dialogue between reality and what might have been in life. With only 92 minutes left to live, the filmmaker fantasizes his desires and some of the things that he didn't have a chance to do. Combining cinematic realism with black comedy, this film is a criticism of the triviality of life and of contemporary values.

Miki Baum (Assi Dayan) is a middle-aged importer of sunglasses who lives in Tel Aviv and is the father of two. One day, Baum is told by his doctor that he has 92 minutes to live. The film, which lasts exactly as long as Baum's remaining life, portrays its hero confronting his Polish mother, his wife, his soldier son and student daughter, a secretary, a business friend, and a Chinese advertiser. Surprised and shocked by his new reality and haunted by the countdown, Baum tries to live his last moments to the fullest. Those around him take new shape and experience new situations in his fantasies. Envisioning his own funeral, he sees all his friends and family in a grotesque situation.

Trilogy: *Life According to Agfa**, *An Electric Blanket**, *Mr. Baum.*

MR. LEON (Adon Leon), 1982.

Dir.: Ze'ev Revach*; Prod.: Nissim Levy, Eitan Even; Sc.: Shimon Yisraeli, Ze'ev Revach; Ph.: Amnon Salomon*; Edit.: Alain Jakubowicz; Music: Dov Seltzer*; Cast: Ze'ev Revach, Nurit Cohen, Ya'ackov Banai, Meir Suissa, Batya Rosenthal, Moshe Ivgi*, Smadar Brenner, Meni Bagar, Mordechai Ben-Ze'ev, Yoel Sher.

An ethnic drama with elements of the absurd, the film portrays family values and intergenerational conflict. It takes place in the Haifa neighborhood of Wali Salib.

Mr. Leon (Ze'ev Revach) is an old-fashioned Moroccan Jew, a man of piety and superstition, deeply dedicated to his wife and daughter. When his daughter, Dahlia (Batya Rosenthal), returns from living in Tel Aviv, he mistakenly thinks that she has given birth to a baby out of wedlock. He obsessively follows her around, looking for proof and searching for the father. The story becomes complicated when Dahlia brings home a baby belonging to her friend. The parents love and care for the child. Finally, the rabbi helps to clear up the situation, and Dahlia's friend, the mother of the baby, marries the father. Leon, however, doesn't want to be parted from the child. There is a big circumcision party for the baby, and Leon is chosen to be the godfather.

MY FATHER'S HOUSE (Beit Avi), 1947.

Dir.: Herbert Kline; Prod.: Meyer Levin, Herbert Kline; Co-prod.: U.S.A.-British Mandatory Palestine; Sc.: Meyer Levin; Ph.: Floyd Crosby; Edit.: Peter Elgar; Music: Henry Brant, Performed by the Palestine Philharmonic Orchestra, Conducted by M. Taube; Cast: Ronnie Cohen, Irene Broza, Yitzhak Danziger, Yoseph Millo, Zalman Levioush, Raphael Klatchkin, Yoseph Sa'adia, Miriam Lazerson, Azaria Rappaport.

American Jewish novelist and journalist Meyer Levin (1905–1981) has created a historical story of the aftermath of the Holocaust using all of Palestine as a backdrop in this film, which he later adapted into a novel. Based on the story of a little boy whom Levin met at the liberation of the Buchenwald concentration camp, the film tells the story of David, a 10-year-old survivor who is brought to Palestine from Europe via the Haganah underground, landing illegally on the beach in the dark of the night. Remembering that his father had told him when they were separated in Cracow during a Nazi roundup that they would meet in Palestine, David immediately asks for his father. American documentary filmmaker Herbert Kline (1909–1999) and cinematographer Floyd Crosby (1899–1985) were brought in from abroad for this production. Crosby was also the co-cinematographer for the award-winning film *Sallah** (1964).

David (Ronnie Cohen) is taken to a kibbutz near the Sea of Galilee, where he is befriended by another survivor, a neighboring Arab boy, and a little kibbutz girl. As it becomes apparent that David cannot adapt and that he believes that his family is still alive, he is sent to a youth aliyah village (boarding school for orphan children from Europe). Since he refuses to believe that he is an orphan like the rest of the children, he runs away, obsessively searching for his father. After fleeing to Jerusalem to continue the search and being hospitalized for an inability to function, there is a happy ending when David eventually learns to adapt to reality.

MY LOVE IN JERUSALEM (Margo Sheli; Alternative title: *My Margo*), 1969.

Dir. & Sc.: Menahem Golan*; Prod.: Menahem Golan, Yoram Globus*; Ph.: Ya'ackov Kallach; Music: Dov Seltzer*; Edit.: Dov Hoenig; Cast: Levana Finkelstein*, Oded Teomi, Bracha Ne'eman, Avner Hezkiyahu, Yoseph Shiloah*.

Set against the backdrop of reunited Jerusalem (produced only two years following the Six Day War and the reunification of the city), the film is a romantic story of a forbidden love between Ashkenazi and Sephardi, between an educated, married man and a young, working-class woman.

A married man (Oded Teomi) meets and falls in love with a young woman, Margo (Levana Finkelstein), who lives at home with her father and works as a hairdresser's assistant. They meet by chance on a rainy day at a bus stop, where he offers her protection under his umbrella. He is unhappily married, a university lecturer, but owes the success of his career to his father-in-law's influence. Family ties cause the lovers to part, though they find each other again.

MY MICHAEL (Micha'el Sheli), 1975.

Dir.: Dan Wolman*; Prod.: David Lipkind, Shlomi Cohen; Sc.: Dan Wolman, Esther Mor, based on a novel by Amos Oz; Ph.: Adam Greenberg*; Edit.: Dani Schik; Music: Alex Cagan; Cast: Oded Kotler*, Efrat Lavie, Irit (Mohr) Alter, Moti Mizrachi, Rafael Tzvi, Devora Halter-Keidar, Arnon Tzafir, Shimon Dotan*.

The film is set in the city of Jerusalem, which was divided in 1948 into an Arab sector and a Jewish sector, an event that split friendships and neighborhoods. A reflection of the divided city in which she lives, the heroine becomes melancholy, isolated, and filled with conflict and tension. The film is a literary adaptation of a novel by Amos Oz, one of Israel's best-known contemporary writers.

Hannah (Efrat Lavie) is a Hebrew literature student at the university, a young woman of sensitivity and desire. She is married to Michael (Oded Kotler), a reticent, sympathetic, hardworking geologist. However, she is unfulfilled by the peaceful, humdrum, conventional life that they are leading. Hannah slowly abandons herself to a world of erotic fantasies and dreams in which both her past attraction to and fear of Arab twin boys, with whom she played as a child, play a major role.

MY MOTHER, THE GENERAL (Eemi Hageneralit), 1979.

Dir.: Yoel Zilberg*; Prod.: Menahem Golan*, Yoram Globus*; Sc.: Eli Tavor, Yoel Zilberg, based on a play by Eli Saguy; Ph.: David Gurfinkel*; Edit.: Irit Raz; Music: Nurit Hirsch; Cast: Gila Almagor*, Tzachi Noy, Uri Sali, Gideon Zinger, Gilat Ankori, Eyal Geffen, Makram Khoury*, David Ram, Avi Pnini.

A comedy of errors, the film portrays a caricature of the domineering Jewish mother who is overly protective of her son. Produced during the period following the Camp David agreements between Israel and Egypt, the story takes place against the background of a cease-fire between the two countries.

A soldier's mother (Gila Almagor) travels to the Sinai desert to bring home-cooked food to her son, the commander of the military base. After many comical incidents on the base, the mother finds herself losing her way, crossing UN lines, and ending up in a nearby Egyptian army base, where she meets her counterpart—a middle-class mother who has come all the way into the Sinai desert to bring home-cooked food to her son, the commander of the Egyptian base.

NADIA, 1986.

Dir.: Amnon Rubinstein*; Prod.: Ehud Ben-Shach; Sc.: Eitan Green, Amnon Rubinstein, based on a book by Galila Ron-Feder; Ph.: Ilan Rosenberg; Edit.: David Tour; Music: Yoni Richter; Cast: Hannah Azoulai-Hasfari*, Yuval Banai, Meir Banai, Meir Suissa, Ossi Hillel, Ree Rozenfeld, Yusuf Abu-Warda, Rifat Charb, Salwa Haddad, Tzvi Korman, Yehuda Efroni, Moscu Alcalay.

Award: Best Actress (Hannah Azoulai-Hasfari), Israel Film Center (1986–1987).

Focusing on a teenage girl from an Arab village who chooses to study at a boarding school for Jewish students, the film tells a sensitive story about the possibilities of overcoming prejudice. Additional feature films based on novels by Galila Ron-Feder are *Final Exams* and *On My Own*.*

Nadia (Hannah Azoulai-Hasfari) wants to become a doctor. Therefore, her father, a middle-class Israeli Arab, agrees to send her to a Jewish boarding school. Nadia intellectually understands the difficulties of being a member of a minority in a Jewish setting but sometimes finds it difficult to cope. She eventually succeeds in proving herself to be an integral part of the student body, even participating in a student strike in support of two students who were expelled.

She forms friendships with the other students; her roommate, Nurit, antagonistic at first, soon becomes her best friend. However, when a bomb, planted by Arab terrorists at a bus station in the nearby city of Hadera, takes Jewish lives, the students silently make Nadia very uncomfortable, accusing her with their eyes, as if all Arabs are to blame. This is her most difficult test of all. She decides to leave the school, unable to face the distrust of her fellow students. Her faith in her friends is rekindled, however, when the entire class arrives at her village for a soccer match.

NOA AT 17 (Noa Bat 17), 1981.

Dir., Prod., & Sc.: Yitzhak (Tzepel) Yeshurun*; Ph.: Yitzhak Oren, Ya'ackov Saporta; Edit.: Tova Asher; Music: Isaac Steiner; Cast: Daliah Shimko, Idit Tzur, Shmuel Shiloh, Moshe Havazeleth, Adi Ne'eman, Osnat Ofer.

Awards: Second Prize, Best Screenplay, Best Actor (Shmuel Shiloh), Israel Film Center (1981).

About the ideology and lifestyle of kibbutzim, the film explores the trauma and bitterness of a family's breakup over ideological issues. The film portrays the dilemmas of youth, the disappointments and dissatisfactions of life, and the difficulties of living by rigid principles. The story takes place against the background of 1950s kibbutz life when kibbutzim were broken apart by ideological disagreements over issues such as rapprochement with the West, the principle against the hiring of outside labor, and the controversy over permitting Holocaust survivors to receive reparations money (from Germany) for their own private use.

Noa (Daliah Shimko) lives with her parents. Her father (Moshe Havazeleth), a farmer at heart, loved kibbutz life. He sacrificed all his principles and desires, however, for the sake of family unity and moved with his wife (Idit Tzur) to live in the city, where he has become a frustrated bureaucrat. Noa's Uncle Shraga (Shmuel Shiloh) is a man suffering from the pain caused by adhering to his principles. His kibbutz was ripped apart, and he does not speak to his own daughter, who has married a man from the other camp. The sensitive Noa falls in love with Uzi, her girlfriend's boyfriend. She has a terrible fight with her friends in the youth movement who talk about the need for personal sacrifice for the good of the commmunal effort. Noa, however, burdened by the pressures of her own parents' ideological turmoil, realizes that she is a nonconformist and believes in self-realization and that she has a right to her own private life; nobody can tell her what to wear or criticize her for the boyfriend whom she has chosen. Uzi, on the other hand, lives for the principles of the movement—communal kibbutz ideology, Zionism, and sacrifice for the group.

NURIT, 1972.

Dir., Prod., & Sc.: George Ovadiah*; Ph.: Yechiel Ne'eman; Edit.: Avi Lifshitz; Music: Shaike Faikov, Boaz Sharabi, Albert Piamante; Cast: Yona Elian*, Sassi Keshet, Tova Katzav, Rachel Furman, Jacques Cohen, Tova Pardo, Ya'ackov Ben-Sira, Arieh Elias, Ezra Dagan, Avraham Ronai.

A sentimental melodrama, the film combines plot elements of young love and tragedy. Despite its minimal character development, simplistic dialogue, and primitive direction, this was a surprisingly popular Israeli film due to its portrayal of clashes between cultures and because it is a tearjerker and a musical at the same time. The film was a box office success.

Moshe (Sassi Keshet) and Shoshana (Yona Elian) are in love. After they are separated by meddling parents, Moshe makes a life with another woman and becomes a famous singer. Meanwhile, Shoshana is hit by the jeep belonging to three very strange characters, and she loses her vision. The three men insist on caring for her and her young baby, Nurit. As Nurit grows up, the group entertains on the street; the three play music, Shoshana sings, and Nurit dances. Shoshana is cured of her blindness by miraculous surgery, and just as Moshe is about to marry another, he hears Shoshana singing outside, and they are reunited.

ODED THE WANDERER (Oded HaNoded), 1932.

Dir.: Haim Halachmi; Prod.: Haim Halachmi, Nathan Axelrod*; Based on a story by Tzvi Lieberman-Livne; Ph. & Edit.: Nathan Axelrod; Music: Emanuel Pugchov; Cast: Shimon Finkel, Shimon Pevsner, Shifra Ashman, Menachem Gnesin, Moshe Chorgal, Dvora Halachmi, Michael Klinger, Moshe Tawil.

The first feature-length, Hebrew-language drama, the film has very little story but rather shows sights of both the Land of the Bible and the newly developing Jewish community. It was made as a silent film with literary Hebrew intertitles. The narrative focuses on a group of children from Nahalal on a school trip in the hills above Jezreel Valley. Ukrainian-born Haim Halachmi (1902–1979) worked in the field of theater. His pioneering efforts in the field of film gave birth to the short drama *Once Upon a Time* (1932) and this feature, *Oded the Wanderer*, which were among the first films produced locally during the prestate period.

Oded's father (Shimon Finkel) has given him a journal in which to keep a record of the school trip. As the trip begins and the children are standing on a mountaintop from which they can see the fields of the valley below, they are told of their responsibility to make the barren land come alive. Oded (Shimon Pevsner) wanders off to write in his new journal. He is mistakenly left behind as his friends continue on their journey. When it is discovered that Oded is missing, a search is mounted. Meanwhile, Oded becomes tired and thirsty and imagines water flowing before his eyes. He falls into a pit and becomes unconscious. When he awakens, he imagines his home at Nahalal, the cows, the bees and the harvesting of the fruit. Finally, Oded is rescued and saved by Bedouin.

ON A NARROW BRIDGE (Gesher Tzar Me'od), 1985.

Dir.: Nissim Dayan*; Prod.: Micha Sharfstein; Sc.: Haim Hefer, Nissim Dayan, based on a story by Haim Hefer; Ph.: Amnon Salomon*; Edit.: Dani Schik; Music: Poldi Shatzman; Cast: Aharon Ipale, Salwa Haddad, Makram Khoury*, Uri Gavrieli, Jacques Cohen, Rahel Dayan, Yusuf Abu-Warda, Tuncel Curtiz.

Award: Best Supporting Actor (Makram Khoury), Israel Film Center (1985).

The film reflects the intolerance of both Jewish and Arab communities; neither society will condone intermarriage. It is also a reflection of the complexity of the cultural, religious, and nationalistic motives behind the regional conflict.

Benny (Aharon Ipale) is a divorced attorney. He does his military reserve duty as a prosecutor for the civil administration in the occupied West Bank, which is run by his friend, the Military Governor (Makram Khoury). Benny's windshield is smashed by a stone-thrower, and the young boy is caught hiding behind the school librarian, Leila (Salwa Haddad). Benny becomes inexplicably attracted to Leila, who is the proud, widowed daughter-in-law of a leading Christian Palestinian of Ramallah (Tuncel Curtiz). The plot is complicated with a terrorist gang opposing her father-in-law's election as mayor, with an Arab collaborator who runs the local garage, and with Benny's ex-wife getting arrested for participating in a peace rally.

Benny and Leila's love grows against a background of stone-throwing and terrorism, until they become obsessed with something that intellectually they know is dangerous and foolish but that emotionally they can no longer control. Benny's love for Leila causes a rift in his family and a crisis in his relations with his army unit. At the same time, Leila is dismissed from her job as librarian in the nearby refugee camp school, and her life is threatened because of the shame that she has brought on her father-in-law. Leila's brother (who had been deported from the West Bank) secretly arrives from Amman to deal with the family's dishonor. When he comes, rather than killing his sister, he convinces her to return with him to Jordan.

ON MY OWN (El Atzmi), 1988.

Dir.: Tamir Paul; Prod.: Ehud Ben-Shach; Sc.: Galila Ron-Feder, Tamir Paul, based on a book by Galila Ron-Feder; Ph.: Ofer Yanov; Edit.: Rachel Yagil; Music: Ilan Wurtzberg; Cast: Arik Ohana, Roy Bar-Natan, Techiya Danon, Roberto Pollack, Ruchama Malka, Eitan Hammus, Noya Lancet.

Awards: First Prizes, Children's Film Festivals, Frankfurt (1988) and Vienna (1989); Best Editing, Israel Film Center (1987–1988).

A story of the disadvantaged through the eyes of a child, the film is based on a series of classic children's books. Depicting a young boy's feelings, doubts, and fears, the film portrays tensions between youngsters, problems of adolescence, difficulties of forming friendships, and the need for belonging. Additional feature films based on novels by Galila Ron-Feder are *Final Exams* and *Nadia**.

Tzion (Arik Ohana) is a streetwise slum child who is sent by his social worker to live with an upper-middle-class Ashkenazi foster family. He is an illiterate and tough 11-year-old whose mother left him and whose father is in prison. Tzion finds adapting to his new surroundings difficult at first and he misses his old neighborhood, especially his grandmother (Ruchama Malka) and his friend Marco, who is into petty crime. When Tzion runs away from the family, it causes tensions. Although the other kids band together to insist that Tzion stay, he finds it difficult to be the foster child in the family and eventually he goes to live on a kibbutz.

ON THE FRINGE (Bouba), 1987.

Dir.: Ze'ev Revach*; Prod.: Ya'ackov Kotzky; Sc.: Hillel Mittelpunkt, Ze'ev Revach, Ya'ackov Kotzky, based on a play by Hillel Mittelpunkt; Ph.: Ilan Rosenberg; Edit.: Zion Avrahamian; Music: Dov Seltzer*; Cast: Ze'ev Revach, Hani Nachmias, Eli Denker, Yona Elian*, Ruth Segal, Yossi Graber, Asher Tsarfati, Raphael Klatchkin.

Awards: FIPRESCI Prize, Rio de Janeiro (1988); Best Actor (Ze'ev Revach), Israel Film Center (1986–1987).

A serious drama, the film grapples with the loneliness and social maladjustment caused by the traumas of war. Based on a stage play about a crazy man, the film adds the additional element of trauma and shell shock. The central character is a war hero who has not been able to return to normal life, a man of the night, a desert wanderer.

Having left his wife and son, Bouba (Ze'ev Revach) works in a desert gas station in the middle of nowhere. When Mona (Hani Nachmias), a young girl from far away, comes to participate in a dance competition in the area, Bouba lets her camp out for a few days in his derelict bus by the gas station. One day, Mona gets Bouba to dance. Just as the frenetic dancing scene leads us to believe that he might come out of his shell, underworld characters come looking for his brother. They beat up Bouba and rape Mona. When Mona becomes pregnant, Bouba wants to fix up his old bus for the baby. Although she doesn't want the baby, she decides to return to live with Bouba. He feels compelled to revenge the murder of his brother. The film concludes with Bouba's dancing, just as Mona taught him, in the prison courtyard.

ONCE WE WERE DREAMERS (Hacholmim; Alternative titles: *Unsettled Land/ The Dreamers*), 1987.

Dir.: Uri Barbash*; Prod.: Ben Elkerbout, Ludi Boeken, Katriel Schory*; Co-prod.: The Netherlands–Israel; Sc.: Benny Barbash*, Eran Preis; Ph.: Amnon Salomon*; Edit.: Tova Asher; Music: Misha Segal; Cast: John Shea, Arnon Zadok*, Kelly McGillis, Christine Boisson, Ohad Shachar, Roberto Pollack, Sinai Peter, Shmuel Shiloh, Amos Lavie (English dialogue).

Awards: Best Cinematography, Best Art Direction (Eitan Levy), Israel Film Center (1987–1988).

The film is about sacrifice and love, trust, and communal life in the early kibbutz movement during the beginning of the twentieth century. Using voice-over from diary entries, the film presents an almost utopian image of Jew and Arab struggling side by side to fight the forces of extremism on both sides and concludes with an overwhelmingly pessimistic message concerning Arab–Jewish relations.

A group of idealistic young Jews has come to settle on a piece of land in the Galilee. The land was purchased from an effendi in Beirut, but Arabs live on it and work it, which is a cause of considerable tension. Amnon (Arnon Zadok) arrives on horseback; he has been sent by the defense organization to help protect the pioneers. He tries to rectify their mistakes in dealing with the local Arabs, but there is shooting as a result of their having plowed a field down into the valley where the Arabs graze their sheep. Amnon, assisted by his friend Muhammed, tries to be the peacemaker.

The young pioneers pool all of their possessions and try to live by their ideals. Anda, who has graduated from medical school in Vienna, and Marcos, a violinist, are in love, but they refrain from indulging their passion because it might tear apart the collective. Ze'ev had been an ultra-Orthodox fanatic in Russia until his family was slaughtered in a pogrom; now he is a fanatic in his support of the secular, communal life. It is a harsh winter. There is not enough to eat. One of the group commits suicide. Blood is shed. The dreams require compromise.

ONE OF US (Echad Mi Shelanu), 1989.

Dir.: Uri Barbash*; Prod.: Tzvi Shpielman, Shlomo Mugrabi; Sc.: Benny Barbash*; Ph.: Amnon Salomon*; Edit.: Tova Asher; Music: Ilan Wurtzberg; Cast: Alon Aboutboul*, Sharon Alexander*, Dalia Shimko, Dan Toren, Arnon Zadok*, Shaul Mizrachi, Alon Neuman, Ofer Shikartzi, Ruby Porat-Shoval, Eli Yatzpan.

Awards: Best Film, Best Director, Best Actress (Dalia Shimko), Best Actor (Alon Aboutboul and Sharon Alexander), Best Cinematography, Best Editing, Best Screenplay, Best Musical Score, Israel Film Center (1988–1989).

The film narrative is concerned with the bonding and solidarity of basic training, the pressures and conflicts of army life, and an army cover-up that takes place during the Palestinian uprising (*intifada*) that began in 1987. On one level, it is the story of three young men and the strong friendship that they form as they suffer together through the humiliations and hardships of basic training. Years later, however, two of them meet again, this time on opposite sides of a military investigation. The film, critical of army procedures and investigations and of Israel's handling of the *intifada*, opens with a panning shot of the pastoral hillside, sounds of the muezzin in the background, and a lone Arab riding over the crest of the hill on his donkey. Then, disturbing the tranquillity, two soldiers suddenly appear, pushing a car that will not start over the hilltop, until it begins to roll down the hill, gather momentum, and come to life. This opening sequence visually portrays the contrast between the Israeli military machine—apparently dysfunctional and out of control—and the supposed tranquillity of Arab life rooted in the land of the West Bank.

Yotam (Alon Aboutboul) is an officer in a combat unit where Rafa (Sharon Alexander) is sent to investigate the death of an Arab terrorist who has been reported shot while escaping. It becomes apparent, however, that the terrorist did not try to escape; rather, he was tortured and killed in revenge for having murdered their friend from the days when the three of them served together during basic training. As details of the murder and the ensuing cover-up come to light, a clash arises between Yotam and Rafa. Pressure is put on Rafa to close the investigation and leave the base, but he is a stubborn man and refuses to give up lightly. The film concludes with Rafa standing over an open fire, contemplating destroying the evidence, if not actually doing so.

ONLY TODAY (Rak Hayom), 1976.

Dir. & Sc.: Ze'ev Revach*; Prod.: Yosef Zovida, Shimon Armeh; Ph.: David Gurfinkel*; Edit.: Alain Jakubowicz; Music: Yair Rosenblum; Cast: Ze'ev Revah, Efrat Lavie, Jacques Cohen, Ilan Dar, Miri Suryano, Raphael Klatchkin, Ya'ackov Banai, Avraham Mor, Tikvah Aziz, Gideon Zinger, Ya'ackov Ben-Sira, Sefi Rivlin, Betty Segal, Rafi Ginai.

Revach's directorial debut, this film is an ethnic comedy that portrays the values shared by Ashkenazi and Sephardi Jews living in the same neighborhood. The intertwining vignettes that illustrate old-world family values appealed to Sephardi immigrant cinemagoers, facing an increasingly secular society.

Sasson (Ze'ev Revah) is a good-natured, small-time tomato vendor with a stall in the outdoor Jerusalem market. His humor and easygoing nature have permitted him to romance two women; one, Dalia (Efrat Lavie), is the daughter of an old friend of his father, while the other is a mature married woman. Both women have been stolen away from humorless Ashkenazi men who are suffering from a socioeconomic problem; they are so involved with their own professional advancement that they do not pay sufficient attention to their personal lives. The film concludes with the sun setting over the Mediterranean Sea as Dalia and Sasson, lovers of differing ethnic backgrounds but with similar values, declare their love for each other.

OPERATION THUNDERBOLT (Mivtza Yonatan), 1977.

Dir.: Menahem Golan*; Prod.: Menahem Golan, Yoram Globus*; Sc.: Clarke Reynolds, Menahem Golan; Ph.: Adam Greenberg*; Edit.: Dov Hoenig; Music: Dov Seltzer*; Cast: Klaus Kinski, Yehoram Gaon*, Gila Almagor*, Assi Dayan*, Shaike Ophir*, Reuven Bar-Yotam, Arik Lavie, Sybil Danning, Shmuel Rodensky*, Mark Heath, Uri Levy, Oded Teomi, Shoshana Shani, Rahel Marcus, Yehuda Efroni, Gabi Amrani, Natan Cogan.

Nomination: Nominated for an American Academy Award for Best Foreign Film (1977).

Awards: Third Prize, Best Cinematography, Best Editing, Israel Film Center (1978).

Based on a true incident of international terrorism, the film tells the story of a planeload of people that was hijacked and taken to Entebbe airport in July 1976. Filmed with the full cooperation of the Israeli army, even to the extent of providing the use of Hercules jets, the film is a thriller that covers many aspects of the story, especially the military rescue operation. Filmmaker Menahem Golan decided to use a prestigious international cast in this portrayal of the story of the hijacking and the many days of agony suffered by the hostages (Jews and non-Jews alike), crew, and even the terrorists. In addition, the film reveals the workings of the Israeli cabinet and portrays the feelings of journalists on the scene, families of hostages, and even Idi Amin Dada. The film was shot with the participation of Yitzhak Rabin, Shimon Peres, and Yigal Alon.

The film tells the story of the hijacking. For six days, the Israeli cabinet pondered the problem of whether or not to give in to the demands of the hijackers. At the same time, Israeli commandos prepared and trained for the rescue mission. The soldiers flew across Africa in four massive Hercules jets, loaded to capacity with jeeps, equipment, and personnel. They even brought along a Mercedes decked out to look as if it was carrying Idi Amin (Mark Heath). On July 4, 1976, the Israeli armed forces, led by Yoni Netanyahu (Yehoram Gaon), rescued 104 hijacked passengers from the hands of terrorists (Klaus Kinski and Sybil Danning) at Entebbe airport. The operation was a success—the terrorists killed, the hostages rescued—all at the cost of only one Israeli soldier and two hostages.

OUT OF EVIL (Mi Klalah Le Brachah), 1950.

Dir.: Joseph Krumgold; Prod.: Leo Hermann, based on a novel by Yehuda Ya'ari; Ph.: Alphonso Frenguelli, Leroy Phelps; Edit.: Larry Katz, Joseph Kay; Music: Daniel Sambursky, Mordechai Zeira, Karol Rathaus; Cast: Azaria (Zuska) Rappaport, Nahum Buchman, Esther Margalit-Ben Yoseph, Yitzhak Shulman, Mordechai Ben-Ze'ev, Roberta Hodes, Eliezer Whartman.

Film within a film: *Balaam's Story*, by Helmar Lerski* and Paul Loewy (1948).

The film is told in flashback. It tells the story of a 1920s kibbutz cooperative settlement, with contemporary elements of the Holocaust. In addition to tackling issues of communal life, the film is a bitter reflection of the feelings of a society trying to understand its own guilt and helplessness in grappling with the tragedy that had so recently fallen on European Jewry. The heavily stylized marionette sequences (film within a film) portray the transformation of a historic curse into a blessing (based on the biblical story of Balaam). American-born film director Joseph Krumgold (1908–1980) made documentary films in the United States. During his short stay in Israel, he made both documentaries and ideological docudramas.

Narrated by Joseph (Eliezer Whartman), the story is about the struggles of his young parents on a kibbutz located in the Lower Galilee. Ya'ackov (Yitzhak Shulman) and Chavah (Esther Margalit-Ben Yoseph) fall in love and receive the permission of the group to marry. When Chavah becomes pregnant, and the special plans and sacrifices required to take care of a baby begin to be prominent in everyone's mind, the young couple slowly realizes that they are a burden to the group. One day, a marionette theater group comes to the settlement. They perform the biblical story of Balaam and the ass (Num. 22), the story of a people cursed with no land. The sentiment on the kibbutz is that the biblical people were cursed because they put the importance of the individual over that of the group and did not succeed in living a truly cooperative life. This lesson makes Ya'ackov and Chavah feel even more uncomfortable, and they decide to return to their native Germany. Years later, after his parents have been killed by the Nazis, Joseph returns to the kibbutz.

OVER THE OCEAN (Me'ever Le'yam), 1991.

Dir.: Ya'ackov (Yankul) Goldwasser*; Prod.: Marek Rozenbaum*, Ronny Ackerman; Sc.: Haim Merin; Ph.: David Gurfinkel*; Edit.: Anat Lubarsky; Music: Shlomo Gronich*; Cast: Arieh Moscuna, Dafna Rechter, Moti Giladi, Uri Alter, Sinai Peter, Mili Avital, Yair Lapid, Oshik Levy, Yossi Graber.

Awards: Best Film, Best Director, Best Actor (Arieh Moscuna), Best Actress (Dafna Rechter), Best Supporting Actress (Mili Avital), Best Screenplay, Best Editing, Best Art Director (Emanuel Amrani), Best Musical Score, Israeli Academy Awards (1991).

Seen through the eyes of a child, the film tells a story that takes place during the early years of the state about immigrants finding it hard to deal with the hardships and reality of life in Israel, and dreaming of leaving but somehow never quite succeeding in breaking away.

Menahem and Rosa Goldfarb (Arieh Moscuna and Dafna Rechter) are Holocaust survivors struggling with the economic reality and secretly making preparations for moving to Toronto to join a friend, Morris (Moti Giladi), who has become successful there. They work together in a small family business. Rosa has two brothers; one died defending the country, and the other lives on a moshav (a cooperative agricultural community). Their 10-year-old son (Uri Alter), together with his friend, is planning a secret trip to Petra, a sure way to get themselves accepted into the paratroops when they get older. The teenage daughter, Miri (Mili Avital), who became involved with a petty criminal, is sent to Canada ahead of the rest of the family. Menahem sells their shop and begins making preparations for leaving. However, things change when it becomes clear that their friend Morris in Toronto is not so successful and is really a scoundrel, that Miri is not very happy there, that their son doesn't want to leave, and that Rosa has changed her mind.

THE PARATROOPERS (Masa Alunkot), 1977.

Dir. & Prod.: Yehuda (Judd) Ne'eman*; Sc.: Daniel Horvitz, Rachel

Ne'eman, Cobi Niv, Renen Schorr*; Ph.: Hanania Bar; Edit.: David Tour; Music: Shem-Tov Levy*; Cast: Gidi Gov, Moni Moshonov, Michael Warshaviak, Yair (Koya) Rubin, Dov Glickman, Geta Munte, Yael Perl, Ezra Kafri, Shimon Cohen, Ami Traub.

Awards: Second Prize, Best Cinematography, Israel Film Center (1978).

The first Israeli feature film to criticize the conformity and the pressures demanded by army basic training, the film portrays the story of one individual's inability to fit into the rigorous atmosphere of army life. The film provides insight into the complex nature of human beings, from one sensitive recruit concerned with his own self-image in the face of the military system to the ambitious squad commander who must make difficult decisions concerning his own life.

Weissman (Moni Moshonov), a young paratroop recruit, finds it difficult to adjust to the pressures and discipline of basic training. As a result, he suffers in his relations with Yair (Gidi Gov), his squad commander, and with the other recruits. The recruit, pushed beyond his limit, is inexplicably killed during a combat exercise. Was it an accident, or was it suicide? Yair is suspended pending the completion of an inquiry. Preoccupied with the incident and confused and burdened by feelings of guilt and remorse, he decides to abandon his military career, even after the verdict is given in his favor. However, he finds himself unable to leave the army and returns to training recruits and leading them on endless hikes.

PASSOVER FEVER (Leyl La'sedah), 1995.

Dir. & Sc.: Shemi Zarhin*; Prod.: Micha Sharfstein, Amitan Menelzon; Ph.: Amnon Zlayet; Edit.: Einat Glaser-Zarhin; Music: Adi Cohen; Cast: Gila Almagor*, Yoseph Shiloah*, Alon Aboutboul*, Miki Kam, Arieh Moscuna, Anat Wachsmann*, Itcho Avital, Esti Zackheim, Dror Keren, Dana Berger, Shoshana Duar.

Awards: Best Screenplay, Montreal (1995); Honorable Mention, Wolgin Competition, Jerusalem (1995); Best Supporting Actress (Esti Zackheim), Israeli Academy Awards (1995).

The film draws a tapestry of authentically evoked personalities, psychological obsessions, and family nostalgia. The Israeli family is seen as a typical dysfunctional family that one might find anywhere; there are divorce, bulimia, paranoia, bickering, and suspicion. At the end, however, all disagreements are washed away with the falling snow in the springtime, a whimsical narrative element that signals hope and renewal for the future.

Yona (Gila Almagor) is the matriarch of the family, which gathers together at the family homestead to celebrate the Passover holiday. All of her five children and their children are there, except for one, Izhar, who died in an army training accident. His memory hovers in the background throughout the film. Yona's husband (Yoseph Shiloah) is preoccupied lately, and therefore Yona becomes worried about her marriage. Tormented by the death of their son, she still harbors resentment against her husband, who went abroad on a business trip shortly after the son's death. Her husband, however, blames her for not having given him the space to mourn also. He is begging to be included in the area of grieving, which had previously been perceived as a uniquely female realm. During the Passover seder, one of the grandchildren climbs up on the roof. When the near-tragedy is averted, the relief is so great that all the family members become reconnected with each other.

PEEPING TOMS (Metzitzim), 1972.

Dir.: Uri Zohar*; Prod.: Yitzhak Kol; Sc.: Uri Zohar, Arik Einstein*; Ph.: Adam Greenberg*; Edit.: Avi Lifshitz; Music: Shalom Hanoch; Cast: Uri Zohar, Arik Einstein, Sima Eliyahu, Mona Silberstein, Tzvi Shissel, Moti Mizrachi, Mordechai Ben-Ze'ev, Mordechai Arnon, Margalit Ankori.

Award: Second Prize, Israel Film Center (1973).

This is the story of a man who never grows up, the embodiment of many recurring traits in the films of Uri Zohar—the individualist yet childish, vulnerable adult, beset by sexual anxieties, who manages to avoid the commitments and responsibilities of mature life. Filled with sexual innuendo (the Tel Aviv beachfront provides the milieu), the film has become a cult film of secular Israelis due to its satirical look at Israeli society, the ultimate negation of the earlier Zionist films that were solely dedicated to the glorification of the new society and that did not dwell at all on the problems of the individual.

Guta (Uri Zohar) is a confirmed bachelor, living the life of an aging beachboy, spending his days renting out beach chairs, selling sodas, and chasing young peeping toms from the windows of the women's dressing area. His friend (Arik Einstein), married and with a child, is a pop singer. Guta is envious of his friend, secretly wishing that he had a wife, yet approaching women in a gruff manner. On the other hand, his friend, who is very successful with women, envies Guta's freedom and uses Guta's beach house for his one-night stands. Guta slowly begins to realize the inevitability of his growing older.

Rereleased in cinemas in a newly restored version in 2002.

Trilogy: *Peeping Toms* (1972), *Big Eyes** (1974), *Save the Lifeguard** (1977)

PICK A CARD (Afula Express), 1997.

Dir.: Julie Shles*; Prod.: Assaf Amir; Sc.: Amit Lior; Ph.: Itzik Portal; Edit.: Maor Keshet; Music: Yuval Shafrir; Cast: Tzvika Hadar, Esti Zackheim, Arieh Moscuna, Orly Perl, Natan Zehavi, Evelyn Kaplun, Pini Kidron, Amit Lior, Tsipor Aizen.

Awards: Silver Prize, Houston (1998); Wolgin Award, Jerusalem Film Festival (1997); Best Film, Best Director, Best Actress (Esti Zackheim), Best Supporting Actor (Arieh Moscuna), Best Supporting Actress (Orly Perl), Best Musical Score, Israeli Academy Awards (1997).

The film is a comedy about love, fantasy, and dreams, portraying quirky, overweight characters with much depth and charm. Its success lies in the small magical moments of humor, intimacy, and serendipity.

Originally from Afula, Davy (Tzvika Hadar) and Batya (Esti Zackheim) live together in Tel Aviv, where Batya is working as a supermarket cashier and Davy is spending his days doing card tricks, rehearsing with his rabbits, and dreaming about becoming a magician. Although they live in a dilapidated apartment building in south Tel Aviv, they seem happy together. As time goes by, Batya grows impatient and wants to return to Afula, where they can settle down and have children. But Davy's dreams are different; he wants to see his name in lights and believes that he can really make it performing magic tricks.

When Batya returns to Afula, Davy joins his friend Shimon (Arieh Moscuna), and together they go on the road, doing magic tricks and enjoying a fair amount of success. The months pass, and the big night of Independence Day arrives; Shimon and Davy are performing in Afula, but the reunion with Batya is complicated, and things do not go as planned.

PILLAR OF FIRE (Amud Ha-Esh), 1959.

Dir.: Larry Frisch*; Prod.: Mordechai Navon*, Yitzhak Agadati, Larry Frisch; Sc.: Hugh Nissenson, based on a story by Larry Frisch, Hugh Nissenson; Ph.: Chaim Shreiber; Edit: Nellie Bogor-Gilad; Music: Moshe Wilensky; Cast:Yitzhak Shiloh, Lawrence Montaigne, Nehama Hendel, Moshe Ya'ari, Amos Mokadi, Uri Zohar*, Yair Pradelski, Alex Peleg, Eli Pen, Shlomo Jacobi.

Set against the background of the 1948 War of Independence, the film deals with issues such as the difficulties of war for the individual, fresh memories of the Holocaust, and the need to make personal sacrifices during wartime. Produced for export, the film speaks English. Nehama Hendel sings the lead song, which became popular at that time.

A struggling new settlement in the northern Negev is under attack from Arab tanks. When the kibbutz members are forced to take shelter in an underground bunker, they are cut off from other settlements, and no reinforcements are forthcoming. Moshe (Moshe Ya'ari), a Holocaust survivor, is reminded of another time and place by the wooden bunks, the barbed wire, and the pillar of smoke (resembling the smoking chimney at Auschwitz) rising from a burning tank. Rahel (Nehama Hendel) has fallen in love with David (Lawrence Montaigne), an American volunteer who has come to fight for Israel. On a mission to scout out enemy tank movements, David is wounded, and the commander and some of the others are killed. Moshe becomes a hero in battle out of his own need to lash out for what was done to him in Europe. Rahel finds herself in the difficult position of having to choose between saving her wounded lover and the desperate need to warn the struggling town of Beersheba of the approaching danger.

THE POLICEMAN (HaShoter Azoulai), 1971.

Dir. & Sc.: Ephraim Kishon*; Prod. Ephraim Kishon, Yitzhak Kol; Ph.: David

Shaike Ophir in *The Policeman* (Ephraim Kishon, 1971). Photo courtesy of the Jerusalem Cinematheque, reprinted with the permission of Ephraim Kishon.

Gurfinkel*; Edit.: Anna Gurit; Music: Nurit Hirsch; Cast: Shaike Ophir*, Avner Hezkiyahu, Zaharira Harifai, Yoseph Shiloah*.

Nomination: Nominated for an American Academy Award for Best Foreign Film.

Awards: Gold Medal Special Jury Award, Atlanta (1972); Cino de Duca Award, Monte Carlo TV (1972); Golden Globe for Best Foreign Language Film, Hollywood Foreign Press Association (1971); Outstanding Foreign Film, Semana Internacional de Cine en Color, Barcelona (1971).

A touching comedy, this film is about a kindhearted, bumbling policeman who is portrayed as a comic-pathetic antihero. Shaike Ophir, as the policeman Azoulai, offers one of Israeli cinema's legendary performances.

Azoulai is completing 20 undistinguished years on the police force. Although inept in his police work, he is also a devout Jew and a loving husband. When Azoulai is told that he is being retired from the force, he imagines himself standing before a firing squad. He has interesting religious ideas; he believes that you don't ask yourself if you believe in God; rather, you behave well enough so that God will believe in you. The Jaffa criminal underworld has come to appreciate Azoulai. Therefore, when they learn of his approaching retirement, they conspire to stage one last robbery in order to give him the chance to catch a criminal and be permitted to remain their local cop on the beat. The concluding scene shows the humiliation of the little guy trying to preserve his last bit of self-respect. It shows Azoulai standing at attention as the young police cadets march by and salute him. His face shows pride, as he has just retired from his career in the force, mixed with sadness and remorse in the knowledge that he never really excelled as a cop.

THE REAL GAME (Hamischak Ha'Amiti), 1980.

Dir.: Avi Cohen; Prod.: David Tour; Sc.: Avi Cohen, Jonathan Aron; Ph.: Dani Shneur, Edit.: Anat Lubarsky; Music: Alona Turel; Cast: Yossi Pollack, Michal Bat-Adam*, Gabi Amrani, Shlomo Vishinksy, Dalia Gur, David Ram, Yuval Moskin, Eli Nissan, Peter Freistadt, Reuven Dayan, Yitzhak Havis.

An insider's look at the world of Israeli politics, the film is about the corruption of politics, money, and power. Film director Avi Cohen has directed numerous television entertainment programs, documentaries, and commercials. His other features include *Joshua, Joshua* (1986) and *The Skipper II* (1989).

Shaul Raz (Yossi Pollack) is a Tel Aviv wunderkind who leaves the world of business to work for the upcoming elections of a political party. He succeeds in rising up the ladder to an influential position and eventually gets himself elected to the Knesset. Along the way, however, he has sacrificed and destroyed the life of a Sephardi party figure in Beersheba, whose trust he has betrayed. In addition, he is responsible for the breakup of the party and for ruining his own family life.

REPEAT DIVE (Tzlila Chozeret), 1981.

Dir. & Sc.: Shimon Dotan*; Prod.: Amos Mokadi, based on a story by Yehudit Hendel; Ph.: Dani Shneur; Edit.: Dani Schik; Advisor: David Perlov*; Music: Zohar Levy; Cast: Doron Nesher, Liron Nirgad, Danny Muggia, Ami Traub, Ze'ev Shimshoni, Yair (Koya) Rubin, Moscu Alcalay, Zaharira Harifai, Dalia Shimko.

Awards: First Prize, Best Director, Best Editing, Israel Film Center (1981).

The film deals with the emotional growth of the members of a navy commando unit and their learning to grapple with the dangers and personal losses involved in serving in such a unit.

Yoav (Doron Nesher) and his close friends are highly trained commandos who bravely volunteer for dangerous underwater missions. After one diver is killed in a tragic encounter with the enemy, his friends develop a relationship with Mira, his bereaved young widow (Liron Nirgad). Suffering from loneliness and desperation, Mira is seen mostly at home, listening repeatedly to a cassette tape left behind by her husband. On the tape her husband brags about sleeping with other women, and he jokingly states in his last will and testament that he leaves his wife to his virgin friend Yoav. Obsessed with the memories of her dead husband, Mira latches onto Yoav and decides that she wants to marry him. She frantically tries to protect him from future dangerous missions, going so far as begging his commander not to send him out on the next mission. Yoav guesses what happened and confronts Mira. After he returns safely from the mission, they marry. But things are not quite right; upon returning home late one night in the rain from the base, Yoav hears her playing the tape again and again.

THE REVENGE OF ITZIK FINKELSTEIN (Nikamato Shel Itzik Finkelstein), 1993.

Dir.: Enrique Rottenberg; Prod.: Sergio Dizenhause, Anat Asulin; Sc.: Enrique Rottenberg, Esteban Gottfried; Ph.: Jorge Gurvich, Edit.: Tali Halter-Shenkar; Music: Shlomo Yidov; Cast: Moshe Ivgi*, Esteban Gottfried, Devora Halter-Keidar, Shmil Ben-Ari, Gilat Ankori, Shmuel Wolf, Ayelet Zuarer, Alexander Cohen, Ezra Kafri, Moscu Alcalay.

Awards: Best Film, Haifa (1994); Best Film, Best Director, Best Supporting Actor (Esteban Gottfried), Best Supporting Actress (Devora Halter-Keidar), Best Screenplay, Best Editing, Best Musical Score, Israeli Academy Awards (1993).

The film is a comedy about a 40-year-old man who is a failure both in business and in his private life. He is helped by an invisible monk to take revenge on those who have made him into such a loser. Argentinian-born Enrique Rottenberg is a successful businessman who produced the films of Amos Gutmann*. This is his first directorial effort.

Itzik (Moshe Ivgi) has failed in his latest business venture, which has left him with thousands of imported, vulgar little key rings of a monk whose penis sticks out when you press the button. Itzik lives at home with his mother and contemplates suicide. One day, in disgust, Itzik throws one of the key rings, which suddenly comes to life as a monk from a secret order whose goal is to bring chaos to the world. Itzik and the monk (Esteban Gottfried) set out together on the path of revenge against all those who have made him into such a loser—his elementary school teacher, his army commander, his first girlfriend, his successful cousin, and, lastly, his Jewish mother. With each confrontation, Itzik gains more self-confidence, until he realizes that he has only himself to blame for his personal failure. Finally, taking matters into his own hands, he succeeds in unloading his tacky key rings for a good price.

RICOCHETS (Shtei Etzba'ot Mi'Tzidon), 1986.

Dir.: Eli Cohen*; Prod.: Eli Dori; Sc.: Tzvika Kretzner, Baruch Navo, Eli Cohen; Ph.: Yechiel Ne'eman; Edit.: Avigdor Weill; Music: Benny Nagari; Cast: Roni Finkovitz, Shaul Mizrachi, Alon Aboutboul*, Dudu Ben-Ze'ev, Boaz Ofri, Nazzy Rabach, Ossi Hillel, Dan Turgeman, Cameo: Micha Shagrir*.

Awards: First Prize, Best Director, Best Supporting Actor (Alon Aboutboul), Best Cinematography, Israel Film Center (1986–1987).

Originally produced by the Israel Defense Forces to encourage discussion about moral ambiguity and "purity of arms," as well as an attempt to provide guidelines for conduct with the civilian population in Lebanon, the film was produced as a series of incidents, later woven together into a feature-length drama. The film raises ethical issues concerning military behavior during wartime and looks critically at a political issue—the uncertainty about what the soldiers were doing in South Lebanon in the first place.

A soldier on routine patrol is attracted to a local Arab girl whom he sees daily hanging laundry on the roof of her home. They smile at each other, and he leaves her a chocolate bar on the stone wall of the house. Only later does it become clear that she is actually signaling to the enemy from her roof, providing information about the movement of Israeli troops.

Raouf (Nazzy Rabach) is an Israeli Druze soldier who has become engaged to a Lebanese Druze girl. He signs on for an additional tour of duty in South Lebanon in order to remain near her, but eventually he gets killed by the Lebanese Phalangists.

Gadi (Roni Finkovitz) is a young officer who, upon completion of his officer training course, is sent directly to Lebanon to serve with an infantry unit. His inexperience and instinctive trust of the local civilian population at first cause difficulties. In the final, climactic sequence, Gadi is faced with a moral dilemma about risking the lives of innocent civilians in order to apprehend armed terrorists. Although pressured by his commanding officer and his men to attack with full strength, he never loses sight of his inner moral code and searches for another route in order to protect the civilians.

ROCKINGHORSE (Sus Etz), 1978.

Dir. & Edit.: Yaki Yosha*; Prod.: Yitzhak Shani, Danny Shalem, Yaki Yosha; Sc: Yaki Yosha, Yoel Kaminsky, Yoram Kaniuk, Shmuel Kraus, based on a book by Yoram Kaniuk; Ph.: Ilan Rosenberg; Music: Shmuel Kraus; Cast: Shmuel Kraus, Gedalia Besser*, Arik Lavie, Judy Katz, Miriam Bernstein-Cohen, Avraham Ben-Yosef, Shoshana Shani, Rahel Marcus, Levana Finkelstein*, Miriam Gavrielli, Daniel Wachsmann*.

Awards: Special Jury Prize and Best Actor (Gedalia Besser), Oxford (1978).

The film is a literary adaptation that works on two levels. On the personal level, it provides a portrait of an artist searching for the reasons for his own failure, his relationship with his aged father, and his inability to compromise in anything concerned with his art. It is also a look at the alienation of the generation that grew up on the classical Zionist upbringing. The film is shot in black and white; in contrast, however, the film within the film is in color, which adds to the authenticity of the memory, and it includes some documentary footage that emphasizes the film's being more than a personal statement, making it a semihistorical statement about an entire generation.

Aminadav Susetz (Shmuel Kraus) returns to Israel after 10 unsuccessful years in New York. He is an artist whose paintings all mysteriously disappeared in a fire on the night before an exhibition of his work. Leaving his wife and child, Aminadav returns to Tel Aviv, where he is shocked to find his mother bitter and lonely and his father dying in a nursing home. With the help of an old friend, Ansberg (Gedalia Besser), who is studying prostitution in the Tel Aviv beach area, he produces a film that searches into his past—the background of his parents, who came to Palestine as immigrants and the circumstances surrounding his birth. When the film is completed and acclaimed by a small group of friends and crew, he takes it out late at night and burns it.

SAINT CLARA (Clara Ha'K'dosha), 1995.

Dir. & Sc.: Ori Sivan, Ari Folman; Prod.: Marek Rozenbaum*, Uri Sabag, based on a story by Pavel and Jelena Kohout; Ph.: Valentin Belanogov; Edit.: Dov Steuer; Music: Barry Sakharov; Cast: Lucy Dubinchek, Halil Elohev, Johnny Peterson, Maia Meron, Yigal Naor, Menashe Noy, Yosef El-Dror, Yevgenia Dodina, Roland Haylovski.

Awards: Special Jury Prize, Karlovy Vary (1996); Best Film, Children's Film Festival, Vienna (1996); Best Film, Haifa (1995); Best Film, Best Directors, Best Actress (Lucy Dubinchek), Best Supporting Actor (Yigal Naor), Best Editing, Best Musical Score, Israeli Academy Awards (1996).

On one level, the film is a story of adolescent love. On another, more complex level, it tells a tale of supernatural powers against an apocalyptic futuristic landscape of power plants spewing forth smoke, bright city lights, swirling fog, and swampy areas. The script is based on a once-banned novel by dissident Czech writer Pavel Kohout and his wife, Jelena Kohout. Prizewinning film directors Ori Sivan (b. 1963 in San Francisco) and Ari Folman (b. 1962 in Warsaw) are documentary filmmakers. This is their first feature film.

Clara (Lucy Dubinchek) is a 13-year-old Russian immigrant living with her family in the harsh reality of a remote industrial town in Israel. Clara has suddenly found that she has strange powers, and weird things begin to occur; her schoolmates have come under her spell, and, surprisingly, all of them excel in their latest math exam. It appears that members of Clara's family acquire amazing supernatural powers the first time they fall in love. Clara's unusually strong powers bring the small town to the brink of chaos; her school bursts into flames, her teacher dreams about wild nights, and an earthquake threatens to destroy everything. Just when Clara has experienced her first taste of young love (Yigal Naor), she must choose between keeping her newly acquired powers or having the opportunity to experience love.

SALLAH (Sallach Shabbati), 1964.

Dir. & Sc.: Ephraim Kishon*; Prod.: Menahem Golan*, Ephraim Kishon, Haim Topol*; Ph.: Floyd Crosby, Nissim (Nitcho) Leon*; Edit.: Dani Schik; Music: Yochanan Zarai; Cast: Haim Topol, Gila Almagor*, Arik Einstein*, Shraga Friedman, Zaharira Harifai, Natan Meisler, Esther Greenberg, Shaike Levi, Mordechai Arnon.

Nomination: Nominated for an American Academy Award for Best Foreign Film.

Awards: Two Golden Globes—Outstanding Foreign Film of '64 and Star of Tomorrow Award (Haim Topol), Hollywood Foreign Press Association (1965); Golden Gate Awards for Best Screenplay and Best Actor (Haim Topol), San

Haim Topol (top) as the patriarch of the family in *Sallah* (Ephraim Kishon, 1964). Photo reprinted with the permission and courtesy of Ephraim Kishon.

Francisco (1964); First Prize for Best Foreign Direction, All American Press—American Distributors (1965); Prize, Viennale (1966).

Having broken all box office records in Israel, selling more than double the number of tickets of any previous film, the film then went abroad and ran for six months at the Little Carnegie Theater in New York City. A fast-paced musical, combining comedy and social satire, the film takes place during the years of the mass immigration immediately following the establishment of the state of Israel.

Sallah (Haim Topol) arrives by plane with his wife and seven children and is sent directly to a transit camp. Relying on his own instincts, Sallah quickly learns to adapt and get along in his new surroundings. He learns about political corruption; his new friend, Goldstein, is an Ashkenazi Jew who advises Sallah of the possibilities for gaining advantage at election time, and Sallah learns his lesson so well that he finds himself on the receiving end of favors from every political party. A nearby kibbutz sends a well-meaning yet inexperienced young social worker (Gila Almagor) to offer advice and assistance. Quickly, the positions are reversed, and Sallah is listening to her problems and offering her solace and advice from his innate wisdom and simple philosophy of life.

Sallah also learns about bureaucratic inefficiency. When he is sent to work in afforestation, where the local bureaucrats are playing a scam by switching the forest's billboard for each visiting donor, Sallah uproots the trees instead of planting them, not so much to register his protest but because he likes being unemployed. Sallah is portrayed as lazy and illiterate and at the same time as lovable, capable of great understanding, with a capacity for homespun wisdom. In a particularly humiliating scene, the chauvinistic father figure, Sallah, finds himself taking his daughter's earnings so that he can go out drinking with the other new immigrant men. Out in the rain, having fallen in the mud, he implores God's benevolence in helping him climb out of the poverty and degradation of life in the transit camp.

SALOMONICO, 1972.

Dir.: Alfred Steinhardt; Prod.: Henry Ohana, David Shapira, Roni Ya'ackov; Sc.: Reuven Bar-Yotam, Eli Tavor; Ph.: Yechiel Ne'eman; Edit.: Anat Lubarsky; Music: Dov Seltzer*; Cast: Reuven Bar-Yotam, Gabi Amrani, Etti Grottes, Yehuda Efroni, Levana Finkelstein*, Ronit Porat, Mani Pe'er, Moscu Alcalay, Ya'ackov Ben-Sira, Jacky Arkin, Rivka Michaeli, Reuven Shefer, Yehuda Fuchs, Arieh Moscuna.

The film portrays the breakdown of the traditional Sephardi family and the difficulties of raising and supporting a family in Tel Aviv. It is a film filled with humor, traditional values, and ethnic music. In addition to directing six feature films, Alfred Steinhardt (b. 1930 in Poland) produced and directed numerous documentaries, army training films, instructional films, and commercials during his career.

Salomonico (Reuven Bar-Yotam) is a Sephardi dockworker, originally from Saloniki, and he is married to a boisterous woman (Levana Finkelstein). After finally arranging the financing to leave their slum neighborhood, they move to the middle-class neighborhood of north Tel Aviv, where they discover that traditional values are considered old-fashioned. The neighbors are all Ashkenazi, the kids use pills, and people complain when Salomonico has a lot of guests. Their daughter gets pregnant, and they have a big wedding—a combination Ashkenazi-Sephardi wedding with both kinds of music. After they decide to move back to the old neighborhood, the father of a girl who has gotten pregnant by their son knocks on the door. Another Ashkenazi–Sephardi marriage is arranged.

Sequel: *The Father* (Alfred Steinhardt, 1975).

SAVE THE LIFEGUARD (Hatzilu et Hamatzil), 1977.

Dir. & Sc.: Uri Zohar*; Prod.: Yitzhak Kol, David Shapira; Ph.: David Gurfinkel*; Edit.: Hadassah Shani; Music: Ronny Weiss; Cast: Uri Zohar, Gila

Almagor*, Gabi Amrani, Yoseph Shiloah*, Hannah Laszlo, Judith Soleh, Arieh Kasbiner, Yosef Bashi, Avner Hezkiyahu, Albert Cohen.

A farce combined with sentimental moments, the film is the third in a trilogy of Tel Aviv beach comedies. The film portrays a devoted family man who treats his wife with love and tenderness, grappling with his desire to be faithful to her while also acknowledging his need for flirtations with other women.

Uri (Uri Zohar) is a lifeguard on the Tel Aviv beach, devoted father of three, still tenderly in love with his wife (Gila Almagor). Uri's friend at the lifeguard station is a bachelor, with whom he argues about the need for roots and about staying in Israel. Somewhat jealous of his friend's lifestyle, he often makes passes at the girls on the beach. His father-in-law, a successful businessman, does not like him and feels that his daughter has married beneath her. Hilarious situations arise when the father-in-law hires an American girl (Hannah Laszlo) to try to seduce Uri and to bring back proof of her success in the form of photographs.

Trilogy: *Peeping Toms** (1972), *Big Eyes** (1974), *Save the Lifeguard* (1977)

SCAR (Tzaleket), 1994.

Dir.: Haim Bouzaglo*; Prod.: David Silber, Micky Rabinovitz, Huguette Elhadad; Co-prod.: France-Israel; Sc.: Haim Bouzaglo, Ronit Elkabetz*; Ph.: Oren Shmukler; Edit.: Ira Lapid; Music: Arkadi Duchin; Cast: Robin Renucci, Ronit Elkabetz, Andréa Ferréol, Sasson Gabai, Muhammed Bakri*, Dalia Shimko, Juliano Mer.

Awards: Best Editing, Best Costume Design (Ruth Shaudinski), Best Musical Score, Best Sound (Eli Yarkoni, Israel David), Israeli Academy Awards (1994).

About the search for metaphysical love and the loss of individual and human identity, the film offers a vision of society in the future. The action takes place everywhere—in New York, Paris, and Israel—and the film speaks many languages. It is about worldwide societal alienation in which one is able to rent relatives and friends for intimate relationships.

A man (Robin Renucci) has a chance passionate encounter with a woman with long black hair and a scar on her thigh. He becomes attracted to her, but having never really seen her face, his search for the woman of his dreams turns into an obsession, a search for that ephemeral love that perhaps can never really be found. She (Ronit Elkabetz) lives with her husband (Muhammed Bakri) in a manor house. He lives alone in a loft and seeks out occasional relationships at a futuristic brothel, a house of fantasy and desire, located near railway lines leading nowhere, where he can pay for someone to talk to, for a child to read a book to, or for an elderly man to be his estranged father. He hires a detective to find her. She leaves her husband, seeking solitude.

SCOUTING PATROL (Sayarim), 1967.

Dir.: Micha Shagrir*; Prod.: Eli Gil; Sc.: Avram Heffner*; Ph.: Yachin Hirsch; Edit.: Tova Biran; Music: Alexander (Sasha) Argov; Cast: Illy Gorlitzky,

Lior Yaeni, Ze'ev Revach*, Eli Cohen*, Yossi Ohana, Assi Dayan*, Jacques Cohen.

Portraying an undercover commando operation, the film tells the story of the bravery and comradeship of four elite soldiers who are sent on a mission across the border into Jordan to capture a terrorist leader. The film is a statement about the dilemmas of Israeli soldiers who take the dangers of their mission in stride.

Eli (Ze'ev Revach), an army officer, and three soldiers set out on a mission to capture an Arab terrorist (Yossi Ohana). They succeed in abducting him. Having almost completed the mission successfully, the group mistakes its way in the desert, prolonging the journey and bringing them under Arab fire. When the soldiers are asleep, the prisoner grabs a gun and shoots and kills one of them. Although they succeed in recapturing the prisoner, they must refrain from harming him since their orders were to bring him back alive. The memory of their dead friend haunts them, however, as they continue on their way home.

SH'CHUR, 1994.

Dir.: Shmuel Hasfari*; Prod.: Yoram Kislev*; Sc.: Hannah Azoulai-Hasfari*; Ph.: David Gurfinkel*; Edit.: Zion Avrahamian; Music: Uri Vadislavski; Cast: Ronit Elkabetz*, Gila Almagor*, Ya'ackov Cohen, Amos Lavie, Hannah Azoulai-Hasfari, Orly Ben-Gerty.

Awards: Special Mention, Berlin (1995); Second Prize, Sorento (1996); First Prize, Montpellier (1994); Best Script, San Sebastian (1994); Best Film, Best Director, Best Actress (Ronit Elkabetz), Best Supporting Actor (Amos Lavie), Best Cinematography, Best Art Direction (Ya'akov Turgeman), Israeli Academy Awards (1994).

A film about cultural conflict, the story deals with superstition, family hardship, and sacrifice. The conflict lies embedded in the childhood memories of the Israeli-born daughter of a traditional and old-fashioned Moroccan family, a family that solves domestic problems through the use of white magic (*sh'chur*) and casting spells.

On the way to her father's funeral, talk-show host Heli (Hannah Azoulai-Hasfari) remembers growing up as the youngest in a traditional Moroccan Jewish family. Heli is the only Israeli-born child in her family. Remembering the last summer before she is sent away to boarding school in Jerusalem, at the age of 13, she recalls her brothers and sisters, strange images of her mother (Gila Almagor) and her retarded older sister, Pnina (Ronit Elkabetz), who together practice white magic. Pnina is possessed of supernatural powers and has a peculiar capacity for creating electrical energy. Heli also remembers her blind father (Amos Lavie), a sometimes unforgiving man, mainly interested in preparing for his participation in the national Bible quiz and "blind" to the world around him, especially the needs of his Israeli-born daughter, growing up in a different cultural milieu. Years later, Heli has an autistic daughter of her own, a girl who is strangely similar to her sister, Pnina.

SHELLSHOCK (Betzaylo Shel Helem Krav), 1988.

Dir. & Sc.: Yoel Sharon; Prod.: Yechiel Yogev, Meir Amsalom, Yoel Sharon; Ph.: Yoav Kosh*; Edit.: Zohar Sela; Music: Arik Rudich; Cast: Asher Tsarfati, Dan Turgeman, Anat Atzmon*, Slava Chaplin, Gili Ben-Uzilio.

Award: Best Musical Score, Israel Film Center (1987–1988).

Exploring the psychological problems of returning to normal life in the aftermath of war, filmmaker Yoel Sharon, himself badly injured in the Yom Kippur War, has simultaneously made a film about his own story, trying to recall certain moments of his life that were missing from his memory. This is his first feature film. The film is the story of two men, in the aftermath of the 1973 Yom Kippur War, who are assigned to share a room in a military hospital. One is a young member of a tank unit, and the other, a paratroop brigade commander; one cannot remember, and the other cannot forget.

Micha (Dan Turgeman), a fashion photographer, recalls that he was taking pictures of his friends around their troop carrier when a bomb fell and destroyed his entire unit. He is unable, however, to remember the important events that followed. He develops the pictures that were in his camera, looking for a clue that might help him to recall. Taking photos of fashion models in a junkyard, he sets the piles of junk alight in order to reconstruct that moment. When Micha finally remembers what has eluded him for so long, he realizes that he killed his friend trying to quiet his moaning as enemy troops were peering in on their burning troop carrier.

Micha's roommate Gideon (Asher Tsarfati) lives with haunting memories of Israeli phantom jets mistakenly bombing his position and wiping out his brigade. He is afraid to leave his hospital room and shakes every time he hears planes overhead. As he slowly recovers, he is looking for a chance to prove himself and he rushes to participate in an attack against terrorists who are holding children hostage in a local school. As he is first to storm the school, he is killed.

SHUROO, 1990.

Dir.: Savi Gabizon*; Prod.: Yonatan Aroch, Yochanan Raviv; Sc.: Savi Gabizon, Yonatan Aroch, Yochanan Raviv; Ph.: Yoav Kosh*; Edit.: Tali Halter-Shenkar; Music: Lior Tevet; Cast: Moshe Ivgi*, Sharon Hacohen, Sinai Peter, Keren Mor, Shmuel Edelman, Ahuva Keren, Ezra Kafri, Natan Zehavi, Yigal Adika, Albert Eluz.

Awards: Wolgin Award and Honorable Mention (Moshe Ivgi), Jerusalem (1991); Best Actor (Moshe Ivgi), Haifa (1991); Best Film, Best Director, Best Screenplay, Best Actor (Moshe Ivgi), Best Editing, Best Sound Recording (Eli Targan), Israeli Academy Awards (1990).

The film satirizes feminism, homosexuality, commitment to one partner, and male chauvinism in Israeli life. It is also a film about city life, intimate fears, and trust. In addition to the quirky characters of the narrative, the film is filled with strange images—a cabdriver who makes comments as he moves through the scenes, an encyclopedia salesman locked in the bathroom all day, yeshivah students passing in the night.

Asher (Moshe Ivgi) is a small-time con artist whose latest venture is involved with the self-realization movement. He has written a book on techniques that provide a new perspective on life—how not to be too serious, how to enjoy yourself naturally without drugs or alcohol, and how to open up to your true feelings. As a result of his new book and an appearance on late-night television, Asher becomes popular with a small group searching for meaning in their lives. When Asher is arrested for fraud, the group disintegrates, but the lives of all the participants have been altered. One woman suffers a breakdown, Asher's wife has the strength to leave him, two of the men admit to their homosexual tendencies, and everyone tries out new relationships.

In a surreal concluding scene, individual members of the group are seen wandering around the cold and misty Tel Aviv streets, streets devoid of other passers-by except for a kibbutz choir. The members of the choir, lost in the night, are all dressed in pure white, like angelic messengers of the socialist dream of the "lost" pioneering generation.

SIEGE (Matzor), 1969.

Dir.: Gilberto Tofano; Prod.: Ya'ackov Agmon; Sc.: Dan Ben-Amotz, Gilberto Tofano, based on an idea by Gila Almagor*; Ph.: David Gurfinkel*; Edit.: Dani Schik; Music: Yochanan Zarai; Cast: Gila Almagor, Yehoram Gaon*, Dan Ben-Amotz, Yael Aviv, Amir Orion, Raviv Oren, Uri Sharoni, Baruch Sadeh, Eran Agmon, Omna Goldstein-Cohen, Micha Cagan.

Awards: Best Actress (Gila Almagor), Chicago (1969); Gold Medal (Gila Almagor), Atlanta (1970); Best Actress (Gila Almagor), Hemisfilm Festival, San Antonio (1970).

Dealing with the psychological effects of coping with loss following the 1967 Six Day War, the film is the story of a society under siege, and the young widow in her loneliness and despair becomes the symbol of that society. The film is filled with the widow's memories and flashbacks. In addition, there is a constant emphasis on the news reports of the daily terrorist incidents on the Jordanian border and the skirmishes at the Suez Canal. Scriptwriter Dan Ben-Amotz (1923–1989) was a novelist and a prominent figure in the Israeli bohemian culture of the 1950s and 1960s. The film *Don't Give a Damn** (Shmuel Imberman, 1987) is based on his book. Italian-born Gilberto Tofano was a theater director, and this is his only feature film.

Tamar (Gila Almagor) is a young widow stifled by the sympathy that she encounters everywhere, especially by the attentions of her dead husband's paratroop buddy, Eli (Yehoram Gaon). There are intimate scenes between Tamar and her little son (Uri Sharoni), as they talk about the dead father. She finally meets a man she can talk to, David (Dan Ben Amotz), a bulldozer driver, who provides her with the opportunity to escape from her grief. After David is called up for reserve duty, an incident is reported on the radio in which two bulldozer drivers are killed. As Tamar frantically sets out to search for David, the film is intercut with clips of news events—violence, war, and rioting. Gila Almagor/Tamar (both in her role and in real life) becomes a symbol for an entire nation in distress. In fact, the film concludes with the actress on the film set as reality creeps in, and the crew listens to the newscast about Israeli soldiers being killed by terrorists. The siege is not only the story of the film; it was also the reality of everyday life for the nation.

SING YOUR HEART OUT (Halahaka; Alternative title: *The Troupe*), 1978.

Dir.: Avi Nesher*; Prod.: Yitzhak Kol; Sc.: Avi Nesher, Sharon Harel; Ph.: Ya'ackov Kallach; Edit.: Yitzhak Tzhayek; Music: Yair Rosenblum; Cast: Gidi Gov, Liron Nirgad, Meir Suissa, Dafna Armoni, Gali Atari, Gilat Ankori, Helli Goldenberg, Sassi Keshet, Smadar Brenner, Eli Gorenstein, Tuvia Tsafir, Dov Glickman.

A musical comedy that became a cult film with young audiences, the film was acclaimed for its authenticity and spontaneity. The story focuses on a uniquely Israeli cultural institution—the army entertainment troupe, which was created to entertain the forces at the front and to develop and train a cadre of young talent toward a career in the musical entertainment field. As a result of their roles in this film, many of the young actors and actresses went on to become popular Israeli entertainers.

Three new soldiers have just joined the Army Entertainment Troupe during the War of Attrition (1968–1969) and are immediately subjected to a barrage of pranks from the veteran troupe members. As the group—both young men and women—is packed into a small bus, forced to spend long months traveling and performing together, friendships form, rivalries and jealousies grow, and ambitions develop. The group works hard at creating musical numbers, rehearsing songs, and performing in front of the troops. Pressure builds as they find out that they are in competition for a coveted spot in an important television show, and the film concludes as all band together to produce a successful television event.

'66 WAS A GOOD YEAR FOR TOURISM (Shnat 66 Hayta Tova La'Tayarut), 1992.

Dir., Prod., Sc. & Narr.: Amit Goren*; Ph.: Eytan Harris; Edit.: Tali Halter; Music: Yo-Go.

Awards: Best Documentary, Israeli Academy Award (1992); Wolgin Award, Jerusalem (1992).

An introspective documentary, the film tells the story of the filmmaker's family. It is about people who uproot themselves and their families, their memories, and resultant issues of rootlessness and belonging. In 1966, the filmmaker's family emigrated from Israel to New York. Since that time, they have been people who belong in many places and at the same time nowhere. The film travels from place to place—Queens, where they lived when they first arrived;

their home on Long Island; the brother's home in Los Angeles; another brother's home in New York; the father's roots in Alexandria; the filmmaker's home in Tel Aviv. The mother is a strong image in this family. She kept up their ties to Israel and never let herself become really American since she refused to believe that they were staying in New York forever. She is an artist, a woman with a strong identity and a warm sense of humor.

THE SKIPPER (Abba Ganuv), 1988.

Dir.: Ya'ackov (Yankul) Goldwasser*; Prod.: Yehuda Barkan*; Co-prod.: Israel-U.S.A.; Sc: Haim Merin, Pincas Eden; Ph.: Ilan Rosenberg; Edit.: Anat Lubarsky; Music: Shlomo Gronich*; Cast: Yehuda Barkan*, Alona Kimchi, Ben Tzion, Keren Mor, Uri Shamir, Geta Luca, Leni Ravitz, Dan Herdan, Zeira Vartinian, Ya'ackov Cohen, Aryeh Cherner, Yarden Ross, Ilana Berkovitz.

Made for children, the film portrays an ideal relationship between father and son. It uses melodrama and humor in its creation of a commercial film that was popular with the Israeli audience.

Chico (Yehuda Barkan) and his son, Ben (Ben Tzion), live on a tourist boat on the Sea of Galilee, and they have a very healthy, loving relationship. Their problems begin when Ben's mother, now married to a millionaire in the United States, returns to try to obtain custody of her son. There are humorous scenes at the expense of the mother's highly paid Tel Aviv lawyer and true drama when Chico loses his son in a preliminary hearing, due to his pride and his refusal to accept the help of a lawyer. A female lawyer (Alona Kimchi), interested in Chico, saves the day and obtains a last-minute restraining order from the judge, preventing the mother and her millionaire husband from taking the boy out of the country.

Sequels: *The Skipper II* (directed by Avi Cohen, 1989) and *The Skipper III* (directed by Ayelet Menachemi, 1991).

SMILE OF THE LAMB (Chi'uch Hagdi), 1985.

Dir.: Shimon Dotan*; Prod.: Yonatan Aroch; Sc.: Shimon Dotan, Shimon Riklin, Anat Levy-Bar, based on a novel by David Grossman; Ph.: Dani Shneur; Edit.: Netaya Anbar; Music: Ilan Wurtzberg; Cast: Tuncel Curtiz, Rami Danon, Makram Khoury*, Danny Muggia, Iris Hoffman.

Awards: Silver Bear, Berlin, for Turkish actor Tuncel Curtiz (1986); First Prize, Best Director, Best Actor (Rami Danon), Best Supporting Actor (Makram Khoury), Best Cinematography, Best Musical Score, Israel Film Center (1985).

Mixing fantasy with reality and adding a heavy dose of folk wisdom, the film is a literary adaptation of a novel by David Grossman (one of Israel's important novelists, whose writings express a particular political agenda) about the occupation of the West Bank. Dealing with the gap in understanding in popular traditional and cultural matters between Jews and Arabs, the film confronts issues of friendship and trust, occupation and coexistence. Turkish actor Tuncel Curtiz also appears in the Israeli film *On a Narrow Bridge**(1985).

Colonel Katzman (Makram Khoury) is appointed to the post of military governor in the West Bank. He invites his liberal friend Dr. Uri Laniado (Rami Danon) to work with him. On a visit to a small village under their supervision, they meet Hilmi (Tuncel Curtiz), the village fool, who lives the life of a hermit in a cave with his memories of the past, eating his food sprinkled with the soil of the land ("When I finish eating all my land, I can die in peace."). The wise old man has tried all his life to stay aloof from any kind of political involvement, even after Yazdi, his son, joins the PLO and disappears from the village. But Yazdi returns, and the story focuses on the growing political awareness of the old man. Hilmi recounts folktales from his past—how he unwittingly aided his father in committing suicide, how his grandfather proved his heroism on safari, and how he used to care for unwed mothers, stigmatized and unaccepted by others. The film tells the story of two triangles—the love triangle in which Laniado's wife is having an affair with his friend Katzman and the political triangle in which Laniado finds himself trapped in the endless argument between his old friend Katzman, providing enlightened government, and Hilmi, an Arab traditionalist turned political activist.

SNAIL (Shablul), 1970.

Dir. & Sc.: Boaz Davidson*; Prod.: Tzvi Shissel; Ph.: Nurith Aviv*; Edit.: Anat Lubarsky; Music: Shalom Hanoch; Cast: Arik Einstein*, Uri Zohar*, Tzvi Shissel, Shalom Hanoch, Judy Katz, Judith Soleh, Ze'ev Revach*, Mordechai Arnon, Alona Einstein, Yossi Pollack.

Full of songs and good music with an infectious beat, the film is a collaboration between two of the biggest Israeli musical talents of the period—Shalom Hanoch and music idol Arik Einstein. An episodic film made up of spontaneity, the narrative revolves around the personal life of a famous music star (played by Arik Einstein), including vignettes loosely intertwined—such as his divorce, his encounters with his recording producer, and an interview with a newspaper reporter. Although a successful and popular singer, the star is seen as a man with personal problems, a man who retreats into his shell when people try to penetrate his protective exterior.

SONG OF THE SIREN (Shirat Hasireneh), 1994.

Dir.: Eytan Fox*; Prod.: Yonatan Aroch; Sc.: Irit Linur, based on her novel; Ph.: Avi Koren; Edit.: Zohar Sela; Music: Adi Cohen; Cast: Dalit Kahan, Boaz Gur-Lavie, Yair Lapid, Orly Zilbershatz-Banai, Avital Decker, Meir Suissa, Dudu Ben-Ze'ev, Cameo appearance: Yaffa Yarkoni.

Awards: Best Supporting Actress (Orly Zilbershatz-Banai), Israeli Academy Award (1994).

The film is a romantic and quirky comedy, rich in texture, color, and humor, set against the stress and absurdity of the Gulf War of 1991 and based on a best-seller by the same name. It is the story of an assertive, professional woman who experiences emotional growth and genuine romance. At the same time, the film is critical of the superficial lifestyle of the trendy Tel Aviv urban set. The title is a play on the air-raid sirens that sounded almost every night during the six weeks of the war.

Talila (Dalit Kahan) is an advertising executive. At a New Year's party, when everyone is poking fun at Saddam Hussein, she notices her manipulative ex-boyfriend (Yair Lapid), who is with his new fiancée. In order to make him jealous, she begins to pay special attention to her boss, the slick and shallow Marco. Sleeping with the boss has certain advantages, and the next day, she is assigned a new account. At the first meeting with the new account, she meets their food engineer, Noah (Boaz Gur-Lavie), an easygoing fellow who lives outside Tel Aviv in a rural community and has more depth and feeling than the shallow members of her Tel Aviv circle. They begin a passionate relationship.

The romantic intrigues of the film develop as Talila and her family are sitting huddled in a sealed room, wearing gas masks, with SCUD missiles hurtling through the sky aimed at Tel Aviv. Noah's ex-girlfriend appears on the scene; Talila's sister (Orly Zilbershatz-Banai) reunites with her cheating husband; and the tensions of wartime bring together Talila's mother (Yaffa Yarkoni) and father after many years of separation. As the Gulf War comes to an end, Noah realizes that he doesn't love his ex, and he arrives on Talila's doorstep.

STALIN'S DISCIPLES (Yaldei Stalin), 1986.

Dir. & Sc.: Nadav Levitan*; Prod.: Doron Eran*; Ph.: Gadi Danzig; Edit.: Shimon Tamir; Music: Hava Alberstein; Cast: Shmuel Shiloh, Yossi Kantz, Hugo Yarden, Rahel Dobson, Aharon Almog, Ezra Dagan, Doron Golan, David Semadar.

Award: Best Actor (Shmuel Shiloh), Israel Film Center (1987–1988).

A satire of kibbutz life, the complex narrative presents quirky characters on a background of ideological crisis. Using the voyeur technique of viewing the action through windows (as in Levitan's previous film, *An Intimate Story**), the film portrays the problem of lack of privacy on the kibbutz. The story touches on the highly emotional issue of accepting reparation money from the German government during the postwar period. The title refers to the admiration of the Israeli Labor Movement for Stalinist Russia before the atrocities and corruption of Stalin became known.

On a kibbutz in 1950s Israel, three comic-pathetic shoemakers (whose work has become obsolete), all sporting bushy Stalin mustaches, express a sense of tragedy when news of Stalin's death reaches them. The story revolves around the schoolteacher, who feels unaccepted because he does not do physical labor, and his wife, who has a heart condition stemming from the physical traumas that she experienced in Nazi Europe. When the oppression and the forced labor camps of Stalinist Russia become known, the kibbutz members burn their red flags and pictures of Stalin.

STIGMA (Ot Kain), 1982.

Dir.: Uri Barbash*; Prod.: Micha Shagrir*; Sc.: Eran Preis, Uri Barbash; Ph.: Dani Shneur; Edit.: Ira Lapid; Music: Yoni Richter; Cast: Arnon Zadok*, Dalik Volonitz, Ofra Weingarten, Ezra Kafri, Roberto Pollack.

Trying with difficulty to rebuild his life after a mental breakdown, the film's hero is pressured both socially and politically to fulfill his military obligations, even though he is not sufficiently healthy to cope.

Ehud (Arnon Zadok) has recently been released from a mental hospital. He returns home to find that his wife, Esti, and son have left him. Ehud tries to live his life as if the mental breakdown had never occurred—continuing with his reserve army service and with friends—and is particularly sensitive to any references to his previous illness. At one point, Ehud accuses his best friend of having an affair with his wife and pulls his Uzi submachine gun on him. Eventually, Ehud realizes that he has a problem that he cannot deny and that he must live with it and conquer it.

STREETS OF YESTERDAY (Rechovot Etmol), 1989.

Dir.: Yehuda (Judd) Ne'eman*; Prod.: Mark Forstater, Ye'ud Levanon*; Co-prod.: Israel-U.K.-Germany; Sc.: Yehuda (Judd) Ne'eman, David Lan; Ph.: Miklos Jancso Jr.; Edit.: Graham Walker; Music: Gary Hughes; Cast: Paul McGann, John Finch, Suzan Sylvester, Alon Aboutboul*, Nadim Sawalha, Hans Peter Hallwachs, Michael Warshaviak, Alona Kimchi.

A political film of intrigue and betrayal, the complex narrative depicts an Israeli who stretches out his hand to assist the Palestinians but is caught in a complicated and irresolvable situation. The film speaks English.

Raz (Paul McGann) is an Israeli student who becomes a fugitive from his own country for having aided his Palestinian friend, Amin (Alon Aboutboul), who was wounded in an attempted terrorist operation against the Israeli minister of foreign affairs. Raz flees by boat and arrives in West Berlin, where he meets Amin's sister, who is a journalist and photographer. In a flashback, Amin is a law student working as a waiter at the King David Hotel. He provides the weapon for a terrorist to assassinate an Israeli government minister. When Amin delivers the weapon, he discovers that the shooter is dead—so who killed the minister? A complicated string of betrayals follows.

SUMMER OF AVIYA (Kayitz shel Aviya), 1988.

Dir.: Eli Cohen*; Prod.: Eitan Even, Gila Almagor*; Sc.: Gila Almagor, Haim Bouzaglo*, Eli Cohen, based on a book by Gila Almagor; Ph.: David Gurfinkel*; Edit.: Tova Ne'eman; Music: Shem-Tov Levy*; Cast: Gila Almagor, Kaipo Cohen, Marina Rossetti, Eli Cohen, Avital Decker-Ben Porat, Dina Avarech, Sandra Sadeh.

Awards: Silver Bear for the film and the actresses (Gila Almagor and Kaipo Cohen), Berlin (1989); Best Foreign Film, San Remo (1989); Golden Spike,

Kaipo Cohen (left) and Gila Almagor in *Summer of Aviya* (Eli Cohen, 1988). Photo courtesy of the Jerusalem Cinematheque, reprinted with the permission of Eitan Even.

Valladolid (1989); Grand Prix, Belgrade (1990); Second Prize, Best Director, Best Actress (Gila Almagor), Israel Film Center (1987–1988).

The film is an intensely human story seen through the eyes and perceptions of a child (played by child actress Kaipo Cohen). It is a portrayal of the growth of understanding, handled sensitively and with maturity, and a triumphant artistic effort. The film, originally a one-woman theater production starring Gila Almagor, tells Almagor's own personal story, an in-depth study of the shame that she felt as a child, growing up with a mother who was forever tortured by her memories.

Almagor, who co-wrote, co-produced, and stars in the film, plays the role of her own mother, Henya, a woman with a number on her arm, a terrible testimony to her experiences in a Nazi concentration camp. In the year 1951, Henya's 10-year-old daughter, Aviya, is studying at a boarding school since her mother has been hospitalized for mental instability. From the first moment that Henya comes to pick up her daughter for the summer vacation, her erratic behavior becomes apparent. Aviya's head is shaven because her mother sees lice in her hair, a reminder of another time and place. Aviya is a sensitive child, and, although it is difficult for her and often embarrassing, she tries hard to help her mother. Mother and daughter settle into a routine in small-town 1950s Israel. Aviya daydreams about her father, whom she has never met, because he died before she was born, fantasizing that he is still alive, building an elaborate story around one of their neighbors, and imagining that he was married to her mother years ago.

Aviya's mother lives with a stigma, and the children of the small town taunt her by turning her heroic title of "partisan" against her. Desiring more than anything else to be like the other little girls, Aviya begs her mother to dress her in a beautiful dress so that she can go to ballet lessons. However, her mother does not understand the need for a fancy dress; if your clothes are clean, that is good enough. As the tension builds, there is a violent clash between the ballet teacher and Aviya. When things are resolved and they eventually become friends, they exchange secrets. The ballet teacher, however, leaks Aviya's secret, which helps Aviya to realize the superficiality of a lifestyle that requires fancy clothes and reinforces her struggle for independence and maturity.

Sequel: *Under the Domim Tree** (Eli Cohen, 1995).

TAKE OFF (Hitromamut), 1970.

Dir.: Uri Zohar*; Prod.: Avraham (Pashanel) Deshe; Sc.: Talila Ben-Zakai, Avraham (Pashanel) Deshe; Ph.: David Gurfinkel*; Edit.: Anna Gurit; Music: Shalom Hanoch; Cast: Yisrael Poliakov, Shaike Levi, Gavri Banai, Uri Zohar, Tikvah Mor, Judy Katz, Tsippi Shavit, Lihi (Hanoch) Efron, Liora Rivlin, Judith Soleh.

An episodic, surrealistic tale of the childish fantasy world of three grown men, the film combines elements of the absurd and the crude and uses interesting artistic techniques such as outrageous camera angles, a female spirit walking through and observing scenes, and an on-camera maestro (Uri Zohar) making humorous observations and comments concerning sexual dilemmas and fantasies.

The film portrays three men and their adolescent sex lives. The three friends (the Gashash Trio—Yisrael Poliakov, Shaike Levi, Gavri Banai)—an analyst, a hairstylist, and a boutique owner—spend hours together dreaming, talking, and thinking about exciting women. In spite of the fact that they each voice ambivalent feelings concerning their own wives and precisely because they do not know how to go about recruiting beautiful girls, they plan an orgy to which each will bring his own wife.

TAKE TWO (Hatzad Hasheni), 1972.

Dir., Prod., & Sc.: Baruch Dienar*; Ph.: Adam Greenberg*; Edit.: David Treuherz; Music: Noam Sheriff; Cast: Uri Levy, Sherry Ren Smith, Gadi Yagil, Albert Cohen, Oriella Veit, Yona Elian*.

Award: Critics' Prize, Venice (1972).

Depicting the tension between artistic and commercial filmmaking, the film deals with the complexities of the political and artistic reality and presents a serious work ethic and a need for a high standard of professionalism.

Sonny (Sherry Ren Smith) is a young American hippie who comes from abroad to learn filmmaking. She encounters and falls for Assi (Uri Levy), an Israeli cameraman/documentary filmmaker who helps her learn the trade. She shoots new immigrants arriving from Russia and is very moved by the material. When it turns out to have been arranged by Assi, however, she is devastated. His chauvinism, dishonesty, and manipulative methods in producing crass commercials and documentary films eventually lead her to reject him.

TEL AVIV–BERLIN, 1987.

Dir. & Sc.: Tsipi Trope*; Prod.: Smadar Azrielli; Ph.: Gadi Danzig; Edit.: Rachel Yagil; Music: Shalom Weinstein; Cast: Shmuel Vilozhny, Rivka Neuman, Anat Harpaz, Zohar Aloni, Yosef Carmon, Constantine Anatol.

Awards: Best Film, Best Actress (Rivka Neuman), Best Supporting Actor (Yosef Carmon), Best Screenplay, Best Art Director (Eli Landau), Israel Film Center (1987–1988).

A study of a man living in the past, the film confronts the difficulties of a Holocaust survivor in adapting to his new environment and portrays him obsessed with memories of a world that was destroyed. Benjamin (Shmuel Vilozhny), a survivor of Auschwitz, is released from a mental institution, where the nurse (Rivka Neuman) has befriended him. Five years later, they are married, and they have a little girl. Benjamin lives with the memories of his family and surrounds himself with the music and art of prewar Berlin. He also extols the sense of morality and justice that he learned when growing up in Germany. But his chess partner, also a survivor from Germany, says that the only thing he got from Germany is the number on his arm.

One night in a nightclub with his wife, Benjamin finds himself attracted to a beautiful and elegant woman from Berlin (Anat Harpaz) who represents for him the world of culture, which he misses so desperately. At the same time, he becomes obsessed with a local blacksmith (Yosef Carmon), who was the brutal *kapo* (concentration camp inmate with authority over a group of Jewish prisoners) in charge of his father's barracks at Auschwitz.

TEL AVIV–LOS ANGELES, 1988.

Dir.: Shmuel Imberman*; Prod.: Shlomo Paz, Rafi Shahar; Sc.: Dudu Topaz, Mickey Goldenberg; Ph.: Nissim (Nitcho) Leon; Edit.: Zion Avrahamian; Music: Eldad Shrem; Cast: Dudu Topaz, Jacques Cohen, Avigail Arieli, Bracha Ne'eman, Amnon Moskin, Yossi Barak.

Featuring one of Israel's popular entertainers, Dudu Topaz, the film tells the story of a stand-up comedian who goes to the United States on tour and is tempted to stay in order to pursue fame and fortune. Moti (Dudu Topaz) is a 40-year-old entertainer. He is unsuccessful in his professional life—telling jokes at bar mitzvahs. When his career begins to take off, he goes to New York on tour, where he is very successful. Moti is tempted to stay in America and make it big. A wealthy older Israeli woman takes him under her wing, and he becomes her gigolo. The months go by. Eventually, Moti decides to go home and returns to his agent in Tel Aviv and to entertaining the troops.

TEL AVIV STORIES (Sipurei Tel Aviv), 1992.

Dir.: Ayelet Menachemi, Nirit Yaron; Prod.: Ehud Bleiberg, Yitzhak Ginsberg; Sc.: Shemi Zarhin*, Ayelet Menachemi, Nirit Yaron; Ph.: Amnon Zlayet, Jorge Gurvich; Edit.: Ayelet Menachemi; Music: Ari Frenkel, Shlomo Gronich*; Cast (*Sweet Sharona*): Yael Abecassis, Sharon Alexander*, Juliano Mer, Shahar Segal, Modi Bar-On, Nuli Omer; (*Operation Cat*): Ruti Goldberg, Rosina Cambos, Dror Keren, Amnon Zlayet, Sa'ar Fine, Anat Zahor; (*Divorce*): Anat Wachsmann*, Sasson Gabai, Michal Matityahu, Shlomo Tarshish, Amnon Moskin, Uri Gavrieli.

Awards: Best Actress (Anat Wachsmann), Best Editor, Best Art Director (Eva Grunovitch, Itamar Neuman, Ariel Glaser), Best Costume Design (Shira Breuer, Neta Ramon), Israeli Academy Awards (1992).

The film is composed of three episodes, all stories about women. Film director Ayelet Menachemi also directed the award-winning short *Crows* (1986) and the feature film *The Skipper III* (1991). Nirit Yaron has directed commercials and the award-winning drama *A Big Girl* (1986).

Sweet Sharona (Sharona Motek) and *Operation Cat* (Mivtzah Chatool) are about working women suffering from alienation in the jungle atmosphere of big-city life. *Sweet Sharona* is about a young art designer (Yael Abecassis) who flits from lover to lover and eventually feels harassed by the men who are crazy about her. *Operation Cat* is about a young female reporter (Ruti Goldberg) who can't juggle all the elements of her private life. She is breaking up with her boyfriend, moving out of her apartment, and doing stories for the newspaper, and, at the same time, she is obsessed with worrying about a cat caught in the sewer near her house.

The third story, *Divorce* (Get), is about a woman willing to resort to desperate means in response to anachronistic rabbinic laws. According to Jewish law, a woman cannot request a divorce; it must be granted to her by her husband. Tikva (Anat Wachsmann) is a 32-year-old mother of two, a policewoman who takes her job very seriously. Working at the Shalom Tower, a skyscraper in the center of Tel Aviv, Tikva spots her husband, Menashe (Shlomo Tarshish), who has been hiding from her, refusing to grant her a divorce. Determined to obtain the divorce that had been denied her for so many years, she grabs hostages and presents demands. One of her hostages, an Orthodox rabbi, arranges by cellular telephone for the ex-husband to be kidnapped by an entire rabbinic court, which will force him to grant the divorce. Tikva realizes that she does not want anything under these circumstances, neither from her ex-husband nor from the rabbinic authorities. With this decision, she finds herself strangely liberated from the desperation and anguish that have plagued her for so long.

TEL AVIV TAXI (Ma'aseh Be'Monit; Alternative title: *Tale of a Taxi*), 1954.

Dir. & Sc.: Larry Frisch*; Prod.: Yitzhak Agadati, Mordechai Navon*, Larry Frisch; Ph.: Nissim (Nitcho) Leon*; Edit.: Nellie Bogor-Gilad; Music: Eddie Halperin; Cast: Shaike Ophir*, Miriam Bernstein-Cohen, Azaria (Zuska) Rappaport, Raphael Klatchkin, Natan Cogan, Shmuel Rodensky*, Gideon Dorn, Hanan Simtai.

The first Israeli feature film to be completely produced in Israel, the film is a comedy comprising a tapestry of vignettes. The film touches on issues of ethnic diversity, memories of the War of Independence, and problems of new immigrants.

Following a Purim parade in Tel Aviv, a taxi driver fills his old taxi with travelers to Jerusalem. Along the difficult climb to Jerusalem, the taxi breaks down. As the driver is repairing the vehicle, his passengers exchange stories in the nearby ruin of an old building. One passenger (Shaike Ophir) tells a story involving a War of Independence incident at the same ruin. One night on guard duty, he left his post to meet a pretty girl. When he returned, he found that Arab soldiers had occupied the building. After succeeding in recapturing the building that he had lost, he is rewarded with a medal.

The second vignette is told by an older woman who lives in an old-age home near Netanya. At a phone booth, she mistakenly exchanges purses with a young girl and unwittingly steals 10 lirot from the girl's purse. The third vignette takes place in Safed, where a religious man complains to his rabbi about his family's cramped living quarters. The concluding vignettes are a story about poisonous mushrooms, a puppet story of Purim, and a Robin Hood story about a bank employee who steals to give money to new immigrants living in a transit camp.

TELL ME THAT YOU LOVE ME (Dibri Alai Ahavah; Alternative title: *Miri*), 1983.

Dir.: Tsipi Trope*; Prod.: Israel Ringel, James Kaufman, Yair Pradelski; Coprod.: Israel-Canada; Sc.: Tsipi Trope, Sandra Kolber; Ph.: David Gurfinkel*; Edit.: Yves Langlois; Music: André Gagnon; Cast: Barbara Williams, Nick Mancuso, Belinda Montgomery, Ken Walsh, André Pelletier, Assi Dayan*.

The film portrays two tales of family life, one about the pressures of a two-career family and the other about physical abuse. In both stories, compromises are needed in order to build mutual understanding and respect. The film speaks English.

Miri (Barbara Williams) and Dan (Nick Mancuso) are married. He expects her to be the perfect housewife and verbally abuses her for not having everything just as he wants it at home. He criticizes her for being too involved in her work, especially when she is offered the position of editor-in-chief of a magazine. Miri is researching a story on the subject of battered women and becomes personally involved with Naomi, a middle-aged woman who refuses to leave her unemployed husband, even though he beats her. Eventually, the situation gets so bad that Naomi is forced to leave him and, with Miri's help, moves to a small

Shmuel Rodensky in *Tevye and His Seven Daughters* (Menahem Golan, 1968). Photo courtesy of the Jerusalem Cinematheque, reprinted with the permission of Yoram Globus.

apartment with her children. Meanwhile, Dan is offered a position to go to New York, and Miri finally asserts herself and decides not to go with him. After Dan leaves and divorce becomes inevitable, she experiences overwhelming loneliness, and her relationships with those around her are severely affected. Just when Naomi is returning to her husband, Miri's own husband flies over from New York for a visit, and their reconciliation begins.

TEVYE AND HIS SEVEN DAUGHTERS (Tuvia Ve'Sheva B'Notav), 1968.

Dir. & Prod.: Menahem Golan*; Sc.: Haim Hefer, Menahem Golan, based on stories by Shalom Aleichem; Ph.: Nissim (Nitcho) Leon*; Edit.: Tova Biran, Dov Hoenig; Music: Dov Seltzer*; Cast: Shmuel Rodensky*, Ninette Dinar, Tikvah Mor, Avital Paz, Judith Soleh, Illy Gorlitzky, Peter van Eyck.

A literary adaptation of Shalom Aleichem's Yiddish stories about Jewish life in the Russian Pale, where traditional Jewish culture thrived, the film includes elements of authenticity, including period costumes, Yiddish expressions, and an entire village built especially as the set for this film. The film was shot both on this village set and partially at a kibbutz in the Upper Galilee. The story is episodic, each daughter's story linked together as tales in a greater drama of an entire people. The same stories were later adapted by filmmaker Norman Jewison in his 1971 classic, *Fiddler on the Roof.*

Oded Teomi and Ninette Dinar in *They Were Ten* (Baruch Dienar, 1960). Photo courtesy of the Jerusalem Cinematheque, reprinted with the permission of Yanky Dienar.

Tevye (Shmuel Rodensky) lives in a small Russian village at the beginning of the twentieth century with his devoted wife and seven daughters. He is a religious Jew who makes a living by delivering milk with his wobbly old horse-drawn wagon. Tevye must use his resourcefulness and his sense of humor in coping with his poverty, the influences of the modern world, and finally a pogrom. Try as he might, Tevye cannot stop his daughters from being exposed to the world that is changing around them. One announces that she is following her revolutionary lover, who has recently been exiled to Siberia; another decides to marry a non-Jew. Then one day, when a pogrom hits the town, Tevye realizes that his whole world is crumbling around him.

THEY WERE TEN (Hem Hayu Asarah), 1960.

Dir. & Prod.: Baruch Dienar*; Sc.: Gabriel Dagan, Baruch Dienar, Menachem Shuval; Ph.: Lionel Banes, Desmond Davis; Edit.: Helga Cranston (Keller), Dani Schik; Music: Gary Bertini; Cast: Oded Teomi, Ninette Dinar, Leo Filler, Yoseph Safra, Bomba Tzur, Gabriel Dagan, Nissim Izikari, Yisrael Rubinchik, Yitzhak Bareket, Amnon Kahanovich.

Awards: Grand Prix, Rencontre du Film pour la Jeunesse, Cannes (1961); Prize CIDALC, Mannheim (1961).

The film tells the heroic story of 10 pioneers—nine men and one woman—who settle a desolate hilltop in the Galilee in the 1880s. The film is significant due to its artistic quality, in-depth characterizations, and striking images, which are reminiscent of American westerns, in which the entire film is seen from the point of view of the "good" guys, and the Arabs are seen as one-dimensional characters.

Joseph (Oded Teomi) and Manya (Ninette Dinar) are a married couple living together with the other pioneers in one large room. Lacking privacy, they are under extreme stress, and Manya is lonely. The pioneers are forced to deal with the resentments of the neighboring Arabs, struggle with the harsh conditions of nature, and learn how to handle the ruling Turkish authorities. They clear the land of rocks, plant their crops with primitive tools, and are constantly on the lookout for marauding thieves and shepherds. In their fight against the Arabs for their rights to the local water well, an argument arises among the pioneers concerning what kind of relationship they want to establish with the Arabs of the region. The difficult lifestyle was not for everyone—some left, and not all who remained survived. Matters eventually work out, however, the internal problems are settled, Manya becomes pregnant, an honorable modus vivendi is found with the Arab neighbors, and the Turkish officer is taken care of. There is a semitragic ending to the film, an ending that leaves the viewer with a sense of hope as the drought ends and the rains begin to fall.

A THIN LINE (Al Chevel Dak), 1980.

Dir. & Sc.: Michal Bat-Adam*; Prod.: Gideon Amir, Avi Kleinberger, Michal Bat-Adam; Ph.: Nurith Aviv*; Edit.: Zion Avrahamian; Music: Alex Cagan; Cast: Gila Almagor*, Alex Peleg, Liat Pansky, Avner Hezkiyahu, Yitzhak Havis, Miri Fabian, Dina Limor, Irit (Mohr) Alter, Esther Zebko.

Awards: First Prize, Best Director, Best Actress (Gila Almagor), Best Cinematography, Israel Film Center (1980).

A psychological study of a woman with emotional problems, the film emphasizes mood, feelings, and facial expressions and focuses on a mother's dependency on her 11-year-old daughter, who struggles to sustain her in times of need. This is an autobiographical film—Bat-Adam herself was sent away to a kibbutz for schooling because her mother was having difficulties coping emotionally and mentally.

On the surface is a typical Israeli family—mother, father, and two children. The older daughter lives away at a kibbutz, and the younger lives at home with her parents. The father, helpless in the face of his wife's problems, works in a camera shop. As the mother's condition is progressively deteriorating—she is not able to keep the house in order, doesn't cook or sleep or clean—the young daughter tries to help her mother in every way that she can.

When the mother (Gila Almagor) is hospitalized, the young daughter is sent to the kibbutz to be with her big sister. Upon the mother's release from the hospital, the daughter returns home to care for her. A relapse, however, is inevitable.

THIS IS THE LAND (Zot Hi Ha'Aretz), 1935.

Dir.: Baruch Agadati*; Prod.: Yitzhak Agadati; Sc.: Avigdor Hame'iri; Documentary footage: Ya'akov Ben-Dov*; Music: Ya'ackov Levanon, Mordechai Zeira; Lyrics: Emanuel Harussi, Alexander Penn; Songs sung by: Hana Kipnis, Yosef Goland; Cast: Shmuel Rodensky*, Raphael Klatchkin, Moshe Chorgal, Yitzhak Katz, Meir Teomi, Bezalel London.

The first sound feature film in Palestine, this film is a combination of documentary and drama—mixing dramatic sequences, documentary footage from AGA newsreels, and documentary footage shot originally by Ya'ackov Ben-Dov.

The film tells the story of 50 years of the history of the pioneers in Palestine since the early Zionist settlers first came to Rishon Letzion in 1882. It also deals with some of the issues of the pioneers, including the problems of kibbutz life, through dramatized sequences. Emphasizing both the farm and the city, the film is a great artistic achievement, combining beautifully photographed visual elements with drama, music, and history. Some of the early footage by Ben-Dov includes remarkable shots of members of the Jewish Legion in full military uniform praying and reading from a Torah scroll at an outdoor service; Sir Herbert Samuel, the first British high commissioner of Palestine, arriving at Jaffa port in 1920; and the opening ceremony of the Hebrew University of Jerusalem on Mount Scopus in 1925, with Lord Balfour speaking.

Rereleased in a new version: *Tomorrow's Yesterday*, 1963, also directed by Baruch Agadati.

A THOUSAND AND ONE WIVES (Eleph Neshotav Shel Naphtali Siman-Tov), 1989.

Dir. & Sc: Michal Bat-Adam*; Prod.: Effi Atad; Based on a novel by Dan Benaya Seri; Ph.: Yoav Kosh*; Edit: Yosef Grunfeld; Music: Alon Olearchik; Cast: Rita Faruz-Kleinstein, Yossi Pollack, Nissim Izikari, Salim Dau*, Yonatan Cherchy, Levana Finkelstein*, Navah Ziv, Etti Grottes, Rivka Bachar, Geula Nuni.

Awards: Best Actress (Rita Faruz-Kleinstein), Best Cinematography, Best Art Director (Yoram Shayer), Israel Film Center (1988–1989).

A tale of superstition and jealousy, the film is a literary adaptation set in the Bucharan quarter of Jerusalem at the end of the nineteenth century. It is a quiet film, filled with memories and beautiful shots of Jerusalem courtyards.

Flora (Rita Faruz-Kleinstein) is a young and inexperienced woman who is married by arrangement to an older man (Yossi Pollack), whose previous two wives died under peculiar circumstances. He therefore superstitiously decides to refrain from physically touching Flora, for fear that something terrible will happen again. Meanwhile, Flora, eager to please her husband yet young and ignorant, is seduced by a local shopkeeper and becomes pregnant. Having been unprepared for marriage, she does not realize that she is pregnant and certainly does not understand what her pregnancy implies. Only her husband knows that she is pregnant by another.

A THOUSAND LITTLE KISSES (Eleph Nishikot K'Tanot), 1981.

Dir. & Sc.: Mira Recanati; Prod.: Tzvi Shpielman, Shlomo Mugrabi; Ph.: David Gurfinkel*; Music: Shlomo Gronich*; Edit.: Jacques Ehrlich; Cast: Dina Doron, Rivka Neuman, Gad Roll, Rina Otchital, Doron Tavori, Nissim Zohar, Nirit Gronich, Daphne Recanati, Cochava Harari, Adi Kaplan.

Awards: Second Prize, Best Musical Score, Best Cinematography, Israel Film Center (1981).

The film portrays the complexities and jealousies in mother–daughter relationships and focuses specifically on a stormy period following the death of the father. Russian-born film director Mira Recanati is a sculptress and artist, and this is her first feature film.

After her father's death, Alma (Rivka Neuman) is inexplicably drawn into his past and discovers that her father had been having a secret affair for many years. Torn between her father's two lives, Alma becomes passionately involved with the other woman's son. Her newly widowed mother (Dina Doron), who already feels betrayed by her husband's infidelity and robbed of her memories ("even my memories are a lie"), now feels even more betrayed by her daughter, who has seemingly abandoned her for the other family. After a claustrophobic sequence in which the mother suffers a monthlong siege of hiding from reality and coming to terms with her own subjugated needs and desires, she overcomes her feelings of betrayal, despite the pain and suffering that she has endured.

THREE DAYS AND A CHILD (Shlosha Yamim Veyeled), 1967.

Dir.: Uri Zohar*; Prod. Amatsia Hiuni; Sc.: Uri Zohar, Dan Ben-Amotz, Amatsia Hiuni, based on a novel by A. B. Yehoshua; Ph.: David Gurfinkel*; Edit.: Jacques Ehrlich; Music: Dov Seltzer*; Cast: Oded Kotler*, Judith Soleh, Germaine Unikovsky, Illy Gorlitzky, Misha Oshorov, Stella Ivni, Nissan Yatir, Baruch David, Shoshana Duar, Shai Oshorov.

Award: Best Actor (Oded Kotler), Cannes (1967).

Although the context of the film is kibbutz and Jerusalem, the thematic content does not deal with Israeli life per se but rather with human problems of jealousy, love, and hate. A psychological drama, the film tells the story of a man—the well-known sabra (native-born Israeli), tough and cynical on the outside yet extremely vulnerable on the inside—who encounters himself as he confronts the child of the woman whom he loves. Three feature films have been produced that are literary adaptations based on a novel by A. B. Yehoshua, a prominent figure of contemporary Hebrew literature—*Three Days and a Child*, *The Lover**, and *The Return from India*.

Eli (Oded Kotler), a botany lecturer at the Hebrew University in Jerusalem, is entrusted for three days with Shai, the young son of his former girlfriend (Germaine Unikovsky). She and her husband have come to Jerusalem from their kibbutz in order to study for university entrance exams. Eli, also a former kibbutz member, is reminded of his past love affair with the child's mother. The child, who might even be his own, arouses ambivalent feels in Eli—Eli loves him for being his mother's son, and at the same time he hates him for perhaps being the son of another man. Although Shai shows some warmth to Eli, Eli gradually begins to react only with hostility, even to the extent of placing the child in dangerous situations.

THREE HOURS IN JUNE (Shalosh Sha'ot Be'Yuni), 1967.

Dir.: Ilan Eldad*; Sc.: Moshe Hadar; Ph.: Nissim (Nitcho) Leon*; Edit.: Esther Feldman, Helga Cranston; Music: Melvin Keller; Narr.: Shraga Friedman, Dina Doron, Moshe Hovev; Narr. (English version): Chaim Herzog.

Produced by the Israel Defense Forces, this documentary covers the military victory of the Six Day War. It tells the story of the role of the Israeli air force during the war and was seen in Israeli cinemas for weeks. The documentary footage includes actual aerial combat shots of dogfights taken by automatic cameras mounted on air force fighters. Flying low over the Mitla Pass in the Sinai desert, the cameras photographed endless lines of destroyed military equipment abandoned in the desert by the retreating Egyptians. These scenes today visually symbolize the triumph of the Israelis against the well-equipped armies of the enemy.

In addition, the film portrays reenacted sequences including personal stories, such as that of a tractor driver from Kibbutz Ha'On near the Sea of Galilee, whose fields and homes were shelled from the Syrian positions and whose children lived in shelters until the Six Day War liberated them from danger. There is also a story of an Israeli pilot, shot down near the Suez Canal, who is rescued by comrades who fly by helicopter across enemy-held territory during darkness to bring him home to safety.

THROUGH THE VEIL OF EXILE (M'Be'ad L'Re'alat Hagalut), 1992.

Dir. & Ph.: David Benchetrit*; Prod.: David Benchetrit, Sini Bar-David, Amos Mokadi; Edit.: Sini Bar-David; Music: Elias Taissir (in Arabic and English).

This documentary film tells the story of three Palestinian women from different backgrounds who live in exile. Their exile is both political and personal. On the political level, their families are refugees and were displaced by the conflict between the Israelis and the Palestinians. On the personal level, these women are out of place, to a certain degree, within their own society. Shot during the period of the first *intifada* (uprising), the camera follows them in their everyday lives, recording the poverty of the refugee camps, the oppression of women within Arab society, and the humiliation of the occupation. This is the human side of the Palestinian–Israeli conflict—a look behind the veil.

Dalal Abu-Kamar is a 33-year-old single Muslim woman living in the dreary Shateh refugee camp. As a youngster, she was politically active, running arms and fingering collaborators. This was her way to gain independence in the suffocating Arab society. Instead, it brought her incarceration by the Israelis for most of her youth. She says that "sorrow is a way of life" in Gaza. She bemoans the fact that she has no independence, even after all that she did for the George Habash PFLP (Popular Front for the Liberation of Palestine), and she is "just another girl from Gaza."

Mary Khass is a 60-year-old English-speaking woman from a Christian family in Haifa. After the Six Day War of 1967, she and her husband decided to move to Gaza City in order to provide their children with a Palestinian identity. As Christian Israeli Arabs, they were considered outsiders in the Muslim society of Gaza, and it took them many years to fit in. They were more successful, however, in providing their children with a newfound identity. Their son, Majed, went to Lebanon to fight against the Israelis, and today he is living in exile in Egypt. Mary, who feels guilty for having made her son into a soldier, goes to the border crossing at Rafiah, where she can shout to him through the barbed wire.

Umm Muhammed is a 53-year-old widowed peasant woman who lives and toils in the shockingly stark and barren Ein Sultan refugee camp near Jericho and who is the mother of eight. She remembers with a smile that she was married at the tender age of 13 and that she used to leave her first baby at home so that she could go out and play with the other children. Living in dire poverty in a mostly abandoned refugee camp, she feels that Allah has forgotten them and says, "We are the phantoms of the desert."

TIME OF FAVOR (Hahesder), 2000.

Dir. & Sc.: Joseph Cedar*; Prod.: David Mandil, Eyal Shiray; Ph.: Ofer Inov; Edit.: Tova Asher; Cast: Aki Avni, Tinkerbell, Assi Dayan*, Idan Alterman, Amnon Wolf.

Awards: Best Film, Best Director, Best Actor (Aki Avni), Best Actress (Tinkerbell), Best Cinematography, Best Screenplay, Best Editing, Israeli Academy Awards (2000).

The film tells the story of modern young Orthodox men, part of the settler movement, who study at a yeshivah in the West Bank and serve in the army in their own platoon. It is a touching story of young love and, at the same time, a compelling story of the dangers of religious extremism. The film works on two levels; on the political level, it reflects the dangers of exploiting religious fervor for political and violent ends; on the more human level, it criticizes the settlement movement for its lack of sensitivity to the needs and suffering of its individual members.

Menachem (Aki Avni) is an officer in the army and has been chosen by the

Aki Avni (center) in *Time of Favor* (Joseph Cedar, 2000). Photo reprinted with the permission and courtesy of Joseph Cedar.

charismatic rabbi of his yeshivah (Assi Dayan) to be the commander of their own company of religious soldiers. His friend Pini (Idan Alterman) is a brilliant Talmud scholar. The rabbi, who preaches religious and political extremism, has chosen Pini to marry his daughter Michal (Tinkerbell). Michal, however, is unwilling to put up with her father's manipulations. Heavily influenced by the memories of her mother, who died years ago of cancer, Michal spurns Pini, and it becomes apparent that she and Menachem are falling in love. As religious young people they are forbidden to touch; instead, they erotically play with each other's hands as they shadow-dance on the wall.

Menachem is working hard at building up his company, teaching the soldiers how to overcome weakness in battle, and is preparing them for their final ceremony at the Western Wall. Pini, harboring resentment about Michal and believing that he understands better than anyone else their role as required by God, plans a shockingly violent and dangerous mission for the same evening. Michal, realizing that a conspiracy is under way, alerts the Israeli secret service. Menachem, the commander of the unit, is humiliated, and the rabbi is incriminated, but the disaster has been averted.

TIME OF THE CHERRIES (Onat Haduvdevanim), 1991.

Dir.: Haim Bouzaglo*; Prod.: Riki Shelach (Nissimoff), Abraham Gedalia, Huguette Elhadad Azran; Sc.: Haim Bouzaglo, Hirsch Goodman; Ph.: Oren Shmukler; Edit.: Ira Lapid; Music: Adi Renart; Cast: Gil Frank, Idit Teperson,

Sasson Gabai, Tzachi Noy, Avi Gilor, David Milton-Jones, David Danino, Dor Zweigenbom; Guest appearances: Shlomo Tarshish, Avi Pnini, Levana Finkelstein*.

Awards: Best Supporting Actor (Sasson Gabai), Best Cinematography, Best Sound (David Lis, Ira Lapid, David Uzichov), Israeli Academy Awards (1991).

Presenting a surrealistic commentary on the futility of war in general and on the 1982 War in Lebanon in particular, the film contains strong visual images—a grenade placed in a doves' nest with eggs waiting to be hatched; slaughtered sheep on a hillside as the nearby shepherd plays a lamentation on his flute.

Mickey (Gil Frank) is a young advertising executive. When his unit is called up for reserve duty toward the end of the war, he begins to be obsessed with his supposed destiny and goes to the nearby cemetery to look at the graves that are being prepared for soldiers killed in Lebanon. An American journalist (Idit Teperson) and her crew become attached to Mickey's unit. They have come to Israel in order to get the big story of the war. As she follows Mickey's unit during their service in Lebanon, she develops a strong relationship with Mickey. Choco (Sasson Gabai), his closest friend, has a brief encounter with danger and suddenly becomes religious. Trembling, he recites a prayer of thanks to God for having saved him from death.

Another member of their unit is a magician, a strange individual who has a soliloquy in which he is hooded, like an executioner or informer, and yells at his own shadow, accusing it of risking his life and bringing him to this "crazy land of slaughter." The magician also presents a show for his friends on their last night in Lebanon, a culmination to the film, in which he "conducts" an imaginary orchestra playing the grand finale from Tchaikovsky's *1812 Overture* over the hills of Lebanon while shells are exploding in the background. In this highly symbolic scene, the magician wears carved dove's wings, the final symbol of the army unit as they depart from Lebanon, having been a bearer of "peace" in a land of civil strife. The cynicism of this symbol is made even clearer when Mickey's unit is caught in the eye of the American television camera as tragedy strikes.

TRANSIT, 1980.

Dir.: Daniel Wachsmann*; Prod.: Ya'ackov (Yankul) Goldwasser*; Sc.: Daniel Horvitz, Daniel Wachsmann; Ph.: Ilan Rosenberg; Edit.: Asher Tlalim*, Levi Zini; Music: Shlomo Gronich*; Cast: Gedalia Besser*, Yitzhak Ben-Tzur, Liora Rivlin, Amnon Moskin, Fanny Lubitsch, Yair Elazar, Ruth Geller, Gideon Zinger, Moti Shirin, Geta Luca, Talia Shapira.

Award: Best Actor (Gedalia Besser), Israel Film Center (1979).

Reflective of Israel as a society of new immigrants, the film portrays people who are cut off from their culture and roots and who feel that they never truly belong. The film is about the alienation of one such immigrant, who finds it too difficult to adjust to the new environment and to deal with the problems of belonging in such strange surroundings.

In the late 1960s, a German refugee, Nussbaum (Gedalia Besser), is living in Tel Aviv. He has not been able to become accustomed to the dirt, the language, the crowds, and their bad manners. Divorced from his wife, who is much younger than he, he has become a lonely man with few friends, a man who does not fit in anywhere. His apartment house is being torn down, and he has to get out, so he moves into a cheap hotel in a depressing area of the city. Finally, Nussbaum decides to leave. Years later, his son, looking back, not understanding why his father left, tells his story.

THE TRAVELER (Oreyach Be'Onah Hametah; Alternative title: *Customer in the Dead Season*; French title: *Le Client de la Morte Saison*), 1970.

Dir.: Moshe Mizrahi*; Prod.: Michel Cousin, Tzvi Shpielman; Co-prod.: France-Israel; Sc.: Moshe Mizrahi, Rachel Fabian; Ph.: Etien Sabo; Music: Georges Moustaki; Edit.: Dov Hoenig; Cast: Hans-Christian Blech, Claude Rich, Henya Sucar-Ziv, Amos Kenan.

An anti-Nazi and pro-French resistance film, the story is about someone who tries to run away from his past. After 20 years of living the life of an average citizen, a former Nazi becomes obsessed not with overcoming his guilt but rather with the possibility of others' discovering his past.

A former Gestapo officer (Hans-Christian Blech) who actively opposed the French resistance during World War II has rebuilt his life as an innkeeper, living in Eilat. One day, a French stranger (Claude Rich) appears and seduces his attractive wife (Henya Sucar-Ziv). The stranger reminds the innkeeper of his past, and he begins to suspect something. Completely overcome with the fear of being discovered, he murders the stranger. Later, returning to his café, he is horrified to find another stranger.

THE TRUE STORY OF PALESTINE (Etz O Palestine), 1962.

Dir.: Nathan Axelrod*, Yoel Zilberg*, Uri Zohar*; Prod.: Nathan Axelrod*, Avraham (Pashanel) Deshe; Sc.: Haim Hefer; Edit.: Leah Axelrod; Music: Yitzhak (Ziko) Graziani; Narr.: Haim Topol*, Uri Levy.

Using newsreels from the Carmel collection (which were produced from 1935 to 1958) and mixing them with an updated and humorous narration, this documentary film looks at the Zionist enterprise, the establishment of the state of Israel, and the early years of the state. Including extraordinary visuals such as water buffalo and the draining of the Hula swamp, harvesting of olives, early farming methods, and cultural events including theater and dance of the 1930s, the film is a fast-paced journey into nostalgia, which was popular with cinema audiences of the time.

A TRUMPET IN THE WADI (Chatzotzrah Be'Vadi), 2001.

Dir.: Lena and Slava Chaplin; Prod.: Riki Shelach (Nissimoff); Sc.: Amit Lior, based on the book by Sami Michael; Ph.: Itzik Portal; Edit.: Bracha Zisman-Cohen; Music: Evyatar Banai; Cast: Alexander Senderovich, Khawlah Hag-

Debsy, Raeda Adon, Salwa (Nakkara) Haddad, Itzhak (Babi) Ne'eman, Imad Gabarin.

Awards: Best Film, Haifa (2001); Best Original Television Drama, Israeli Academy Awards (2001).

A literary adaptation, the film is the tragic story of two young lovers trying to bridge the gap between Israeli Arabs and Jews. The film takes place against the background of the difficult political period of the first *intifada* (1987–1991), when tensions were high.

Mary and Huda are Christian Arab sisters, living with their mother and grandfather in a poor area of Haifa. Huda, the older sister, has not yet found a suitor. Mary is currently breaking up with her boyfriend, a neighborhood hooligan. Alex (Alexander Senderovich), a new immigrant from Russia, moves into the roof apartment in their building. In a moving scene, he saves the family from an attack by the hooligan. Although Alex is short and Jewish and expresses himself poorly in Hebrew, Huda finds his strong sense of responsibility toward his neighbors, his extraordinary sense of humor, and his trumpet playing very compelling. Soon they fall in love, but the story takes place during a difficult time, and Huda's family does not approve of their relationship. Although Huda decides to commit her life to Alex and to have his child, the story ends in tragedy.

TWO KUNI LEMEL (Shnei Kuni Lemel; Alternative title: *The Flying Matchmaker*), 1966.

Dir.: Yisrael Becker; Prod.: Mordechai Navon*; Sc.: Yisrael Becker, Alexander Maimon, based on a play by Avraham Goldfaden; Ph.: Adam Greenberg*, Romolo Gorani; Music: Shaul Barzovsky, Moshe Sahar; Edit.: Nellie Bogor-Gilad; Adviser: David Perlov*; Cast: Mike Burstyn*, Firman Onikovsky, Rina Ganor, Shmuel Rodensky*, Raphael Klatchkin, Aharon Moskin, Elisheva Michaeli, Oshik Levy, Hanan Goldblatt, Mordechai Arnon, Shlomo Vishinsky, Pesach'ke Burstein.

Inspired by classical Yiddish literature, the film is a musical comedy. It tells the story of a schlemiel who lives in a shtetl in Eastern Europe at the beginning of the twentieth century. The comedy of errors that ensues when the hero dresses up like the schlemiel is a metaphor for the ambivalent issues of identity of the Jew in the modern period. The grand finale of the musical, which includes songs and dance, is performed by the people of the entire shtetl. Polish-born film director Yisrael Becker (b. 1917), is an artist and actor in Habima Theater. In addition to this film, he wrote the script and starred in the Holocaust film classic *Lang ist der Weg* (Herbert Fredersdorf, 1947).

Caroline (Rina Ganor), the daughter of a wealthy man (Shmuel Rodensky), is in love with Max (Mike Burstyn). Max visits Caroline as her French tutor, but it doesn't take her father long to realize that he's not really a tutor, and he throws him out. Her father asks Kalman the matchmaker (Raphael Klatchkin) to find his daughter a match. Kalman finds the son of a rich man from a nearby town, but the young man, Kuni Lemel (also played by Mike Burstyn), limps, and stutters, and is very shy. Max, realizing that he might lose his girlfriend, develops a strategy. He dresses up like Kuni Lemel, and when the real Kuni Lemel is on his way to meet the bride, Max's friends divert him from the correct road. Meanwhilc, Max presents himself as the groom. When the real Kuni Lemel finally arrives, a comedy of errors ensues as people go in and out of rooms and mistaken identities are the name of the game. At the end, Kuni Lemel chooses to marry the daughter of Kalman, the matchmaker, and Max marries Caroline.

Sequels: *Kuni Lemel in Tel Aviv* (Yoel Zilberg, 1976), *Kuni Lemel in Cairo* (Yoel Zilberg, 1983).

UNDER THE DOMIM TREE (Etz HaDomim Tafus), 1995.

Dir.: Eli Cohen*; Prod.: Gila Almagor*, Eitan Even; Sc: Gila Almagor, Eyal Sher; Ph.: David Gurfinkel*; Edit.: Dani Schick; Music: Benny Nagari; Cast: Kaipo Cohen, Juliano Mer, Riki Blich, Orly Perl, Ohad Knoller, Genia Katzan, Aya Shiftel, Gila Almagor, Alex Peleg, Ohad Shachar, Uri Avrahami, Yael Perl.

Awards: Wolgin Award, Jerusalem (1995); Best Cinematography, Best Art Director (Eitan Levy), Best Costume Design (Rona Doron), Israeli Academy Awards (1995).

A sequel to *Summer of Aviya** and based on autobiographical elements of Gila Almagor's childhood, the film portrays the painful struggles of a group of Holocaust survivor children all living together in a youth village (boarding school) during the early 1950s.

Aviya (Kaipo Cohen) is a sabra (native-born Israeli) pupil at a youth village. Most of the other children, however, are survivors. Her mother (Gila Almagor), who fled Europe and went to Palestine before the war, is a survivor in the sense that she lost everyone who was important to her, friends, family, her entire world. She even lost her husband to Arab gunfire in 1939 Palestine, before Aviya was born. Her guilt and grief for having survived, when her entire family perished, have caused her to live in a world of memories and fears. One of the children, wise beyond his years, explains this behavior to Aviya: "There are those who were there and want to forget, and there are those who live as if they were there."

Aviya's boyfriend has serious emotional problems. He is inseparable from his friend; together they survived the war living like animals in the forests of Europe. Late at night, they prowl the grounds of the school, howling like wolves. A new girl, Miri, hides when her parents visit the school; she insists that they are not her real parents. The entire matter eventually goes to court, where it becomes shockingly clear that these apparently good-hearted people simply wanted Miri in place of the child whom they had lost.

UNDER WESTERN EYES (Leneged Einayim Ma'araviyot), 1996.

Dir. & Sc.: Joseph Pitchhadze*; Prod.: Dubi Baruch, Joseph Pitchhadze; Ph.:

Shai Goldman; Edit.: Dov Steuer; Music: Barry Sakharof; Cast: Eyal Shechter, Liat Glick, Ezra Kafri, Carmel Betto.

Awards: Ecumenical Jury Prize for Best Feature Film, Berlin (1997); Outstanding Auteur Film Prize and Special Mention of FIPRESCI Jury, Belgrade (1997); Wolgin Award, Jerusalem (1996).

The film is a combination road movie and detective story. Using slow and measured pacing, it includes remarkable photography and beautiful desert scenery.

Gary (Eyal Shechter) is a young man, an architect, living in Berlin. His father, who was imprisoned 20 years ago for spying for the Soviets against Israel, has escaped from the prison hospital. Two detectives, obsessed with the case, send Gary a phony fax saying that his father has died, in order to coax him to come to Israel, and convince him to cooperate in finding the escaped convict.

Gary, however, is a complicated young man, with ambivalent feelings toward his father. Arriving at the airport, he picks up a young woman, an actress (Liat Glick), and together they go to the desert in search of his father. They search out Joshua, his father's cellmate from prison. Gary gradually builds up his willingness to confront his past and finally see his father, only to be disappointed when he finds him, murdered by one of the detectives, in a shack not far from Joshua's place.

URBAN FEEL (Kesher Ir), 1998.

Dir. & Sc.: Jonathan Sagall*; Prod.: Eyal Shiray, Jonathan Sagall, David Mandil, Michael Tapuach; Ph.: Dror Moreh; Edit.: Dalia Kastel; Music: Joseph Bardanashvili; Cast: Dafna Rechter, Sharon Alexander*, Jonathan Sagall, Asi Levy, Shmil Ben-Ari, Techiya Danon, Ziv Baruch, Zachi Dichner, Alon Dahan.

Awards: Golden Palm Tree, Valencia (1999); Bulgarian Film Critics' Award, Varna, Bulgaria (2000); Best Film, Haifa (1998); Best Actress (Dafna Rechter), Best Supporting Actress (Asi Levi), Israeli Academy Awards (1998).

A film of real emotions, the story is about the fleeting nature of love and the reality of marriage. Much of the film is seen peeking through windows and doors, often from the vantage point of the little boy in the family, symbolizing relationships that have no depth and that are not always what they appear. Not shying away from showing the human body, the film uses elements of the surreal to portray the human condition of loneliness and despair.

Emanuel (Jonathan Sagall) returns from an extended stay in the Far East and crashes at the home of his ex-girlfriend (Dafna Rechter), whose husband searches for sexual partners in the want ads. The ensuing sexual relationship between Emanuel and the young wife stems not only from reawakened feelings but also from the boredom of the contemporary family situation.

VARIATIONS ON A LOVE THEME (Isha Becheder Hasheni; Alternative title: *The Woman in the Other Room*), 1967.

Dir., Prod., & Sc.: Yitzhak (Tzepel) Yeshurun*; Ph.: Yachin Hirsch; Edit.: Tova Biran; Music: Melvin Keller; Cast: Natan Cogan, Ruth Segal, Tziona Tuchterman, Amnon Berenson.

Made in the style of the European intellectual filmmaking of the period, the film is a study of the dynamics of relationships, without much dialogue or action. Feelings of tension, jealousy, and depression are strongly conveyed, as are misunderstandings, needs, and the fear of expressing them.

A young couple (Amnon Berenson, Tziona Tuchterman) invites older friends over for the weekend. The older man (Natan Cogan) is attracted to his hostess, while his wife (Ruth Segal) is having a nervous breakdown. Hurt and frustrated, the young host takes an interest in the other's wife. Each sleeps with the other. A new day dawns. Nothing is said.

THE VULTURE (Ha'Ayit), 1981.

Dir., Prod., & Sc.: Yaki Yosha*, based on the novel *The Last Jew* by Yoram Kaniuk; Ph.: Ilan Rosenberg; Edit.: Anat Lubarsky; Music: Jacob Rotblit; Cast: Shraga Harpaz, Shimon Finkel, Nitza Shaul, Hannah Meron*, Andy Richman, Ami Weinberg, Anat Atzmon*, Ophelia Shtruhl, Yoel Sher.

A literary adaptation, the film is about the effects of war on the souls of young Israelis and the understandable need for grieving parents to idealize their young sons who have been sacrificed in battle. The film examines the tension between the battle-weary soldier's desire to return to normal life after war and his need to cling to the memories of the past, a tension that affected an entire generation of young people in the aftermath of the 1973 Yom Kippur War.

Boaz (Shraga Harpaz) returns from the Yom Kippur War feeling guilty that he is alive and that his friend, Menachem, has been killed in a pointless battle during the last moments before the cease-fire. During a visit to Menachem's parents (Shimon Finkel and Hannah Meron), Boaz suddenly finds himself making up things in an effort to make his parents proud. Menachem died for the cheap thrill of killing a few Egyptians, even after the cease-fire went into effect. Yet Boaz talks about the poetry that Menachem supposedly wrote, and he becomes caught up in the lie of trying to make Menachem into something that he was not. Boaz, sensitive to the needs of others and confused about his feelings, carries on an affair with Menachem's girlfriend (Andy Richman). Feeling unable to return to normal life, he spends his time memorializing those who have died and becomes obsessed, preparing commemorative albums and memorial ceremonies and, like a bird of prey, living off the memories of war.

WEDDING IN GALILEE (Chatunah Be'Galil), 1987.

Dir. & Sc.: Michel Khleifi; Prod.: Georges Khleifi, Jacqueline Louis, Bernard Lorain; Co-prod.: France-Belgium-Palestine; Ph.: Walter van den Ende; Edit.: Marie Castro-Vasquez; Music: Jean Marie Sinaya; Cast: Ali Al Akili, Makram Khoury*, Yusuf Abu-Warda, Bushara Karaman, Juliano Mer, Anna Achadian, Sonia Amar, Nazih Akleh.

The film portrays the tensions between Israeli military authorities and Arab villagers in the Galilee (within the state of Israel). The first feature film to be directed by an Israeli Arab, the film deals with generational differences in political consciousness, family tensions, and sexual inadequacies, all against the background of the Israeli military control of the Galilee (which ended in 1966). Film director Michel Khleifi (b. 1950 in Nazareth) has been based in Belgium since the 1970s.

The village elder (Ali Al Akili) wants to give his son a proper, traditional wedding, which will last into the night. The village, however, is under military curfew. The Military Governor (Makram Khoury) finally agrees to permit the wedding to take place at night, on the condition that he and his retinue are invited. Many younger radicals, including the groom, are angered by this development. As the wedding takes place, tension develops as to whether or not the village radicals will implement a violent action and take the Military Governor hostage. As the evening progresses, the groom's impotence is revealed (a narrative element that was heavily criticized in Arab countries).

WEST SIDE GIRL (Na'arat Haparvarim), 1979.

Dir.: George Ovadiah*; Prod.: Michael Shvili, Benny Shvili; Sc.: Bezalel Aloni, Michael Shvili; Ph.: Achsani Kodarella; Edit.: Zion Avrahmian; Music: Shaike Faikov; Cast: Ofra Haza, Menachem Einay, Uri Selah, Avner Dan, Nahum Shalit, Shish Koller, Ruth Bikel, Uri Alon, Reuven Dayan, Yossi Segal.

Combining melodrama and musical elements, the film tells the story of the discovery of a great singer, a fairy-tale story from the street to fame and success. The story is reminiscent of Charlie Chaplin's *City Lights*, about the main character's love for a blind flower vendor.

Vered (Ofra Haza) is a simple blind girl who sells cigarettes and chocolates on the street. She is also a beautiful young woman, serious and thoughtful, and a very talented singer. Three surprisingly simple yet well-intentioned young men, who become her friends, will do anything to raise the money necessary for the surgery she needs in order to see again. One of the three is falling in love with her and decides to steal the money for her operation from the local moneylender. Two of them get arrested while the third takes her to the hospital. Finally cured of her blindness, she gets picked up by a fancy musician who begins to arrange her career for her. When her friends get out of prison, they search for her and find her at a singing performance in Jerusalem. All ends well as it is clear that she has not forgotten her friends.

WHAT A GANG! (Chavura She'Ka'Zot), 1962.

Dir.: Ze'ev Havatzelet; Prod.: Mordechai Navon*, Yitzhak Agadati, Bomba Tzur; Sc.: Yisrael Wessler, Shaul Biber, Bomba Tzur, based on a story by Yisrael (Putcho) Wessler; Ph.: Nissim (Nitcho) Leon*; Edit.: Anna Gurit; Music: Alexander (Sasha) Argov; Cast: Yossi Banai, Bomba Tzur, Oded Teomi, Avner

Hezkiyahu, Gila Almagor*, Miriam Sharon, Shoshana Duar, Gideon Zinger, Natan Cogan, Emmanuel Ben-Amos, Illy Gorlitzky.

A comedy about a young recruit in the elite Palmach underground army during the period prior to the establishment of the state of Israel, the film pokes fun at Israel's preoccupation with the military. Film director Ze'ev Havatzelet (1922–1962) studied film in Italy, where he had the opportunity to work with Rossellini, Fellini and De Sica. He died in a tragic accident one week before the film was released to the cinema.

Tel Aviv, 1946. Yossinu (Yossi Banai) leaves his mother (Shoshana Duar) and his home to join a group of youngsters as new members of Kibbutz Palmachim. The newest member of the group, Yossinu finds himself the butt of much healthy humor, as he slowly adjusts to his new surroundings. Under the supervision of their commander, the group learns to grapple with the everyday life on the kibbutz—working in the fields, military training, face-to-face combat, target practice, and planning anti-British actions. Meanwhile, as Yossinu's mother attempts to convince him to leave the cooperative lifestyle and return to Tel Aviv, it is time for Yossinu and his friends to prepare to receive the next group of recruits.

WHEN NIGHT FALLS (Ad Sof Halaylah; Alternative title: *Into the Night*), 1985.

Dir. & Sc.: Eitan Green; Prod.: Micha Sharfstein; Ph.: Amnon Salomon*; Edit.: Ira Lapid; Music: Yitzhak Klepter; Cast: Assi Dayan*, Yoseph Millo, Orna Porat, Danny Roth, Haya Pik-Pardo, Lasha Rosenberg, Amos Lavie, Irit Sheleg, Ilana Badash, Rafi Adar, Shmuel Tenneh.

Awards: Second Prize, Best Screenplay, Israel Film Center (1985).

The film portrays the alienation caused by city life, focusing on the cheating, violence, and drinking. The darkness of Tel Aviv is contrasted with the brightness and airiness of Nahariya, where the protagonist's parents live. The film focuses entirely on the owner of a Tel Aviv pub whose family crises are a metaphor for societal crises. Film director Eitan Green is also a film critic and edited books about film; his other feature films include *Lena* (1982) and *American Citizen** (1992).

Giora (Assi Dayan) runs a bar and dreams of opening a restaurant. He has made a mess of his life—his marriage is in trouble, since he is pathologically cheating on his wife; his parents (Yoseph Millo and Orna Porat) have separated; and his father arrives for an extended visit from Nahariya. Giora spends time with his army buddies, recalling their experiences during the War in Lebanon. His father is undergoing a major life crisis and finds both the loneliness of the city and his son's lifestyle unappealing. As a non-Jew in a Jewish society, he feels estranged, an outsider who has never been able to adapt, and contemplates suicide. Eventually, Giora's parents decide to attempt a reconciliation, until tragedy strikes.

WHITE NIGHT (Layla Lavan), 1995.

Dir.: Arnon Zadok*; Prod.: Arnon Zadok, Doron Eran*; Sc.: Yoav Halevy, Arnon Zadok; Ph.: Ofer Harari; Music: Adi Renart; Edit.: Dani Schik; Cast: Shalom Shmuelov, Sharon Alexander*, Shmil Ben-Ari, Liora Rivlin, Arnon Zadok.

Award: Prix de la Jeunesse, Cannes (1996).

With a clear antidrug addiction message, the film tells a hard-hitting story of the brutality and humiliation of prison life and the terrible difficulties faced by those trying to break a drug addiction. There is a clear tension within the prison between those struggling to break their addictions and those who are pushing the drugs because of the power that it brings them.

A white-collar inmate (Sharon Alexander) becomes the cellmate of Charlie, a hardened criminal (Shalom Shmuelov). One is Ashkenazi, and the other is Sephardi. The two eventually become soulmates, and the white-collar inmate helps his new friend break his cocaine habit.

WINTER GAMES (Mischakim Ba'Horef), 1988.

Dir.: Ram Loevy*; Prod.: Baruch Aboulouf; Sc.: Dita Gerry, Meir Doron, Gilad Evron, Ram Loevy, based on a story by Yitzhak Ben-Nir; Ph.: Yechiel Cohen; Edit.: Ira Lapid; Music: Ilan Wurtzberg; Cast: Gal Yachas, Moshe Ivgi*, Dov Navon, Constantin Anatol, Rae Roz, Ruth Geller, Tuvia Gelber, Varda Ben-Chor, Manny Savir, Arieh Elias.

A historical drama, the film depicts life in a small Jewish town outside Haifa during the end of the British Mandate period and explores themes of maturity, friendship, and trust. Eli and Adina are changed by their relationship with a newcomer to their village (Moshe Ivgi). Eli is 11 years old, and Adina is a few years older. Each, in his or her own way, shoulders the burden of caring for and hiding the wounded Jewish terrorist.

WOMEN (Nashim), 1996.

Dir. & Sc.: Moshe Mizrahi*; Prod.: Micha Sharfstein, Amitan Menelzon, based on the story *Bi'kedusha* by Yehuda Burla; Ph.: Amnon Zlayet; Edit.: Tova Asher; Music: Avihu Medina; Cast: Michal Bat-Adam*, Amos Lavie, Ilor Harpaz, Yoseph Shiloah*, Rivka Gur, Geula Nuni.

Award: Best Actor (Amos Lavie), Israeli Academy Awards (1996).

The film takes place in Jerusalem of the nineteenth century, with beautiful photography of the old alleyways and stone courtyards of the Old City. It is a story about love, jealousy, barrenness, the difficulties of two women vying for the attentions of one man, and, ultimately, about intimacy and friendship. These are traditional Jews who quote the Bible and believe in living by its teachings.

Rivka (Michal Bat-Adam) is the devoted wife of Ya'akov, a kabbalist (Amos Lavie). After 15 years of a childless marriage, Rivka decides to take her young cousin, Sultana, as a second wife to her husband. At first, Ya'akov is opposed to the idea, but he eventually gives in to his wife's devotion and insistence.

Sultana comes to live with them, and things seem good at first, but eventually Rivka cannot deny the jealousy that is growing within herself. When she runs away, Sultana finds her and tells her that she is willing to live with Ya'akov only if Rivka is with her—she loves Rivka and wants to live with Rivka more than she desires Ya'akov. Sultana is pregnant, and both women decide to return together.

THE WOODEN GUN (Roveh Chuliot), 1979.

Dir. & Sc.: Ilan Moshenson; Prod.: Eitan Even, Richard Sanders, John Hardy; Ph.: Gadi Danzig; Edit.: Zion Avrahamian; Music: Yossi Mar-Chaim; Cast: Judith Soleh, Michael Kafir, Leon Young, Ophelia Shtruhl, Louis Rosenberg, Arik Rosen, Nadav Brenner, Nissim Eliaz.

Awards: Best Screenplay, Best Music, Israel Film Center (1979).

Evoking the early years following independence, the film interweaves elements concerning the centuries-old longing of the people to return to their homeland, the trauma of the Holocaust, the ideology of the founding generation of Zionist leaders, and the consciousness of a nation living in the shadow of war. The narrative construct portrays a deep psychological struggle through the games of children. In addition to this film, director Ilan Moshenson directed films for educational television and one additional feature film, *Crazy Weekend* (1986).

Yoni (Arik Rosen), whose mother escaped from Europe just prior to World War II, is a sensitive and intelligent 10-year-old boy. The tense atmosphere of the times is portrayed through his escapades with his friends and their encounters with the adults in their world—his father, his schoolteacher, the school principal, and an earthy woman named Palestina (Ophelia Shtruhl), a Holocaust survivor haunted by nightmares who lives in a hut on the beach. Yoni's growing understanding and awareness become apparent as he watches a friend and his family pack to leave the country, when he shoots a boy in a rumble with an opposing gang—ironically, he has shot the boy who plays Theodor Herzl in the school play—and when he is soothed by Palestina.

WORLDS APART (Al Tishalu Im Ani Ohev; Alternative title: *Don't Ask Me If I Love*), 1979.

Dir.: Barbara Noble; Prod.: Amos Kollek*, Rafi Reibenbach; Sc.: Amos Kollek, Mark Dickerman, based on a book by Amos Kollek; Ph.: David Gurfinkel*; Edit.: Alain Jakubowicz; Music: Nurit Hirsch; Cast: Amos Kollek, Shelby Livingston, Joe Cortez, Shraga Harpaz, Yossi Yadin, Lia Koenig, Liron Nirgad, Gidi Gov, Yossi Pollack, Avi Lugia.

A romance about a young man who falls for an American tourist visiting Jerusalem, the story revolves against the background of the Arab–Israeli conflict and shows that things are usually more complicated than they seem at first.

Assaf (Amos Kollek) and Ram serve together on military reserve duty in the Judean Hills. Assaf strikes up a relationship with Lee (Shelby Livingston), an American tourist who is spending a lot of time in the Old City of Jerusalem.

Evelyn Kaplun and Moscu Alcalay in *Yana's Friends* (Arik Kaplun, 1999). Photo courtesy of the Jerusalem Cinematheque, reprinted with the permission of Marek Rozenbaum.

Late one night, after a party, Ram recognizes a terrorist from a skirmish in the Judean Hills. He chases him through the alleys of the Old City and is killed. Having heard the shot, Assaf runs to him and sees the terrorist escaping. When Assaf goes to the jail to find out why Mustafa, a friend of Lee's, has been jailed, he recognizes him right away as the terrorist who killed Ram. After Mustafa is released, Assaf drives him out into the desert, intending to kill him. Meanwhile, Assaf's romance with Lee is developing, until tragedy strikes.

YANA'S FRIENDS (Haverim Shel Yana), 1999.

Dir.: Arik Kaplun*; Prod.: Uri Sabag, Einat Bikel, Marek Rozenbaum*, Moshe Levinson; Sc.: Arik Kaplun, Simeon Vinokur; Ph.: Valentin Belanogov; Edit.: Tali Halter-Shenkar, Einat Glazer-Zarhin; Music: Avi Binyamin; Cast: Nir Levi, Evelyn Kaplun, Shmil Ben-Ari, Moscu Alcalay, Dalia Friedland, Lucy Dubinchek, Israel Demidov.

Awards: Grand Prix Crystal Globe and Special Mention of Ecumenical Jury, Best Actress (Evelyn Kaplun), Karlovy Vary (1999); Artistic Expression Award, Rome (1999); Public Prize, Montpellier (1999); Best Director, Moscow (1999); Best Foreign Film, Houston (2000); Wolgin Award, Jerusalem (1999); Best Film, Best Director, Best Actor (Nir Levi), Best Actress (Evelyn Kaplun), Best Supporting Actor (Moscu Alcalay), Best Supporting Actress (Dalia Friedland), Best Cinematography, Best Screenplay, Best Editing, Best Art Direction (Ariel Rochko), Israeli Academy Awards (1999).

The film, which takes place against the background of the Gulf War, portrays a variety of quirky characters, many of whom are immigrants from the former Soviet Union, and reflects the difficulties of new immigrants in a foreign land. The protagonist, feeling lonely and vulnerable in Tel Aviv, finds that she is able to make love to her Israeli-born flatmate only during an air-raid siren and with a gas mask covering her face. Not only does the gas mask protect her from chemical warfare, but it also hides her limitations in the new language and hides her identity. It is the great equalizer between new immigrant and veteran Israeli.

Yana (Evelyn Kaplun) is a new immigrant from the former Soviet Union. On the day that she moves into a room in an apartment in Tel Aviv, her husband returns to Russia. Her new flatmate, Eli (Nir Levi), is a video cameraman who makes a living photographing weddings. Enjoying his role as voyeur, he intrudes into the lives of others, videotaping private moments. As Yana realizes that she has been abandoned by her husband and discovers that she is pregnant, she slowly turns to Eli for support. The Gulf War begins, and they find themselves huddling together in a sealed room. Slowly, Eli learns to relate to Yana as a human being, instead of just one of his video projects, and Yana becomes less restless and better adjusted to her new life in Tel Aviv.

Some of the in-depth colorful characters include a decorated Russian soldier (Moscu Alcalay) and Yana's landlord (Dalia Friedland), who discover that they are long-lost lovers from almost 50 years before.

YELLOW ASPHALT—THREE DESERT STORIES (Asphalt Tzahov), 2000.

Dir., Prod., & Sc.: Dan (Nokyo) Verete; Ph.: Yoram Millo; Edit.: Rachel Yagil, Anna Finkelstein, Jak Hana; Music: Yves Touati; Cast: Sami Samir, Motti Katz, Tatiana Blacher, Raeda Adon, Moshe Ivgi*, Abed Zuabi, Zevik Raz, Hagit Keller, members of the Jahalin Bedouin tribe.

Awards: Special Jury Prize at Cologne (2001); Best Feature, Haifa (2000).

A trilogy portraying the lifestyle of a desert tribe, the film depicts the complex situations that arise from the encounter between the Bedouin traditional culture and that of modern Israel. The cinematography, providing striking desert landscapes, and the music track both complement the enthographic elements. In addition to this film, film director Dan (Nokyo) Verete was a co-scriptwriter for *Hamsin** (Daniel Wachsmann, 1982) and directed *Koko at 19** (1985).

The first vignette, *Black Spot*, is the story of two truckers (Moshe Ivgi, Zevik Raz) who carelessly run over and kill a Bedouin child in the middle of the desert. Realizing what they have done, they throw his body into a ditch and attempt to flee. Meanwhile, a small group of silent but angry Bedouin men congregate around them. Fearful for their lives, they must find a way out of a potentially explosive situation. *Here Is Not There* tells the story of a woman (Tatiana Blacher) who years ago fell in love with a Bedouin man (Abed Zuabi). After they marry and have two daughters, she realizes that things are different from what she had expected, and she requests to return to her father's home. However, Bedouin tradition prevents her from leaving her husband. *Red Roofs* is a drama that tells the story of two Bedouin who work at a nearby Jewish settlement. Suhilla (Raeda Adon) does domestic work for a Jewish family, and Abed (Sami Samir) is the hired hand. When Suhilla's husband becomes suspicious that she is having an affair with the Jewish boss (Motti Katz), matters take a violent turn, and Abed discovers that he is not comfortable living between two worlds.

YOU'RE IN THE ARMY, GIRLS (Banot), 1985.

Dir.: Nadav Levitan*; Prod.: Nissim Levy, Harvey Adinovich; Sc.: Assi Dayan*; Ph.: Marcello Mashioki; Edit.: Nissim Mossek; Music: Yaroslav Yackobovitz; Cast: Helli Goldenberg, Hannah Azoulai-Hasfari*, Anat Topol, Irit Frank, Caroline Langford, Ariella Rabinovich, Sigal Cohen, Orna Rotenberg, Raheli Hiamian, Amos Lavie.

The film combines comedy and drama to present the development of relationships and the growth of group feeling and solidarity among young women undergoing the discipline and rigors of basic training. The story concerns an extremely diversified group of girls, all of whom are eventually transformed into a committed and unified group of young women.

Shuli (Hannah Azoulai-Hasfari) is a Sephardi girl from a development town. Niva (Helli Goldenberg) is a wealthy Ashkenazi "daddy's girl" from north Tel Aviv. Karen (Caroline Langford) is a new immigrant from Canada. Shirley (Irit Frank) is a "druggy" who is resisting serving in the army. Anna (Orna Rotenberg) is a cheerful girl who enjoys indulging in food. Tali (Anat Topol), the squad commander, takes a dislike to Shuli, who gets back at her by getting her boyfriend to make a pass at her. Karen's father wants her back in Canada, but Karen will go to any extreme, even suicide, rather than return. The stories develop as the girls set their sights on their future jobs in the army, following the basic training. More than anything else, Niva wants to join the Entertainment Troupe of the army, and she gets Shuli to pass the test for her. Much to her disappointment, it is actually Shuli who gets accepted.

ZOHAR: MEDITERRANEAN BLUES (Zohar), 1993.

Dir.: Eran Riklis*; Prod.: Micha Sharfstein, Amitan Menelzon, Sc.: Moshe Zondar, Amir Ben-David; Ph.: Amnon Zlayet; Edit.: Einat Glaser-Zarhin; Music: Zohar Argov; Cast: Shaul Mizrachi, Daphna Deckel, Gabi Amrani, Juliano Mer, Menachem Einay, Yitzhak Ne'eman.

Awards: Best Actor (Shaul Mizrachi), Best Sound (Israel David, Rifka Yogev), Israeli Academy Awards (1993).

The film tells the biographical story of Zohar Argov, the Israeli singer who rose to fame during the late 1970s and 1980s and committed suicide in 1987. It is a tragic story of cocaine and how it can destroy someone's life. A success at the box office, the film includes uplifting ethnic music.

As a child, Zohar (Shaul Mizrachi) was ashamed of his drunken father. As a grown man, he remained pitifully in love with his ex-wife, who had moved on and no longer cared for him. Having risen to stardom and known as the "King" of Mizrachi music, he shouldered the intense burden of trying to prove what a Sephardi Jew from a difficult background was capable of achieving. Drugs were his undoing.

THE MEN AND WOMEN OF ISRAELI FILM

As in the case with other national cinemas, the cinema of Israel is the fruit of the labor of many individuals. Some of them have made greater contributions and some of them lesser. However, all of their achievements have contributed to the success and growth of Israeli cinema, both as an art form and as an industry. This chapter is devoted to their contributions and their biographies.

The personalities who appear in this listing have been chosen due to their qualitative and quantitative contributions to Israeli cinema. In addition, recognition in the form of awards has also been taken into consideration. This chapter includes film directors, producers, scriptwriters, actors and actresses, cinematographers, and composers. For reasons of space, biographies for art directors and film editors are not included, even though their important contributions should not be overlooked. Each entry includes biographical information and filmography:

- The filmographies include *only* Israeli productions, even though many of the personalities have also contributed to foreign productions, many of which are mentioned in the biographical entries.
- A wide variety of genres have been included in the filmographies, including feature films, TV dramas, docudramas, shorts, and documentaries. Due to the fact that the focus of this book is feature films, if there is no mention of the genre in a filmography entry, it should be assumed that the film mentioned is a full-length feature film.
- In order to read more about the films listed in each filmography, credits and synopses appear in the main body of this book for those films marked with an asterisk.
- Filmographies refer to each person's role (such as director, actor, etc.) for each film entry. It should be assumed that the role relates to the role stated at the beginning of the biographical entry, unless otherwise stated. For example, if a person is a director,

filmography entries that state "also" imply that he/she is director in addition to other roles for that film. "Only" annuls his/her role as director. In the event that a person is both a director and an actor, or a director and a producer, then "only" and "also" have not been used. Instead, the roles are listed in full for each film entry.

ABOUTBOUL, ALON (Tel Aviv, 1965). Actor.

Aboutboul is an actor of stage and screen whose first major appearance was in Eli Cohen's* film *Ricochets** (Israel Film Center award for his supporting role) in which he appeared as a brash young soldier serving during the war in Lebanon. Aboutboul won an Israel Film Center award for Best Actor for another military role, in Uri Barbash's* *One of Us**. One of Aboutboul's most memorable performances was as the bartender in Amit Goren's* short film *The Cage*, in which he plays a soldier who becomes scarred in his interpersonal relations due to his recent reserve duty on the occupied West Bank.

Filmography

The Guitar, 1982, short / *Cordonia*, 1982, short / *Fun Forever*, 1983 / *Bar 51**, 1984 / *Ricochets*, 1985 / *Mondo Condo*, 1986 / *Prom Queen*, 1986 / *A Place by the Sea*, 1987 / *Photo Roman*, 1988 / *The Cage*, 1989, short / *Streets of Yesterday**, 1989 / *One of Us*, 1989 / *Dual Entity*, 1992 / *Passover Fever**, 1995 / *Yours Forever*, 1996, TV drama / *Egoz*, 1996, TV drama / *Degree*, 1996, TV drama / *First Love*, 1997, TV drama / *Pisces*, 1997, TV drama / *The Other Half*, 1997, TV drama / *Marco Polo**, 1996 / *Saturdays and Holidays*, 1999, TV series / *The Order*, 2000, TV drama / *A Five Minute Walk*, 2002.

AGADATI, BARUCH (Bessarabia, 1895–Lakewood, Ohio, 1976). Producer and Director.

Agadati (original name: Kaushansky) went to live in Palestine in 1910 and began his studies at the Bezalel Academy of Art in Jerusalem. In 1914 he returned to Europe to visit his family and was caught in the throes of World War I. In 1919 he returned to Palestine and lived in Tel Aviv. Agadati was a leading cultural figure and a versatile artist, known as a dancer (having performed Israeli dances abroad), a painter, and the organizer of the Purim carnivals of Tel Aviv.

Together with his brother, Yitzhak Agadati, he opened the AGA Film Company, which produced a small number of newsreels and also produced the first sound feature film in Palestine, *This Is the Land** (1935). The film, telling the story of modern Zionism, is a combination of documentary and drama and showcased Agadati's artistry in producing montage sequences that juxtaposed visual elements.

Filmography

This Is the Land, 1935, docudrama (director) / AGA Newsreels (co-producer) / *Tomorrow's Yesterday*, 1963 (director, producer, co-scriptwriter, cinematographer).

ALEXANDER, SHARON (Tivon, 1962). Actor.

Having studied acting at the Beit Tzvi School in Ramat Gan, Alexander has become a successful actor of stage and screen. He teaches acting and is the founding director of a school of acting. He is well known in Israel for the varied roles that he has played, and he has received two acting awards—the Israel Film Center Award (in Uri Barbash's* *One of Us**) and an Israeli Academy Award (in Assi Dayan's* *Life According to Agfa**).

Filmography

*Growing Pains**, 1979 / *Teacher's Room*, 1981, TV series / *Torn Apart**, 1989 / *One of Us*, 1989 / *Cup Final**, 1990 / *The Deserter's Wife*, 1991 / *Sarah Aharonson*, 1991 / *Amazing Grace**, 1992 / *Tel Aviv Stories**, 1992 / *Life According to Agfa*, 1992 / *Religious Murder*, 1992, TV series / *A Different Light*, 1993, TV drama / *Murder at the Dead Sea*, 1994, TV series / *White Night**, 1995 / *Marco Polo**, 1996 / *Deep Blue*, 1997, TV series / *Café Paris*, 1997, TV series / *Options*, 1997, TV drama / *Chronicle of Love*, 1998 / *Children's Games*, 1999, TV drama / *Cause of Death: Murder*, 1999, TV series / *Urban Feel**, 1999 / *White Lies*, 1999 / *Five Minutes by Foot*, 2000 / *Borovsky House*, 2000 / *A Protected Species*, 2001, TV drama / *A Five Minute Walk*, 2002 / *A Group Portrait with a Woman*, 2002.

ALMAGOR, GILA (Haifa, 1940). Actress.

Almagor grew up in dire poverty in Petah Tikvah. As an only child she cared for her mother, who had lost her entire family in the Holocaust and was slowly losing her grip on reality. Almagor studied at the Habimah Theater's Drama School. She was affiliated with the Cameri Theater for eight years, appeared in theater productions of Habimah, and then began working in film. She has continued to work simultaneously in both theater and film throughout her entire career and is one of Israel's leading ladies of stage and screen.

Almagor won international recognition at the Chicago, Atlanta, and San Antonio Film Festivals for her sensitive portrayal of a war widow in *Siege** (Gilberto Tofano, 1969). In 1986 Almagor published an autobiographical novel for young adults, which told the story of her special relationship with her Holocaust survivor mother. The book became a best-seller, was translated into 16 languages, and became part of the official high school curriculum in Israel. She adapted the book into a one-woman theatrical performance and later into an award-winning film, *Summer of Aviya**, for which she won Best Actress awards—a Silver Bear at Berlin (1989) and an Israeli Film Center Award. A few years later she wrote a sequel, *Under the Domim Tree**, about the friendships that she made while living in the youth village of Hadassim.

Almagor has been a member of the City Council of Tel Aviv since 1998 (in charge of Arts and Cultural Affairs) and has appeared in more than 30 Israeli feature films and dozens of stage plays and television dramas. She was awarded a Life Achievement Award from the Jerusalem Film Festival (1996) and one from the Israeli Academy of Film (1997).

Filmography

*Blazing Sands**, 1960 / *What a Gang!** 1962 / *Eldorado**, 1963 / *Not a Word to Morgenstein*, 1963 / *Sallah**, 1964 / *Trunk to Cairo*, 1966 / *The Girl from the Dead Sea**, 1966 / *Ervinka**, 1967 / *Motive to Kill*, 1967 / *Sabra—Death of a Jew*, 1969 / *Siege*, 1969 (also script idea) / *Highway Queen** 1971 (also co-scriptwriter) / *Escape to the Sun**, 1972 / *The House on Chelouche St.**, 1973 / *Operation Thunderbolt**, 1977 / *Save the Lifeguard**, 1977 / *My Mother, the General**, 1979 / *Hide and Seek**, 1980 / *A Thin Line**, 1980 / *On the Air*, 1981 / *Dead End Street**, 1982 / *First Love**, 1982 / *Summer of Aviya*, 1988 (also co-producer, co-scriptwriter, author) / *Life According to Agfa**, 1992 / *Sh'chur**, 1994 / *Passover Fever**, 1995 / *Under the Domim Tree*, 1995 (also co-producer, co-scriptwriter) / *Dangerous Acts*, 1998 / *The Other Woman*, 2000, TV series.

ALTER, NAFTALI (Tel Aviv, 1947). Producer and Composer.

Alter graduated from the London Film School in 1971. His contribution to Israeli filmmaking has been in a number of areas. For 15 years he worked at producing, composing musical scores, and jointly writing scripts with Assi Dayan*. Alter also directed three feature films—*Irit Irit**, *The Wild Crazy and the Lunatics*, and *Attraction**. He received an Israeli Academy Award for the Original Musical Score for *Life According to Agfa** (Assi Dayan). In addition, he served as the general manager of the Fund for the Promotion of Quality Films (1994-1998) and teaches at the Sam Spiegel Film and Television School in Jerusalem. Alter is also a songwriter and has produced documentary films and commercials.

Filmography

C.O.D., Crime on Delivery, 1973 (producer, co-scriptwriter, composer) / *Saint Cohen*, 1975 (producer, co-scriptwriter, composer) / *Beautiful Troubles*, 1976 (co-producer, co-scriptwriter, composer, actor) / *Halfon Hill Doesn't Answer**, 1976 (co-producer, co-scriptwriter, composer) / *King for a Day*, 1980 (producer, co-scriptwriter, composer) / *Final Exams*, 1983 (producer, co-scriptwriter, composer) / *Irit, Irit*, 1985 (director, co-scriptwriter, composer) / *The Wild, Crazy and the Lunatics*, 1986 (director, composer) / *Attraction**, 1988 (director, co-scriptwriter) / *Photo Roman*, 1988 (only composer) / *April Fool*, 1989 (actor) / *Yossele, How Come*, 1989 (producer, composer, co-scriptwriter) / *Life According to Agfa*, 1992 (composer).

ATZMON, ANAT (Tel Aviv, 1959). Actress.

Atzmon's career in acting began with her service in the Army Entertainment Troupe. She studied theater at Tel Aviv University. Her film debut was made with the immensely popular *Lemon Popsicle** (Boaz Davidson*), which placed her, at a young age, along a successful career track. Her role in *Dead End Street** (Yaki Yosha*) won her an Israel Film Center award for Best Actress. Atzmon has also appeared on stage with her father, Shmuel Atzmon, actor and director of the Yiddish Theater in Tel Aviv. She is also a successful singer and released her first album in 1989.

Filmography

Lemon Popsicle, 1978 / *Dizengoff 99**, 1979 / *The Vulture**, 1981 / *Dead End Street*, 1982 / *Forced Testimony**, 1984 / *Sunstroke*, 1984 / *Love Contract*, 1986 / *Shellshock**, 1988 / *Angels on the Wind*, 1992 / *Double Edge**, 1992 / *Minotaur*, 1997 / *Frank Sinatra Is Dead*, 1999, TV drama / *Seven Days*, 1999, TV drama.

AVIV, NURITH (Tel Aviv, 1945). Cinematographer.

Aviv studied cinematography in Paris and returned to Israel in 1969. Her first film as cinematographer was a feature film, *Snail** (Boaz Davidson*). Since that time Aviv has established herself as a successful cinematographer who works both in Europe and in Israel. She has served as the cinematographer for numerous films, both documentaries and features, with Israeli directors such as Amos Gitai*, Michal Bat-Adam*, and Boaz Davidson. She also worked with European directors as diverse as Agnès Varda (*L'une chante, L'autre pas*, 1976; *Daguerreotypes*, 1975; *Documenteur*, 1982; *Jane B. par Agnès V.*, 1987), René Allio, Ruth Beckerman, Claude Berri, and Jacques Doillon. Aviv won an award for Best Cinematography from the Israel Film Center for *A Thin Line** (Michal Bat-Adam). Her first entry into the field of directing was with the film *Kafr Qar'a, Israel*, a documentary about the resentments of the Arabs of Israel.

Filmography

Snail, 1970 / *Circles**, 1980 (co-cinematographer) / *A Thin Line*, 1981 / *Field Diary**, 1982, documentary / *Boy Meets Girl**, 1983 / *Atalia**, 1984 / *Esther*, 1986 / *Aquabat Jabert, vie de passage*, 1986 / *Kafr Qar'a, Israel*, 1989, documentary (also director) / *Berlin–Jerusalem**, 1989 / *Wadi*, 1991, documentary / *The European Tribe*, 1992, documentary / *Jerusalem—Borderline Syndrome*, 1994, documentary / *Work, Place*, 1998, documentary (also director) / *A Sign from Heaven*, 1999, documentary / *Circumcision*, 2000, documentary (also director) / *A Love beyond Words*, 2001, documentary / *Wadi, Grand Canyon*, 2001, documentary (co-cinematographer) / *Purity*, 2002, documentary (co-cinematographer).

AXELROD, NATHAN (Poltava, Russia, 1905–Tel Aviv, 1987). Director and Producer.

Axelrod emigrated to Palestine in 1926. Almost immediately he improvised filmmaking equipment and began filming. In the late 1920s he worked with Yerushalayim Siegel at Moledeth Films. By 1934 he was editing his materials into weekly newsreels. Using two wooden shacks, Axelrod created a film laboratory, where he mixed his own chemicals. This studio served his company for many years as it grew into the Carmel Film Company, which produced the Carmel Newsreels on a regular basis from 1934 to 1958 (except for the years of World War II).

Axelrod is remembered for recording for posterity the events of the prestate pioneering period through his newsreels. He captured historical moments, such as major British Mandatory events, the arrival of new immigrants by ship, and the opening ceremonies of airports, parks, schools, and settlements. In addition, his newsreels show everyday life during that period—sports, education, health, agriculture, holiday celebrations, and entertainment.

Not only did he create a vast documentary collection through the production of his newsreels, but Axelrod was also a pioneer of dramatic filmmaking in the prestate period. Together with Haim Halachmi, he produced the first locally made fiction films—*Once upon a Time*, a short, silent comedy about a Purim carnival, and *Oded the Wanderer**, a feature-length silent film. As the years went on, Axelrod directed three feature-length dramas and worked as a partner on the production of a full-length documentary, *The True Story of Palestine** (together with Uri Zohar* and Yoel Zilberg*), which was based on his newsreel collection.

Catalogs of the Carmel Newsreel Collection, *The Nathan Axelrod Collection, vol. I* (1994) and *The Nathan Axelrod Collection, vol. II* (1996), were published by Flicks Books of Trowbridge, England, in cooperation with the Israel Film Archive—Jerusalem Cinematheque.

Filmography

Once upon a Time, 1931, silent, short (co-producer, scriptwriter, cinematographer) / *Oded the Wanderer*, 1932, silent (co-producer, cinematographer, editor) / *Carmel Newsreels*, 1934-1958 (director, producer) / *Over the Ruins*, 1938 (co-director, producer, cinematographer) / *Dan Quixote and Sa'adia Pancha*, 1956 (director, producer) / *The True Story of Palestine*, 1962, documentary (co-director, co-producer) / *Girls' Paradise Eilat*, 1964 (co-director, producer, co-scriptwriter).

AZOULAI-HASFARI, HANNAH (Beersheba, 1960). Actress.

Following her service in the Army Entertainment Troupe, Azoulai-Hasfari studied theater for a short time at Tel Aviv University. She is an actress of stage and screen. Her first major screen role was as a new army recruit in *You're in the Army, Girls** (Nadav Levitan*) and she received attention for her role as an Israeli Arab girl attending a Jewish boarding school in *Nadia** (Amnon Rubinstein*). Searching for her own cultural roots, Azoulai-Hasfari wrote the screenplay for *Sh'chur**, which is based partially on her own Moroccan family's story. She won two Israeli awards for acting for her roles in *Nadia* and *Lovesick on Nana St.** (Savi Gabizon*).

Filmography

You're in the Army, Girls, 1985 / *Rage and Glory*, 1985 / *Nadia*, 1986 / *Braids**, 1989, TV drama / *Torn Apart*, 1989 / *The Quarry*, 1990 / *Sh'chur*, 1994—(also script) / *Lovesick on Nana St.*, 1995.

BAKRI, MUHAMMED (Al-Bina, 1954) Actor.

Bakri studied at Tel Aviv University during the early 1970s, at which time he was the only Arab in the theater department. He began acting in the Haifa Theater ensemble, and since that time he has acted in dozens of theater productions, films, and a one-man play, which brought him much recognition. The play, adapted for the stage by Bakri himself, was called *The Opsimist* (a combination of "the optimist" and "the pessimist"), based on the novel by Israeli Arab writer Emile Habibi.

Bakri's first major role on the screen was as the Palestinian political prisoner in *Beyond the Walls**, directed by Uri Barbash (Best Actor, Israel Film Center Awards). He appeared as the leader of a Palestine Liberation Organization (PLO) unit in the award-winning *Cup Final** (Eran Riklis*). Bakri has also appeared in a number of international films, including *Anna K.* (Costa Gavras) and *Haifa* (by Palestinian filmmaker Rashid Mashrawi).

A documentary film, *Not a Beginning, nor an End*, directed by Lena Chaplin, about Bakri and his family portrays the issues of dual identity of a Palestinian living in the state of Israel, issues that are present in Bakri's life. Bakri himself has turned to directing. He has directed for the theater and made documentary films. His film *1948* discusses the tragic events that took place during the period of Israel's war of independence, when thousands of Palestinians became refugees.

Filmography

*Fellow Traveler**, 1983 / *Beyond the Walls*, 1984 / *On a Clear Day You Can See Damascus*, 1984 / *Esther*, 1985 / *Shelter*, 1989, short / *Double Edge**, 1992 / *Cup Final*, 1991 / *Beyond the Walls II*, 1992 / *Scar**, 1994 / *Haifa*, 1996 / *The Milky Way**, 1998 / *1948*, 1998, documentary (only director) / *Desperado Square**, 2000 / *Jenin, Jenin*, 2002, documentary (only director).

BARBASH, BENNY (Beersheva, 1951). Scriptwriter.

Barbash studied history at Tel Aviv University. One of the only people in Israel who have successfully made a career out of scriptwriting, Barbash writes scripts for political feature films and television dramatic series. He has also written theater plays and novels. Barbash won Israel Film Center awards for Best Screenplay for *Beyond the Walls** and *One of Us**, both directed by his brother, Uri Barbash.

Filmography

Beyond the Walls, 1984 / *Once We Were Dreamers**, 1987 / *One of Us*, 1989 / *Crossfire**, 1989 / *Where Eagles Fly*, 1990 / *Real Time*, 1991 / *Beyond the Walls II*, 1992 / *Licking the Raspberry*, 1992 / *Power of Attorney*, 1993–1994, TV series / *Siton*, 1995–1996, TV series / *Basic Training*, 1998–1999, TV series / *My First Sony*, 2001, TV series.

BARBASH, URI (Beersheba, 1946) Director.

Barbash received his B.A. in Hebrew language and theater from Tel Aviv University and subsequently earned a degree from the London Film School. After returning to Israel in 1973 and serving in the reserves during the Yom Kippur War, his first efforts at directing were television dramas. His *Sentenced for Life* (1979) concerns the difficulties of breaking away from a criminal background, and *Gabi Ben Yakar* (1982) tells the story of a young criminal who is successfully reformed during his army training.

Barbash has directed dozens of features and television dramas during his career. He is best known for *Beyond the Walls** (1984), an unrestrained portrayal of Arab–Jewish relations in the brutal environment of an Israeli prison. Nominated for an American Academy Award for Best Foreign Film, winner of the Critics' Jury Prize at Venice, First Prize at Salerno, and Israel Film Center Awards, the film was popularly acclaimed worldwide. His feature films and many of his television dramatic series reflect his own political consciousness and willingness to confront difficult issues. His film *One of Us**, winner of Israel Film Center awards, is critical of an army cover-up that takes place against the background of the first *intifada* (Palestinian uprising). His television miniseries *Kastner Trial* was awarded the prize for Best Original Television Drama by the Israeli Academy Awards (1994).

Barbash has become known for his artistic honesty, leading the circle of filmmakers interested in a critical look at Israeli political issues and dealing with issues of contemporary reality in a harsh and uncompromising fashion. He is a member of the faculty at the Sam Spiegel School of Film and Television in Jerusalem.

Filmography

Sentenced for Life, 1979, TV drama / *Gabi Ben Yakar*, 1982, TV drama / *Stigma**, 1982 (also co-scriptwriter) / *Near Ones, Dear Ones*, 1983, TV series (co-director) / *Beyond the Walls*, 1984 / *Once We Were Dreamers**, 1987 / *One of Us*, 1989 / *Where Eagles Fly*, 1990 / *Real Time*, 1991 / *Licking the Raspberry*, 1992 / *Beyond the Walls II*, 1992 / *Power of Attorney*, 1994, TV drama / *Kastner Trial*, TV miniseries, 1994 / *Siton*, 1995, TV series / *Bus 300*, 1997, TV miniseries / *Basic Training*, 1998, TV series / *The Institution*, 2000, TV series / *My First Sony*, 2001, TV series.

BARKAN, YEHUDA (Netanya, 1945). Actor and Director.

Barkan served in the Army Entertainment Troupe and began his screen career as an actor in ethnic films produced by Menahem Golan*. He later turned to directing and producing candid camera films. Barkan's most popular films have been *The Skipper** (Ya'ackov Goldwasser*) and its two sequels, which are sentimental films about a single parent (played by Barkan himself) who runs a tourist boat on the Sea of Galilee. Barkan is well known to Israeli audiences for his rare combination of melodrama and comedy.

Filmography

*Lupo**, 1970 (actor) / *Highway Queen**, 1971 (actor) / *Katz and Carrasso*, 1971 (actor) / *Two Heartbeats*, 1972 (actor) / *Escape to the Sun**, 1972 (actor) / *Charlie and a Half**, 1974 (actor) / *Snooker*, 1975 (actor) / *Lupo Goes to New York*, 1976 (actor) / *Million Dollar Heist*, 1977 (actor) / *Millionaire in Trouble*, 1978 (actor) / *You've Been Had, You Turkey*, 1980 (co-director, producer, actor) / *Smell and Smile*, 1985 (director, producer, actor) / *Born to Laugh*, 1988 (director, producer, actor, scriptwriter) / *The Skipper*, 1988 (producer, actor) / *Crazy Camera*, 1989 (actor) / *The Big Gag*, 1989 (director, producer, actor) / *The Skipper II*, 1989 (producer, actor) / *The Day We Met*, 1990 (producer, actor) / *The Skipper III*, 1991 (producer, actor) / *Lady, Open Up, It's Me*, 1992 (director, producer, scriptwriter) / *Bogie and Alexis*, 1993 (producer, actor).

BAT-ADAM, MICHAL (Afula, late 1940s). Director and Actress.

Bat-Adam went to school at Kibbutz Merhavia and, as a young woman, studied to become a musician at the Tel Aviv Academy of Music. After an impulsive decision to change her career from music to acting, she attended the Beit Zvi School in Ramat Gan. Her stage experience included leading roles in repertory theaters in Israel. Her first major role on the film screen was in 1972 with the film *I Love You, Rosa**, directed by Moshe Mizrahi* (later to become her life partner). Following this success, Bat-Adam appeared in a number of Mizrahi's films including *The House on Chelouche St.**, *Daughters, Daughters**, and his American Academy award-winning French film *Madame Rosa (La vie devant soi)*.

The first Israeli-born woman to direct a feature film, Bat-Adam began her directing and scriptwriting career with the acclaimed French–Israeli co-production *Moments** (winner of the Israel Film Center Award, 1979), which tells the story of a chance encounter between two women. Since that time, Bat-Adam has written and directed additional features; two are literary adaptations (*The Lover** and *A Thousand and One Wives**) and the others are autobiographical in nature. Her film *A Thin Line** won awards from the Israel Film Center (1980).

Bat-Adam's films portray complex family relationships, providing tremendous sensitivity and painting portraits of women who expose their inner selves. In relying heavily on the interweaving of elements of past and present, she has created a uniquely Israeli genre that mixes intimate emotions and passions with historical context. All of her films deal with complex relationships, unique friendships, loving portrayals of the elderly, and passionate loves of women.

Filmography

*The Big Escape**, 1970 (actress) / *I Love You, Rosa*, 1972 (actress) / *The House on Chelouche St.*, 1973 (actress) / *Daughters, Daughters*, 1973 (actress) / *Rachel's Man*, 1976 (actress) / *Moments*, 1979 (director, scriptwriter, actress) / *The Real Game**, 1980 (actress) / *A Thin Line*, 1980 (director, scriptwriter, co-producer) / *Boy Meets Girl*, 1983 (director, scriptwriter) / *Fellow Traveler**, 1983 (guest appearance) / *Atalia**, 1984 (actress) / *The Lover*, 1986 (director, co-scriptwriter, actress) / *A Thousand and One Wives*, 1989 (director, scriptwriter) / *The Deserter's Wife*, 1992 (director, scriptwriter) / *The Flight of Uncle Peretz*, 1992, TV drama (director, scriptwriter, actress) / *Aya: An Imagined Autobiography**, 1994 (director, scriptwriter, actress) / *Women**, 1996 (actress) / *Love at Second Sight**, 1998 (director, producer, scriptwriter) / *Life Is Life*, 2003 (director, scriptwriter).

BENCHETRIT, DAVID (Casablanca, Morocco, 1954). Director.

Benchetrit emigrated to Israel with his family as a teenager in 1967. He studied filmmaking at the Beit Tzvi School in Ramat Gan. He works as a documentary filmmaker and has directed and produced films on political and social issues. His first full-length documentary film, *Through the Veil of Exile** (Golden Gate Award at San Francisco, 1994), portrays issues of national exile through portraits of three Palestinian women. He was awarded the Wolgin Prize at Jerusalem for his documentary film *Kaddim Winds—A Moroccan Chronicle.*

Filmography

The Bedouin, 1979, documentary (also producer, cinematographer) / *Nadia*, 1984, documentary / *Through the Veil of Exile*, 1992, documentary (also co-producer, cinematographer, co-scriptwriter) / *Born on the 13th of September*, 1994, documentary (also producer, cinematographer) / *Sami Michaeli*, 1995, documentary (also producer, cinematographer) / *The Dream and Its End*, 1995, documentary (only producer) / *South: Alice Never Lived Here*, 1998, documentary (only co-producer, cinematographer) / *They Shoot and Cry*, 2000, documentary (also producer, cinematographer) / *Ruach Kadim—A Moroccan Chronicle*, 2002, documentary (also producer, co-scriptwriter, cinematographer).

BEN-DOR (NIV), ORNA (Kfar Saba, 1954). Director.

Ben-Dor (Niv) began her higher education with studies in architecture and later in philosophy and Jewish thought. She then decided to study at the Department of Film and Television at Tel Aviv University. She completed a one-year course in the management of cultural institutions at Tel Aviv University (1997).

Ben-Dor is a director of documentaries, television dramas, and one feature film. Her docudrama *Manya Shohat—The Diary of a Journey* won an award for Best Documentary from the Israel Film Center. Her groundbreaking documentary *Due to That War** was one of the first Israeli films to deal with the complex and sensitive subject of second-generation survivors of the Holocaust (FIPRESCI Prize at Berlin, Honorable Mention at Leningrad, and Critics' Jury Prize at Haifa).

Following a fruitful period of filmmaking, Ben-Dor worked as the first director of the New Foundation for Film and Television (1994–1999). She has taught film and has worked on a number of television magazine programs.

Filmography

A View of the Situation, 1982, short / *The Story of Every Woman*, 1982, documentary / *Manya Shohat—The Diary of a Journey*, 1986, docudrama / *Due to That War*, 1988, documentary / *Cloud Fragment*, 1989, documentary / *Sarah*, 1991, TV drama (also co-scriptwriter) / *Shoah Tovah*, 1993, TV drama / *Newland*, 1994 / *Sweet was the Mud*, 2002, documentary (only scriptwriter).

BEN-DOV, YA'AKOV (Yekaterinoslav, Ukraine, 1882–Tel Aviv, 1968). Director and Cinematographer.

Ben-Dov was the first local filmmaker. He emigrated to Palestine in 1907 and began work as a still photographer. Believed to have owned the first movie camera in Palestine, Ben-Dov was a highly skilled cameraman who understood the art form. In fact, he taught photography at the Bezalel Academy of Art in Jerusalem. In 1917 he photographed the historical entrance of General Allenby into Jerusalem, which was the official moment of the end of Turkish rule in the area and the beginning of the British period (which continued until 1948). Ben-Dov established a film company called Menorah, and the documentary films that he made portray the achievements of the Zionist enterprise as they were unfolding.

His film *Return to Zion* (1920–1921) incorporates important historical footage of special events, including Winston Churchill's 1921 visit to Palestine, with early scenes of the pioneers rebuilding the land. This film was widely screened abroad and the screening in Prague was mentioned in Kafka's memoirs. Baruch Agadati's* documentary film *This Is the Land** (1935) integrates large amounts of footage shot by Ben-Dov.

Filmography

Judea Liberated, 1917, documentary (director, cinematographer) / *Return to Zion*, 1920–1921, documentary (director, cinematographer) / *Palestine Awakening*, 1923, documentary (director, cinematographer) / *Romance of a New Palestine*, documentary (director, cinematographer) / *Rebirth of a Nation*, 1926 (director, cinematographer) / *Eretz Israel at Work*, 1926, documentary (director, cinematographer) / *Young Palestine*, 1926, documentary (director, cinematographer) / *Springtime in Eretz Israel*, 1928, documentary (director, cinematographer) / *We Will Rise and We Have Built*, 1929, documentary (director, cinematographer) / *Kfar Yeladim*, 1930, short (cinematographer) / *This Is the Land*, 1935, documentary (co-cinematographer).

BESSER, GEDALIA (Kalish, Poland, 1939). Actor.

Besser's career began in 1965 as an actor in the Cameri Theater. He has worked in the field of theater both as an actor and as a director. On screen, his acting debut was in a film directed by Yaki Yosha. Besser has won awards for his screen performances—as Nussbaum, the outsider planning on returning to his country of origin in *Transit** (Daniel Wachsmann*) from the Israel Film Center and as a sociologist interested in prostitution in *Rockinghorse** (Yaki Yosha) from the Oxford Film Festival. More recently he was acclaimed for his role as the understated father in two films—*Blind Man's Bluff** (Aner Preminger*) and *Aya, an Imagined Autobiography** (Michal Bat-Adam*).

Filmography

Rockinghorse, 1978 / *Transit*, 1980 / *On the Air*, 1981 (also co-scriptwriter) / *The Owl*, 1988 / *The Duel*, 1993, short / *Blind Man's Bluff*, 1993 / *On the Edge*, 1994 / *New Land*, 1994 / *Aya, an Imagined Autobiography*, 1994.

BOUZAGLO, HAIM (Jerusalem, 1952). Director.

Following his army service, Bouzaglo studied literature and theater at Hebrew University in Jerusalem, and then later he studied cinema in France. His first feature film, *Marriage of Convenience**, won him the prize for Best Film and

Best Director of the Israel Film Center Awards (1988–1989). Due to its use of humor and its political insight, the film is an important statement about Arab–Jewish relations in the contemporary period. Repeating his successful recipe for combining humor with political insight, Bouzaglo's *Time of the Cherries** is a critical view of the War in Lebanon using elements of the surreal. He has also won awards for his television dramatic series *Yarkon Files* (Israeli Academy Award) and *Zinzana* (Jerusalem Film Festival award). In addition, Bouzaglo is a scriptwriter and has directed numerous television commercials.

Filmography

*Summer of Aviya**, 1988 (only co-scriptwriter) / *Marriage of Convenience*, 1988 (also co-scriptwriter) / *Time of the Cherries*, 1991 (also co-scriptwriter) / *Scar**, 1994 (also co-scriptwriter) / *Yarkon Files*, 1997, TV series (co-director) / *Zinzana*, 1999, TV drama (also scriptwriter) / *Peacefulness*, 2002, TV series (also scriptwriter) / *Illusions*, 2002, TV series.

BUKAEE, RAFI (Tel Aviv, 1957). Director.

After completing his army service in 1978, Bukaee studied at the University of Tel Aviv (1979–1981). The student film that won him his degree in the Department of Film served as the basis for his first feature, *Avanti Popolo**, which won an award at Locarno and Haifa, and an Israel Film Center award. Although the film was ahead of its time in its understanding of the plight of the Egyptian soldier within the context of the Six Day War of 1967, it eventually won critical acclaim worldwide and was screened at festivals and broadcast on television throughout Europe. According to Bukaee, the film was the antithesis of those documentaries produced following the war which made fun of the Egyptian soldiers who fled barefoot in the hot sands of the Sinai Peninsula, leaving behind mounds of shoes. In contrast, Bukaee's film is an honest attempt at looking behind the uniform and understanding the Arab enemy—his background, his plea for understanding, his humanity. In a sense, Bukaee has tried to stand in the shoes of the Egyptians.

In his second feature film, *Marco Polo—The Missing Chapter**, Bukaee combined a historical tale with political allegory. The stories of Christian religious martyrdom of Marco Polo's time certainly have parallels in the religious fanaticism, both Jewish and Muslim, as seen within the contemporary context.

Filmography

Avanti Popolo, 1986 (also producer, scriptwriter) / *Fear of the Jews*, 1991, TV drama / *Eddie King*, 1992 (only co-producer) / *Life According to Agfa**, 1992 (only co-producer) / *Marco Polo—The Missing Chapter*, 1996 (also producer, scriptwriter).

BURSTYN, MIKE (New York, 1945). Actor.

Born to the Yiddish stage performers Lillian Lux and Pesach'ke Burstein, the young Burstyn, together with his twin sister, grew up in the theater, performing since the age of seven. The documentary film *The Komediant** (Arnon Goldfinger, 1999) relates the story of the family. Burstyn made a name for himself with his first big film success, *Two Kuni Lemel** (Israel Becker, 1966), and from there went on to additional films (both in Israel and abroad) and to a successful career on Broadway.

Filmography

*Sallah**, 1964 / *Shabbat Hamalka*, 1965, TV drama / *Two Kuni Lemel*, 1966 / *The Dybbuk*, 1968, TV drama / *Kuni Lemel in Tel Aviv*, 1976 / *Hershele*, 1977 / *The Children's Festival*, 1980 / *Kuni Lemel in Cairo*, 1983 / *Minotaur*, 1997.

CEDAR, JOSEPH (New York, 1968). Director.

Cedar emigrated to Israel with his family at the age of five. He studied philosophy and history of theater at Hebrew University (B.A.) and later studied at the Tisch School of the Arts at New York University (B.F.A., 1995). He teaches scriptwriting at the Ma'aleh Film School in Jerusalem.

Cedar's first full-length feature film, *Time of Favor**, works on two levels. On the political level it reflects the dangers of exploiting religious fervor for political and violent ends; on the more human level it criticizes the settlement movement for its lack of sensitivity to the needs and suffering of its individual members. The film, which was screened at many international festivals and was acclaimed by critics for its relevance to timely issues in Israeli society, won Israeli Academy Awards (2000)—an impressive achievement for a young filmmaker's first film.

Filmography

Uri and Aliza, 1992, short (also scriptwriter) / *Psalms*, 1994, short (also scriptwriter) / *Time of Favor*, 2000 (also scriptwriter).

COHEN, ELI (Hadera, 1940). Director.

Cohen studied at Tel Aviv University in theater arts and philosophy (B.A.). He worked for a few years as a theater actor, playing lead roles in plays of the Habimah National Theater. When he then decided to change his career, he went to London to study filmmaking and graduated from the London Film School in 1971.

Having directed some of the important, prizewinning feature films produced in Israel, Cohen's first feature, *Ricochets**, was produced as a training film for the Israeli army and was shot on location in Southern Lebanon. The film, which deals with the War in Lebanon and was originally conceived as a series of discussion films for soldiers on issues of moral ambiguity, won Israel Film Center awards (1986–1987). Shortly thereafter, Cohen directed *Summer of Aviya**, a memory film that was acclaimed internationally for its sensitive depiction of a Holocaust survivor and her 10-year-old daughter in 1950s Israel. It earned awards at Berlin (1989), Valladolid (1989), San Remo (1989), and Belgrade (1990) and an Israel Film Center award (1987–1988). The film's sequel, also directed by Cohen, produced a few years later, *Under the Domim Tree**, won a prize at the Jerusalem Film Festival (1995).

Abroad, Cohen directed the Canadian film *The Quarrel* (1992), based on the story by the well-known author Chaim Grade, which grapples with theological and philosophical issues of faith following the Holocaust. He also directed the U.S. film *Soft Kill* (1994). Cohen teaches scriptwriting and directing at Tel Aviv University, Camera Obscura, and Ma'aleh Film Schools.

Filmography

*Scouting Patrol**, 1967 (only actor) / *He Walked through the Fields*, 1967 (only actor) / *Prisoners of Freedom*, 1968 (only actor) / *To Stand on One's Feet*, 1975, documentary / *Waiting for Godot*, 1976, TV drama (also actor) / *The Ayland Affair*, 1980, TV drama (also scriptwriter) / *The Man with Two Brains*, 1983 (only costume designer) / *Ricochets*, 1986 (also co-scriptwriter) / *Summer of Aviya*, 1988 (also co-scriptwriter, actor) / *The Wordmaker*, 1991, TV drama (also co-scriptwriter) / *Under the Domim Tree*, 1995 / *Family Secrets*, 1998 (only actor) / *Buzz*, 1998, TV drama / *Egoz*, 1999, TV drama / *Altermania*, 2001, documentary (also scriptwriter) / *Electric Man*,* 2001.

DAU, SALIM (Bena, 1950). Actor.

Dau studied acting in Paris and at the Beit Tzvi School in Ramat Gan. He is an actor of film and stage, a director, storyteller, and scriptwriter. In addition, he teaches theater at the University of Haifa and has appeared in dozens of theater and film productions in Israel and abroad. He served as the artistic director of the Beit Geffen Theater in Haifa (1986–1998) and teaches in the Department of Theater at Haifa University.

Dau's role of the Egyptian soldier in *Avanti Popolo** (Rafi Bukaee*), who recites Shylock in an attempt to plead for human understanding from the Israeli soldiers, won a prize for best actor at the Haifa Film Festival. An Israeli documentary film, *Arlecchino: Behind the Masks* (David Noy, 2000), tells the story of Dau's life and discusses some of the issues involved in being an Israeli Palestinian Arab actor.

Filmography

*Hamsin**, 1982 / *Avanti Popolo*, 1986 / *The Cage*, 1989, short / *Shelter*, 1989, short / *A Thousand and One Wives**, 1989 / *The Quarry*, 1990 / *The Mountain*, 1990, short / *Cup Final**, 1991 / *The Flying Camel**, 1994 / *Max and Morris*, 1994 / *The Milky Way**, 1998 / *Aviv*, 1998, short / *White Lies*, 1999 / *Abramov*, 2001, short / *Grossman, the Great*, 2002, TV drama.

DAVIDSON, BOAZ (Tel Aviv, 1943). Director.

Davidson graduated from the London International Film School in 1970 and returned to Israel to begin his career as a film director. He is well known for his ethnic comedies and irreverent humor. In his collaboration with Uri Zohar*, Arik Einstein*, and Tzvi Shissel, a team of great talent that made television productions and feature films, he co-directed *Lool* (1969, 1988) and directed and scripted *Snail** (1970).

Davidson's most popular films in Israel were *Lemon Popsicle**, which won Israel Film Center awards (1978), and its sequel, *Going Steady* (1979). Both films are period pieces of nostalgia for the 1950s and portray teenage pranks and explicit adolescent sexuality. Their commercial success depended largely on their innovative style—fast pacing, authenticity, humor, period music, and cinematographic quality.

Davidson is also a director and producer of films in the United States, where he has been working since the 1980s. His films include *The Last American Virgin* (1982), *Lunarcorp* (1994), *American Cyborg: Steel Warrior* (1994), and *Macarena* (1998). He is the managing director of New Age Cinema, Los Angeles, since 1998.

Filmography

Lool, 1969, TV series (co-director) / *Snail*, 1970 (also scriptwriter) / *Fifty-Fifty**, 1971 (also co-scriptwriter) / *Azit, the Paratrooper Dog*, 1972 (also co-scriptwriter) / *Charlie and a Half**, 1974 / *Snooker*, 1975 / *Lupo Goes to New York*, 1976 (also co-scriptwriter) / *Tzanani Family*, 1976 / *It's a Funny, Funny World*, 1978, candid camera (only co-scriptwriter, actor) / *Lemon Popsicle*, 1978 (also co-scriptwriter) / *Going Steady*, 1979 (also co-scriptwriter) / *Hot Bubblegum*, 1981 (also co-scriptwriter) / *Private Popsicle*, 1982 (also co-scriptwriter) / *Private Maneuvers*, 1983 (only co-scriptwriter) / *Alex in Love*, 1986 (also scriptwriter) / *Lool*, 1988 (co-director) / *Crazy Camera*, 1989 (also co-producer) / *A Bit of Luck**, 1992 (only co-producer) / *Licking the Raspberry*, 1992 (only co-producer).

DAYAN, ASSI (Nahalal, 1945). Director and Actor.

After his military service in the paratroops, Dayan studied philosophy and English literature at Hebrew University in Jerusalem, following which he worked as a theater actor. Dayan quickly switched to the screen and has worked in both international and Israeli cinema.

During his early filmmaking, Dayan was known for his light "ethnic" films. This period is also characterized by social satires such as *Halfon Hill Doesn't Answer**, which has become a cult film with young audiences due to its sharply satirical view of army life and relations with Arabs across the border, and *Saint Cohen* (Special Jury Prize at Bergamo, 1975) which is about a poet in the Galilee who attempts suicide.

By the early 1990s Dayan's filmmaking changed. In a rebellion against the self-sacrificing image of his war hero father (Moshe Dayan), Dayan's filmmaking has come to portray heroes and antiheroes who stubbornly maintain their individuality and unabashedly look inward. He focuses on issues of the decaying urban society with *An Electric Blanket** and *Life According to Agfa**. The latter shocked the Israeli public by actually depicting the "apocalypse," a violent nightmare that takes place in a Tel Aviv pub. The film, a serious political statement of honesty and perhaps despair, won Honorable Mention at Berlin (1993). As one of the provocative and outspoken filmmakers of Israel of the 1990s, Dayan also won Israeli Academy Awards for *Life According to Agfa, Mr. Baum**, and *An Electric Blanket* (also Best Film, Valencia, 1998).

Dayan's special talent as an actor can be seen in many of his own films and also in the memorable roles that he has played in films by other directors (both Israeli and international)—*A Walk with Love and Death* (John Huston, 1969), as the young kibbutznik in *He Walked through the Fields** (Yoseph Millo), as the conscientious objector in *Beyond the Walls** (Uri Barbash*), and as the extremist rabbi who incites his yeshivah students to violence in *Time of Favor** (Joseph Cedar*). Dayan is also a writer, contributing satirical columns in newspapers, a poet, and a novelist. He was awarded recognition by the Jerusalem Film Festival (1998) and was the recipient of a special homage by the Israeli Ministry of Culture for his contribution to Israeli cinema (1990).

Filmography

*Scouting Patrol**, 1967 (actor) / *He Walked through the Fields*, 1967 (actor) / *Five Days in Sinai*, 1969 (actor) / *Sabra, Death of a Jew*, 1969 (actor) / *Boys and Girls*, 1970* (actor) / *Fifty-Fifty**, 1971 (co-producer, co-scriptwriter, actor) / *C.O.D., Crime on Delivery*, 1973 (director, co-scriptwriter) / *Saint Cohen*, 1975 (director, co-scriptwriter) / *Three and One*, 1975 (actor) / *Halfon Hill Doesn't Answer*, 1976 (director, co-scriptwriter) / *Beautiful Troubles*, 1976 (director, co-scriptwriter) / *Operation Thunderbolt**, 1977 (actor) / *The Uranium Conspiracy*, 1978 (actor) / *Shlager*, 1979 (director, scriptwriter) / *Moments**, 1979 (actor) / *King for a Day*, 1980 (director, co-scriptwriter) / *The Impotent*, 1981 (director, scriptwriter) / *The Man Who Flew in to Grab*, 1981 (actor) / *Tell Me That You Love Me**, 1983 (actor) / *Final Exams*, 1983 (director, co-scriptwriter) / *When Night Falls**, 1985 (actor) / *Irit, Irit**, 1985 (co-scriptwriter) / *You're in the Army, Girls**, 1985 (scriptwriter) / *Beyond the Walls*, 1986 (actor) / *The Good, the Bad and the Not So Bad*, 1986 (director, co-producer, co-scriptwriter, actor) / *Mondo Condo*, 1986 (scriptwriter) / *The Owl*, 1987 (actor) / *Photo Roman*, 1988 (co-producer, scriptwriter) / *Where Eagles Fly*, 1990 (co-scriptwriter) / *Real Time*, 1991 (actor) / *Life According to Agfa*, 1992 (director, scriptwriter) / *Overdose*, 1993 (co-scriptwriter) / *An Electric Blanket*, 1994 (director, scriptwriter) / *Devarim*, 1995 (actor) / *Orchids and Spears*, 1995, TV drama (actor) / *No Names on the Door*, 1996 (actor) / *A Whale on Sheraton Beach*, 1997, TV miniseries (actor) / *Ben-Gurion*, 1997, TV drama (actor) / *The Guide for Low Profile*, 1997, TV drama (director, actor) / *Mr. Baum*, 1997 (director, scriptwriter, actor) / *How to Cover Your Ass*, 1998, TV drama (director, scriptwriter, actor) / *As If Nothing Happened*, 1999, TV drama (actor) / *Time of Favor*, 2000 (actor) / *A Matter of Reputation**, 2000 (actor) / *The News According to God*, 2001 (director) / *The Return from India*, 2002 (actor) / *The Brown Girls*, 2002, TV series (actor) / *The Glow*, 2002 (actor) / *Grossman, the Great*, 2002, TV drama (actor).

DAYAN, NISSIM (Tel Aviv, 1946). Director.

Dayan studied acting at the Nissan Nativ School in Tel Aviv and began his career as an actor at the Habimah Theater. He went on to filmmaking and has directed shorts, features, television dramas, and documentaries. His feature films deal with social and political issues—reflections on life in a deteriorating social structure (*Light Out of Nowhere** and *The End of Milton Levy**) and Arab–

Jewish relations (*On a Narrow Bridge**). His most ambitious project was the production of the internationally acclaimed television miniseries *Michel Ezra Safra and Sons*, a family saga about the conflicts between traditional and modern cultures within the Syrian-Jewish community, spanning its roots in Syria to its relocation in Israel.

Dayan teaches film at the Sam Spiegel Film School in Jerusalem, appears as a television talk-show host, worked as the artistic director of the Haifa International Film Festival (1988 and 1992), and writes film criticism.

Filmography

Man on the Edge, 1971, short / *Floch**, 1972 (assistant director) / *The Dog, Linda*, 1973, documentary (also scriptwriter) / *Light Out of Nowhere*, 1973 (also co-scriptwriter) / *Joy of Mitzvah*, 1974, documentary (also scriptwriter) / *Janna and Yael*, 1974, documentary (also scriptwriter) / *I Remember Weizmann*, 1974, documentary (also scriptwriter) / *Simon*, 1974, documentary (also scriptwriter) / *Love of Hadassah*, 1975, documentary (also scriptwriter) / *The Last Ghetto*, 1975, documentary (also scriptwriter) / *Mashed*, 1977, documentary (also scriptwriter) / *The Drafting Party*, 1977, documentary (also scriptwriter) / *Kamikaze*, 1978, documentary (also scriptwriter) / *Beauty Queen*, 1978, documentary (also scriptwriter) / *Mazzot*, 1978, documentary (also scriptwriter) / *Identification Card*, 1978, documentary (also scriptwriter) / *The Seventh Year*, 1979, documentary (also scriptwriter) / *The End of Milton Levy*, 1981 (also co-producer, scriptwriter) / *Lena*, 1982 (producer) / *Michel Ezra Safra and Sons*, 1983, TV miniseries / *Villa Emma*, 1983, docudrama / *On a Narrow Bridge*, 1985 (also co-scriptwriter) / *One Crime Free*, 1989–1992, TV series (only producer) / *Flight No. 016*, 1989–1992, TV series (only producer) / *Yael's Friends*, TV drama (only producer) / *A Local Story*, 1995, TV drama / *A Woman in Gray*, 1997, TV series.

DIENAR, BARUCH (Hamburg, Germany, 1923–Tel Aviv, 1997). Director.

Dienar immigrated to British Mandatory Palestine in 1934. He studied Bible and psychology at Hebrew University in Jerusalem. Dienar was a teacher who freelanced as a film critic for a local radio station. When he decided to enter film production, he went to New York to study at Columbia University to learn scriptwriting. After a year apprenticing in Hollywood, Dienar returned to Israel to make his first documentary, *The New Pioneers*, distributed worldwide by Paramount.

Dienar made sponsored documentary films as ordered by Jewish national organizations, which dealt with the achievements of the modern state of Israel. In addition, he produced and wrote, in cooperation with the Israel Motion Picture Studios, a compelling short drama, *Tent City* (Aryeh Lahola, 1951), about the tensions and difficulties of life in the new immigrant transit camps during the early 1950s.

Dienar tackled the subject of Arab–Jewish relations head-on in a classic feature drama, *They Were Ten**, which won the Grand Prix, Rencontre du Film pour la Jeunesse, Cannes (1961) and CIDALC Prize, Mannheim (1961). He was the first Israeli filmmaker to receive international distribution—*They Were Ten* was distributed in 24 countries by Twentieth Century Fox—and to win the struggle for government support of his film. His second feature, *Take Two**, won the Critics' Prize at Venice (1972). Dienar served for many years (1979–1989) as the head of the Fund for Promotion of Quality Films, the government-sponsored agency that, beginning in 1979, partially funded the production of many Israeli feature films. He received a Life Achievement Award from the Haifa Film Festival (1995).

Filmography

The New Pioneers, 1949, documentary (also producer) / *Two Thousand and Three*, 1951, documentary / *Tent City*, 1951, short (producer, scriptwriter) / *We Chose Life*, 1952, documentary / *Deadline for Danny*, 1953, documentary / *The Lachish Story*, 1955, documentary / *Report on the Holy Land*, 1956, documentary / *Israel in the Family of Nations*, 1958, documentary / *They Were Ten*, 1960 (also producer, co-scriptwriter) / *Run No More*, 1964, documentary / *Land of a Thousand Faces*, 1964, documentary / *The Sand Curtain*, 1966, documentary / *Ben Gurion—Builder of a Nation*, 1966, documentary / *And on the Seventh Day*, 1967, short (also producer, co-scriptwriter) / *Bon Voyage*, 1968, documentary / *Speaking of Israel*, 1969, documentary / *Take Two*, 1972 (also producer, scriptwriter) / *The Will to Do*, 1974, documentary / *From Every Mountainside*, 1975, documentary / *A Letter from Or Akiba*, 1976, documentary / *A Touch of Magic*, 1992, TV drama.

DOTAN, SHIMON (Adjud, Romania, 1949). Director.

Dotan immigrated to Israel with his family at the age of 10. He studied filmmaking at Tel Aviv University and received Israeli prizes for his short films. His features *Repeat Dive** and *Smile of the Lamb** offer insight into issues of Israeli society, both social and political, and received critical acclaim and received awards from the Israel Film Center. Dotan has produced and directed films in the United States and Canada, including *Warriors* (1994), *Coyote Run* (1996), and *You Can Thank Me Later* (1998).

Filmography

Seven in Nature, 1975, short / *My Michael**, 1975 (only actor) / *Meir in Seven Pictures*, 1976, short / *Repeat Dive*, 1981 (also scriptwriter) / *83*, 1983 (co-director) / *Smile of the Lamb*, 1985 (also co-scriptwriter).

EINSTEIN, ARIK (Tel Aviv, 1939). Actor.

Einstein is a well-known actor and popular singer. He began his career in the Army Entertainment Troupe, worked in a satirical theater group, and then became a successful singer. In the field of film he is known for artistic work with Uri Zohar*, especially in his films *Peeping Toms** and *Big Eyes**, two beach comedies about hedonistic life in Tel Aviv that became popular with young audiences in later years.

Filmography

Nini, 1962 / *Dalia and the Sailors**, 1964 / *Sallah**, 1964 / *Dreamboat**, 1964 / *Lool*, 1969, TV series (also co-scriptwriter) / *Snail**, 1970 / *Peeping Toms*, 1972 (also co-scriptwriter) / *Big Eyes*, 1974 / *Lool*, 1988 (also co-scriptwriter) / *Cables*, 1992 (also co-scriptwriter).

ELDAD, ILAN (Subotica, Yugoslavia, 1929). Director.

Eldad (original name: Ivan Lengyel) graduated from the Academy of Cinematic Art in Belgrade. He immigrated to Israel in 1950 and served in the aerial photography department of the air force for two years. He worked as assistant director for Thorold Dickinson, Otto Preminger, Christian Jaque, and Daniel Mann and studied filmmaking in England. In addition to a successful career as a theater director and producer at Habimah and Beit Lessin Theaters, he has directed dozens of commercials, documentaries, television dramas, and multimedia shows and a small number of feature films.

Eldad's first feature film, *Clouds over Israel**, about tolerance between Arabs and Jews in the region, was ahead of its time. His full-length documentary *Three Hours in June** (using his experience in aerial photography) showed a creative approach, integrating both documentary footage and reenacted sequences.

Filmography

Clouds over Israel, 1962 / *Shabbat HaMalka*, 1965, TV drama (also co-scriptwriter) / *Three Hours in June*, 1967, documentary / *The Dybbuk*, 1968 (also co-scriptwriter) / *The Children's Festival*, 1980 / *The Megillah**, 1983 (also co-scriptwriter).

ELIAN, YONA (Jaffa, 1949). Actress.

Elian has played in numerous feature films and is known for her first screen role in George Ovadiah's* *Nurit** and for the fact that she fell in love with her life partner, Sassi Keshet, on the film's set. In *The Last Winter** (Riki Shelach Nissimoff) Elian played a professional woman whose husband is missing in action, and she has appeared in starring roles in Eyal Halfon's* *The Italians Are Coming** as the single mother turned kibbutz manager and in Benny Torati's *Desperado Square** as the elegant widow. She has also appeared in a number of television dramas and is familiar to Israeli audiences as a television talk-show host.

Filmography

Nurit, 1972 / *They Call Me Shmil*, 1973 / *Take Two**, 1972 / *The Father*, 1975 / *Diamonds*, 1975 / *Three and One*, 1975 / *Sixtieth St.*, 1976 / *Beautiful Troubles*, 1976 / *Million Dollar Heist*, 1977 / *The Last Winter*, 1982 / *Kasach*, 1984 / *On the Fringe**, 1987 / *Lend Me Your Wife*, 1988 / *Kastner Trial*, 1994, TV drama / *The Italians Are Coming*, 1996 / *Zinzana*, 1999, TV drama / *Desperado Square*, 2000 / *The Other Woman*, 2000, TV series / *Peacefulness*, 2002, TV series / *Grossman, the Great*, 2002, TV drama.

ELKABETZ, RONIT (Beersheba, 1964). Actress.

Elkabetz began her career as a model at the age of 16. She is an actress of stage and screen, working both in Israel and in France. Elkabetz won attention in Israel with her first screen role as the demonic Lilith character in *The Appointed** (Daniel Wachsmann*) and appeared again as a woman with special powers when she played the mentally challenged sister in *Sh'chur** (Shmuel Hasfari*), a role that won her the Israeli Academy Award for Best Actress. Elkabetz won awards for her role in Dover Kosashvilli's* *Late Marriage**—at Thessaloniki (2001), Buenos Aires (2002), and an Israel Academy Award. She appeared in the French film *Origine controlée*, directed by Zakia and Ahmed Bouchaala.

Filmography

The Appointed, 1990 / *Eddie King*, 1992 / *Sh'chur*, 1994 / *Scar**, 1994 (also co-scriptwriter) / *Ben Gurion*, 1997, TV drama / *Late Marriage*, 2001 / *The Lawyers*, 2002, TV series.

ERAN, DORON (Ramat Gan, 1955). Producer.

During his military service, Eran worked with youth at risk, and his college studies were in the field of education. Since 1983 he has produced more than 30 feature films and television dramas. His films have represented Israel at film festivals worldwide and won awards—*Burning Land** (Serge Ankri) won the Critics' Prize at Torino, *Beyond the Walls II* (Uri Barbash*) won a prize at Valencia, and *White Night** (Arnon Zadok*) won Prix de la Jeunesse at Cannes.

Eran has directed feature films and produced many films for television on subjects dealing with social issues, especially the problems of development towns. He also works on a co-production basis with European film companies. Eran was one of the initiators and producers of the Children's International Film Festival, which began in Holon in December 2001.

Filmography

Fun Forever, 1983 / *Burning Land*, 1984 (co-producer) / *Dawn*, 1985 (co-producer) / *Joshua, Joshua*, 1986 / *Stalin's Disciples**, 1986 / *Flash*, 1986 (only director) / *Crazy Weekend*, 1986 (co-producer) / *All My Loving*, 1986 (co-producer) / *Magic Samson*, 1988 / *April Fool*, 1989 / *Leave My Wife Alone*, 1989 / *Torn Apart*, 1989 (co-producer) / *The Voice of Ein Harod*, 1990 (director, co-producer) / *Where Eagles Fly*, 1990 (co-producer) / *Real Time*, 1991 (co-producer) / *Beyond the Walls II*, 1992 / *Strangers in the Night*, 1993 / *Overdose*, 1993 (co-producer) / *White Night*, 1995 (co-producer) / *Ingil*, 2001 / *God's Sandbox*, 2002 (only director).

FINKELSTEIN, LEVANA (Sofia, Bulgaria, 1947). Actress.

Finkelstein studied acting at Beit Tzvi School in Ramat Gan (graduated 1967). Following her service in the Army Entertainment Troupe, she continued her studies in New York at Hunter College. She has appeared in dozens of roles on the Israeli stage and has also appeared in the theater in New York. She established a puppet theater in New York in 1980.

On the Israeli screen, Finkelstein is well known for her roles as the Sephardi Jewish mother who radiates love, warmth, and traditional values to her family. She won the Anat Pirchi Award at the Jerusalem Film Festival for her role in the TV drama *Voices from the Heartland—Mother V* (Shachar Rozen).

Filmography

*My Love in Jerusalem**, 1969 / *I Love You, Rosa**, 1972 / *Salomonico**, 1972 / *Tzanani Family*, 1976 / *Midnight Entertainer*, 1977 / *Rockinghorse**, 1978 / *A Thousand and One Wives**, 1989 / *Time of the Cherries**, 1991 / *The Heritage*, 1993 / *Dreams of Innocence**, 1993 / *Aya, an Imagined Autobiography**, 1994 / *Jewish Revenge*, 1997, TV drama / *Basic Training*, 1998, TV series / *Egoz*, 1999, TV drama / *Voices from the Heartland—Mother V*, 2001, TV drama.

FOX, EYTAN (New York City, 1964). Director.

Fox immigrated to Israel with his family at a young age and grew up in Jerusalem. He studied at the Department of Film and Television at Tel Aviv University. He made two films about homosexuality in the Israeli army: *Time-Off* is a short drama which won First Prize at the Munich Student Film Festival; *Yossi and Jagger* won the Anat Pirchi Honorable Mention for TV drama at the Jerusalem Film Festival. Fox's first feature film, *Song of the Siren**, based on the acclaimed novel by Irit Linur, was one of the most popular Israeli films of the 1990s. His dramatic television series *Florentene*, based on the American TV model of *Friends*, which examines the lives of young people in Tel Aviv, won First Prize in the television category at Jerusalem (1997). His short musical comedy, *Gotta Have Heart*, won a prize for Best Short at the New York NewFest (1999).

Fox's films deal with strongly delineated characters, professional women, and homosexuality and reflect a strong use of artistic design and aesthetic elements.

Filmography

Time-Off, 1990, short / *Song of the Siren*, 1994 / *Florentene*, 1997–1999, TV series / *Gotta Have Heart*, 1997, short / *Yossi and Jagger*, 2002, TV drama.

FRISCH, LARRY (Indianapolis, 1929). Director.

Frisch began his career as a child actor for CBS-TV and as a documentary filmmaker. He studied clinical psychology and then went on to study filmmaking. His first film, *This Is My School*, which was nominated for an Oscar, was produced in 1945 while he was studying cinema at the University of Southern California. In 1950 he made *The Story of a Teenage Drug Addict*. He later went on to direct a pioneering CBS-TV documentary program.

After immigrating to Israel in 1954, Frisch established a documentary film unit for the Israeli Government Press Office. He made three feature films and a number of documentaries during the 1950s and into the 1960s in Israel, which established him as one of the pioneers of Israeli filmmaking. His best-known feature, *Tel Aviv Taxi**, was the first Israeli feature to be completely produced in Israel. The film was made simultaneously in both Hebrew and English, and the laboratory work was carried out at the new Geva Studio in Givatayim, near Tel Aviv, which was also the production company.

Frisch lives primarily in Israel and has worked as the overseas correspondent for news agencies. He has also produced and directed films about the Jewish communities in Ethiopia, Yemen, and India.

Filmography

Tel Aviv Taxi, 1954 (also co-producer, scriptwriter) / *Pillar of Fire**, 1959 (also co-producer, co-author of original story) / *Casablan*, 1962 (also co-producer) / *Miracle of Survival*, 1969, documentary.

FRYE, PETER (Montreal, Canada 1915–London, U.K., 1991). Director.

Frye grew up in Canada; at the age of 18 he left home and joined the world of New York theater. He fought with the International Brigade in Spain and was badly wounded. When he returned to New York he became a theater director and acting teacher. During the period of McCarthyism in the United States he fell under suspicion due to his involvement in the Spanish civil war. He left the United States and immigrated to Israel in 1952.

Frye's first filmmaking job in Israel was on the film classic *Hill 24 Doesn't Answer** (Thorold Dickinson). As a result of strongly differing opinions with his backers, he was forced to leave that project. However, he is credited onscreen as a co-producer and co-scriptwriter. Frye went into directing and producing for theater and radio and was one of the founding teachers at the Drama School of Tel Aviv University (1961). He became a major theater director in Israel and was the artistic director of the Ohel Theater. His wife, Thelma Ruby, was also a major theater personality, starring in many West End productions.

In the field of filmmaking Frye directed two important features, *I Like Mike** and *The Hero's Wife**. Both films portray strong female images. In *I Like Mike* the main character is a domineering Jewish mother, and in *The Hero's Wife* she is a Holocaust survivor who lost her lover years ago and finds it difficult to love again.

Frye and his wife wrote a joint autobiography, entitled *Double or Nothing: Two Lives in the Theatre—The Autobiography of Thelma Ruby and Peter Frye*, which has been published in both English (Janus Publishing Co., 1997) and Hebrew (Zemora-Bitan Publishers, 1992).

Filmography

Hill 24 Doesn't Answer, 1954 (only co-producer, co-scriptwriter) / *I Like Mike*, 1962 (also scriptwriter) / *The Hero's Wife*, 1963 (also co-producer) / *The Dybbuk*, 1968, TV drama (only actor) / *Two Heartbeats*, 1972 (only actor).

GABIZON, SAVI (Kiryat Yam, 1960). Director.

Gabizon studied film and television at Tel Aviv University and received his B.A. in 1987. He teaches scriptwriting and directing at Tel Aviv University (since 1993), at the Sam Spiegel Film and Television School in Jerusalem and at Camera Obscura in Tel Aviv and directs the programming development department for an Israeli television broadcasting company.

Gabizon directed two feature films dealing with societal disaffection, *Shuroo** and *Lovesick on Nana St.**, both of which won Israeli Academy Awards and the coveted Wolgin Prize at Jerusalem. *Lovesick on Nana St.* was also awarded international recognition at Mannheim and São Paolo.

Filmography

They Call Me Itzik, 1986, short / *Shuroo*, 1990 (also co-scriptwriter) / *Lovesick on Nana St.*, 1995 (also co-producer, scriptwriter).

GAON, YEHORAM (Jerusalem, 1939). Actor.

Gaon grew up in a Sephardi household steeped in Ladino culture and served in the Nahal Entertainment Troupe of the army. He directed and produced a cinematic musical ode to Jerusalem, *I Was Born in Jerusalem**, in which he sings as he points out places of interest in the city. He then went on to study acting in the United States and television directing at the RCA Institute. He returned to Israel in 1973 to star in Menahem Golan's* film spectacular *Kazablan**, which depicts the discrimination suffered by Jews of Sephardi background during the early years of the state of Israel.

Gaon has appeared in leading roles in numerous films and in more than 600 stage performances and is well known in Israel for his songs in both Ladino and Hebrew. He has produced numerous albums, many of which are solo performances. He serves on the Jerusalem City Council, responsible for the portfolio of culture, and is an Israeli talk-show personality. He has published two books, which are collections of songs, stories, and pictures of the Ladino culture, and has four times received an Israeli Grammy award for his music.

Filmography

*Every Bastard a King**, 1968 / *Siege**, 1969 / *The Big Escape*, 1970 / *I Was Born in Jerusalem*, 1971, documentary (only director, co-producer, co-scriptwriter, singer) / *Kazablan*, 1973 / *Joker*, 1976 / *Operation Thunderbolt**, 1977 / *Dead End Street**, 1982 / *The Lover**, 1986 / *From Toledo to Jerusalem*, 1989, documentary (only scriptwriter, singer) / *Mr. Mani*, TV series / *Neighbors*, TV series / *Jerusalem Investigator*, TV series.

GITAI, AMOS (Haifa, 1950). Director.

Gitai served in the Yom Kippur War of 1973 as a reserve soldier, at which time his helicopter was shot down. In 1977 he began directing documentary films for Israel Television. After his film *House* was censored by the television authorities, and when his subsequent film *Field Diary** met with much criticism in Israel, Gitai moved abroad. He trained as an architect at the University of California at Berkeley (Ph.D., 1986) and lived in Paris for many years. He returned to live in Israel in 1993. Gitai's films deal with themes of exile, emigration, and political issues relevant to the current reality in Israel. In addition, his films experiment with the traditional definitions of narrative and explore the boundaries of a critical view from within. His film *Berlin–Jerusalem** is a shattering view of the Zionist dream, and *Kippur** is a graphic antiwar film (based on some of his own experiences during the Yom Kippur War). His trilogy

Devarim, *Day after Day**, and *Kadosh** takes place in Haifa, Tel Aviv, and Jerusalem and explores, with a critical eye, societal issues in each of those cities.

A prolific and controversial filmmaker, Gitai is one of the Israeli directors who have received much recognition worldwide—Nyon, 1982 (*Field Diary*); European Council, 1991 (*Golem—The Spirit of Exile*); Venice, 1989; Istanbul, 1990 (*Berlin–Jerusalem*); and Jerusalem, 1998 (*Day after Day*). He was awarded the distinction of Cavalier of the Arts from the Minister of Culture of France (1999) and an achievement award from the Jerusalem Film Festival (2002).

Filmography

Political Myth, 1977, documentary / *Wadi Rushmia*, 1978, documentary / *Wadi Salib Riots*, 1979, documentary / *House*, 1980, documentary / *Wadi*, 1981, documentary / *In Search of Identity*, 1981, documentary / *Field Diary*, 1982, documentary / *Esther*, 1985 (also producer, co-scriptwriter) / *Berlin–Jerusalem*, 1989 (also scriptwriter) / *Wadi, Ten Years Later*, 1991, documentary / *Give Peace a Chance*, 1994, documentary / *Devarim*, 1995 (also co-scriptwriter) / *The Arena of Murder*, 1996, documentary / *Milim*, 1996 / *War and Peace in Vesoul*, 1997, improvised fiction and documentary / *A House in Jerusalem*, 1998, documentary / *Zion, Auto-Emanicipation*, 1998, documentary / *Tapuz*, 1998, documentary (also co-producer, scriptwriter) / *Day after Day*, 1998 (also script) / *Kadosh*, 1999 (also co-producer, co-scriptwriter) / *Kippur**, 2000 (also co-producer, co-scriptwriter) / *Wadi, Grand Canyon*, 2001, documentary (also co-producer, scriptwriter) / *Eden*, 2002 (also co-producer, co-scriptwriter) / *Kedma*, 2002.

GLOBUS, YORAM (Tiberias, 1941). Producer.

Globus grew up working in his father's cinema in Haifa, where he got his first taste of the film industry. Following his studies in business and service in the Israeli army he joined his cousin, Menahem Golan*, and in 1963 they formed Noah Films. Their film company was responsible for many Israeli productions, including hits such as *Lemon Popsicle** (Boaz Davidson*) and an entire series of sequels, and *Kazablan** (Menahem Golan). In addition, they jointly produced four Israeli feature films that were nominated for an American Academy Award for Best Foreign Film—*Operation Thunderbolt** (Menahem Golan), *The House on Chelouche St.** (Moshe Mizrahi*), *I Love You, Rosa** (Moshe Mizrahi), and *Sallah** (Ephraim Kishon*).

In 1979 Golan and Globus purchased controlling shares in Cannon Films, an independent film production company headquartered in Los Angeles. Globus has co-produced more than 160 films in both Israel and in the United States and received a Life Achievement Award from the Israeli Academy of Film (1999).

Filmography

Fortuna, 1966 (co-producer) / *A Miracle in the Town*, 1968 (co-producer) / *My Margo*, 1969 (co-producer) / *The Big Escape*, 1970 (co-producer) / *Lupo**, 1970 (co-producer) / *Highway Queen**, 1971 (co-producer) / *Katz and Carrasso*, 1971 (co-producer) / *The Great Telephone Robbery*, 1972 (co-producer) / *I Love You, Rosa*, 1972 (co-producer) / *Daughters, Daughters**, 1973 (co-producer) / *Kazablan*, 1973 (co-producer) / *Diamonds*, 1975 (co-producer) / *Lupo Goes to New York*, 1976 (only executive producer) / *Operation*

Thunderbolt, 1977 (co-producer) / *It's a Funny, Funny World*, 1978 (co-producer) / *Lemon Popsicle*, 1978 (co-producer) / *Going Steady*, 1979 (co-producer) / *Marriage Tel Aviv Style*, 1979 (co-producer) / *My Mother, the General**, 1979 (co-producer) / *Hot Bubblegum*, 1981 (co-producer) / *Private Popsicle*, 1982 (co-producer) / *Mute Love*, 1982 (co-producer) / *Private Maneuvers*, 1983 (co-producer) / *Baby Love*, 1984 (co-producer) / *Forced Testimony**, 1984 (co-producer) / *The Lover**, 1985 (co-producer) / *Up Your Anchor*, 1985 (co-producer) / *Prom Queen*, 1986 (co-producer) / *Theater of Illegal People*, 2002, documentary / *Sleeping Diagonal*, 2002, documentary.

GOLAN, MENAHEM (Tiberias, 1929). Producer and Director.

Golan studied theater directing at London's Old Vic, and after working as a director of theater for a number of years in Israel he decided to change course and to go into filmmaking. He studied film in New York City and received film experience working for Roger Corman. Upon his return to Israel in 1963 he directed his first film, *Eldorado**.

Golan was instrumental in developing an active industry and providing jobs and training for many film professionals, including technicians and cast, on a continuous basis during the 1960s and 1970s. Golan's low-budget ethnic films were the forerunners of a popular genre entitled "bourekas" films (named for the fluff pastry)—films that portray stories and humor made mostly at the expense of Sephardi ethnic stereotypes. The best known of this genre was *Sallah** (Ephraim Kishon*), which he produced. The prolific and diverse Golan has produced and directed adolescent sex comedies, musicals, crime stories, and thrillers. He directed the first Israeli musical spectacular, *Kazablan**, which was hugely popular due to its combination of fast-paced choreography with ethnic tension and romance.

Golan has worked together as a team with his cousin, Yoram Globus*, in a production company (Noah Films) since 1963. After many successful years and a growing international reputation, the two formed the international Golan-Globus company in 1976 and purchased the controlling interest in Cannon Films, a U.S. independent film production and distribution company, in 1979. For the next 10 years they produced dozens of commercial action films, including *Delta Force* (Menahem Golan, 1985), *American Ninja* (Sam Firstenberg, 1985), and *Cobra* (George Cosmatos, 1986), and they worked with world-class directors such as Jean Luc Godard (*King Lear*, 1987), Franco Zeffirelli (*Otello*, 1986), Alexander Konchalovsky (*Shy People*, 1987), and Barbet Shroeder (*Barfly*, 1987).

Personally responsible for the production and/or direction of over 175 films internationally (of which approximately 40 were Israeli features), Golan's style is one of popularized filmmaking. He produced many of the biggest box office successes in Israel, which were not necessarily also the critics' choices. Notwithstanding the taste of the critics, some of Golan's films have won international recognition. Over the years, six Israeli feature films have been nominated for an American Academy Award for Best Foreign Film. Golan jointly produced four of these six films together with his partner, Yoram Globus—Kishon's *Sallah*, two directed by Moshe Mizrachi* (*I Love You, Rosa** and *The House on Chelouche St.**), and one that was directed by Golan himself, *Operation Thunderbolt**. Golan's contribution to Israeli cinema was recognized when he received a Special Citation from the Minister of Industry and Trade (1985) and a Life Achievement Award from the Israeli Academy Awards (1994).

Filmography

Eldorado, 1963 (director, co-scriptwriter) / *Dalia and the Sailors**, 1964 (director) / *Eight Against One**, 1964 (director, co-producer) / *Sallah*, 1964 (producer) / *The Girl from the Dead Sea**, 1966 (director, co-producer, scriptwriter) / *Trunk to Cairo*, 1966 (director, producer) / *Aliza Mizrachi*, 1967 (director, producer, scriptwriter) / *A Miracle in the Town*, 1968 (co-producer) / *Tevye and His Seven Daughters**, 1968 (director, producer, co-scriptwriter) / *My Love in Jerusalem**, 1969 (director, co-producer, scriptwriter) / *The Big Escape*, 1970 (director, co-producer, co-scriptwriter) / *Lupo**, 1970 (director, co-producer, scriptwriter) / *The Highway Queen**, 1971 (director, producer, co-scriptwriter) / *Katz and Carasso*, 1971 (director, co-scriptwriter) / *Escape to the Sun**, 1972 (director, producer, co-scriptwriter) / *The Great Telephone Robbery*, 1972 (director, co-producer, co-scriptwriter) / *I Love You, Rosa*, 1972 (producer) / *Kazablan*, 1973 (director, producer, co-scriptwriter) / *Daughters, Daughters**, 1973 (producer) / *The House on Chelouche St.*, 1973 (producer) / *Diamonds*, 1975 (director, co-producer, scriptwriter) / *Lupo Goes to New York*, 1976 (producer, scriptwriter) / *Operation Thunderbolt*, 1977 (director, co-producer, co-scriptwriter) / *It's a Funny, Funny World*, 1978 (co-producer) / *Lemon Popsicle**, 1978 (co-producer) / *Going Steady*, 1979 (co-producer) / *Marriage Tel Aviv Style*, 1979 (co-producer) / *My Mother, the General**, 1979 (co-producer) / *Hot Bubblegum*, 1981 (co-producer) / *Mute Love*, 1982 (co-producer) / *Private Popsicle*, 1982 (co-producer) / *Private Maneuvers*, 1983 (co-producer) / *Baby Love*, 1984 (co-producer) / *Forced Testimony**, 1984 (co-producer) / *Up Your Anchor*, 1985 (co-producer) / *The Lover**, 1986 (co-producer) / *Prom Queen*, 1986 (co-producer) / *The Wild, Crazy and the Lunatics*, 1986 (co-producer, co-scriptwriter) / *Hannah's War*, 1987 (director, co-producer, co-scriptwriter) / *The Return from India*, 2002, (director, producer).

GOLDWASSER, YA'ACKOV (YANKUL) (Tel Aviv, 1950). Director.

Two of Goldwasser's feature films, *The Skipper** and *Over the Ocean**, deal with family issues as portrayed through the eyes of a young boy. In *The Skipper*, which was very popular with the Israeli filmgoing public, the narrative construct deals with issues of divorce and a father–son relationship. In the historical film *Over the Ocean* (winner of Israeli Academy Awards), which takes place during the early years of the state, the family is finding it difficult to manage and is considering leaving Israel.

Goldwasser's TV series *Reaching for Heaven* won an Israeli Academy Award (2001) and the Anat Pirchi Prize at Jerusalem (2000). Goldwasser has also produced local commercials and many films abroad.

Filmography

Re'ut, 1970, short / *Shalom, Prayer for the Road*, 1973 (only editor) / *Once You Loved Picnics with Daddy*, 1974, short / *Transit**, 1980 (only producer) / *Big Shots*, 1982 (also co-scriptwriter) / *The Skipper*, 1988 / *Over the Ocean*, 1991 / *Max and Morris*, 1994 / *Reaching for Heaven*, 2000, TV series (co-director).

GOREN, AMIT (Tel Aviv, 1957). Director.

Goren studied film at the Tisch School of the Arts, Film and Television Department at New York University (B.A.). He is a documentary filmmaker whose films have been seen at numerous film festivals and broadcast on television stations worldwide. He has made many award-winning documentary films that deal with societal issues—*'66 Was a Good Year for Tourism** (Wolgin Award, Jerusalem and Israeli Academy Award); *6 Open, 21 Closed* (Prix Futura at Berlin, 1996, and the Gold Medal at FIPA, Biarritz, 1995); *Good or Bad, Black and White* (Wolgin Award, Jerusalem and Award from the New Foundation for Cinema and Television); *Another Land* (Wolgin Award at Jerusalem). Goren teaches filmmaking at the Sam Spiegel Film and Television School in Jerusalem, Sapir College and at the Beit Berl Art Academy.

Filmography

The Cage, 1989, short (also scriptwriter) / *Israeli Salad*, 1991, documentary (also scriptwriter) / *'66 Was a Good Year for Tourism*, 1992, documentary (also producer, scriptwriter) / *6 Open, 21 Closed*, 1994, documentary (also producer, scriptwriter) / *Good or Bad, Black and White*, 1995, documentary (also producer, scriptwriter) / *Ever Shot Anyone*, 1995, documentary (only producer) / *119 bullets + Three*, 1996, documentary (only producer) / *Thy Father's Name*, 1996, documentary (also scriptwriter) / *Test Run*, 1998, TV drama (also producer, scriptwriter) / *Another Land*, 1998, documentary (also producer, scriptwriter) / *Babylon and Jerusalem*, 1998, documentary (also scriptwriter) / *Moscow on the Mediterranean*, 1999, documentary (only producer) / *Perets and the Wolf*, 1999, documentary (also producer, scriptwriter) / *Your Nigger Talking*, 1999, video installation (also scriptwriter) / *Ullman's Earth*, 2000, documentary (also producer, scriptwriter) / *Makom Project*, 2001, TV series (only producer) / *Apropos Mizrachi*, 2001, documentary (also producer, scriptwriter) / *Golan*, 2002, documentary (also producer, scriptwriter).

GREENBERG, ADAM (Cracow, Poland, 1937). Cinematographer.

Greenberg began his professional career in the Israeli army as an air force cameraman. He worked for the Geva Studios, photographing the newsreels, and then began to do documentary and feature films. He has served as cinematographer, working with many of the outstanding Israeli directors, including Moshe Mizrachi* (*I Love You, Rosa**, *Daughters, Daughters**, and *The House on Chelouche St.**), Dan Wolman* (*My Michael**), Menahem Golan* (*Operation Thunderbolt**), and Boaz Davidson* (*Lemon Popsicle** and its sequel, *Going Steady*). Some of his films were nominated for American Academy Awards, and he won two awards for cinematography from the Israel Film Center in the same year (1978)—*Operation Thunderbolt* and *Lemon Popsicle*.

Greenberg has also served as the cinematographer for many foreign films, including *Sister Act* (Emile Ardolino) and *Terminator 2* (James Cameron). He was nominated for an American Academy Award for his cinematography for the latter.

Filmography

In Jerusalem, 1963, documentary / *Two Kuni Lemel**, 1966 / *Sha'ar Hagay*, 1966, abstract documentary / *Slow Down*, 1968, short / *Before Tomorrow*, 1969 / *Lool*, 1969 / *Ben Gurion, 42:6*, 1970, documentary / *Get Zorkin*, 1971 / *I Was Born in Jerusalem**, 1971, documentary / *Take Two**, 1972 / *Peeping Toms**, 1972 / *The Pill*, 1972 / *I Love You, Rosa*, 1972 / *The House on Chelouche St.*, 1973 / *Daughters, Daughters*, 1973 / *Diamonds*, 1975 / *My Michael*, 1975 / *Operation Thunderbolt*, 1977 / *Half a Million Black*, 1977 / *A Movie and Breakfast*, 1977 / *Uranium Conspiracy*, 1978 / *It's a Funny, Funny World*, 1978 / *Lemon Popsicle*, 1978 / *Belfer*, 1978 / *Going Steady*, 1979 / *Private Popsicle*, 1982 / *Private Maneuvers*, 1983 / *Lool*, 1988.

GRONICH, SHLOMO (Hadera, 1949). Composer.

Gronich has composed the music for theater, dance performances, musicals, and feature films. He won Israeli awards for Best Musical Score for *A Thousand Little Kisses** (Mira Recanati), *Over the Ocean** (Ya'ackov Goldwasser*), and *Circus Palestine** (Eyal Halfon*). His music brings together differing influences from around the world, integrating them with his Israeli and Jewish roots. He established and made famous the Shva Choir, which is composed of children who emigrated to Israel from Ethiopia, and he is its musical director and conductor.

Filmography

*Transit**, 1980 / *A Thousand Little Kisses*, 1981 / *Big Shots**, 1982 / *The Skipper**, 1988 / *The Owl*, 1988 / *Over the Ocean*, 1991 / *Tel Aviv Stories**, 1992 (co-composer) / *Max and Morris*, 1994 / *Abraham's Journey*, 1997, documentary / *Circus Palestine*, 1999.

GROSS, NATHAN (Cracow, Poland, 1919). Director.

Gross studied filmmaking at the Lodz film school. Following the war he directed two Yiddish feature films as part of the Polish cooperative "Kinor." One of these, *Unzere Kinder* (1949), starring the comic duo Dzigan and Shumacher and Jewish children of Lodz, became one of the most important postwar Holocaust films, a tribute to the children's indomitable strength and will to survive.

After coming to live in Israel in 1950, Gross made Geva newsreels and commercials and later became an independent documentary filmmaker. In his career he has directed numerous documentaries, most of them dealing with the early years of the state of Israel and with Jewish subjects. His feature *The Cellar** won the Jugend Film Prize at Berlin.

Gross wrote film criticism for the newspaper *Al Hamishmar* for 20 years (1962–1982). Together with his son, Ya'akov Gross, he wrote a reference book on the history of early Israeli filmmaking entitled *HaSeret Ha'Ivri* (*Hebrew Film—Chapters in the History of Silent and Sound Film in Israel*), published in 1991. Nathan Gross was given a Life Achievement Award by the Israel Academy Awards (1991) and by the Jerusalem Cinematheque (2001).

Filmography

Tel Aviv, 1950, documentary / *The Red Shoelace*, 1954, documentary / *The Hula Valley*, 1954, documentary / *Brit Damim*, 1956, documentary / *The Open Border*, 1956, documentary / *The Town of Nazareth*, 1957, documentary / *Song of Songs*, 1957, documentary / *Gadna: Israel Youth Brigade*, 1958, documentary / *The Fourth Maccabiah*, 1958, documentary / *From Beersheva to Eilat*, 1958, documentary / *Degania*, 1960, documentary / *Arad*, 1963 / *The Cellar*, 1963 / *How Goodly Are Thy Tents*, 1965, documentary / *Carmiel*, 1965, documentary / *Remember*, 1965, documentary / *Knesset Israel*, 1965, documentary / *Ashdod*, 1966, documentary / *The Magic Circle*, 1967 / *Water, Water*, 1969, documentary / *A Leader in Israel*, 1969, documentary / *Sir Moses*, 1970, documentary / *Yossele Rosenblatt*, 1978, documentary / *The Yellow Star*, 1978, documentary.

GURFINKEL, DAVID (Tel Aviv, 1939). Cinematographer.

Following his army service as a cameraman, Gurfinkel worked for the Geva newsreels and eventually became one of Israel's most prolific and outstanding cinematographers. Gurfinkel's first feature film, *Hole in the Moon**, was directed by Uri Zohar*, with whom he continued to work on many films. He worked with directors such as Ephraim Kishon* (*The Big Dig**, *The Fox in the Chickencoop**, and *The Policeman**), Michal Bat-Adam* (*The Lover**), Avram Heffner* (*Aunt Clara**, *The Last Love Affair of Laura Adler**), Uri Zohar* (*Every Bastard a King**—Best Color Photography Prize, Chicago, 1968), and Ze'ev Revach* (*Only Today**). Gurfinkel won Israel Film Center awards for Best Cinematography for *A Thousand Little Kisses** (Mira Recanati) and *Rage and Glory* (Avi Nesher*) and Israeli Academy Awards for *Under the Domim Tree** (Eli Cohen*), *Sh'chur** (Shmuel Hasfari*), and *Dangerous Acts* (Shemi Zarhin*). He has also been the cinematographer for Israeli television dramas and documentaries and numerous American films that were produced by Cannon Films, such as *Delta Force* (Menahem Golan), *The Naked Face* (Bryan Forbes), and *Appointment with Death* (Michael Winner).

Filmography

Hole in the Moon, 1965 / *Moishe Air-Condition**, 1966 / *Three Days and a Child**, 1967 / *Every Bastard a King*, 1968 / *Fish, Football and Girls**, 1968 / *Iris**, 1968 / *The Big Dig*, 1969 / *Siege**, 1969 / *Lool*, 1969, TV series / *The Policeman*, 1970 / *Take-Off**, 1970 / *Highway Queen**, 1971 / *Katz and Carasso*, 1971 / *Fifty-Fifty**, 1971 / *The Great Telephone Robbery*, 1972 / *Escape to the Sun**, 1972 / *Kazablan**, 1973 / *Big Eyes**, 1974 / *The Father*, 1975 / *Snooker*, 1975 / *Only Today*, 1976 / *Hershele*, 1977 / *Save the Lifeguard**, 1977 / *Aunt Clara*, 1977 / *Million Dollar Heist*, 1977 / *The Fox in the Chicken Coop*, 1978 / *The Magician from Lublin**, 1979 / *Marriage Tel Aviv Style*, 1979 / *My Mother, the General**, 1979 / *Worlds Apart**, 1979 / *The Man Who Flew in to Grab*, 1981 / *A Thousand Little Kisses*, 1982 / *Hamsin**, 1982 / *Mute Love*, 1982 / *Tell Me That You Love Me**, 1983 / *Rage and Glory*, 1985 / *The Lover*, 1985 / *Once We Were Dreamers**, 1987 / *Lool*, 1988 / *Summer of Aviya**, 1988 / *The Last Love Affair* *of Laura Adler*, 1990 / *Across the Ocean**, 1992 / *Cable*, 1992 / *Choice and Destiny**, 1993, documentary (co-cinematographer) / *Sh'chur*, 1994 / *Under the Domim Tree*, 1994 / *Shiva'a*, 1995, TV drama / *The House Where Cockroaches Live to a Ripe Old Age*, 1996 / *Minotaur*, 1997 / *Three Sisters*, 1998, documentary (co-cinematographer) / *Purple Lawns*, 1998, TV drama / *Dangerous Acts*, 1998 / *Begin*, 1998, TV drama / *Electric Man**, 2000.

GUTMANN, AMOS (Oradea, Romania, 1954–Tel Aviv, 1993). Director.

Gutmann immigrated to Israel in 1962. He studied film at Beit Zvi Film School in Ramat Gan and at New York University. Before his untimely death at the age of 39 he directed four feature films, which portray young people suffering from the limitations of a narrow-minded society and depict the director's own background, milieu, and sensitivities. His distinct stylistic elements include dealing with relations between mother (or mother figure) and son, modest yet erotic male love scenes, nostalgia for the old-fashioned, strong emotions, the use of darkness and shadow to create a claustrophobic environment, and images set in decaying and seedy surroundings.

Gutmann's film *Himmo, King of Jerusalem** (based on the novel by the well-known Israeli author Yoram Kaniuk) deals with the trauma of soldiers wounded in war and has a historical setting. His three additional films, *Drifting**, *Bar 51**, and *Amazing Grace**, form a trilogy, examining issues of homosexuality. *Amazing Grace*, the first Israeli feature film to squarely confront the loneliness and pain of AIDS, won the Silver Palm at Valencia, Honorable Mention at Houston and Torino, the Wolgin Award at Jerusalem, and the Critics' Jury Prize at Haifa.

Filmography

Repeat Premieres, short / *Safe Place*, short / *Nagua*, 1979, short / *Drifting*, 1983 (also co-scriptwriter) / *Bar 51*, 1985 (also co-scriptwriter) / *The Fabric Story*, documentary / *Himmo, King of Jerusalem*, 1987 / *Amazing Grace*, 1992 (also scriptwriter).

HALFON, EYAL (Netanya, 1956). Director.

Halfon received a B.A. from Tel Aviv University in film and television. He worked as a journalist (1985-1995) and makes dramatic and documentary films. In the area of feature film production he wrote the script for *Cup Final** (Eran Riklis*) and directed *The Italians Are Coming** and *Circus Palestine** (Israeli Academy Awards). Halfon teaches in the Department of Film and Television at Tel Aviv University.

Filmography

Tonight a Film, 1990, TV drama (also producer) / *Cup Final*, 1991 (only scriptwriter) / *Back to the Yarkon*, 1992, documentary / *The Italians Are Coming*, 1995 (also co-scriptwriter) / *Hoummous for Two*, 1997, documentary (also producer) / *Circus Palestine*, 1998 (also scriptwriter) / *Theo and His Friends*, 1998, documentary (also producer) / *Family Hip-Hop*, documentary (only producer) / *Manilla Casino*, 1999, documentary (also producer) / *You Must Make a Move Out of This*, 2000, TV series (also producer) /

Diamonds in Pita, 2001, documentary (also producer) / *Bagdad Bandstand*, 2002, documentary (also producer).

HASFARI, SHMUEL (Tel Aviv, 1954). Director.

Hasfari studied theater and philosophy at Tel Aviv University (1976–1980). An important figure of Israeli theater, he has written and directed many plays, including *A Trumpet in the Wadi* (based on the book by Sami Michael), *Kiddush* (which ran for many seasons), and *Eliko* (which won First Prize at the Acre Fringe Theater Festival, 1982). He established an acting group called the Pashut Theater and has been the artistic director of the Cameri Theater (1991–1993) and the Acre Fringe Theater Festival (1990–1991).

Hasfari wrote the script for the award-winning film *The Appointed** (Daniel Wachsmann*). His important contribution to Israeli film is his feature film *Sh'chur**, based on a script written by his wife, the actress Hannah Azoulai-Hasfari*, which won Special Mention at Berlin (1995), Second Prize at Sorento (1996), and Israeli Academy Awards (1994).

Filmography

The Appointed, 1990 (only scriptwriter) / *What's Different on This Night*, 1990, TV drama / *Kol Nidre*, 1991, TV drama / *Sh'chur*, 1994.

HAVILIO, RON (Jerusalem, 1950). Director.

Havilio received his B.A. (1974) from Hebrew University in Jerusalem in art history and Middle Eastern studies. He received his M.A. (1986) from Tel Aviv University in film studies and in art history. He is a prizewinning still photographer and an instructor in aikido and has worked as a building contractor in Jerusalem. He has taught cinema history and the history of art at the Sam Spiegel Film and Television School in Jerusalem since 1989.

Havilio's epic prizewinning film on Jerusalem, *Fragments—Jerusalem**, is a six-hour documentary that took more than 10 years to produce. The film, made in the style of a personal documentary, which won prizes at Edinburgh, Berlin, Yamagata, and Jerusalem, is a diary interwoven with archaeological layers of the city of Jerusalem.

Filmography

Diary, 1985, documentary (also cinematographer) / *Fragments—Jerusalem*, 1986–1996, documentary (also producer, scriptwriter, cinematographer).

HEFFNER, AVRAM (Haifa, 1935). Director.

Heffner served as an actor in the Entertainment Troupe of the army before attending Hebrew University in Jerusalem, where he studied philosophy and English literature (1956–1958). Later he studied philosophy, linguistics, and American studies at the Sorbonne (1958–1961) and then Film at the City College of New York (1961–1962). While in Paris he worked as assistant director to Jacques Becker (*Le Trou*) and Lazlo Benedek (*Recours en grace*).

Heffner returned to Israel in 1963, and shortly thereafter he appeared in a leading role in Uri Zohar's* *Hole in the Moon**. His directorial debut was a prizewinning short, *Slow Down* (Best Short Film, Venice, 1968), based on a short story by Simone de Beauvoir. Heffner is an auteur filmmaker and three of his films show a preoccupation with the illusory past. *But Where Is Daniel Wax?** (Israel Film Center Awards, 1973) is about middle-aged soul-searching and dissatisfaction; *The Last Love Affair of Laura Adler** (Wolgin Award, Jerusalem, 1990 and Best Film, Best Director, Haifa, 1991) is a look at the world of Yiddish theater; and *Cover Story** is an investigation into an unsolved murder from the 1930s. His fourth film, *Aunt Clara**, offers a satirical look at the sacrificing and meddling Jewish mother.

In addition to his filmmaking, Heffner is an accomplished novelist; his first novel, *Aeval*, appeared in 1968, and since that time he has written seven more. He teaches directing and screenwriting at Tel Aviv University in the Department of Film and Television. He has also taught at New York University and at the Ecole Cantonale d'Art in Lausanne. Heffner received a Life Achievement Award from the Jerusalem Film Festival (2000).

Filmography

Hole in the Moon, 1965 (only actor) / *Sinai Commando*, 1967 (only actor) / *Scouting Patrol**, 1967 (only scriptwriter) / *Slow Down*, 1968, short (also producer, scriptwriter) / *Seance*, 1969, short / *But Where Is Daniel Wax?*, 1972 (also scriptwriter) / *Aunt Clara*, 1977 (also scriptwriter) / *Fantasia on a Romantic Theme**, 1978 (also actor) / *Cover Story*, 1979, TV drama (also scriptwriter) / *Ma Karah* (*What's Wrong*), 1988, short (also scriptwriter) / *The Last Love Affair of Laura Adler*, 1990 (also scriptwriter) / *Big Man, Small Country*, 1998, TV series.

IMBERMAN, SHMUEL (Moshav Be'er Tuvia, 1936). Director.

Imberman is a filmmaker working in the areas of feature film production, television dramas, commercials, and educational and documentary filmmaking. He has worked as the head of the Department of Cinema and Television at the Tel Aviv College of Management.

During his career, in which he produced numerous projects, Imberman also directed feature films. His *Don't Give a Damn** is a groundbreaking film about a subject that was taboo in Israeli society for many years—the physical and psychological wounds of disabled war veterans. His hard-hitting film *Overdose* also breaks a taboo and deals seriously with the effects of drug abuse and crime in society.

Filmography

Hedva and I, 1970, TV series / *Two Heart Beats*, 1972 / *Million Dollar Heist*, 1977 / *I Like Mike*, 1978, TV drama / *Chambers of the Heart*, 1979, TV drama / *Five and Five Musical*, 1980 (also co-scriptwriter) / *Deadly Fortune*, TV series / *Don't Give a Damn*, 1987 / *Tel Aviv–Los Angeles**, 1988 / *They Will Arrive Tomorrow*, 1990, TV drama / *From Toledo to Jerusalem*, 1989, documentary / *Twice Abraham*, TV drama / *The Shapira Affair*, TV drama / *Dana*, TV drama / *Dom Lev*, TV series / *Overdose*, 1993 / *Back* *to the USSR*, documentary / *Too Many Graves*, documentary / *A Bottle in the Cellar*, 1994, documentary (also scriptwriter) / *Wings*, 2002, TV series.

IVGI, MOSHE (Casablanca, Morocco, 1954). Actor.

Ivgi's family immigrated to Israel when he was a child. Today he is one of Israel's most popular actors and an active member of Israel's Screen Actors' Guild. He has appeared in television dramas, numerous feature films, shorts, and many and varied plays performed on the Israeli stage.

On the screen Ivgi has made famous the role of the Israeli "little" guy, a well-meaning, regular fellow who has become a tragic victim of societal circumstances, in films such as *Shuroo** (Savi Gabizon*), *Cup Final** (Eran Riklis*), *Max and Morris* (Ya'ackov Goldwasser*), *Lovesick on Nana St.** (Savi Gabizon), and *The Investigation Continues** (Marek Rozenbaum*).

Ivgi has received much recognition for his diverse roles, including an Israeli Academy Award for *Shuroo* (1990), Jerusalem Film Festival Honorable Mention and Haifa Film Festival Prize for Best Actor for *Shuroo* and *Cup Final* (1991), and awards for *Lovesick on Nana St.*—Israeli Academy Award (1995), Critics' Prize at Haifa (1996), and Special Mention at Mannheim (1996).

Filmography

Indiani in the Sun, 1981, TV drama / *Gabi Ben Yakar*, 1982, TV drama / *Big Shots*, 1982 / *Mr. Leon**, 1982 / *Kuni Lemel in Cairo*, 1983 / *Night Movie*, 1985, short / *Mondo Condo*, 1986 / *Bread**, 1986, TV drama / *Attraction**, 1988 (only editor) / *Winter Games**, 1988, TV drama / *Shuroo*, 1990 / *Cup Final*, 1991 / *Angels on the Wind*, 1992 / *Revenge of Itzik Finkelstein**, 1993 / *Dreams of Innocence**, 1993 / *Max and Morris*, 1994 / *Lovesick on Nana St.*, 1995 / *The Dybbuk of the Holy Apple Field**, 1997 / *Cause of Death: Murder*, 1997, TV drama / *Day After Day**, 1998 / *Dangerous Acts*, 1998 / *Aaron Cohen's Debt*, 1998, TV drama / *Begin*, 1998, TV drama / *On Air*, 1999, TV drama / *Yellow Asphalt**, 2000 / *The Investigation Continues*, 2000 / *The Lawyers*, 2002, TV series / *The Postwoman*, 2002, TV drama.

KAPLUN, ARIK (Moscow, Russia, 1958). Director.

Kaplun immigrated to Israel at the age of 20 and studied directing in Tel Aviv. Following a period of two years in Los Angeles, he returned to Israel in 1991 and began to develop the idea behind his first feature film, *Yana's Friends**. The film, which deals with the frustrations of new immigrants to Israel, was an expressive tool for portraying the difficulties of those immigrants who came in the large wave of immigration from the former Soviet Union during the early 1990s. The story takes place against the background of the Gulf War and stars the wife of the director, Evelyn Kaplun, as Yana. The film won much local attention (Israeli Academy Awards and Wolgin Award at Jerusalem) and awards at international film festivals (Karlovy Vary, Moscow, Rome, Houston, and Montpellier).

Kaplun teaches directing in Tel Aviv at the Camera Obscura film school and at the Open University.

Filmography

Solo for Tuba, 1987, short / *Yana's Friends*, 1999 (also co-scriptwriter).

KHOURY, MAKRAM (Jerusalem, 1945). Actor.

Khoury studied acting in London and was accepted into the Haifa Theater Ensemble in the late 1970s. Since that time he has appeared in dozens of theater productions with all of the major theater groups in Israel. He is also a star of film and television.

As an Israeli Palestinian Arab actor, Khoury has played Arab roles in films. However, he is well known for his performance as the Jewish military governor of the West Bank in *Wedding in Galilee** (Michel Khleifi) and in *Smile of the Lamb** (Shimon Dotan*). Khoury won Israel Film Center awards for Best Supporting Actor for his roles in *Smile of the Lamb* and *On a Narrow Bridge** (Nissim Dayan*), both in the same year. Khoury was awarded the coveted Israel Prize for Achievement in the field of Theater, Television, and Film (1987).

Filmography

*My Mother, the General**, 1979 / *Big Shots*, 1982 / *Michel Ezra Safra and Sons*, 1983, TV drama / *Kasach*, 1984 / *On a Narrow Bridge*, 1985 / *Smile of the Lamb*, 1985 / *Wedding in Galilee*, 1987 / *Torn Apart*, 1989 / *The Scapegoat*, 1991, TV drama / *Double Edge**, 1992 / *The Milky Way**, 1998 / *A Man of the Police*, 1999–2000, TV series.

KISHON, EPHRAIM (Budapest, Hungary, 1924). Director.

Kishon (original name: Ferenc Hoffman) studied at the Art Academy and at Budapest University. After surviving a concentration camp, he immigrated to Israel in 1949. With his flair for language and talent for writing, he became one of the nation's foremost humorists and satirists. He has written satirical columns for an Israeli daily newspaper (*Ma'ariv*), books, satires, novels, and plays. He directed and scripted five feature films that are political and social satires. With these five films, which criticized many aspects of Israeli life—the political parties, the inept government bureaucracy, the well-meaning liberals, unemployment, and the comic-pathetic "little" guy who is the victim of the system—Kishon succeeded in raising the level of Israeli satire to an international level.

Kishon's first film, *Sallah**, was critically acclaimed and very successful with Israeli audiences. The film received awards at San Francisco, from the Hollywood Foreign Press Association (1965) and All American Press–American Distributors (1965), and Vienna (1966) and the nomination for an American Academy Award for Best Foreign Film (1964). *The Big Dig** won awards at Barcelona (1969) and Monte Carlo (1971). *The Policeman** won awards at Atlanta (1972), Monte Carlo (1972), Barcelona (1971), and from the Hollywood Foreign Press Association (1971).

Kishon received an honorary doctorate from Tel Aviv University (1990), was presented with a Life Achievement Award by the Israeli Film Academy (1993), and received a special Life Achievement Award for Literature and Cinema within the framework of the coveted Israel Prize (2002). He has received recognition internationally for his work and has been awarded many literary prizes, including the Order of Merit for Literature, Republic of Hungary (1999); the Bialik Literature Prize of Israel (1998); the Grand Prize of Literature, Budapest (1996); and the Austrian State Prize for Culture and Literature, First Class (1995).

Filmography

Sallah, 1964 (also scriptwriter) / *Ervinka**, 1967 (also co-producer, scriptwriter) / *The Big Dig*, 1969 (also producer, scriptwriter) / *The Policeman*, 1971 (also co-producer, scriptwriter) / *The Fox in the Chicken Coop**, 1978 (also co-producer, scriptwriter).

KISLEV, YORAM (Bialystock, Poland, 1956). Producer.

Kislev studied Semitic and ancient languages at Tel Aviv University and then switched to the film department and completed his degree in 1985. He worked as the assistant director on a number of feature films, both in Israel and abroad, before he began his career as a producer of Israeli films, dealing also with their foreign distribution. In 2000 he directed a feature film, *A Matter of Reputation**.

Filmography

The Owl, 1988 (only assistant director) / *Joshua, Joshua*, 1986 (only executive producer) / *Torn Apart*, 1989 (only assistant director) / *A Thousand and One Wives**, 1989 (only assistant director) / *Stalin's Disciples**, 1986 (only executive producer) / *The Voice of Ein Harod*, 1990 (co-producer) / *Where Eagles Fly*, 1990 (co-producer) / *What's Different on This Night*, 1990, TV drama / *Kol Nidre*, 1991, TV drama / *Fear of the Jews*, 1991, TV drama / *Life According to Agfa**, 1992 (co-producer) / *Sh'chur**, 1994 / *An Electric Blanket**, 1994 / *Mr. Baum**, 1997 (co-produer) / *A Small Country, a Big Man*, 1998, TV series (co-producer) / *A Matter of Reputation*, 2000 (only director, scriptwriter) / *The News According to God*, 2001.

KLAUSNER, MARGOT (Berlin, Germany, 1905–Tel Aviv, 1975). Producer.

Klausner was an author, film producer, and founding owner of the first film laboratory in Israel. She studied theater and art history in Berlin before immigrating to Palestine in 1926. Together with her husband, Yehoshua Brandstatter, she was influential in bringing the Habimah Theater from Moscow to Palestine on its first tour in 1927 and served as part of the management of the theater after it settled in Palestine (1932–1936). In 1933 they established Urim, a film production company. In cooperation with Keren Hayesod they produced their first film, *Land of Promise** (Judah Leman), which won a prize at the Venice Film Festival (1935).

In 1949 Klausner and Brandstatter invested all their personal resources in the building of the first film studio in Israel, known as the Israel Motion Picture Studios Herzliyah Ltd. In 1956 Klausner acquired Carmel Newsreels, and from that time until the demise of newsreels (with the beginnings of Israeli television in 1968) the studios produced hundreds of weekly Carmel-Herzliyah Newsreels. During the first 25 years of the studios Klausner produced five feature films and invested in some of the most important films of the period. During this period, the laboratory of the studios processed hundreds of documentaries, advertising films, newsreels, television productions, and feature films. Klausner wrote a short book about her work in the film industry entitled *The Dream Industry, Memories and Facts—Twenty-five Years of the Israel Motion Picture Studios* (Tel Aviv, 1974).

Filmography

Land of Promise, 1934 (co-producer) / *Yonatan and Tali*, 1953 / *The Hero's Wife**, 1963 (only author of story) / *The Boy Across the Street*, 1966 (co-producer) / *Sabina and Her Men*, 1967 / *The Prodigal Son*, 1968 / *Tamar Wife of Er*, 1972 (co-producer).

KOLLEK, AMOS (Jerusalem, 1947). Director.

Kollek studied psychology and philosophy at the Hebrew University in Jerusalem (B.A., 1971) and took lessons in acting at the Lee Strasberg Acting Studio in New York. He writes articles and short stories, which have been published in newspapers and magazines in Israel, the United States, and Germany. In addition, he has published five novels—*Don't Ask Me If I Love* (1971), *The Girl Who Brought the War* (1974), *After They Hanged Him* (1977), *The Apple, the Singing and the Gold* (1980), and *Approximately Clint Eastwood* (1995). Amos Kollek is the son of Teddy Kollek, longtime mayor of Jerusalem, and together they wrote the nonfiction book *For Jerusalem, a Life* (1979).

Kollek's films provide a unique perspective on moral and social issues. He co-scripted and acted in *Worlds Apart** (based on one of his novels, directed by Barbara Noble) and directed and scripted *Goodbye, New York* and a political thriller, *Double Edge**, in which he appears on-screen together with Faye Dunaway. In addition, Kollek has written, produced, and directed feature films abroad—*Forever Lulu* (1987), *High Stakes* (1989), *Bad Girls* (1994), *Sue* (1997), *Fiona* (1998), *Fast Food, Fast Women* (1999), and *Queenie in Love* (2001). Kollek has achieved international acclaim for his film portrayals of the problems of women against the urban landscape; *Sue* won the Critics' Award and the Jury Award at Berlin (1998), and *Fast Food, Fast Women* won the Jury Award at Cannes (2000).

Filmography

Worlds Apart, 1979 (only co-producer, co-scriptwriter, actor) / *Goodbye, New York*, 1985 (also producer, scriptwriter) / *Double Edge*, 1992 (also scriptwriter, co-producer, actor) / *Teddy Kollek: From Vienna to Jerusalem*, 1997, documentary.

KOSASHVILLI, DOVER (Oni, Georgia, 1966.) Director.

Kosashvilli immigrated to Israel with his family at the age of six. He studied philosophy and cinema at Tel Aviv University. After his prizewinning debut film, *With Rules* (Cine Foundation Prize at Cannes, 1999 and Best Short Film at Jerusalem, 1999), he surprised audiences with his fresh approach and powers of observation with his first feature, *Late Marriage** (Wolgin Award and Lipper

Prize for Best Screenplay at Jerusalem, Israeli Academy Awards, Best Screenplay and Jury Award at Thessaloniki, Best Film at Kiev, and International Critics' Award at Buenos Aires). The film is about the Georgian immigrant community and portrays a man who finds it impossible to break away from the strict demands of his traditional parents.

Filmography

With Rules, 1999, short (also scriptwriter) / *Late Marriage*, 2001 (also scriptwriter).

KOSH, YOAV (Rosh Pina, 1953). Cinematographer.

Kosh studied film and television at Tel Aviv University (1976–1981). In 1986 he served as the cinematographer for his first feature film, *Avanti Popolo** (Rafi Bukaee*). Since that time he has shot Israeli features for a large number of Israeli directors and won numerous awards—an Israel Film Center award for *A Thousand and One Wives** (Michal Bat-Adam*) and Israeli Academy Awards for *The Heritage* (Amnon Rubinstein*) and *Life According to Agfa** (Assi Dayan*).

Filmography

Avanti Popolo, 1986 / *Shellshock**, 1988 / *Missing Picture*, 1989, documentary (co-cinematographer) / *A Thousand and One Wives*, 1989 / *Burning Memory**, 1989 / *Shuroo**, 1991 / *Dual Entity**, 1992 / *A Bit of Luck**, 1992 / *Life According to Agfa*, 1992 / *The Heritage*, 1993 / *On the Edge*, 1994 / *Aya, Imagined Autobiography**, 1994 / *The Flying Camel**, 1994 / *Lovesick on Nana St.**, 1995 / *Shuli's Boy*, 1997, TV drama / *Thunder Cats*, 1997, TV drama / *Forever and Ever*, 1997, TV drama / *Love at Second Sight**, 1998 / *Aaron Cohen's Debt*, 1999, TV drama.

KOTLER, ODED (Tel Aviv, 1937). Actor.

Kotler served in the Army Entertainment Troupe and studied acting in the United States. He served as the artistic director of the Haifa Theater, director of the Cameri Theater, chairman of the Acre Fringe Theater Festival, and head of the Drama Department of Israel Television. He received much attention for his screen roles in Dan Wolman's* *My Michael** and Uri Zohar's* *Three Days and a Child**, for which he won Best Actor at Cannes (1967). He also directed a feature film, *Again, Forever**, in 1985.

Filmography

*Blazing Sands**, 1960 / *Sands of Beersheba**, 1964 / *The Simchon Family*, 1964 / *Three Days and a Child*, 1967 / *Every Bastard a King**, 1968 / *C.O.D., Crime on Delivery*, 1973 / *My Michael*, 1975 / *The Uranium Conspiracy*, 1978 / *Cover Story**, 1979 / *Again, Forever*, 1985 (only director).

LEON, NISSIM (NITCHO) (Plovdiv, Bulgaria, 1931–Tel Aviv, 2000). Cinematographer.

Leon immigrated to Israel at the age of nine. As part of his army service he worked as an assistant cameraman in the army film unit. Following his release from the army he received his professional experience by working as a cameraman for the Geva Newsreels and worked his way up to chief cameraman for the Geva Studios. During his long career he was also a partner in Roll Films, where he worked together with Yisrael Ringel and Yair Pradelski on dozens of film projects. Leon also worked as chief cinematographer on numerous films abroad. In 1996 he received an achievement award from the Israel Academy Awards.

Filmography

*Tel Aviv Taxi**, 1956 / *I Like Mike**, 1962 / *What a Gang**, 1962 / *Pound a Piece*, 1963 / *Eldorado**, 1963 / *Dreamboat**, 1964 / *Sallah**, 1964 (co-cinematographer) / *Three Hours in June**, 1967, documentary (co-cinematographer) / *Sinai Commando*, 1967 (co-cinematographer) / *Aliza Mizrachi*, 1967 / *Tevye and His Seven Daughters**, 1968 / *Two Heartbeats*, 1972 / *Kuni Lemel in Tel Aviv*, 1976 / *Millionaire in Trouble*, 1978 / *Growing Pains*, 1979 / *Five and Five Musical*, 1980 / *Giveaway**, 1982 / *A Married Couple*, 1983 / *Kuni Lemel in Cairo*, 1983 / *Don't Give a Damn**, 1987 / *Tel Aviv–Los Angeles**, 1988 / *The Quarry*, 1990.

LERSKI, HELMAR (Strasbourg, France, 1871–Zurich, Switzerland, 1956). Director.

At the age of 17, Lerski (born Schmuklerski) emigrated to the United States, where he worked as an actor and later took up still photography. In 1915 he returned to Europe, became a successful cameraman in Germany, and gained invaluable experience in silent filmmaking. During these years he worked as the cameraman on expressionist films for directors such as Paul Leni and Fritz Lang. At the age of 60 Lerski moved to Palestine, where he lived from 1932 until 1948.

During his years in Palestine Lerski made documentary films for the institutions of the state in the making. His first major production in Palestine was called *Avodah**, a monumental documentary film, made in the style of social realism, memorable for its cinematographic technique. Lerski's last documentary in Palestine, *Adama*, which included some fictional elements, was renamed *Tomorrow Is a Wonderful Day* when it was shortened for distribution in the United States. Together with Paul Loewy, Lerski directed a short puppet film entitled *Balaam's Story*, which was later incorporated into *Out of Evil** (Joseph Krumgold, 1950).

Filmography

Avodah, 1935, documentary (also cinematographer) / *Adama*, 1947, documentary / *Balaam's Story* (within *Out of Evil*), 1948, short (co-director).

LEVANON, YE'UD (Haifa, 1952). Director.

Before entering the field of filmmaking, Levanon worked as a journalist and broadcaster for army radio (1970–1974). He served on the editorial staff of the newspaper *Yediot Achronot* (1974–1983) and was a member of the editorial Board of *Kolnoa*, a quarterly film publication (1978–1980). His filmmaking background stems from his experience at Universal Studios, Los Angeles. Levanon is also a novelist and scriptwriter and has taught film at Tel Aviv University (1993–1996).

Among the feature films that Levanon directed, *Black Box**, an adaptation of the novel by the well-known Israeli author Amos Oz, won the most attention. As a producer he has worked with directors such as Judd Ne'eman*, Serge Ankri, Amit Goren*, and the well-known Hungarian director Miklos Jancso. In recent years Levanon has been working as the director and producer of documentary films. His award-winning documentary *119 Bullets + Three*, on right-wing extremists in Israel, won the Special Jury Prize, FIPA, at Biarritz (1996).

Filmography

Something Else, 1972, short / *The Honey Connection*, 1978, short / *On the Air*, 1981 (also co-scriptwriter) / *Fun Forever*, 1983 / *Streets of Yesterday**, 1989 (only co-producer) / *Flash*, 1986 (only producer) / *All My Loving*, 1986 (only co-producer) / *Crazy Weekend*, 1986 (only co-producer) / *Burning Land**, 1984 (only co-producer) / *Dawn*, 1985 (only co-producer) / *Hasamba, The Undercover Kids*, 1985 (only co-producer) / *Black Box*, 1993 (also co-scriptwriter) / *119 Bullets + Three*, 1995, documentary (also producer, scriptwriter) / *Another Land*, 1998, documentary (only co-producer) / *Perets and the Wolf*, 1999, documentary (only co-producer) / *Moscow on the Mediterranean*, 1999, documentary (also co-producer, scriptwriter) / *Missing*, 2000 (only scriptwriter) / *Islands on the Shore*, 2002 (also scriptwriter).

LEVITAN, NADAV (Kibbutz Masaryk, 1944). Director.

Levitan is a graduate of the Department of Theater at Tel Aviv University. He worked as a stage director of musicals and as a newspaper and radio journalist, and has produced documentaries for Israel Television (1975–1980). He has published poetry and a volume of short stories.

Among his feature films, Levitan directed *You're in the Army, Girls**, about the transformation of a number of young women from diverse backgrounds into a motivated and unified military group. Born and bred on a kibbutz in Israel, he made his major contribution to Israeli filmmaking in his critical look at the communal life of kibbutz—*An Intimate Story**, *Stalin's Disciples**, and *No Names on the Door*.

Filmography

A Woman in the Garden, 1970, short / *Outside*, 1972, short / *An Intimate Story*, 1981 (also co-scriptwriter) / *The Bride*, 1985 / *You're in the Army, Girls*, 1985 / *Stalin's Disciples*, 1986 (also scriptwriter) / *Yael's Friends*, 1991, TV drama / *Murder on a Saturday Morning*, 1992, TV drama / *Groupie*, 1993 (also producer, scriptwriter) / *No Names on the Door*, 1996 (also scriptwriter) / *Real Father*, 1998 / *Frank Sinatra Is Dead*, 1999, TV drama (also scriptwriter) / *The Mevorach Brothers*, 2000 (also scriptwriter).

LEVY, SHEM-TOV (Rehovot, 1950). Composer.

Levy has written original musical scores for numerous Israeli feature films and television programs. He won Israeli Academy Awards for Best Musical

Score for *The Last Love Affair of Laura Adler** (Avram Heffner*), *Desperado Square** (Benny Torati), and *Provence United* (Ori Inbar). He has released a number of albums, including some as the primary composer for the well-known Israeli singer Arik Einstein.

Filmography

Slow Down, 1968, short / *The Paratroopers**, 1977 / *Little Man**, 1978 / *Sweet and Sour*, 1979 / *Pillar of Fire*, 1979, TV documentary series / *Again, Forever**, 1985 / *Summer of Aviya**, 1988 / *Diary**, 1988 / *The Last Love Affair of Laura Adler*, 1990 / *Dreams of Innocence**, 1993 / *The Flying Camel**, 1994 / *Desperado Square*, 2000 / *Electric Man**, 2001 / *Voices from the Heartland: Slaves of the Lord*, 2002, TV drama / *Provence United*, 2002.

LOEVY, RAM (Tel Aviv, 1940). Director.

After serving in the Nahal unit of the army, Loevy studied economics at the Hebrew University of Jerusalem (B.A., 1966) and received a diploma in filmmaking from the London Film School (1968). He returned to Israel to join the staff of Israel Television (Channel One) from its beginnings in 1968. Loevy served as a senior director at Israel Television (1968–1999), where he directed numerous TV dramas and documentaries.

Loevy's films deal with difficult social issues such as discrimination, poverty, major economic inequality, and political issues. His film *Khirbet Hiza'a* caused a major controversy at Israel Television; the management decided to censor the film and it was broadcast only after the workers committee intervened. His television drama *Indiani in the Sun* won an Israel Television Prize. Three of his films were produced as made-for-television feature films: *Bread** (Prix Italia for TV drama), *Winter Games**, and *Bucha*.

Loevy teaches on the faculty of Tel Aviv University and Beit Tzvi School in Ramat Gan and served for one year (1981–1982) as a Neimann Fellow at Harvard University. He was awarded the coveted Israel Prize for his contribution to television (1993).

Filmography

My Name Is Ahmed, 1966, documentary (only executive producer, scriptwriter) / *Brides, Grooms and Everything Else*, 1969, documentary / *Open the Gates*, 1970, TV drama / *Israel 80*, 1971, documentary / *Don't Think Twice*, 1972, documentary / *Rosewater from Port Said*, 1972, TV drama / *The Fifth Hand*, 1972, TV drama / *Barricades*, 1972, documentary / *The Bride and the Butterfly Hunter*, 1974, TV drama / *Stella*, 1975, TV drama / *Time Out*, 1975, documentary / *Hardship: Second Generation*, 1976, documentary / *Khirbet Hiza'a*, 1978, TV drama / *Spirits and Angels*, 1979, documentary / *Nebuchadnezzer in Caesarea*, 1980, documentary / *Indiani in the Sun*, 1981, TV drama (also co-scriptwriter) / *The Buck Stops in Brazil*, 1982, documentary / *83*, 1983 (co-director) / *End of the Season*, 1983, documentary / *Survival*, 1983, TV drama / *Each Scanner, A Million Dollars*, 1984, documentary / *Bread*, 1986 (also also co-scriptwriter) / *Voice of the Masses*, 1987, documentary / *Winter Games*, 1988 (also co-scriptwriter) / *A Crown on the Head*, 1989, TV drama / *A Woman Who Stopped Eating*, 1991, TV drama / *The Seventh Art*, 1991, documentary / *Bucha*, 1992 (also co-scriptwriter) / *The Boy that Dreams*, 1994, TV drama / *Mr. Mani*, 1996, TV series (also co-scriptwriter) / *A Man of the Police*, 1999–2000, TV series / *Murder on Television*, 2001, TV series (also co-scriptwriter) / *Close. Closed. Closure*, 2002, documentary (also scriptwriter).

MERON, HANNAH (Berlin, Germany, 1923). Actress.

Before immigrating to Israel in 1933, Meron appeared as a child in Fritz Lang's film classic *M* (1931). During the 1940s she studied acting at the studio of Habimah. In 1946 Meron was among the original members of the Cameri Theater, where she appeared in multiple roles until her retirement.

Meron is a well-known actress of stage and screen and a radio personality. She is especially loved by Israeli audiences for her role in the television sitcom series *Near Ones, Dear Ones* (Uri Barbash* and Yitzhak Shauli), for her screen personality as the classic Jewish mother in *Aunt Clara** (Avram Heffner*), and as a more radical kind of mother in *Day after Day** (Amos Gitai*). Meron has directed student plays for the Theater Department of Tel Aviv University and for Beit Tzvi School in Ramat Gan. She was honored for her contribution to Israeli theater with the coveted Israel Prize in 1976 and has received honorary doctorates from Tel Aviv University and from Hebrew University in Jerusalem.

Filmography

Every Mile a Stone, 1954 / *Aunt Clara*, 1977 / *The Vulture**, 1981 / *Dead End Street**, 1982 / *Near Ones, Dear Ones*, 1983, TV series / *Real Time*, 1991 / *Day after Day*, 1998.

MIZRAHI, MOSHE (Alexandria, Egypt, 1931). Director.

Mizrahi immigrated to prestate Israel at the age of 14. As a young man he worked as a Youth Aliyah emissary, as a social worker, and as a journalist, and then at the age of 27 he went to France to learn filmmaking. He started from the bottom and worked his way up, until he became a producer/director for French television. In 1969 he returned to Israel to direct his first feature film, a French–Israeli co-production, *The Traveler**, about a former Gestapo officer who hides out and tries to rebuild his life in Eilat.

Mizrahi is one of the major artistic filmmakers of the Kayitz movement (Young Israeli Cinema of the 1960s and 1970s). His Israeli films are all Sephardi cultural films: *I Love You, Rosa** (which won the Israel Film Center's Best Film Award, 1973), a touching and thoughtful love story; *The House on Chelouche St.**, an autobiographical portrait; *Daughters, Daughters**, a satire on male chauvanism that was popular with the Israeli filmgoing public; and *Women**, set in Jerusalem of the nineteenth century.

Mizrahi, influenced by his Sephardi upbringing, has made a major contribution to Israeli filmmaking with his sensitive and intimate portrayals of cultural conflicts. His films address the central theme of love (often forbidden love) and portray ethnic characters as idealistic rather than stereotypic. Living in both Paris and Tel Aviv, he is best known for his American Academy award-winning French film *Madame Rosa* (*La vie devant soi*, 1977), starring Simone Signoret.

One of Israel's most prominent film directors, Mizrahi has achieved international acclaim; two of his films, *I Love You, Rosa* and *The House on Chelouche St.*, were nominated for American Academy awards for Best Foreign Film. *I Love You, Rosa* featured a young actress, Michal Bat-Adam*, who later became a film director and Mizrahi's life partner. Mizrahi, who has also produced some of Bat-Adam's films, was presented with a Life Achievement Award by the Israeli Academy Awards (2001).

Filmography

The Traveler, 1970 (also co-scriptwriter) / *I Love You, Rosa*, 1972 (also scriptwriter) / *The House on Chelouche St.*, 1973 (also co-scriptwriter) / *Daughters, Daughters*, 1973 (also co-scriptwriter) / *Rachel's Man*, 1976 (also co-scriptwriter) / *Moments**, 1979 (only producer) / *Women*, 1996 (also scriptwriter).

NASSAR, ALI (Arrabeh, 1954). Director.

Nassar studied film directing in Moscow (M.A., 1981). Following his return from Moscow he established a theater group in his village in the Galilee. He then worked as a photojournalist for a Haifa newspaper. His first feature film, *The Babysitter*, was shot in Romania and was never released in Israel. His second feature, *The Milky Way**, was received with considerable interest. As an Israeli Palestinian Arab filmmaker, Nassar recognizes the difficulties of being a film director from a particular minority group and is especially conscious of the burden that this imposes upon him.

Filmography

The Story of the City by the Beach, 1983, documentary (also scriptwriter) / *The Babysitter*, 1993 (also co-producer) / *The Milky Way*, 1998 (also producer, scriptwriter) / *The Ninth Month*, 2002 (also producer, scriptwriter).

NAVON, MORDECHAI (Zabrjczja, Poland, 1908–Tel Aviv, 1966). Producer.

Navon immigrated to prestate Israel in 1923 and entered his family's Tel Aviv textile business. He moved to Australia in 1939, where he became a successful businessman. Returning to Israel, he joined forces with Yitzhak Agadati, who had established Geva Films in 1949. Navon's business grew as he worked with the government agencies that were responsible for major productions of the time. Navon's first feature film, *Tel Aviv Taxi**, was made with a young American director, Larry Frisch*. They worked together again on *Pillar of Fire** in 1959.

Although it was not clear at the time, Navon's most important film came as a result of his agreeing to invest in Uri Zohar's* *Hole in the Moon**. The film is recognized today as a brilliant satire, based on improvisation that, many years ahead of its time, poked fun at the sacred cows of Israeli life.

Filmography

Tel Aviv Taxi, 1954 / *Pillar of Fire*, 1959 / *I Like Mike**, 1962 / *Eldorado**, 1963 / *What a Gang**, 1962 / *Hole in the Moon*, 1963 / *Dalia and the Sailors**, 1964 / *A Night in Tiberias*, 1965 / *Two Kuni Lemel**, 1966.

NE'EMAN, YEHUDA (JUDD) (Tel Aviv, 1936). Director.

Ne'eman served as an officer in the paratroopers and was decorated for valor during the Six Day War (1967). He studied medicine at Hebrew University and worked as a doctor at Ichilov Hospital in Tel Aviv for one year. He then changed to the field of philosophy and theater and studied at Tel Aviv University. He is a tenured member of the faculty of the Department of Film and Television at Tel Aviv University and has served as the chairman of the department (1980-1983, 1991-1995) and as the head of the Graduate Studies Department (2001-2002).

Ne'eman is a prolific writer in the field of cinematic discourse and has authored dozens of journalistic and academic articles and a number of essays in books on film. His first feature, *Boys and Girls**, a trilogy of three short films, showed an obsession with the alienation of the individual in the urban setting. Ne'eman turned his attention to the individual in the military with his groundbreaking film *The Paratroopers**, the first Israeli film to present a critical attitude toward the army and toward "sacred cow" issues in Israeli society (Second Prize from Israel Film Center). He also directed two additional political films, *Streets of Yesterday** and *Fellow Travelers** (both co-productions with Channel Four in London), which deal with complicated issues of betrayal in relations between Arabs and Jews.

Filmography

Boys and Girls, 1970 (also producer, co-scriptwriter) / *Around the Point*, 1970, TV drama (also co-scriptwriter) / *Milk and Honey Experience*, 1971, docu-drama (also producer, co-scriptwriter) / *Bedouin in Sinai*, 1972, documentary (also producer, scriptwriter) / *The Courtyard of Momo the Great*, 1972, TV drama / *The Small Physician of Abyssinian Street*, 1973, TV drama (also producer, co-scriptwriter) / *Observation on Acco*, 1975, documentary (also scriptwriter) / *The Paratroopers*, 1977 (also producer) / *Seamen's Strike*, 1981, documentary (also scriptwriter) / *On the Air*, 1981 (only co-producer) / *83*, 1983 (*The Night the King Was Born*) (co-director) / *Fellow Travelers*, 1983 (also co-producer, co-scriptwriter) / *Streets of Yesterday*, 1989 (also co-producer, co-scriptwriter) / *Heart's Delight*, 2001, TV drama (also producer).

NESHER, AVI (Ramat Gan, 1952). Director.

Nesher studied at Columbia University in New York City. He has directed films both in Israel and in the United States. He began his career directing a few short films, followed by feature films which made a name for him in Israel—*Sing Your Heart Out** and *Dizengoff 99**, both of which were very popular with the young Israeli filmgoing public. The former is about the pressures and satisfactions of working in the Army Entertainment Troupe; the latter was considered controversial at the time due to the permissive lifestyle portrayed and was almost barred by the censorship board. Nesher began working in Hollywood as a scriptwriter and then moved over to directing with films such as *Time Bomb* (1989), *Automatic* (1994), *Mercenary* (1996), *Taxman* (1999), and

Ritual (2001). Nesher's international film credits often appear under the pseudonym Patrick (Ripley) Highsmith.

Filmography

Sing Your Heart Out, 1978 (also co-scriptwriter) / *Dizengoff 99*, 1979 (also scriptwriter) / *The Cowards*, 1980 (also co-scriptwriter) / *Shovrim*, 1985 (also co-producer, scriptwriter / *Rage and Glory*, 1985 (also co-producer, scriptwriter).

OPHIR, SHAIKE (Jerusalem, 1928—Tel Aviv, 1987). Actor.

Ophir (original name: Yishayhu Goldstein) grew up in an ultra-Orthodox neighborhood of Jerusalem. He served in the Palmach (1948-1950) of the Israeli army and then went on to study acting as a pupil at the Ohel Theater in Tel Aviv and then as a student of mime in Paris. In 1954 he was instrumental in opening a school of pantomime at the Cameri Theater.

Ophir appeared in dozens of theater productions, numerous Israeli feature films, and television programs. As one of the most outstanding Israeli comic performers, he was memorable for his role as the comic-pathetic policeman in Ephraim Kishon's* films *The Policeman** and *The Big Dig**. In addition to being an actor, Ophir directed one feature film, *Half a Million Black*.

Filmography

*Tel Aviv Taxi**, 1954 / *Lacking a Homeland**, 1956 / *Eldorado**, 1963 / *Dalia and the Sailors**, 1964 / *Eight against One**, 1964 / *Hole in the Moon**, 1965 / *Moishe Air-Condition*, 1966 / *Ervinka**, 1967 / *Fish, Football and Girls*, 1968 (also co-scriptwriter) / *The Big Dig*, 1969 / *The Policeman*, 1971 / *The Great Telephone Robbery*, 1972 / *Daughters, Daughters**, 1973 (also co-scriptwriter) / *The House on Chelouche St.**, 1973 / *Diamonds*, 1975 / *The Father*, 1975 / *Half a Million Black*, 1977 (also director, co-scriptwriter) / *Operation Thunderbolt**, 1977 / *To Cheat a Cheat*, 1977 / *The Garden*, 1977 / *The Fox in the Chicken Coop**, 1978 / *Wrong Number*, 1979 (also co-scriptwriter).

OVADIAH, GEORGE (Bagdad, Iraq, 1925–Holon, 1996). Director.

Ovadiah moved from Baghdad to Iran in 1949, where he became a pioneer in the field of film production. In 1967, he directed an Israel–Iran co-production, *Harbor of Love*, set in Haifa. After relocating to Israel in 1969, Ovadiah continued his previously successful directing style, including improvisation and heavy emotionalism. During the 1970s and early 1980s, Ovadiah directed feature films, all melodramas and comedies. His early Israeli box office successes, *Arianna** and *Nurit**, popular for their heartbreaking subject matter and fairy-tale, romantic conclusions, were produced during the same period as his military comedies, *Fishke Goes to War* and *Nahtche and the General*, featuring good-hearted fools serving in the army.

One of Israel's most prolific film directors, Ovadiah contributed to Israeli filmmaking in the area of what later was called "bourekas" films—melodramas and comedies that portray ethnic stereotypes. A tribute was paid to his memory by the Israeli Film Academy (1996).

Filmography

Harbor of Love, 1967 / *Arianna*, 1971 (also co-scriptwriter) / *Fishke Goes to War*, 1971 / *Nurit*, 1972 (also producer, scriptwriter) / *Nahtche and the General*, 1972 / *They Call Me Shmil*, 1973 (also co-producer) / *Sarit*, 1974 (also co-producer) / *Day of Judgment*, 1975 (also producer) / *Sixtieth St.*, 1976 / *Midnight Entertainer*, 1977 (also producer, scriptwriter) / *West Side Girl**, 1979 / *Nurit II*, 1983 (also producer, co-scriptwriter) / *The Auntie from Argentina*, 1984 (also co-producer).

PERLOV, DAVID (Belo Horizonte, Brazil, 1930). Director.

Perlov studied painting and engraving in São Paolo and left Brazil in 1952 to study art in Paris. While there he changed direction and began a lifelong romance with the field of filmmaking. Before going to live in Israel in 1958 he worked in Paris with the great documentary filmmaker Joris Ivens.

As one of the primary Israeli figures working in the field of artistic documentary filmmaking, Perlov is known for his intimate documentary style, which includes stream of consciousness. His short documentary *In Jerusalem* is an artistic look at the divided city of Jerusalem in 1963. During the following years he directed a large number of television films and documentaries. Following his feature-length dramatic film *The Pill* (1972) he made a documentary portrait of himself and his family, *Diary**, which was 10 years in the making (1973–1983). A six-hour epic filmed in real time, the film points clearly to Perlov's nostalgia for distant places that are part of his spiritual roots.

Through his teaching at the Department of Film and Television at Tel Aviv University (from 1973 until his retirement in 1999), Perlov trained an entire generation of documentary filmmakers. He received the coveted Israel Prize (1999) for his contribution to Israeli cinema and an Achievement Award from the Israeli Film Academy (1995). Two documentary films about Perlov have been produced—one directed by Asher Tlalim* (1980s) and one by Lior Atzmor (1999).

Filmography

In Jerusalem, 1963, documentary / *In Thy Blood Lives*, documentary / *Fisherman in Jaffa*, documentary / *At Tel Katzir*, documentary / *Old Age Home*, documentary / *Biba*, documentary / *Ben Gurion 42:6*, 1970 / *The Pill*, 1972 / *Repeat Dive**, 1981 (only advisor) / *Diary**, 1988, documentary / *Tel Katzir 93*, 1993, documentary / *Meetings with Nathan Zach*, 1996, documentary / *Updated Diary*, 1990–1999.

PITCHHADZE, JOSEPH (Tbilisi, Georgia, 1965). Director.

Pitchhadze immigrated to Israel with his family in 1972. He graduated from the Department of Film and Television at Tel Aviv University. He directed, produced, and wrote the screenplay for unique and fresh award-winning feature films: *Under Western Eyes**, a road movie, and *Besame Mucho**, a combination love story and crime thriller. *Under Western Eyes* won prizes at Berlin (1997) and at Belgrade (1997). Both of his films, which reflect an international flavor, won the Wolgin Award at Jerusalem.

Filmography

Dreaming in Russian, 1990, short (also scriptwriter) / *Bad Days*, 1993, short (also scriptwriter) / *Under Western Eyes*, 1996 (also co-producer, scriptwriter) / *Besame Mucho*, 2000 (also co-producer, scriptwriter).

PREMINGER, ANER (Tel Aviv, 1955). Director.

Preminger studied physics at Tel Aviv University (B.Sc., 1974) before going abroad to study cinema at New York University's Graduate School of Film and Television (M.F.A., 1983). He completed his Ph.D. in cinema studies from Tel Aviv University (2001).

Since 1986, Preminger has worked as a filmmaker—producing, directing, and writing scripts for documentaries and feature films. His documentaries have classified him as a filmmaker who chooses highly sensitive and personal subjects. His documentary *Ransom of the Father*, about the work of the sculptor Tzvi Lachman, won the Mayor's Prize for best film in the category of the Jewish Experience at Jerusalem (2000). His feature film *Blind Man's Bluff** won prizes at Montpellier, Montevideo, Cancun, and Jerusalem.

Preminger wrote a book on cinema entitled *Enchanted Screen: A Chronology of Media and Language* (Open University of Israel, 1995) and teaches film.

Filmography

Interlock, 1980, short / *Time*, 1981, short / *Darkroom*, 1981, short / *Two Cups*, 1982, short / *24 Hours*, 1984, short / *Front Window*, 1990, short / *Blind Man's Bluff*, 1993 (also co-scriptwriter) / *On My Way to Father's Land*, 1995, documentary / *Last Resort*, 1999 (also producer, co-scriptwriter) / *Ransom of the Father*, 2000, documentary / *Russian Compound*, 2001, documentary (also scriptwriter) / *Theater of Truth and Reconciliation*, 2001, documentary (also producer, scriptwriter).

REIBENBACH, TSIPI (Dzerzonyov, Poland, 1947). Director.

Reibenbach immigrated to Israel with her parents in 1950 and grew up in Lod. After she studied mathematics and physics at Tel Aviv University (B.Sc., 1969), she went on to study at the Department of Film and Television at Tel Aviv University (B.F.A., 1980). Her most important documentary film, *Choice and Destiny**, sensitively portrays her Holocaust survivor parents. The film received much international acclaim (prizes at Nyon, Paris, Créteil, and Yamagata).

Reibenach directed two additional full-length documentaries—*Widow Plus*, which portrays five women widowed during the Yom Kippur War, and *Three Sisters*, which portrays the loneliness of old age through the lives of three women, one of whom is her own mother.

Filmography

Hangers, 1980, short / *Widow Plus*, 1981, documentary / *Choice and Destiny*, 1993, documentary / *Three Sisters*, 1998, documentary / *A City With No Pity*, 2002, documentary.

REVACH, ZE'EV (Rabat, Morocco, 1940). Actor and Director.

Revach immigrated to Israel at the age of nine as part of the large wave of immigration from North African countries. His films focus on those immigrants who have a similar experience. He grew up in Jerusalem in a religious milieu, began his career in the Army Entertainment Troupe, and studied acting at the Beit Zvi School in Ramat Gan. For many years he worked as a stage actor and then moved to screen acting, where he developed a unique screen persona. He has also appeared in foreign films.

When he began directing, Revach created the ethnic character of Sasson (played by himself). Having already figured out his "place" in Israeli society, Sasson plays a self-effacing role when dealing with the outside world but reveals innate wisdom and insight when among his own kind. Sasson is the main character in a number of Revach's films: *Only Today**, *To Cheat a Cheat*, *Sweet and Sour*, *Batito*, and *Lend Me Your Wife*. In addition to these ethnic comedies, Revach has directed films of social comment, *Little Man** and *On the Fringe** (FIPRESCI prize at Rio de Janeiro, 1988). Revach's melodrama *A Bit of Luck** was seen in cinemas in Morocco, the only Israeli feature film to have been sold for distribution to an Arab country. Revach won an Israeli Academy Award for his role in *Provence United* (Ori Inbar).

One of Israel's most prolific film directors, Revach is popular with the Israeli filmgoing audience for his comedies and melodramas, which were not always the critics' choices.

Filmography

Sabina and Her Men, 1967 (actor) / *Scouting Patrol**, 1967 (actor) / *Blaze on the Water*, 1969 (actor) / *Five Days in Sinai*, 1969 (actor) / *Snail**, 1970 (actor) / *Get Zorkin**, 1971 (actor) / *Charlie and a Half**, 1974 (actor) / *Snooker*, 1975 (actor) / *Only Today*, 1976 (director, scriptwriter, actor) / *Beautiful Troubles*, 1976 (actor) / *Half a Million Black*, 1977 (actor) / *To Cheat a Cheat*, 1977 (director, scriptwriter, actor) / *Little Man*, 1978 (director, co-producer, co-scriptwriter, actor) / *Growing Pains*, 1979 (director, scriptwriter) / *Sweet and Sour*, 1979 (director, scriptwriter, actor) / *Wrong Number*, 1979 (director, co-scriptwriter, actor) / *The Man Who Flew in to Grab*, 1981 (co-scriptwriter, actor) / *Mr. Leon**, 1982 (director, co-scriptwriter, actor) / *The Ladies' Hairdresser*, 1984 (director, co-scriptwriter, actor) / *Batito*, 1987 (director, co-producer, scriptwriter, actor) / *On the Fringe*, 1987 (director, co-scriptwriter, actor) / *Lend Me Your Wife*, 1988 (director, co-scriptwriter) / *A Bit of Luck*, 1992 (director, co-scriptwriter, actor) / *The Buskila Twins*, 1998 (director, scriptwriter) / *Provence United*, 2002 (actor).

RIKLIS, ERAN (Jerusalem, 1954). Director.

Riklis was educated and raised in Canada, the United States, Brazil, and Israel. After he studied film at Tel Aviv University (1975–1977), he continued his studies in England and graduated from the National Film School at Beaconsfield (1982).

Riklis directs dramas, documentaries, and commercials for television. His documentary *Borders*, about people who live and work along Israel's borders with its neighbors, won prizes at Munich, Houston, and Mexico. Among his feature films, the dramatic film *Cup Final**, about an Israeli soldier who is captured by a PLO unit during the war in Lebanon, was critically acclaimed (prize at Valencia), and the tragic story of Israeli singer Zohar Argov, in the film *Zohar: Mediterranean Blues**, was a box office hit in Israel.

Filmography

Easy Listenin' Blues, 1977, short / *On a Clear Day You Can See Damascus*, 1984 (also producer, co-scriptwriter) / *The Immigrants*, 1985, documentary / *Cup Final*, 1991 (also original idea) / *Zohar: Mediterranean Blues*, 1993 / *Straight Forward*, 1994, TV series / *Me and My Family*, 1995, TV series / *Deadly Fortune*, 1996, TV series / *Radio One*, 1996–1997, TV series / *Lucky*, 1997, TV drama / *The Poetics of the Masses*, 1997, TV documentary series / *Death by Murder*, 1998, TV series / *Vulcan Junction*, 1999 / *Borders*, 1999, documentary.

RODENSKY, SHMUEL (Smorgon, Russia, 1902–Tel Aviv, 1989). Actor.

Rodensky went to live in prestate Israel in 1924 and became a popular actor, working with many theater groups. His first film appearance was in the prestate docudrama *This Is the Land** (Baruch Agadati*). In 1949 he joined the Habimah Theater and became one of its permanent actors, appearing in dozens of roles during his career.

In film he is best remembered for his role as Tevye the milkman in *Tevye and His Seven Daughters** (Menahem Golan*), the Israeli version of Norman Jewison's *Fiddler on the Roof*, based on the same Shalom Aleichem stories. Rodensky also appeared in television and film roles in Germany and Switzerland. He was awarded the coveted Israel Prize in 1983 for his contribution to Israeli theater.

Filmography

This Is the Land, 1935 / *Tel Aviv Taxi**, 1954 / *A Pound a Piece*, 1963 / *Sallah**, 1964 / *Tomorrow's Yesterday*, 1964 / *Shabbat Hamalka*, 1965 / *Impossible on Saturday*, 1965 / *Two Kuni Lemel**, 1966 / *Tevye and His Seven Daughters*, 1968 / *Katz and Carasso*, 1971 / *Operation Thunderbolt**, 1977 / *Hershele*, 1977 / *Aunt Clara**, 1977 / *Alex in Love*, 1986.

ROZENBAUM, MAREK (Wroszczowe, Poland, 1952). Producer.

Rozenbaum immigrated to Israel in 1968 and he studied both cinema and social work at Tel Aviv University (1972–1976). He established Transfax Films, his own production company (1988). In addition to producing feature films and international co-productions, Rozenbaum has produced numerous documentaries and dramas for Israeli television. He held the position of chairman of Israel's Film and Television Producers Association (1994–2000) and Israel Film Academy (from 2001).

Rozenbaum is the director of one feature film, *The Investigation Continues**, and the producer of many acclaimed films, including *Late Marriage** (Dover Kosashvilli*), *Yana's Friends** (Arik Kaplun*), *Circus Palestine** (Eyal Halfon*), *Saint Clara** (Ori Sivan and Ari Folman), *Aya, an Imagined Autobiography** (Michal Bat-Adam*), and *Over the Ocean** (Ya'ackov Goldwasser*). Rozenbaum's films have won four Israeli Oscars, two Wolgin Awards, and various prizes in international festivals.

Filmography

Green, 1983 / *Berlin–Jerusalem**, 1989 / *Crossfire**, 1989 / *The Last Love Affair of Laura Adler**, 1990 / *Over the Ocean*, 1991 / *An American Citizen**, 1991 / *The Deserter's Wife*, 1992 / *Dreams of Innocence**, 1993 / *The Heritage*, 1993 / *Aya, an Imagined Autobiography*, 1994 / *The Flying Camel**, 1994 / *Max and Morris*, 1994 / *Saint Clara*, 1995 / *Jewish Vendetta*, 1996 / *Exile in Shanghai*, 1997, documentary / *Circus Palestine*, 1998 / *Yana's Friends*, 1999 / *Emile Habibi—I Stayed in Haifa*, 1997, documentary / *The Investigation Continues*, 2000 (also director) / *Sister Wife*, 2000, documentary / *Late Marriage*, 2001 / *Lahola*, 2001, documentary / *The King of Ratings*, 2001, documentary.

RUBINSTEIN, AMNON (Nahalal, 1948). Director.

Rubinstein received a B.A. in political science from Hebrew University in Jerusalem (1972) and worked as an editor of documentary and music programs at Israel Radio. When he switched to filmmaking, he went abroad to study and received a diploma from the London Film School (1975). After his return from London he worked directing, writing, and producing feature films, television dramas, documentaries, and educational films. His feature film *Nadia** brought him much attention. In addition, he has won recognition for his documentaries—*Children of War* (First Prize at Haifa) and *Armenians in Jerusalem* (prize at the New York TV Festival).

Filmography

Once upon a Dream, 1975, TV drama (also scriptwriter) / *Four in a Tank*, 1977, documentary (also scriptwriter) / *Street of Prophets*, 1978, documentary (also scriptwriter) / *Armenians in Jerusalem*, 1979, documentary / *Criss-Cross Thread*, 1982, docudrama (also scriptwriter) / *My Name Is Dana and I'm an Alcoholic*, 1982, TV drama / *New Horizons*, 1983, documentary (also scriptwriter) / *David's Tower*, 1983, documentary (also scriptwriter) / *Nadia*, 1985 (also co-scriptwriter) / *The Owl*, 1987 / *Ruthy Naim*, 1989, TV drama (also co-scriptwriter) / *Mekomon*, 1991, TV miniseries / *The Heritage*, 1992 / *On the Edge*, 1994 / *Children of War*, 1995, documentary (also scriptwriter) / *Café Paris*, 1997–1998, TV series / *A Night in Addis*, 1998, TV drama / *Herzl*, 1998, TV drama (also scriptwriter) / *Enemy Zone*, 1999, TV miniseries / *Chihuli in the Light of Jerusalem*, 2000, documentary (also scriptwriter).

SAGALL, JONATHAN (Toronto, Canada, 1964). Actor.

Sagall graduated from the Guildhall School of Music and Drama in London. In addition to being an author and repertory member of Israel's Habima Theater, he is a successful film actor. He has appeared in a number of international films, including Steven Spielberg's *Schindler's List* and George Roy Hill's *Little Drummer Girl*. He is well known to Israeli audiences for his role as a teenager in Boaz Davidson's *Lemon Popsicle** and its sequel, *Going Steady*. He won an Israel Film Center award for Best Actor for his role in Amos Gutmann's *Drifting**.

Sagall wrote and directed short films and wrote two stage plays, which were produced by the Haifa Municipal Theater and seen also at the La Mama Theater in New York. His directorial debut, *Urban Feel**, won prizes at Valencia (1999), Varna (2000), and Haifa. Sagall worked as a staff writer on the Israeli–Palestinian series of *Sesame Street*, which began broadcasting in 1998.

Filmography

Lemon Popsicle, 1978 / *Going Steady*, 1979 / *Hot Bubblegum*, 1981 / *Private Popsicle*, 1982 / *Drifting*, 1983 (also co-producer) / *The Megillah**, 1983, TV drama (also narrator) / *Baby Love*, 1984 / *Zerach Lipshitz' Last Little Vacation*, 1985, short (only director, scriptwriter) / *Young Love*, 1987 / *At Home*, 1988, short (only director, scriptwriter) / *Urban Feel**, 1998 (also director, co-producer, scriptwriter) / *Sesame Street*, 1998, TV series (staff writer) / *Lipstikonn*, 2001, TV drama (only scriptwriter).

SALOMON, AMNON (Tel Aviv, 1940). Cinematographer.

Salomon began his career as an assistant cameraman in 1961 working with David Gurfinkel* and then progressed to becoming a newsreel photographer. From there he became a cinematographer and has photographed shorts, films for television, documentaries, commercials, and numerous feature films. He served as cinematographer on Uri Barbash's* acclaimed films, *Beyond the Walls** and *One of Us**, and worked with Israeli directors as diverse as Riki Shelach, Boaz Davidson*, Ze'ev Revach*, Avram Heffner*, and Uri Barbash. He won Israel Film Center awards for Best Cinematography for *The Last Winter**, *Once We Were Dreamers**, *One of Us, The Skipper II*, and *Marriage of Convenience**, and a Life Achievement Award from the Haifa Film Festival in 1995.

Filmography

A Woman's Case, 1969 (also co-scriptwriter) / *Before Tomorrow* (*Spring*), 1969 / *The War after the War*, 1969, documentary (co-cinematographer) / *The Trip*, 1971, short / *Neither by Day nor by Night*, 1972 / *But Where Is Daniel Wax?** 1972 / *Sarit*, 1974 / *Tzanani Family*, 1976 / *The Last Winter*, 1982 / *The Ladies' Hairdresser*, 1984 / *Beyond the Walls*, 1984 / *When Night Falls**, 1985 / *Once We Were Dreamers*, 1987 / *Marriage of Convenience*, 1988 / *One of Us*, 1989 / *The Skipper II*, 1989 / *Beyond the Walls II*, 1992 / *Tears Fall by Themselves*, 1996 / *The Milky Way**, 1998 / *Zur Hadassim*, 1999 / *Yolande Remembered*, 1999, documentary (co-cinematographer) / *In the Ninth Month*, 2002.

SCHORR, RENEN (Jerusalem, 1952). Director.

Schorr served in the Army Entertainment Troupe and graduated from the Department of Film at Tel Aviv University. He served as head of production for the Cinema Department at the Beit-Zvi School in Ramat Gan (1982–1985). He is the founder of the Sam Spiegel Film and Television School in Jerusalem

(1989) and has been the school's director since that time. He has served as the president of the Association of European Film Schools.

Schorr's feature film *Late Summer Blues** (winner of Israel Film Center Award) was widely acclaimed by both the critics and the Israeli filmgoing public for its powerful and refreshing look at the issues and dilemmas facing young people in Israel as they approach army age. He is the initiator and creator of the award-winning television drama series, *Voices from the Heartland*, which includes 10 dramas being written and directed by young filmmakers.

Filmography

After Duty, 1977, short / *The Paratroopers*, 1977 (only co-scriptwriter) / *The Battle of Fort Williams*, 1980, short / *On the Air*, 1981 (only co-producer) / *Fellow Traveler**, 1983 (only co-producer) / *A Wedding in Jerusalem*, 1985, documentary / *Late Summer Blues*, 1986 (also co-producer, co-scriptwriter) / *Black to the Promised Land*, 1991, documentary (only producer) / *Black Box**, 1993 (only actor) / *Voices from the Heartland*, 2001, TV series (only creator of series).

SCHORY, KATRIEL (Tel Aviv, 1947). Producer.

Schory studied filmmaking at New York University. He worked as the head of productions for Kastel Films (1973–1980), responsible for the production of a large number of documentary films and television dramas and worked as a television bureau producer for ZDF in Washington, D.C. (1980–1983). He has been the producer and managing director of his own production company, Belfilms, since 1984. The company has produced two Israeli features, television dramas, and documentaries and provides production services for foreign films. In 1998 Schory was appointed as the managing director of the Fund for the Promotion of Israeli Quality Films. He has held public positions that helped to further government support of Israeli filmmaking, including chairman of Israel's Film and Television Producers' Association (1990–1994) and chairman of the board of the Fund for the Promotion of Israeli Quality Films (1995–1998). He has taught film at Tel Aviv University (1986–1992).

Filmography

*Beyond the Walls**, 1984 (associate producer) / *Once We Were Dreamers**, 1987 (co-producer) / *Fifty Plus*, TV series / *Missing Picture*, 1989, documentary / *Haute Cuisine Goes Kosher in Jerusalem*, TV series (co-producer) / *Seven Days in November*, TV documentary / *The Reconstruction—The Danny Katz Murder Case*, 1994, TV documentary / *Yankee Samurai*, TV documentary (also director) / *At Nature's Grace*, TV documentary series / *Prototype*, TV documentary series / *The State of Israel vs. John Ivan Demjanjuk*, TV documentary / *The Wordmaker*, 1991, TV drama / *Dreams of Innocence**, 1993 / *Tkuma—The First 50 Years*, 1998, TV documentary series / *Purple Lawns*, 1998, TV drama.

SELTZER, DOV (DUBI) (Yassy, Romania, 1932). Composer.

Seltzer has appeared widely in musical performances, has composed and played for many recordings, and has accompanied and written music for the widely known singer Theodore Bikel. He has composed musicals for stage, including a few that have been performed on Broadway, a small number of symphonies for the Israeli Philharmonic, and the musical score for numerous films, both Israeli and international. Seltzer won awards for his theater musicals *Utz Li, Gutz Li* (1967) and *Kazablan* (1968). He won a Life Achievement Award from the Israel Musician's Society (1984) and an Israel Film Center award for Best Musical Score for the film *The Megillah** (Ilan Eldad*).

Filmography

The Simchon Family, 1964 / *Dreamboat**, 1964 / *Eight Against One**, 1964 / *Trunk to Cairo*, 1965 / *The Girl from the Dead Sea**, 1966 / *Three Days and a Child**, 1967 / *Ervinka**, 1967 / *Tevye and His Seven Daughters**, 1968 / *My Love in Jerusalem**, 1969 / *The Big Escape*, 1970 / *Eshkol*, 1970, documentary / *Highway Queen**, 1971 / *I Was Born in Jerusalem**, 1971, documentary / *I Love You, Rosa**, 1972 / *Escape to the Sun** 1972 / *Salomonico**, 1972 / *The Great Telephone Robbery*, 1972 / *Kazablan**, 1973 / *The Father*, 1975 / *Kuni Lemel in Tel Aviv*, 1976 / *Operation Thunderbolt**, 1977 / *Hershele*, 1977 / *Half a Milllion Black*, 1977 / *Uranium Conspiracy*, 1978 / *Millionaire in Trouble*, 1978 / *Mr. Leon**, 1982 / *The Megillah*, 1983 / *Forced Testimony**, 1984 / *The Lover**, 1986 / *On the Fringe**, 1987 / *A Place by the Sea*, 1988 / *A Bit of Luck**, 1992 / *The Road to Glory*, 1996 / *The Return from India*, 2002 / *Tow Shot*, 2002, documentary.

SHAGRIR, MICHA (Linz, Austria, 1937). Producer and Director.

Shagrir studied at the Hebrew University of Jerusalem and completed a one-year course for senior producers at the BBC in London (1964). He has produced and directed numerous television series and documentary films, which have been broadcast in Israel and abroad.

A number of Shagrir's films deal with the Six Day War; he directed the feature film *Scouting Patrol** and the documentary *The War after the War*, and he co-produced the acclaimed feature *Avanti Popolo** (Rafi Bukaee*). He was involved in important international television projects such as *Hello Jerusalem*, an ongoing television magazine (1983–1989), and *2000 Today*, an international new millennium event, broadcast live in over 80 countries around the world.

Shagrir is the managing director of Shiba Enterprises and Tapuz Communications, two production companies that are active in developing and producing television and film productions. He founded and headed Kastel Communications (1968–1988).

Filmography

Scouting Patrol, 1967 (director) / *The War after the War*, 1969, documentary (director) / *To Stand on One's Feet*, 1975 (producer) / *Diary of an Egyptian Soldier*, 1981, documentary (director) / *Stigma**, 1982 (producer) / *Ricochets**, 1986 (cameo appearance) / *Avanti Popolo*, 1986 (co-producer) / *Time of the Camel*, 1991 (co-producer) / *Brothers*, 1994, documentary (producer) / *The Inheritors*, 1995, documentary (producer) / *Lev Pashov*, 1995, documentary (producer) / *Zimna*, 1995, documentary (producer) / *David Rubinger—Eyewitness*, 1996, documentary (producer) / *Bat Yam—New York*, 1996–

1999, TV series (producer) / *Borderline*, 1997, documentary (director) / *Mom's First Olympics*, 1997, documentary (producer) / *Via Dolorosa*, 1998, documentary (producer) / *Street Corners*, 1998–1999, documentary (producer) / *The Secrets of Kinneret*, 1998–1999, TV series (producer) / *Ammunition Hill Take 3*, 2001, documentary (co-scriptwriter) / *Take Away*, 2001, TV series (producer) / *The Barbecue People*, 2002 (co-producer) / *Stromboli*, 2002, documentary (director).

SHECHORI, IDIT (Jerusalem, 1955). Director.

Shechori studied film at Beit Zvi School in Ramat Gan (1975–1977). She directed and wrote two feature films, *Circles** and *In the Name of Love*, which are psychological portrayals of women, their relationships, and their search for self-definition in life. *In the Name of Love* won First Prize at the Minneapolis–St. Paul Film Festival (1996). Shechori has also written stage plays.

Filmography

In Place of a Dream, 1978, short (also producer, scriptwriter) / *Circles*, 1980 (also scriptwriter) / *In the Name of Love*, 1994 (also producer, co-scriptwriter).

SHILOAH, YOSEPH (Cenah, Kurdistan, 1941). Actor.

Shiloah immigrated to Israel in 1951. He is a member of the first graduating class of the School of Performing Arts in Ramat Gan (1961–1963). He has worked as a stage actor since 1963 and has appeared in more than 80 films, of which more than 30 are Israeli feature films. He is known to Israeli filmgoers for his leading ethnic roles in acclaimed films such as Moshe Mizrahi's* *The House on Chelouche St.**, *Daughters, Daughters**, and *Women**, Ephraim Kishon's* *The Policeman**, Assi Dayan's* *Saint Cohen*, Shemi Zarhin's* *Passover Fever**; and, more recently, Benny Torati's *Desperado Square**, for which Shiloah won an Israeli Academy Award. Shiloah has also directed two documentary films. He received a tribute from the Israeli Film Academy (1998).

Filmography

*Sinai Commando**, 1967 / *My Love in Jerusalem*, 1969 / *The Big Escape*, 1970 / *The Policeman*, 1971 / *Katz and Carasso*, 1971 / *I Love You, Rosa**, 1972 / *Tamar Wife of Er*, 1972 / *Big Guss, What's the Fuss*, 1973 / *The House on Chelouche St.*, 1973 / *Daughters, Daughters*, 1973 / *Saint Cohen*, 1975 / *Snooker*, 1975 / *Diamonds*, 1975 / *Tzanani Family*, 1976 / *Sixtieth St.*, 1976 / *Half a Million Black*, 1977 / *Save the Lifeguard**, 1977 / *Marriage Tel Aviv Style*, 1979 / *Pillar of Salt*, 1979, TV drama / *Morning Star*, 1980 / *King for a Day*, 1980 / *The End of Milton Levy**, 1981 / *Private Popsicle*, 1982 / *Green*, 1983 / *Private Maneuvers*, 1983 / *The Auntie from Argentina*, 1984 / *Up Your Anchor*, 1985 / *The Wild, Crazy and the Lunatics*, 1986 / *The Good, the Bad and the Not So Bad*, 1986 (also co-scriptwriter) / *Alex in Love*, 1986 / *Braids**, 1989 / *Passover Fever*, 1995 / *Women*, 1966 / *Son*, 1997, TV drama / *Dreams*, documentary (director) / *Moments of Grace*, 1999, documentary (only co-director, co-producer, scriptwriter) / *Desperado Square*, 2000.

SHLES, JULIE (Johannesburg, South Africa, 1960). Director.

Shles immigrated to Israel with her family in 1962. She studied film at Beit Zvi School in Ramat Gan, where she received a prize for directing. She directed two prizewinning documentaries—*St. Jean*, about new immigrants living in a caravan park, and *Baba Luba*, which portrays a well-known Israeli rock singer (Dani Bassan) who is reunited with his family in Brazil after 35 years of separation. Shles' feature film, *Pick a Card** (Silver Prize, Houston, 1998), a comedy noted for its complex, quirky characters, won much attention from the Israeli public. All three films were winners of Israeli Academy Awards.

Filmography

St. Jean, 1993, documentary / *If You Hear, Answer*, 1994, documentary / *Baba Luba*, 1995, documentary / *Pick a Card*, 1997 / *Seamstresses from Mitzpeh*, 2001, TV series / *Sewing for Bread*, 2002, documentary (co-director, co-producer, co-scriptwriter).

SOMER, YOSSI (Haifa, 1956). Director.

Following army service as a combat paramedic, Somer entered the field of cinema. He graduated from the London International Film School (1983) and began his career working as a prop man and then advancing to art director for feature films. He has directed videos and training films for the army medical corps, one of which, *Battle Reaction*, won first prize in the army's annual Instructional Film Competition. His first feature, *Burning Memory**, was a brutally honest film about shell shock. His second feature, *The Dybbuk of the Holy Apple Field**, a modern adaptation of the Sholem Ansky theater classic, won the prize for Best Foreign Film at Houston (2000).

Filmography

Burning Memory, 1988 (also co-scriptwriter) / *The Dybbuk of the Holy Apple Field*, 1997 (also co-producer, co-scriptwriter).

TLALIM, ASHER (Tangier, Morocco, 1950). Director.

Tlalim studied film at the Beit Tzvi School of Film in Ramat Gan (1971–1973) and art and architecture at the Bezalel Art Academy in Jerusalem (1973–1977). Before becoming a documentary film director he edited numerous documentaries and feature films as a freelancer (1976–1986), including working as the co-editor of Daniel Wachsmann's* *Transit**. He has directed prizewinning documentary films—*A People and Its Music* (Final Award at New York), *All the Lonely People* (Wolgin Award at Jerusalem), and *Don't Touch My Holocaust** (an Award for Excellence at Jerusalem and an Israeli Academy Award).

Tlalim has taught film at numerous film schools in Israel and has also taught film editing at the National Film and Television School in Beaconsfield, England.

Filmography

The Valley of Tears, 1980, documentary (also editor) / *Holocaust and Revolt* (within the TV documentary series: *Pillar of Fire*, 1981 (also editor) / *Encounter in the Desert*,

1983, TV drama (also scriptwriter, editor) / *A Day in a Diary*, 1984, documentary (also scriptwriter, editor) / *The Last Nomad*, 1986, documentary (also scriptwriter, editor) / *Battle for the Hermon*, 1988, documentary (also scriptwriter) / *Missing Picture*, 1989, documentary (also scriptwriter) / *All the Lonely People*, 1990, documentary (also scriptwriter, editor) / *The Time of the Camel*, 1991 (also co-producer, scriptwriter, editor) / *Don't Touch My Holocaust*, 1994, documentary (also scriptwriter, editor) / *Violence in Art*, 1995, documentary (also scriptwriter, editor) / *Shalom Haver*, 1998, documentary (also scriptwriter, editor) / *All the Lonely People*, 1990, documentary / *Hitchhikers*, 1998, TV drama (also editor) / *A People and Its Music*, 1992–1998, documentary series (also scriptwriter) / *Between the Carob and the Olive Tree*, 1998, documentary (also editor, scriptwriter) / *Sounds Looking for a Home*, 1999, documentary (also scriptwriter, editor) / *My Yiddishe Mama's Dream*, 1999, documentary (also co-producer, scriptwriter, co-cinematographer, co-editor).

TOPOL, HAIM (Tel Aviv, 1935). Actor.

Topol began his acting career in an amateur theater group for the army's Nahal Entertainment Troupe. Following his army service he founded a satirical theater, the Spring Onion, which performed around the country. Topol's first film role was in Peter Frye's* comedy *I Like Mike**. Following that he starred in the award-winning film *Sallah** (Ephraim Kishon*). Topol's memorable acting and singing performance as the Moroccan patriarchal figure in this film brought him recognition (Golden Gate Award for Best Actor at San Francisco, 1964 and Golden Globe from the Hollywood Foreign Press Association, 1965). Although he starred in a number of additional Israeli films, Topol went on to international success in the arena of foreign theater and film.

In 1967 Topol played Tevye the Milkman for the first time in the London musical production of *Fiddler on the Roof.* This was the role that catapulted him to fame. In 1971 he played Tevye in the film version, directed by Norman Jewison (Golden Globe and nomination for an American Academy Award). Topol's many foreign film appearances include *Cast a Giant Shadow* (Melville Shavelson), *Before Winter Comes* (J. Lee Thompson), *Galileo* (Joseph Losey), *The House on Garibaldi Street* (Peter Collinson), *Flash Gordon* (Mike Hodges), the James Bond film *For Your Eyes Only* (John Glenn), and *Left Luggage* (Jeroen Krabbe). Topol won many awards, including a Tony Award as Best Actor on Broadway, a Golden Gate Award, a David Donatello Award (Italian Oscar), and Man of the Year of Great Britain.

Topol's autobiography, *Topol by Topol*, was published by Weindenfel and Nicholson in London. In addition, he compiled and illustrated *Topol's Treasure of Jewish Humour, Wit and Wisdom*, which was published by Robson Books in London. Two BBC-TV programs were made with and about Topol—*It's Topol* and *Topol's Israel.*

Filmography

I Like Mike, 1962 / *The True Story of Palestine**, 1962, documentary (only narrator) / *Eldorado**, 1963 / *Sallah*, 1964 / *Ervinka**, 1967 (also co-producer) / *Every Bastard a*

*King**, 1968 (also co-producer) / *Fish, Football and Girls*, 1968 (also co-producer) / *The Rooster*, 1971 / *Again Forever**, 1985.

TROPE, TSIPI (Tel Aviv, 1940s). Director.

Trope is a graduate of the Academy of Music and Department of Sociology at Tel Aviv University and the University of Michigan at Ann Arbor (M.A. and Ph.D. in film and television, 1975). She teaches film both in Israel and in New York City at Columbia University and New York University. She has written and directed documentaries, television dramas, and feature films. Her short film *Close–Far* won prizes at Golden Gate Festival in San Francisco and New York Expo for Short Films.

Trope is an auteur filmmaker. Two of her films are intense studies of the relationships between husband and wife, both of which deal with domestic abuse—*Tell Me That You Love Me** and *Chronicle of Love*. Her prizewinning film *Tel Aviv–Berlin** (Israel Film Center Awards) analyzes how a Holocaust survivor's traumatic past can force him to make difficult moral choices.

Filmography

Piano Lesson, 1977, documentary (also scriptwriter) / *A Free Day*, 1978, documentary (also scriptwriter) / *Close–Far*, short (also scriptwriter) / *Tell Me That You Love Me*, 1983 (also co-scriptwriter) / *Tel Aviv–Berlin*, 1987 (also scriptwriter) / *Six Million Pieces* (also scriptwriter) / *Adella*, 1993, TV drama (also scriptwriter) / *Chronicle of Love*, 1998 (also producer, scriptwriter).

VAN LEER, LIA (Balti, Romania, 1924). Pioneer in the field of film culture.

Lia van Leer (born Greenberg) immigrated to Palestine in 1940. She is the pioneering founder of the Haifa Cinematheque, the Jerusalem Cinematheque, the Israel Film Archive, and the Jerusalem Film Festival.

During the 1950s, together with her husband, Wim van Leer (1913–1992), an engineer, pilot, journalist, playwright, and film producer, she established the first film club in the country, later to develop into the Haifa Cinematheque. As their personal film collection grew, it was formally established as the Israel Film Archive in 1960 and accepted into the Federation Internationale des Archives du Film in 1963. The collection developed over the years to more than 26,000 films and includes classics of international cinema, Israeli features and documentaries, and also the historically important collection of Carmel Newsreels (1934–1957). When the van Leers moved to Jerusalem in 1973, Lia van Leer founded the Jerusalem Cinematheque and built a magnificent permanent home for it overlooking the Walls of the Old City. The new premises, which opened in 1981, also house the Israel Film Archive and the Jerusalem Film Festival (established in 1984).

Van Leer's lifework has been recognized by many honors and awards, among them the President's Citation for Volunteerism, presented by President Chaim Herzog (1988); the Israeli Ministry of Education Medal for Contribution to Cinema; the Ordre du Merite, France, presented by President François Mitterrand; the Chevalier des Arts et des Lettres, France; the Chevalier de la Legion d'Honneur, Ministry of Culture, France; and the Life Achievement Award, Israel Film Academy (1998).

WACHSMANN, ANAT (Jaffa, 1962). Actress.

Wachsmann studied acting at Beit Zvi in Ramat Gan and received her degree in 1984. She has appeared in many theater productions. She is well known for her roles in award-winning films such as Shemi Zarhin's* *Passover Fever**, Aner Preminger's* *Blind Man's Bluff**, and Ayelet Menahemi and Nirit Yaron's *Tel Aviv Stories** (for which she won the Israeli Academy Award for Best Actress).

Filmography

The Wild, Crazy and the Lunatics, 1986 / *Don't Give a Damn**, 1987 / *Havatzelet*, 1989, short / *Tel Aviv Stories*, 1992 / *Blind Man's Bluff*, 1993 / *The Wordmaker*, 1991, TV drama / *Passover Fever*, 1995 / *Kinneret's Secrets*, 1998, TV drama / *Life Isn't Everything*, 2001, TV series; *Round-trip*, 2003, TV drama.

WACHSMANN, DANIEL (Shanghai, China, 1946). Director.

Wachsmann emigrated to Israel with his parents in 1948 and was brought up in the mixed Arab–Jewish city of Nazareth. He studied film at the London Film School and at Beit Zvi in Ramat Gan. He has directed prizewinning shorts, such as *My Father* (first prize at Mannheim, 1975). Many of his films deal with the Galilee, an area of hills and agricultural areas in northern Israel—the area where he has made his home, near the mystical city of Safed—including the prize-winning films *The Appointed** and *Hamsin** and the television drama *Song of the Galilee* (prizes at Haifa, 1996, and at Chicago, 1997).

Wachsmann is known for his groundbreaking films that deal with the breakdown of myths in Israeli society. His first feature, *Transit**, portrays the ambivalent feelings of a new immigrant who cannot find his place in Israel and decides to return to his native Germany. His *Hamsin* (Silver Leopard at Locarno, 1983, Human Rights Prize at Strasbourg, 1984, and Israel Film Center Awards, 1982) was the first Israeli feature film to offer an in-depth analysis of the tensions between Arabs and Jews within the borders of Israel. His acclaimed *The Appointed* (Wolgin Award at Jerusalem, 1990) portrays the corruption and exploitation of religious leadership in contemporary Israel.

Wachsmann has taught film at Beit Tzvi School in Ramat Gan, Camera Obscura in Tel Aviv, Tel Aviv University, and at the Sam Spiegel School of Film and Television in Jerusalem. His documentary film *Menelik*, about young immigrants from Ethiopia, won the New Foundation Award at Jerusalem (1997).

Filmography

My Father, 1975, short / *Elvira*, 1977, short / *Rockinghorse**, 1978 (only actor) / *Transit*, 1980 (also co-scriptwriter) / *Big Shots*, 1982 (only actor) / *Hamsin*, 1982 (also co-scriptwriter) / *On a Clear Day You Can See Damascus*, 1984 (only actor) / *The Red*

Heifer, 1986, short / *The Appointed*, 1990 (also co-scriptwriter) / *Song of the Galilee*, 1996, TV drama (also actor) / *The Stone and the Olive Tree*, 1997, documentary / *Menelik*, 1999, documentary / *The Forest*, 1999.

WOLMAN, DAN (Jerusalem, 1941). Director.

Following his military service, Wolman went abroad to study filmmaking at New York University. His early films, which he wrote and directed himself, included two award-winning shorts: *The Race* (Golden Eagle Award, Photography Society of America Film Festival, 1966) and *The Gospel* (Best Film, New York Film Festival, 1967).

Wolman is a leading auteur filmmaker of the Kayitz movement (Young Israeli Cinema of the 1960s and 1970s). His first features, *The Dreamer** (1970) and *Floch** (1972), both look at the problems and hardships of old age. Wolman's third feature, *My Michael** (1975), is about solitude, set in 1950s Jerusalem. It is a faithful adaptation of the celebrated novel by Amos Oz, the well-known Israeli author. Also set against the background of Jerusalem, Wolman's fourth feature, *Hide and Seek** (1980), deals with the problems and tensions of living in a society in conflict during the British Mandate period. His award-winning *The Distance** again takes up themes from his previous films with its story of the responsibilities of a son toward his aging parents. His most recent feature film, *Foreign Sister** (Wolgin Award, Jerusalem, 2000), sensitively deals with the problems of foreign workers within Israel.

Wolman's complex narrative films mix the private with the national—his films are subtle, poetic studies of complex people and relationships against backgrounds heavy with symbolism and political meaning. He is one of Israel's most important humanistic filmmakers and has achieved international recognition. Wolman was presented with a Life Achievement Award at the Jerusalem Film Festival (1999), and he also has directed numerous television films.

Filmography

Habit, 1965, short (also scriptwriter) / *The Living*, 1965, short / *The Race*, 1966, short / *The Gospel*, 1967, short / *The Dreamer*, 1970 (also scriptwriter) / *Floch*, 1972 (also co-scriptwriter) / *My Michael*, 1975 (also co-scriptwriter) / *Gimpel the Fool*, 1976, TV drama (also scriptwriter) / *The Story of Basha*, 1977, TV drama (also scriptwriter) / *To Touch a City*, 1978, documentary (also scriptwriter) / *Hide and Seek*, 1980 (also co-producer, co-scriptwriter) / *The Man Who Par-am-Pam-Pam*, 1982, TV drama (also scriptwriter) / *Nana*, 1983 / *Soldier of the Night*, 1984 (also producer, scriptwriter) / *Baby Love*, 1984 (also scriptwriter) / *Up Your Anchor*, 1985 (also co-scriptwriter) / *Love Contract*, 1986 (also co-producer, co-scriptwriter) / *The Scapegoat*, 1991, TV drama (also co-scriptwriter) / *The Distance*, 1994 (also producer, scriptwriter) / *Lovesick on Nana St.**, 1995 (only cameo performance) / *Yolande Remembered*, 1999, documentary (also producer) / *Foreign Sister*, 2000 (also producer, scriptwriter) / *A Protected Animal*, 2001, TV drama (also producer, scriptwriter) / *Treasures of the Red Sea*, 2001.

YESHURUN, YITZHAK (TZEPEL) (Tel Aviv, 1936). Director.

Yeshurun studied English literature and philosophy at the Hebrew University of Jerusalem and at the Sorbonne (1958-1963). He was influenced by the French Nouvelle Vague, having been trained in cinema in Paris.

Although he is also a documentary filmmaker, Yeshurun is known for his dramatic filmmaking—for its credibility and authenticity, for confronting issues boldly, and for refusing to take the easy road. His themes include love, the breakdown of ideology, social conflict, and intergenerational portrayals. *Noa at 17** and *A Married Couple** won Israel Film Center Awards, and *Green Fields** won the Grand Prize at Rio de Janeiro. Yeshurun directed one film abroad, *Zero Cool* (United States), in 1993.

Filmography

Eradicating Illiteracy, 1966, documentary (also scriptwriter) / *Variations on a Love Theme**, 1967 (also producer, scriptwriter) / *Joker*, 1976 (also producer, scriptwriter) / *Kobi and Mali*, 1978, TV drama (also scriptwriter) / *Noa at 17*, 1981 (also producer, scriptwriter) / *A Married Couple*, 1983 (also scriptwriter) / *Prom Queen*, 1986 (also co-producer, scriptwriter) / *Green Fields*, 1989 (also scriptwriter) / *Love Games*, 1993, TV series (also scriptwriter) / *A Short History of Love*, 1996 (also producer, scriptwriter) / *On Air*, 1999, TV drama (also producer, scriptwriter); *Fight for Jerusalem*, 2003, TV miniseries.

YOSHA, YAKI (Tel Aviv, 1951). Director.

Yosha's narrative feature films created controversy and won international attention due to their subject matter and uncompromising grappling with political issues in an artistic fashion. His first film, *Shalom, Prayer for the Road*, is a lyrical, autobiographical film, using improvisation and experimental techniques and portraying a young man's dissatisfaction with the militarism of his surroundings. His second film, *Rockinghorse** (Special Jury Prize, Oxford), is about the alienation of the Palmach generation. Yosha has also directed films in the United States.

Filmography

Shalom, Prayer for the Road, 1973 (also scriptwriter, composer, co-producer) / *Rockinghorse*, 1978 (also co-producer, co-scriptwriter, editor) / *The Vulture**, 1981 (also producer, scriptwriter) / *Dead End Street**, 1982 (also co-scriptwriter) / *Summertime Blues*, 1985, documentary / *Night Shift*, 1995, TV series / *Cops*, 1998–1999, TV documentary series / *Junkie*, 1998, TV drama / *Joint*, 1999, TV drama / *Inherit the Earth, 2001, documentary / Investigation Committee*, 2001, documentary.

ZADOK, ARNON (Ramat Gan, 1949). Actor and Director.

Zadok has appeared in numerous films in his acting career. He won the Israel Film Center Award for Best Actor for his memorable role as the leader of the Jewish inmates in *Beyond the Walls** (Uri Barbash*). In addition, he has directed a number of feature films—*White Night**, dealing with drug addiction, which won Prix de la Jeunesse, Cannes (1996), *Primal Justice*, and *Ingil*. Zadok has also directed several television dramatic series.

Filmography

On the Air, 1981 (actor) / *Stigma**, 1982 (actor) / *Beyond the Walls*, 1986 (actor) / *Once We Were Dreamers**, 1987 (actor) / *One of Us**, 1989 (actor) / *Torn Apart*, 1989 (actor) / *The Voice of Ein Harod*, 1990 (actor) / *Where Eagles Fly*, 1990 (co-producer) / *Real Time*, 1991 (co-producer) / *Beyond the Walls II*, 1992 (actor) / *Overdose*, 1993 (co-producer) / *White Night*, 1995 (director, producer, co-scriptwriter, actor) / *Primal Justice*, 1998 (director, actor) / *Real Father*, 1998 (co-producer) / *Ingil*, 2001 (director) / *Azanni Family*, TV series (director, actor) / *Sweet Dreams*, TV series (director).

ZARHIN, SHEMI (Tiberias, 1961). Director.

Zarhin studied journalism and public relations and then received a B.A. (1986) from Tel Aviv University in the Department of Film and Television. His short graduation film, *The Last of Grandpa's Magic*, won a German TV Award at Munich (1986). Zarhin taught filmmaking at Tel Aviv University (1989-1994) and then at the Sam Spiegel Film and Television School in Jerusalem (1990-1999). He has written film criticism for *Hadashot*, a daily newspaper, and edited a textbook on writing scripts for feature films. He directed and scripted two award-winning, complex narrative films about family issues: *Passover Fever** (Best Screenplay at Montreal and Honorable Mention, Wolgin Competition at Jerusalem) and *Dangerous Acts* (Israeli Academy Award for Best Director).

Filmography

Holes in the Hands, 1986, short (only co-editor) / *The Last of Grandpa's Magic*, 1986, short (also scriptwriter) / *Tolerance*, 1988, documentary (also scriptwriter) / *Jacky*, 1988, short (only co-scriptwriter) / *A Cupboard*, 1991, short (only scriptwriter) / *Melodrama*, 1991, short (only scriptwriter) / *Tel Aviv Stories**, 1992 (only co-scriptwriter) / *Passover Fever*, 1995 (also scriptwriter) / *Dangerous Acts*, 1998 (also scriptwriter) / *Family Secrets*, 1998 (only scriptwriter) / *The Other Woman*, 2000, TV series.

ZILBERG, YOEL (JOEL) (Tel Aviv, 1927). Director.

Zilberg served in the Army Entertainment Troupe during the 1948 War of Independence and studied theater directing at the Old Vic in London. He became a successful theater director with a specialty in musicals. He began his filmmaking career as an assistant director for American productions shot in Israel, including *Exodus* (Otto Preminger, 1960) and *Judith* (Daniel Mann, 1966). Together with Uri Zohar* and Nathan Axelrod* Zilberg directed the documentary film classic *The True Story of Palestine** (1962). His feature film *Get Zorkin** won the Gran Premio Platero at the Gijon Festival for Youth in 1972. In addition to the feature films that he made in Israel, Zilberg has been directing films in Hollywood since the 1980s, including the box office success *Breakin'* (1984).

Filmography

The True Story of Palestine, 1962, documentary (co-director) / *The Simchon Family*, 1964 / *Get Zorkin*, 1971 / *Marriage Jewish Style**, 1973 / *Kuni Lemel in Tel Aviv*, 1976 (also scriptwriter) / *Hershele*, 1977 (also co-scriptwriter) / *Millionaire in Trouble*, 1978 (also scriptwriter) / *Marriage Tel Aviv Style**, 1979 (also scriptwriter) / *My Mother, the*

*General**, 1979 (also co-scriptwriter) / *Mute Love*, 1982 (also co-scriptwriter) / *Kuni Lemel in Cairo*, 1983 (also scriptwriter) / *Ramat Aviv Gimmel*, 1995, TV series.

ZOHAR, URI (Tel Aviv, 1936). Actor and Director.

After serving in the Army Entertainment Troupe, Zohar studied philosophy and literature at the Hebrew University of Jerusalem. During the 1960s and 1970s he became one of the central figures of the Israeli cultural world, performing in theater, film, television, and radio and directing films that have become widely popular. Known for his irreverence, Zohar is a director/actor in films that portray his beatnik lifestyle, spontaneity, and cutting sense of humor. He directed 10 feature films and numerous shorts and was the first film director to receive the prestigious Israel Prize for his cultural contribution to Israeli life. Zohar's slang, creativity, and spontaneity have created an authentically Israeli film style.

With his first films (*Hole in the Moon** and *Moishe Air-Condition*) Zohar quickly established himself as a director of comedy. However, his next films (*Three Days and a Child** and *Every Bastard a King**—Best Direction at Chicago, 1968) show that he was influenced by the French Nouvelle Vague and capable of directing serious drama. His last few films (*Fish, Football and Girls*, *Take Off**, *The Rooster*, *Peeping Toms**, *Big Eyes**, and *Save the Lifeguard**) were adolescent sex comedies bordering on the vulgar and, at the same time, reflecting a strong criticism of the hedonistic lifestyle.

During his career, Zohar turned away from his classical Zionist upbringing and the society that had nurtured him. Following this shift to the self-indulgence of Tel Aviv secular society, he decided to make another, more significant change. Negating the secularism and arrogance that he had embraced so wholeheartedly, he left the world of film in 1977 to become a newly Orthodox Jew. He had come full circle, from the serious university student to the secularism and satire that shattered the myths of his parents' generation, then to the more mature filmmaker who used nonconformity as a rebellion against religion and tradition, and finally to the middle-aged adult who found solace and an end to his existential searching in the form of ultra-Orthodox religious practice and spirituality.

Filmography

*Pillar of Fire**, 1959 (actor) / *Blazing Sands**, 1960 (actor) / *The True Story of Palestine**, 1962, documentary (co-director) / *Dreamboat**, 1964 (actor) / *Hole in the Moon*, 1965 (director, actor) / *Moishe Air-Condition*, 1966 (director) / *Motive to Kill*, 1967 (actor) / *Aliza Mizrachi*, 1967 (actor) / *Sabina and Her Men*, 1967 (actor) / *Three Days and a Child*, 1967 (director, co-scriptwriter) / *Every Bastard a King*, 1968 (director, co-scriptwriter) / *Fish, Football and Girls*, 1968 (director) / *Lool*, 1969, TV series (director, co-scriptwriter) / *Snail**, 1970 (actor) / *Take Off*, 1970 (director, actor) / *The Rooster*, 1971 (director, actor) / *Peeping Toms*, 1972 (director, co-scriptwriter, actor) / *Big Guss, What's the Fuss*, 1973 (actor) / *They Call Me Shmil*, 1973 (actor) / *Big Eyes*, 1974 (director, co-scriptwriter, actor) / *Save the Lifeguard*, 1977 (director, scriptwriter, actor) / *Lool*, 1988 (co-director, co-scriptwriter, actor).

APPENDIX: INTERNATIONAL AWARDS WON BY ISRAELI FEATURE FILMS

1935 **Venice Film Festival: Prize**—*Land of Promise* (Judah Leman)

1955 **Cannes Film Festival: Homage of the Jury to Actress**—Chaya Hararit—*Hill 24 Doesn't Answer* (Thorold Dickinson)

1961 **Cannes, Rencontre du Film pour la Jeunesse: Grand Prix**—*They Were Ten* (Baruch Dienar)

Mannheim Film Festival: CIDALC Prize—*They Were Ten* (Baruch Dienar)

1963 **Berlin Film Festival: Jugend Film Prize**—*The Cellar* (Nathan Gross)

1964 **San Francisco Film Festival (Golden Gate Awards): Best Screenplay**—Ephraim Kishon for *Sallah* (Ephraim Kishon); **Best Actor**—Haim Topol

1965 **Hollywood Foreign Press Association (Golden Globes): Outstanding Foreign Film of 1964**—*Sallah* (Ephraim Kishon); **Star of Tomorrow**—Haim Topol

All American Press-American Distributors: First Prize for Best Foreign Direction—*Sallah* (Ephraim Kishon)

1966 **Viennale: Prize**—*Sallah* (Ephraim Kishon)

San Francisco Film Festival (Golden Gate Awards): Best Screenplay—*Sallah* (Ephraim Kishon); **Best Actor**—Haim Topol

All American Press-American Distributors: First Prize for Best Foreign Direction—*Sallah* (Ephraim Kishon)

1967 **Cannes Film Festival: Best Actor**—Oded Kotler for *Three Days and a Child* (Uri Zohar)

1968 **Chicago Film Festival: Best Direction**—*Every Bastard a King* (Uri Zohar); **Best Color Photography**—David Gurfinkel

1969 **Chicago Film Festival: Best Actress**—Gila Almagor for *Siege* (Gilberto Tofano)

Barcelona XI Semana de Cine en Color: Lady of Umbrella—*The Big Dig* (Ephraim Kishon)

1970 **Atlanta Film Festival: Gold Medal**—Gila Almagor for *Siege* (Gilberto Tofano)

San Antonio Hemisfilm Festival: Best Actress—Gila Almagor for *Siege* (Gilberto Tofano)

1971 **Hollywood Foreign Press Association (Golden Globe): Best Foreign Language Film**—*The Policeman* (Ephraim Kishon)

Barcelona Semena Internacional de Cine en Color: Outstanding Foreign Film—*The Policeman* (Ephraim Kishon)

Monte Carlo TV Festival: FIPRESCI Special Mention—*The Big Dig* (Ephraim Kishon)

1972 **Venice Film Festival: Critics' Prize**—*Take Two* (Baruch Dienar)

Monte Carlo TV Festival: Cino de Duca Award—*The Policeman* (Ephraim Kishon)

Gijon Festival for Youth, Spain: Gran Premio Platero—*Get Zorkin* (Yoel Zilberg)

Atlanta Film Festival: Gold Medal Special Jury Award—*The Policeman* (Ephraim Kishon)

1975 **Bergamo Festival "Autore": Special Jury Prize**—*Saint Cohen* (Assi Dayan)

1978 **Oxford Film Festival: Special Jury Prize**—*Rockinghorse* (Yaki Yosha); **Best Actor**—Gedalia Besser

1983 **Locarno Film Festival: Silver Leopard**—*Hamsin* (Daniel Wachsmann)

1984 **Venice Film Festival: Critics' Jury Prize**—*Beyond the Walls* (Uri Barbash)

Strasbourg Film Festival: Human Rights Prize—*Hamsin* (Daniel Wachsmann)

Salerno Film Festival: First Prize—*Beyond the Walls* (Uri Barbash)

1986 **Berlin Film Festival: Silver Bear**—Actor Tuncel Kurtiz (Turkey) for *The Smile of the Lamb* (Shimon Dotan)

Locarno Film Festival: Golden Eye of the Leopard—*Avanti Popolo* (Rafi Bukaee)

Prix Italia for TV drama—*Bread* (Ram Loevy)

Torino Film Festival: Critics' Prize—*Burning Land* (Serge Ankri)

1988 **Rio de Janeiro Film Festival: FIPRESCI Prize**—*On the Fringe* (Ze'ev Revach)

Frankfurt Children's Film Festival: First Prize—*On My Own* (Tamir Paul)

1989 **Berlin Film Festival: Silver Bear**—*Summer of Aviya* (Eli Cohen); **Actresses**—Gila Almagor and Kaipo Cohen

Rio de Janeiro Film Festival: Grand Prize—*Green Fields* (Yitzhak Tzepel Yeshurun)

San Remo Festival: Best Foreign Film—*Summer of Aviya* (Eli Cohen)

Valladolid Film Festival: Golden Spike—*Summer of Aviya* (Eli Cohen)

Vienna Children's Film Festival: First Prize—*On My Own* (Tamir Paul)

Venice Film Festival: Special Citation, Italian Film Critics' Association—*Berlin-Jerusalem* (Amos Gitai)

1990 **Istanbul Film Festival: Special Jury Prize**—*Berlin-Jerusalem* (Amos Gitai)

Belgrade Film Festival: Grand Prix—*Summer of Aviya* (Eli Cohen)

1991 **Valencia Film Festival: Second Prize**—*Cup Final* (Eran Riklis)

1992 **Salerno Film Festival: Best Actress**—Rita Zohar for *Last Love Affair of Laura Adler* (Avram Heffner)

Valencia Film Festival: Silver Palm—*Amazing Grace* (Amos Gutmann)

Houston WorldFest: Honorable Mention—*Amazing Grace* (Amos Gutmann)

Torino Film Festival: Honorable Mention—*Amazing Grace* (Amos Gutmann)

1993 **Berlin Film Festival: Honorable Mention**—*Life According to Agfa* (Assi Dayan)

Montpellier Film Festival for Mediterranean Cinema: Antigone d'Or—*Blind Man's Bluff* (Aner Preminger)

Valencia Film Festival: Prize—*Beyond the Walls II* (Uri Barbash)

1994 **Montevideo Film Festival: First Prize for first film**—*Blind Man's Bluff* (Aner Preminger)

Cancun Film Festival in Mexico: Golden Jaguar, Special Jury Prize—*Blind Man's Bluff* (Aner Preminger)

San Sebastian Film Festival: Best Script—*Sh'chur* (Shmuel Hasfari)

Montpellier Mediterranean Film Festival: First Prize—*Sh'chur* (Shmuel Hasfari)

1995 **Berlin Film Festival: Special Mention**—*Sh'chur* (Shmuel Hasfari)

Montreal World Film Festival: Best Screenplay—Shemi Zarhin for *Passover Fever* (Shemi Zarhin)

1996 **Karlovy Vary Film Festival: Special Jury Prize**—*Saint Clara* (Ori Sivan, Ari Folman)

Cannes Film Festival: Prix de la Jeunesse—*White Night* (Arnon Zadok)

Minneapolis-St. Paul Film Festival: First Prize in the Narrative Feature Category—*In the Name of Love* (Idit Shechori)

Vienna Children's Film Festival: Best Film—*Saint Clara* (Ori Sivan, Ari Folman)

Sorento Film Festival: Second Prize—*Sh'chur* (Shmuel Hasfari)

Children and Young People Film Festival, Ragazzi Belinzona, Switzerland: First Prize—*There Was No War in '72* (David Kreiner)

Fort Lauderdale Film Festival: Special Jury Award—*There Was No War in '72* (David Kreiner)

Mannheim Film Festival: Audience Award—*Lovesick on Nana St.* (Savi Gabizon); **Special Mention for Acting**—Moshe Ivgi

São Paolo Film Festival: Jury Award—*Lovesick on Nana St.* (Savi Gabizon)

1997 **Berlin Film Festival: Ecumenical Jury Prize for Best Feature Film**—*Under Western Eyes* (Joseph Pitchhadze)

Belgrade Festival of Auteur Films: Outstanding Auteur Film Prize and Special Mention of FIPRESCI Jury—*Under Western Eyes* (Joseph Pitchhadze)

1998 **Valencia Film Festival: Best Film**—*An Electric Blanket* (Assi Dayan); **Best Actor**—Suheil Hadad for *The Milky Way* (Ali Nassar)

Houston WorldFest: Silver Prize—*Pick a Card* (Julie Shles)

1999 **Karlovy Vary Film Festival: Grand Prix Crystal Globe and Special Mention of Ecumenical Jury**—*Yana's Friends* (Arik Kaplun); **Best Actress**—Evelyn Kaplun

Valencia Film Festival: Golden Palm Tree—*Urban Feel* (Jonathan Sagall)

Montpellier Mediterranean Film Festival: Public Prize—*Yana's Friends* (Arik Kaplun)

Medfilm Festival Rome: Artistic Expression Award—*Yana's Friends* (Arik Kaplun)

Houston WorldFest: Best Foreign Film—*The Dybbuk of the Holy Apple Field* (Yossi Somer)

Moscow Film Festival: Best Director—*Yana's Friends* (Arik Kaplun)

2000 **Houston WorldFest: Best Foreign Film**—*Yana's Friends* (Arik Kaplun)

Varna: Bulgarian Film Critics' Award—*Urban Feel* (Jonathan Sagall)

2001 **Thessaloniki Film Festival: Best Script and Jury Award**—*Late Marriage* (Dover Kosashvilli); **Best Actress**—Ronit Elkabetz

Kiev Film Festival: Best Film—*Late Marriage* (Dover Kosashvilli)

Houston WorldFest: Best Foreign Film—*The Investigation Continues* (Marek Rozenbaum)

Montpellier Mediterranean Film Festival: Antigone d'Or—*Desperado Square* (Benny Torati)

Cologne Mediterranean Film Festival: Special Jury Prize—*Yellow Asphalt—Three Desert Stories* (Dan [Nokyo] Verete)

2002 **Tokyo Film Festival: Grand Prix**—*Broken Wings* (Nir Bergman)

Valencia Film Festival: Bronze Tree and Best Script—*Desperado Square* (Benny Torati)

Buenos Aires Film Festival: International Critics Award—*Late Marriage* (Dover Kosashvilli); **Best Actress**—Ronit Elkabetz

2003 **Palm Springs Film Festival: Prize for first film**—*Broken Wings* (Nir Bergman)

Berlin Film Festival: Prize of the Churches of the Ecumenical Jury, International Confederation of Art Cinemas Prize, Panorama Audience Prize—*Broken Wings* (Nir Bergman)

BIBLIOGRAPHY

Avisar, Ilan. "The Holocaust Complex in Israeli Cinema: The Psychology and Politics of National Memory." Unpublished paper presented at the Eleventh World Congress of Jewish Studies, Jerusalem, June 24, 1993.

Cooper-Weill, Judy. "The Life in a Day of Danny Wolman." *Israel Scene* (December 1985), p. 32.

Dayan, Nissim. "From the Bourekas Back to the Ghetto Culture." *Kolnoa* 11 (Autumn 1976), pp. 54–56 (in Hebrew).

Dayan, Nissim. "The Second Stop on the Road to Salvation." *Kolnoa* 14 (Summer 1977), pp. 3–4 (in Hebrew).

Dienar, Baruch. *Israeli Films Reach Out Across the World*. Tel Aviv: Fund for the Promotion of Israeli Quality Films, June 1988 (pamphlet).

Downing, Taylor. *Palestine on Film*. London: Council for the Advancement of Arab-British Understanding, 1979.

Erens, Patricia. "Israeli Cinema." *Film Comment* 17:1 (1981), pp. 60–64.

Erens, Patricia. "Patricia Erens from Israel." *Film Comment* 16:1 (1980), pp. 4, 6.

Friedman, Jane. "Israel's 'New Wave' Directors Take Root in a Harsh Climate." *New York Times*, June 29, 1980, pp. 15–16.

Friedman, Regine Mihal. "Between Silence and Abjection: The Film Medium and the Israeli War Widow." *Film Historia* 3:1–2 (1993), pp. 80–81.

Gertz, Nurit. "Historical Memory in Israeli Literature and Cinema." Unpublished paper presented at the Eleventh World Congress of Jewish Studies, Jerusalem, June 28, 1993.

Gertz, Nurit. *Motion Fiction: Israeli Fiction in Film*. Tel Aviv: Open University of Israel, 1993 (in Hebrew).

Gross, Nathan. "The Best over Sinai." *Al Hamishmar*, December 15, 1967 (in Hebrew).

Gross, Nathan, and Ya'akov Gross. *Hebrew Film: Chapters in the History of Silent and Sound Film in Israel*. Jerusalem: Nathan and Ya'akov Gross, 1991 (in Hebrew).

Hoberman, J. "Michel Khleifi: Man from Galilee." *Village Voice*, June 28, 1988, p. 84.
Horak, Jan-Christopher. "The Penetrating Power of Light: The Films of Helmar Lerski." *Image* 36 (Autumn/Winter 1993), pp. 40–53.
Israel Film Centre Bulletin. Jerusalem: Israel Film Centre (published annually).
Kaufman, Azriel. "Cinema of the Streets: An Interview with Nissim Dayan." *Kolnoa* 1 (March 1974), pp. 70–77 (in Hebrew).
Klausner, Margot. *The Dream Industry: Memories and Facts—Twenty-Five Years for the Israeli Motion Picture Studios*. Tel Aviv: Israel Publishing, 1974 (in Hebrew).
Kronish, Amy W. *World Cinema: Israel*. Trowbridge, Wiltshire: Flicks Books; Cranbury, NJ: Associated University Presses, 1996.
Kronish, Amy, Edith Falk, and Paula Weiman-Kelman (eds.). *The Nathan Axelrod Collection, vol. 1*. Trowbridge, Wiltshire: Flicks Books, 1994.
Kut, Hagar. "Super Ram." *Davar*, February 5, 1993 (in Hebrew).
Loshitzky, Yosefa. "The Bride of the Dead: Phallocentrism and War in *Himmo, King of Jerusalem*." *Film Literature Quarterly* 21:3 (1993), pp. 218–229.
Luft, Herbert G. "Moshe Mizrachi." *Films in Review* (April 1984), pp. 228–230.
Plutzker, Savor. "Interview with Avram Heffner." *Kolnoa* 2 (May 1974), pp. 8–13 (in Hebrew).
Rosen, Miriam. "The Architecture of Documentary Filmmaking: An Interview with Amos Gitai." *Cineaste* 18:3 (1990), pp. 48–50.
Rosen, Miriam. "Beyond the Walls." *Cineaste* 14:3 (1986), pp. 47–50.
Schnitzer, Meir. *Israeli Cinema: Facts/Plots/Directors/Opinions*. Tel Aviv: Kinneret Publishing, 1994 (in Hebrew).
Schorr, Renen. "40 Years Filmmaking in Israel." *Ariel* 71–72 (1988), pp. 106–127.
Shohat, Ella. "Anomalies of the National: Representing Israel/Palestine." *Wide Angle* 11: 3 (1989), p. 39.
Shohat, Ella. "Israel." In William Luhr (ed.), *World Cinema since 1945*. New York: The Ungar Publishing Company, 1987, pp. 330–346.
Shohat, Ella. *Israeli Cinema: East/West and the Politics of Representation*. Austin: University of Texas Press, 1989.
Tryster, Hillel. *Israel before Israel*. Jerusalem: Steven Spielberg Jewish Film Archive, 1995.
Warth, Daniel. "Feature Film Listing." *Salute to Israeli Cinema*, Cinematheque Tel Aviv (November–December 1989), pp. 34–43 (in Hebrew).
Warth, Daniel (ed.). *Israeli Films 1987–1990*. Tel Aviv: Israel Film Institute, 1990 (pamphlet).
Yakir, Dan. "Eye on Zion." *Film Comment* 19:3 (1983), p. 60.
Zertal, Edith. "The Films of Dan Wolman." *Ariel* 44 (1977), p. 88.

INDEX OF FILM TITLES

This index includes English titles, alternative titles, and Hebrew titles of films. All film entries and all films mentioned in the introductory chapter are included. Page numbers that appear in **bold** indicate a complete entry on the specific film. *Note*: this index does not include the films that appear in the filmographies of the biographical entries.

INDEX OF PERSONALITIES

Page numbers that appear in **bold** indicate a full biographical entry.

INDEX OF SUBJECTS

About the Authors

AMY KRONISH is a freelance film consultant from Jerusalem who has lectured, written, taught, and produced extensively and internationally. For 15 years she worked at the Jerusalem Cinematheque/Israel Film Archive, where she served as Curator of Jewish and Israeli Film. She is the author of *World Cinema: Israel* (1996).

COSTEL SAFIRMAN is the Head of Research and Library Services at the Jerusalem Cinematheque/Israel Film Archive, where he has worked since 1988. Prior to this he lived in Romania, where he directed documentary films and wrote historical and critical articles on film.